ADOBE® PREMIERE® PRO CS4

CLASSROOM IN A BOOK®

The official training workbook from Adobe Systems

www.adobepress.com

Adobe® Premiere® Pro CS4 Classroom in a Book®

Adobe Systems Incorporated, 345 Park Avenue, San Jose, California 95110-2704, USA

Adobe Press books are published by Peachpit, a division of Pearson Education located in Berkeley, California. For the latest on Adobe Press books, go to www.adobepress.com. To report errors, please send a note to errata@peachpit.com. For information on getting permission for reprints and excerpts, contact permissions@peachpit.com.

Writer: Curt Wrigley
Senior Editor: Karyn Johnson
Developmental Editor: Stephen Nathans-Kelly
Production Editor: Kate Reber
Copyeditor: Kimberly Wimpsett
Technical Editor: David Basulto
Compositor: Kelli Kamel
Indexer: FireCrystal Communications
Cover design: Eddie Yuen
Interior design: Mimi Heft

Printed and bound in the United States of America

ISBN-13: 978-0-321-57385-8
ISBN-10: 0-321-57385-4

9 8 7 6 5 4 3 2 1

WHAT'S ON THE DISC

Here is an overview of the contents of the Classroom in a Book disc

Lesson files … and so much more

The *Adobe Premiere Pro CS4 Classroom in a Book* disc includes the lesson files that you'll need to complete the exercises in this book, as well as other content to help you learn more about Adobe Premiere Pro CS4 and use it with greater efficiency and ease. The diagram below represents the contents of the disc, which should help you locate the files you need.

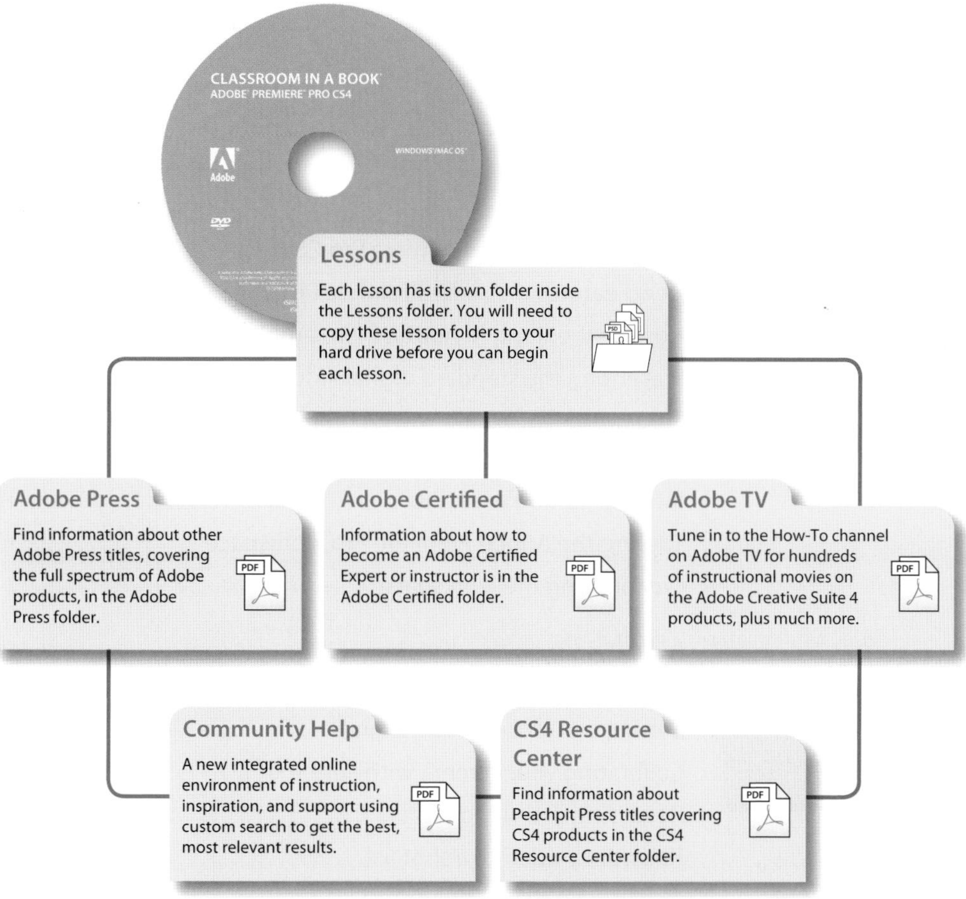

CONTENTS

GETTING STARTED

Adobe® Premiere® Pro CS4, the essential editing tool for video enthusiasts and professionals, enhances your creative power and freedom. Adobe Premiere Pro is the most scalable, efficient, and precise video-editing tool available. Whether you're working with DV, HD, HDV, AVCHD, P2 DVCPRO HD, XDCAM, or any other format, the superior performance of Adobe Premiere Pro lets you work faster and more creatively. The complete set of powerful and exclusive tools lets you overcome any editorial, production, and workflow challenge to deliver the high-quality work you demand.

About Classroom in a Book

Adobe Premiere Pro CS4 Classroom in a Book® is part of the official training series for Adobe graphics and publishing software. The lessons are designed so that you can learn at your own pace. If you're new to Adobe Premiere Pro, you'll learn the fundamental concepts and features you'll need to use the program. *Classroom in a Book* also teaches many advanced features, including tips and techniques for using the latest version of this software.

The lessons in this edition include opportunities to use new features, such as improved audio options, improved editing efficiency, tapeless media, and the ability to send a sequence to Adobe® Encore® CS4 without rendering or intermediate exporting to be output to DVD, Blu-ray Disc, or Adobe® Flash® CS4 Professional. Exporting has gotten more powerful and convenient through the ability to batch export through the Adobe® Media Encoder. Breakthrough new features such as speech-to-text transcription can save hours locating specific frames of a project. Adobe Premiere Pro CS4 is available for both Windows and Mac OS.

Prerequisites

Before beginning to use *Adobe Premiere Pro CS4 Classroom in a Book*, make sure your system is set up correctly and that you've installed the required software and hardware. You should have a working knowledge of your computer and operating system. You should know how to use the mouse and standard menus and commands, and also how to open, save, and close files. If you need to review these techniques, see the printed or online documentation included with your Microsoft Windows or Mac OS system.

Installing Adobe Premiere Pro CS4

You must purchase the Adobe Premiere Pro CS4 software separately from this book. For system requirements and complete instructions on installing the software, see the document Adobe Premiere Pro ReadMe.html on the software DVD.

Install Adobe Premiere Pro from the Adobe Premiere Pro CS4 software DVD onto your hard disk; you cannot run the program from the DVD. Follow the onscreen instructions. The installation process also installs Adobe® Encore® CS4, Adobe® OnLocation™ CS4, Adobe® Bridge CS4, and some shared components.

Make sure your serial number is accessible before installing the application; you can find the serial number on the registration card or on the back of the DVD case.

Optimizing performance

Editing video is memory- and processor-intensive work for a desktop computer. A fast processor and a lot of memory will make your editing experience much faster and more efficient; 1 GB of memory is the minimum, and 2 GB is recommended for editing HDV or HD media. Adobe Premiere Pro CS4 takes advantage of multicore processors on Windows and Macintosh systems, and will run on Macintosh computers with multicore Intel processors.

▶ **Tip:** A common disk configuration is to put the operating system and applications on drive 1, video and audio files on drive 2, and export files on drive 3. For HD work, drive 2 should be a RAID 0 striped disk array or SCSI disk subsystem.

A dedicated 7200 RPM or faster hard drive is recommended for SD or HDV media. A RAID 0 striped disk array or SCSI disk subsystem is recommended for HD. Performance will be significantly affected if you attempt to store media files and program files on the same hard drive.

Copying the lesson files

The lessons in *Adobe Premiere Pro CS4 Classroom in a Book* use specific source files, such as image files created in Adobe® Photoshop® CS4 and Adobe® Illustrator® CS4, audio files, and videos. To complete the lessons in this book, you must copy all the files from the *Adobe Premiere Pro CS4 Classroom in a Book* DVD (inside the back cover of this book) to your hard drive. You will need about 4.7 GB of storage space in addition to the 12 GB you need to install Adobe Premiere Pro CS4.

Although each lesson stands alone, some lessons use files from other lessons, so you'll need to keep the entire collection of lesson assets on your hard drive as you work through the book. Here's how to copy those assets from the DVD to your hard drive:

1 Open the *Adobe Premiere Pro CS4 Classroom in a Book* DVD in My Computer or Windows Explorer (Windows) or in the Finder (Mac OS).

2 Right-click (Windows) or Control-click (Mac OS, if you're not using a super mouse or pen, in which case you can right-click) the folder called Lessons, and choose Copy.

3 Navigate to the location you set to store your Adobe Premiere Pro CS4 projects.

The default location is My Documents\Adobe\Premiere Pro\4.0 (Windows) or Documents/Adobe/Premiere Pro/4.0 (Mac OS).

4 Right-click (Windows) or Control-click (Mac OS) the 4.0 folder, and choose Paste.

That will load all the lesson assets to your local folder. This process may take a few minutes to complete, depending on the speed of your hardware.

How to use these lessons

Each lesson in this book provides step-by-step instructions for creating one or more specific elements of a real-world project. The lessons stand alone, but most of them build on previous lessons in terms of concepts and skills. So, the best way to learn from this book is to proceed through the lessons in sequential order.

The organization of the lessons is workflow-oriented rather than feature-oriented, and uses a real-world approach. The lessons follow the typical sequential steps video editors use to complete a project, starting with acquiring video, laying down a cuts-only video, adding effects, sweetening the audio track, and ultimately exporting the project to DVD, Blu-ray Disc, or Flash.

Note: You can control many aspects of Adobe Premiere Pro CS4 using multiple techniques, such as menu commands, context menus, and keyboard shortcuts. Sometimes more than one of the methods are described in any given procedure so that you can learn different ways of working, even when the task is one you've done before.

Additional resources

Adobe Premiere Pro CS4 Classroom in a Book is not meant to replace the documentation that comes with the program or to be a comprehensive reference for every feature in Premiere Pro CS4. Only the commands and options used in the lessons are explained in this book. For comprehensive information about program features, refer to any of these resources:

Note: If Premiere Pro detects that you are not connected to the Internet when you start the application, choosing Help > Premiere Pro Help opens the Help HTML pages installed with Premiere Pro. For more up-to-date information, view the Help files online or download the current PDF for reference.

- Adobe Premiere Pro CS4 Community Help, which you can view by choosing Help > Premiere Pro Help. Community Help is an integrated online environment of instruction, inspiration, and support. It includes custom search of expert-selected, relevant content on and off Adobe.com. Community Help combines content from Adobe Help, Support, Design Center, Developer Connection, and Forums—along with great online community content so that users can easily find the best and most up-to-date resources. Access tutorials, technical support, online product help, videos, articles, tips and techniques, blogs, examples, and much more.
- Adobe Premiere Pro Help and Support Center, where you can find and browse support and learning content on Adobe.com. Visit www.adobe.com/support/premierepro/.
- Adobe TV, where you will find programming on Adobe products, including a channel for professional photographers and a How To channel that contains hundreds of movies on Premiere Pro CS4 and other products across the Adobe Creative Suite 4 lineup. Visit http://tv.adobe.com/.

Also check out these useful links:

- The Premiere Pro CS4 product home page at www.adobe.com/products/premierepro/.
- Premiere Pro user forums at www.adobe.com/support/forums/ for peer-to-peer discussions of Adobe products.
- Premiere Pro Exchange at www.adobe.com/cfusion/exchange/ for extensions, functions, code, and more.
- Premiere Pro plug-ins at www.adobe.com/products/plugins/premierepro/.

Adobe certification

The Adobe training and certification programs are designed to help Adobe customers improve and promote their product-proficiency skills. There are four levels of certification:

- Adobe Certified Associate (ACA)
- Adobe Certified Expert (ACE)
- Adobe Certified Instructor (ACI)
- Adobe Authorized Training Center (AATC)

The Adobe Certified Associate (ACA) credential certifies that individuals have the entry-level skills to plan, design, build, and maintain effective communications using different forms of digital media.

The Adobe Certified Expert program is a way for expert users to upgrade their credentials. You can use Adobe certification as a catalyst for getting a raise, finding a job, or promoting your expertise.

If you are an ACE-level instructor, the Adobe Certified Instructor program takes your skills to the next level and gives you access to a wide range of Adobe resources.

Adobe Authorized Training Centers offer instructor-led courses and training on Adobe products, employing only Adobe Certified Instructors. A directory of AATCs is available at http://partners.adobe.com.

For information on the Adobe Certified programs, visit www.adobe.com/support/certification/main.html.

Checking for Updates

Adobe periodically provides updates to software. You can easily obtain these updates through Adobe Updater, as long as you have an active Internet connection.

1 In Premiere Pro, choose Help > Updates. The Adobe Updater automatically checks for updates available for your Adobe software.

2 In the Adobe Updater dialog box, select the updates you want to install, and then click Download and Install Updates to install them.

Note: To set your preferences for future updates, click Preferences. Select how often you want Adobe Updater to check for updates, for which applications, and whether to download them automatically. Click OK to accept the new settings.

1 TOURING ADOBE PREMIERE PRO CS4

Topics covered in this lesson

- What's new in Adobe Premiere Pro CS4
- Nonlinear editing in Adobe Premiere Pro CS4
- Standard digital video workflow
- Incorporating Adobe® Creative Suite® 4 Production Premium into the workflow
- Touring the Adobe Premiere Pro workspace
- Customizing the workspace

This lesson will take approximately 40 minutes.

Before you make your first edit or apply your first transition, you will see a brief overview of video editing and how Adobe Premiere Pro fits into the video production workflow, as well as get an introduction to some of the new features of this release. Even those who are old hands at editing will find the tour useful for a glimpse of the many enhancements and new features in Adobe Premiere Pro.

Introducing Adobe Premiere Pro CS4

As video editors, we've come a long way from clunky old videotape machines and expensive production equipment to professional-level editing on a desktop computer. Adobe Premiere Pro CS4 extends our capabilities even further. To get started, we'll begin by looking at some of the exciting new features included with Adobe Premiere Pro CS4. We'll review the basic workflow most video editors follow and see how Adobe Premiere Pro fits within the different versions of Adobe Creative Suite. Finally, you'll be introduced to custom workspaces in Adobe Premiere Pro CS4.

New Features in Adobe Premiere Pro CS4

Although this is not a complete list of every new feature in Adobe Premiere Pro CS4, it will give you an idea of some of the improvements you can look forward to as you learn this exciting application. We will use many of these features in the lessons throughout the book.

Effects

- **Apply effects to multiple clips**: Speed up your editing by selecting multiple clips in a sequence, and drag one or more effects from the Effects panel to the selected clips.
- **Use multiple effects in presets**: Now you can save one or multiple effects as a preset that you can apply to one or multiple clips in a sequence or project panel.
- **Remove all effects**: Quickly remove all effects from one or more clips. There are also new options to allow you to remove selected effects from a clip.
- **Use blending modes**: Each clip now has blending modes available that are similar to the same feature in Adobe Photoshop® CS4 and Adobe After Effects® CS4. Photoshop images with blending modes applied are recognized and supported when imported into Adobe Premiere Pro CS4.

Audio

- **Zoom waveforms vertically**: Zoom in to the waveform in the Source Monitor to get a better view of amplitude.
- **Scrub audio in a waveform**: In the past, it was necessary to scrub by using the current-time indicator in the Source Monitor. Now you can scrub right on the waveform.

- **Normalize master tracks**: Easily adjust the volume of your mix by normalizing the master track to a peak value in decibels (dB).
- **Use additional audio gain options**: Now you can set gain to a specific value, adjust gain by an amount relative to the current value, normalize to the maximum peak, or normalize to a specific peak value.
- **Transcribe speech**: Transcribe a video interview to text in order to search for words or to find a specific frame of video without having to listen to the audio frame by frame.

Sequence editing

- **Move the current-time indicator to the end of a pasted clip**: This is a simple but useful improvement when pasting the same content multiple times.
- **Return to previous zoom level**: Often, editors want to zoom in to a specific frame and then zoom back to see more of the sequence. A new shortcut makes this easy.
- **Change destination tracks in the Timeline while dragging clips**: Now you can determine the combination of destination tracks of your choice when dragging a clip to the Timeline.
- **Change the speed and duration of multiple clips**: This is a powerful new feature that will save a lot of time when you need to manipulate time.
- **Use new keyboard shortcuts to jump to the head/tail of a clip**: These new shortcuts work in the Timeline, Program Monitor, Reference Monitor, Effect Controls, and Audio Mixer panels.
- **Snap a clip when moving between tracks**: With this new option, it is easy to keep a clip in the same location in time as you drag it between tracks.
- **Snap keyframes to align them**: Now it is a simple task to align the keyframes of multiple effects.
- **Apply the default transition to multiple clips**: This is a huge time-saver when you want to apply the same transition to one or many clips.
- **Nest sequences quickly**: Nested sequences have been a powerful feature of Adobe Premiere Pro, and now they are even more flexible. Quickly create a nest from a continuous or noncontiguous selection of clips.
- **Drag subclips from the Timeline**: Now you can drag a subclip from the Timeline directly to a bin.
- **Set In and Out points around a clip**: In addition to the traditional In and Out points of a sequence, now you can create In and Out points around a clip in a sequence.

- **Track synchronization during edits**: Easily control which tracks remain in sync during a ripple or insert edit.
- **Use source patch indicators**: Map each source track containing multiple audio tracks to specific destination tracks.

Managing assets

- **Search faster and better in the Project panel**: Search faster, across all columns on the Project panel.
- **Leverage the improved metadata**: Tab between columns and edit the fields right in the Project panel.
- **Import layers with the enhanced PSD support**: Integration with Photoshop is even better in Adobe Premiere Pro CS4. There are now options for merging all layers, merging selected layers, selecting individual layers, and importing selected layers to a sequence.
- **Import Photoshop video**: Now you can import Adobe Photoshop video into Adobe Premiere Pro CS4, and it will play back as it does in Adobe Photoshop.
- **Replace footage**: Similar to the old Replace With Clip feature, this feature allows more flexibility.
- **Browse for files with Media Browser**: Media Browser is a panel in Adobe Premiere Pro CS4 that allows you to quickly locate and import footage. Thanks to Media Browser, you no longer need to move to your operating system's file manager to browse for files.
- **Explore the improved support for tapeless formats**: Using the new Media Browser, media from Panasonic P2 or Sony XDCAM is automatically filtered to display importable media. Adobe Premiere Pro CS4 also supports and maintains metadata from tapeless media.

Project and sequences

- **Save media locations within projects**: Rather than using a global setting, you can specify a different scratch disk path for each project, if desired.
- **Separate your sequence and project settings**: Now you can now create sequences with different media types in the same project. You can also import a specific sequence from one project rather than importing the entire project.
- **Replace clips with an Adobe After Effects composition**: Select a group of clips and easily convert them to an After Effects composition, which instantly becomes a dynamic link in Adobe Premiere Pro CS4.
- **Dynamically link to Adobe Encore CS4**: Save a lot of time and disk space by sending a sequence to Encore without rendering or exporting an intermediate file.

Nonlinear editing in Adobe Premiere Pro CS4

Adobe Premiere Pro is a nonlinear editor (NLE). Unlike older videotape-editing systems, where you generally need to lay down edits consecutively and contiguously, Adobe Premiere Pro lets you place, replace, trim, and move clips anywhere you want in your final edited video.

On videotape systems, if you decide to insert a sound bite in the middle of a story already edited on tape, you need to insert that sound bite over your existing edits and reedit everything after it. Or you can make a *dub* (copy) of the story segment after the new edit point and rerecord that part after adding the sound bite (causing generation quality loss in the process).

Adobe Premiere Pro lets you do things nonsequentially. With Adobe Premiere Pro (and other NLEs), you can make changes by simply dragging clips or segments around within your final video. You can edit video segments separately and tie them together later. You can even edit the closing sequence first.

NLEs have another huge benefit over videotape-editing systems: immediate access to your video clips. No longer do you need to endlessly fast-forward or rewind through tons of tape to find that one elusive-but-essential shot. With Adobe Premiere Pro, it's a mouse click away.

Adobe Premiere Pro supports the new tapeless media formats including Panasonic P2 and Sony XDCAM. With this new tapeless technology, media acquisition has also become nonlinear.

Presenting the standard digital video workflow

There is a basic workflow for creating videos with NLEs such as Adobe Premiere Pro. After a while, it'll become second nature. Generally, that workflow follows these steps:

1 Shoot the video.

2 Capture (transfer) the video to your hard drive. With tapeless media, Adobe Premiere Pro can read the media directly. Or, use Adobe OnLocation CS4 to record video directly to your workstation hard drive (bypassing the capture step).

3 Build your edited video by selecting, trimming, and adding clips to the Timeline.

4 Place transitions between clips, apply video effects to clips, and composite (layer) clips.

5 Create text, credits, or basic graphics, and apply them to your project.

Note: Audio can also be the first thing you lay down when editing a video.

6 Add audio—be it narration, music, or sound effects.

7 Mix multiple audio tracks, and use transitions and special effects on your audio clips.

8 Export your finished project to videotape, to a file on your desktop computer, to streaming video for Internet playback, or to a DVD or Blu-ray Disc.

Adobe Premiere Pro supports each of these steps with industry-leading tools. Since this book is geared to the beginning and intermediate video editor, becoming proficient with these standard workflow tools is the primary goal of the upcoming lessons.

Enhancing the workflow with high-level features

Adobe Premiere Pro goes well beyond providing a full-featured toolset for standard digital video editing. It's loaded with extra features that can enhance the video production process and improve the quality of your finished product.

You're not likely to incorporate many of these features in your first few video projects. But as you ramp up your skills and expectations, you'll begin to tap these high-productivity features. The following topics will be covered in this book:

- **Advanced audio editing**: Adobe Premiere Pro provides audio effects and editing unequaled by any other nonlinear editor, or by most audio software. Create and place 5.1 surround-sound audio channels, make sample-level edits, apply multiple audio effects to any audio clip or track, and use the included state-of-the-art plug-ins and other Virtual Studio Technology (VST) plug-ins.
- **Color correction**: Correct and enhance the look of your footage with advanced color-correction filters.
- **Keyframe controls**: Adobe Premiere Pro CS4 gives you the precise control you need to fine-tune your visual and motion effects without requiring you to export to a compositing application.
- **Broad hardware support**: Choose from a wide range of capture cards and other hardware to assemble a system that best fits your needs and budget. Adobe Premiere Pro CS4 support extends from low-cost computers for digital video (DV) and compressed high-definition video (HDV) format editing up to high-performance workstations capturing high-definition (HD) video. When it's time to upgrade your hardware to work with HD and film, you don't need to leave the familiar Adobe Premiere Pro interface—unlike with some proprietary systems that use different interfaces for different formats.

- **Clip notes**: Speed your client review-and-approval process by embedding Adobe Premiere Pro projects in PDF documents. Your client watches the video with Adobe® Reader®, enters comments into the feedback form in the PDF file, and then e-mails the comments to you.
- **GPU-accelerated video effects**: Use the graphics-processing unit (GPU) on modern graphics cards to create real-time page curls, page rolls, spheres with video mapped on them, and other image distortion effects that typically require expensive hardware or long render times.
- **High-definition video support**: Work with every high-definition format, including HDV, AVCHD, XDCAM HD, DVCPRO HD, D5-HD, and 4K film scans. Adobe Premiere Pro CS4 supports these formats at any resolution (720p, 1080i, 1080p) and frame rate (24 fps, 23.98 fps, 30 fps, 60 fps, and so on).
- **Support for tapeless workflows**: Adobe Premiere Pro CS4 supports tapeless media—such as P2 and other flash-based formats—natively, without the need to convert the files.
- **Multicam editing**: You can easily and quickly edit any production shot with multiple cameras. Adobe Premiere Pro displays all the camera tracks in a split-view monitor, and you set the edits by clicking in the appropriate screen or by pressing keys.
- **Project Manager**: Manage your media through a single dialog box. View, delete, move, search for, and reorganize clips and bins. Consolidate your projects by moving just the media actually used in a project and copying that media to a single location. Then reclaim drive space by deleting unused media.

Incorporating other Creative Suite components into the editing workflow

Even with all the exciting extra features in Adobe Premiere Pro, it cannot perform some digital video production tasks. These include the following:

- High-end 3D motion effects
- Detailed text animations
- Layered graphics
- Vector artwork
- Music creation
- Advanced audio mixing, editing, and effects processing

To incorporate one or more of these features into a production, you can turn to the other applications included in the Adobe Creative Suite 4 Production Premium product family. It has all the components you need to produce some absolutely amazing videos.

Here's a brief description of the nine other components in Adobe Creative Suite 4 Production Premium:

- **Adobe® After Effects® CS4**: The tool of choice for motion graphics and visual effects artists.
- **Adobe® Photoshop® CS4 Extended**: The industry standard image-editing and graphic-creation product.
- **Adobe® Soundbooth™ CS4**: Easy yet powerful audio editing, audio cleanup, audio sweetening, and music creation.
- **Adobe® Encore® CS4**: A high-quality DVD-authoring product designed to work closely with Adobe Premiere Pro, After Effects, and Photoshop CS4. Encore publishes to standard DVD, Blu-ray Disc, and interactive SWF files. Encore CS4 is included with Adobe Premiere Pro CS4 when it's purchased outside the Creative Suite 4 Production Premium suite.
- **Adobe® Illustrator® CS4**: Professional vector graphics creation software for print, video production, and the Web.
- **Adobe® Dynamic Link**: A cross-product connection that allows you to work in real time with native After Effects files in Adobe Premiere Pro and Encore CS4 without rendering first.
- **Adobe® Bridge CS4**: A visual file browser that provides centralized access to your Creative Suite project files, applications, and settings.
- **Adobe® Flash® CS4 Professional**: The industry standard for creating rich, interactive web content.
- **Adobe® OnLocation® CS4 (now available for Windows and Mac)**: Powerful direct-to-disk recording and monitoring software to help you produce superior-quality results from your video camera.

Adobe Creative Suite 4 Production Premium workflow

Your Adobe Premiere Pro/Adobe Creative Suite Production Premium workflow will vary depending on your production needs. Here are a few mini-workflow scenarios:

- Use Adobe OnLocation to record video direct to disk.
- Use Photoshop CS4 to touch up still images from a digital camera, a scanner, or an Adobe Premiere Pro video clip. Then export them to Adobe Premiere Pro.
- Create layered graphics in Photoshop CS4, and then open them in Adobe Premiere Pro. You can opt to have each layer appear on a separate track in the Timeline, allowing you to apply effects and motion to selected layers.
- Build custom music tracks using Adobe Soundbooth CS4, and then export them to Adobe Premiere Pro.
- Use Adobe Soundbooth to do professional-quality audio editing and sweetening on an existing Adobe Premiere Pro video or a separate audio file.
- Using Dynamic Link, open Adobe Premiere Pro video sequences in After Effects CS4. Apply complex motion and animation, and then send those updated motion sequences back to Adobe Premiere Pro. You can play After Effects compositions in Adobe Premiere Pro CS4 without first waiting to render them.
- Use After Effects CS4 to create and animate text in ways far beyond the capabilities of Adobe Premiere Pro. Export those compositions to Adobe Premiere Pro.
- Send video projects created in Adobe Premiere Pro into Encore CS4 using Dynamic Link, without rendering or saving an intermediate file. Use Encore to create a DVD, Blu-ray Disc, or interactive Flash application.

Most of this book will focus on a "standard" workflow involving only Adobe Premiere Pro. However, several lessons will demonstrate how you can incorporate Adobe Creative Suite 4 Production Premium components within your workflow for even more spectacular results.

Touring the Adobe Premiere Pro workspace

You'll dive into nonlinear editing in the next lesson. At this point, you'll take a brief tour of the video-editing workspace. In this exercise, you will use an Adobe Premiere Pro project from this book's companion DVD:

1 Make sure you've copied all the lesson folders and contents from the DVD to your hard drive. The suggested directory is My Documents\Adobe\Premiere Pro\4.0\Lessons (Windows) or Documents/Adobe/Premiere Pro/4.0/Lessons (Mac OS).

Note: It's best to copy all the lesson assets from the DVD to your hard drive and leave them there until you complete this book; some lessons refer to assets from previous lessons.

2 Start Adobe Premiere Pro.

3 Click Open Project.

In Adobe Premiere Pro's welcome screen, you can start a new project or open a saved one.

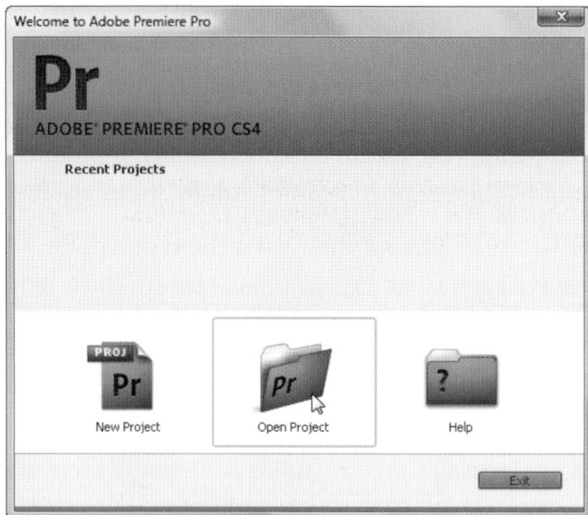

4 In the Open Project window, navigate to the Lesson 01 folder in the Lessons folder, and then double-click the Lesson 01.prproj project file to open the first lesson in the Adobe Premiere Pro workspace.

All Adobe Premiere Pro project files have a .prproj extension.

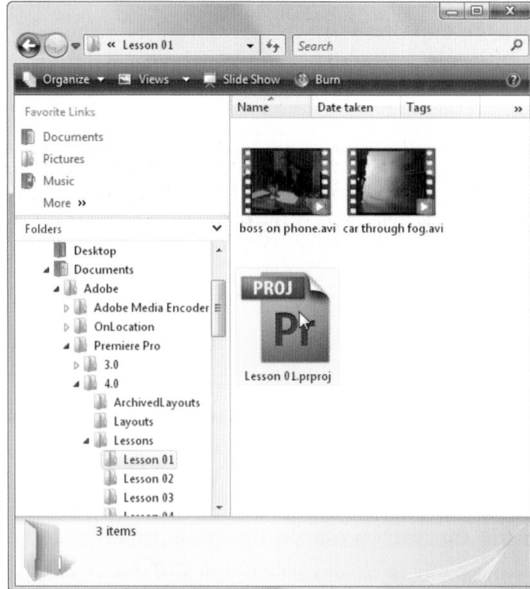

● **Note:** You may be prompted with a dialog box asking where a particular file is. This will happen when the original files are saved on a hard drive other than the one you're using. You'll need to tell Adobe Premiere Pro where the file is. In this case, navigate to the Lesson 01 folder, and select the file that the dialog box is prompting you to open.

The workspace layout

If you've never seen a nonlinear editor, the default workspace might overwhelm you. Don't worry. A lot of careful consideration went into its design and layout. The principal elements are identified in the figure shown here.

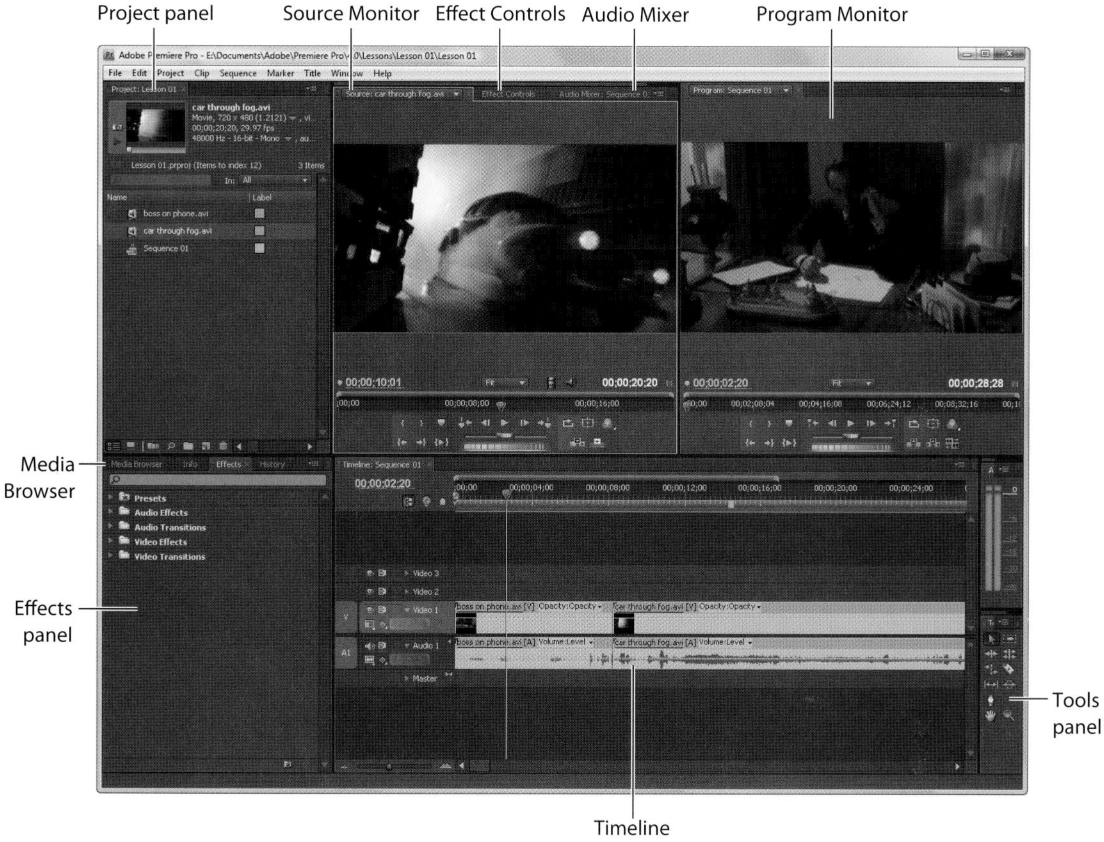

Each workspace item appears in its own panel. You can dock multiple panels in a single frame. Some items with common industry terms stand alone, such as Timeline, Audio Mixer, and Program Monitor. The main workspace elements are as follows:

- **Timeline**: This is where you'll do most of your actual editing. You create sequences (Adobe's term for edited video segments or entire projects) in the Timeline. One strength of sequences is that you can nest them—place sequences in other sequences. In this way, you can break up a production into manageable chunks.

More tracks than you can use: You can layer—or composite—video clips, images, graphics, and titles in an unlimited number of tracks. Video clips in higher-numbered tracks cover whatever is directly below them on the Timeline. Therefore, you need to give clips in higher-numbered tracks some kind of transparency or reduce their size if you want to let clips in lower tracks show through. Compositing will be covered in several upcoming lessons.

- **Monitors**: You use the Source Monitor (on the left) to view and trim raw clips (your original footage). To place a clip in the Source Monitor, double-click boss on phone.avi in the Project panel. The Program Monitor (on the right) is for viewing your project-in-progress.

  Single- or dual-monitor view: Some editors prefer working with only one monitor screen. The lessons throughout this book reflect a two-monitor workflow. You can change to a single-monitor view if you choose. Click the Close button in the Source tab to close that monitor. In the main menu, choose Window > Source Monitor to open it again.

- **Project panel**: This is where you place links to your project's assets: video clips, audio files, graphics, still images, and sequences. You use bins—or folders—to organize your assets.
- **Media Browser panel**: This is where you can browse your file system to quickly locate a file to examine or import.

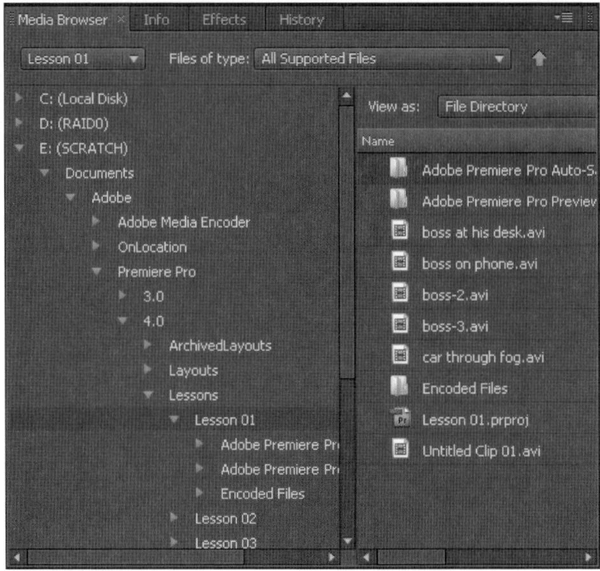

Media Browser allows fast, easy access to files in your operating system.

- **Effects panel**: Click the Effects tab (docked, by default, with the History and Info tabs) to open the Effects panel (shown below, on the left). Effects are organized by Presets, Audio Effects, Audio Transitions, Video Effects, and Video Transitions. If you open the various effects bins, you'll note that they include numerous audio effects to spice up your sound; two audio crossfade transitions; video scene transitions, such as dissolves and wipes; and many video effects to alter the appearance of your clips.
- **Audio Mixer**: Click the Audio Mixer tab to the right of the Effect Controls tab to open the Audio Mixer. This interface looks a lot like audio production studio hardware, with its volume sliders and panning knobs—one set of controls for each audio track in the Timeline, plus a master track.

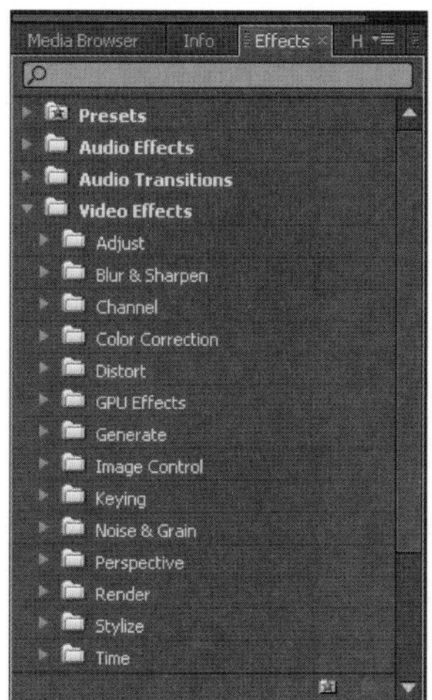

Effects panel

Audio Mixer

- **Effect Controls panel**: Click the Effect Controls tab, and then click any clip in the Timeline to display that clip's effect parameters in the Effect Controls panel (shown on the next page). This will give you a small taste of many lessons to come. Two video effects are always present for every video, still, or graphic: Motion and Opacity. Each effect parameter (in the case of Motion: Position, Scale height and width, Rotation, and Anchor Point) is adjustable over time using keyframes. The Effect Controls panel is an immensely powerful tool that gives you incredible creative latitude. It comes up in many of this book's lessons.

- **Tools panel**: Each icon in this panel represents a tool that performs a specific function, typically a type of edit. The Selection tool is context-sensitive, which means it changes appearance to indicate the function that matches the circumstances.

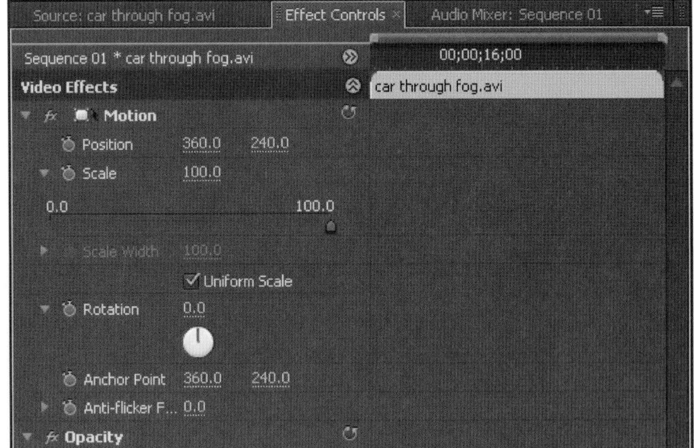

Effect Controls panel

Tools panel

- **Info panel**: Click the Info tab to the left of the Effects tab. The Info panel that appears (shown below, on the left) presents a data snapshot of any asset you've selected in the Project panel or any clip or transition selected in a sequence.
- **History panel**: Click the History tab to the right of the Effects tab to open the History panel. This panel tracks every step you take in your video production and lets you back up if you don't like your latest efforts. When you back up to a previous condition, all steps that came after that point are also undone. In other words, you cannot extract a single misstep buried within the current list.

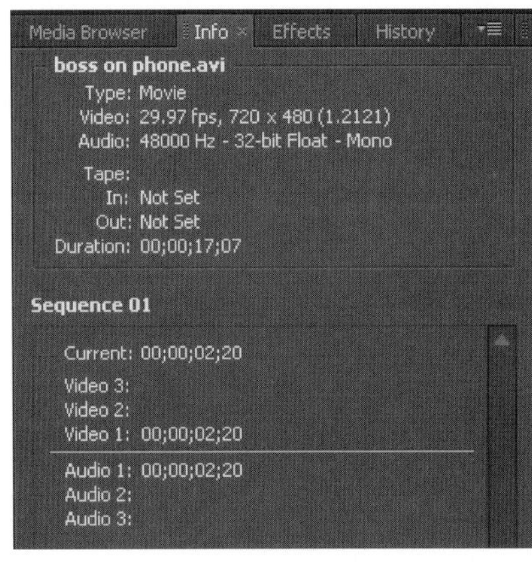

Info panel

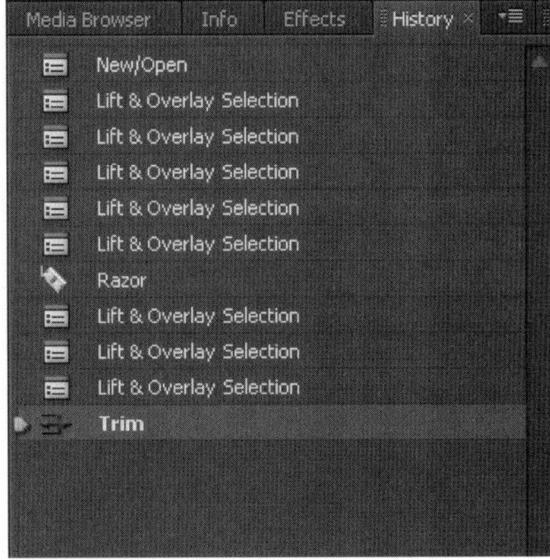

History panel

Customizing the workspace

You can customize the workspace to create a layout that works best for you:

- As you change the size of one frame, other frames change size to compensate.
- All panels within frames are accessible via tabs.
- All panels are dockable—you can drag a panel from one frame to another.
- You can drag a panel out of a frame to become a separate floating panel.

You can save your workspace as a custom workspace, and you can save as many custom workspaces as you like.

In this exercise, you'll try all these functions and save a customized workspace. Before changing the interface layout, though, you'll adjust its brightness:

1 Choose Edit > Preferences > Appearance (Windows) or Premiere Pro > Preferences > Appearance (Mac OS).

2 Drag the Brightness slider to the left or right to suit your needs. When done, click OK.

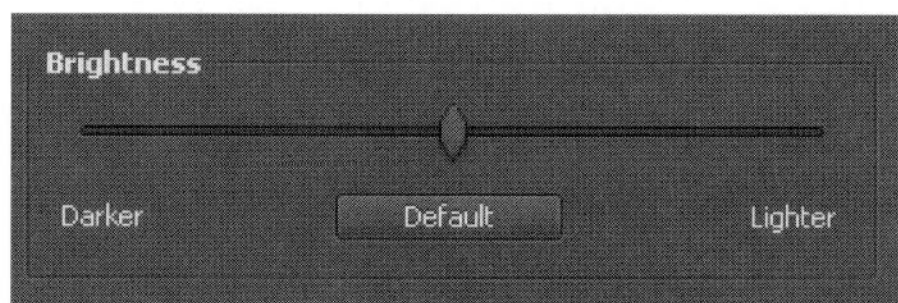

Cave-like editing bays: As you approach the darkest setting, the text switches to white on gray. This is to accommodate those editors who work in editing bays in darkened rooms.

3 Click the Effects tab, and then position your pointer on the vertical divider between the Effects panel and the Timeline. Then, click and drag left and right to change the sizes of those frames.

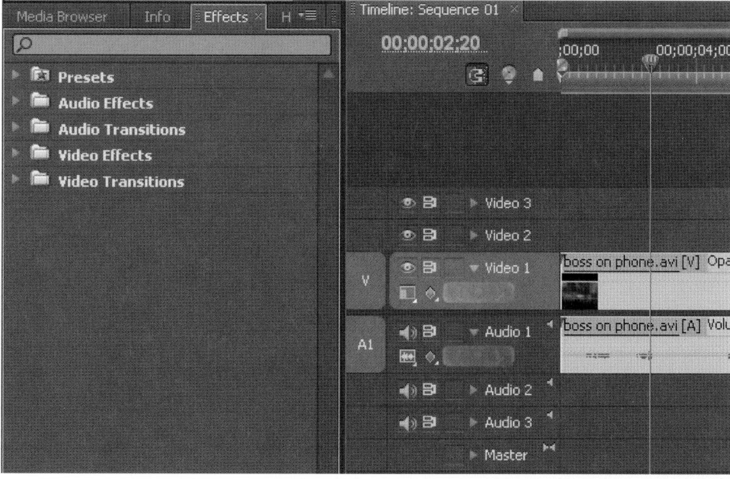

4 Place the pointer on the horizontal divider between the Effect Controls panel and the Timeline. Click and drag up and down to change the sizes of these frames.

Note: As you move a panel around, Adobe Premiere Pro displays a drop zone. If the panel is a rectangle, it will go into the selected frame. If it's a trapezoid, it'll go into its own frame.

5 Click the drag handle in the upper-left corner of the History tab, and drag it to the top of the interface, next to the Project tab, to dock the History panel in that frame.

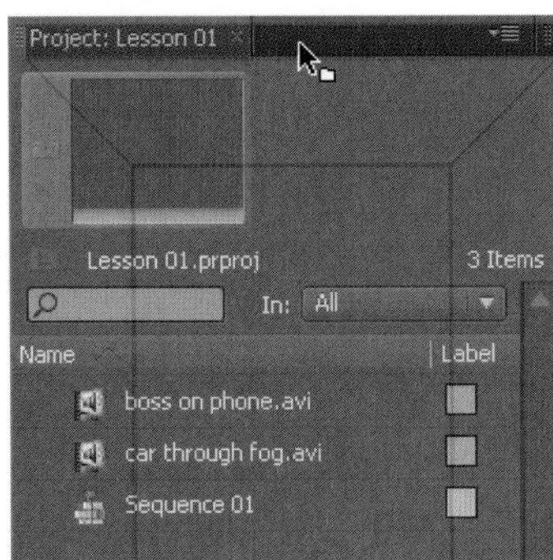

Rectangular drop zone

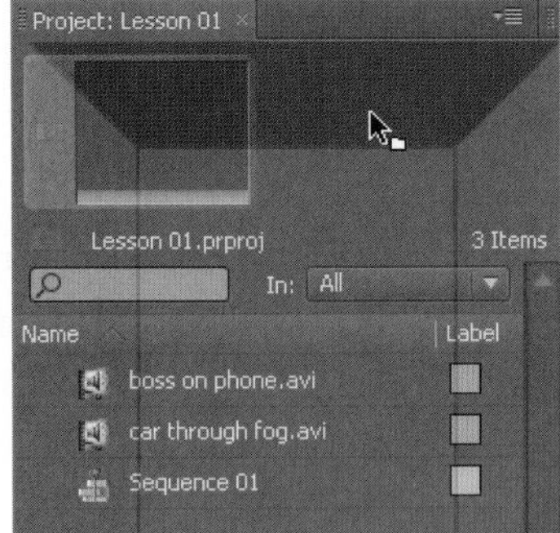

Trapezoidal drop zone

Dealing with a crowded frame: When the History panel is added to the frame with the Project panel, you may not be able to see all the tabs. In this case, a slider appears above the tabs. Slide it left or right to reveal all the tabs. You can also open a hidden (or any other) panel directly from a menu by choosing Window and then clicking a panel name.

6 Drag the Effect Controls drag handle to a point near the bottom of the Project panel to place it in its own frame.

As shown here on the left, the drop zone is a trapezoid that covers the lower portion of the Project panel. Release the mouse button, and your workspace should look something like the one shown here on the right.

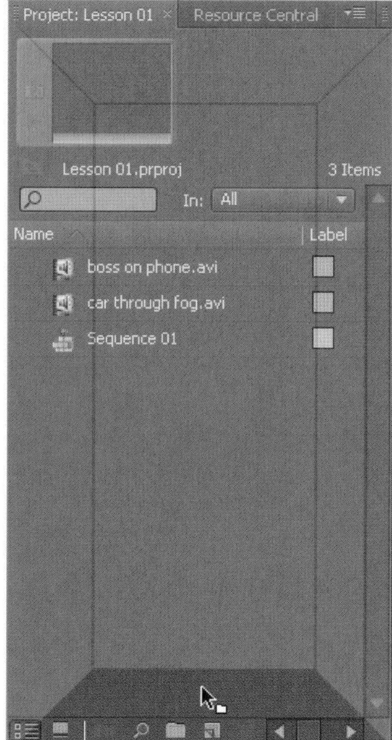

7 Click the Program Monitor's drag handle, and hold down the Control (Windows) or Command (Mac OS) key while dragging it out of its frame. Its drop zone image is much more distinct, indicating you are about to create a floating panel.

8 Drop the Program Monitor anywhere, creating a floating panel. Expand it by dragging from the corner.

9 As you gain editing acumen, you might want to create and save a customized workspace. To do so, choose Window > Workspace > New Workspace. Type a workspace name and click OK.

10 If you want to return the workspace to its default layout, choose Window > Workspace > Reset Current Workspace.

Review questions

1 Why is Adobe Premiere Pro considered a nonlinear editor?

2 Describe the basic video-editing workflow.

3 What is the difference between the Project panel and Media Browser?

4 Can you save a customized workspace?

5 What is the purpose of the Source Monitor? What is the purpose of the Program Monitor?

6 Describe how OnLocation works with Premiere Pro.

Review answers

1 Adobe Premiere Pro lets you place video, audio, and graphics anywhere on a sequence (in the Timeline), rearrange media clips within a sequence, add transitions, apply effects, and do any number of other video-editing steps in just about any order that suits you.

2 Shoot your video; transfer it to your computer; create a sequence of video, audio, and still-image clips on the Timeline; apply effects and transitions; add text and graphics; edit your audio; and export the finished product.

3 The Project panel contains links to files on your computer that have been imported into Adobe Premiere Pro. Media Browser is a convenient way to browse your computer's file system from within Adobe Premiere Pro.

4 Yes. Any customized workspace can be saved by choosing Window > Workspace > New Workspace.

5 You use the monitor panels to view your project and your original clips. When working with two monitors—Source and Program—you can view and trim your raw footage in the Source Monitor and use the Program Monitor to view the Timeline sequence as you build it.

6 OnLocation provides a way to capture video and audio from a camera directly to disk. You can import these files directly into Adobe Premiere Pro without capturing them.

2 EXPLORING ADOBE ONLOCATION CS4

Topics covered in this lesson

- Connecting your camcorder to Adobe OnLocation CS4
- Calibrating your camera with SureShot
- Recording live video
- Recording video to a shot list
- Analyzing video with Adobe OnLocation
- Analyzing audio with Adobe OnLocation

This lesson will take approximately 40 minutes.

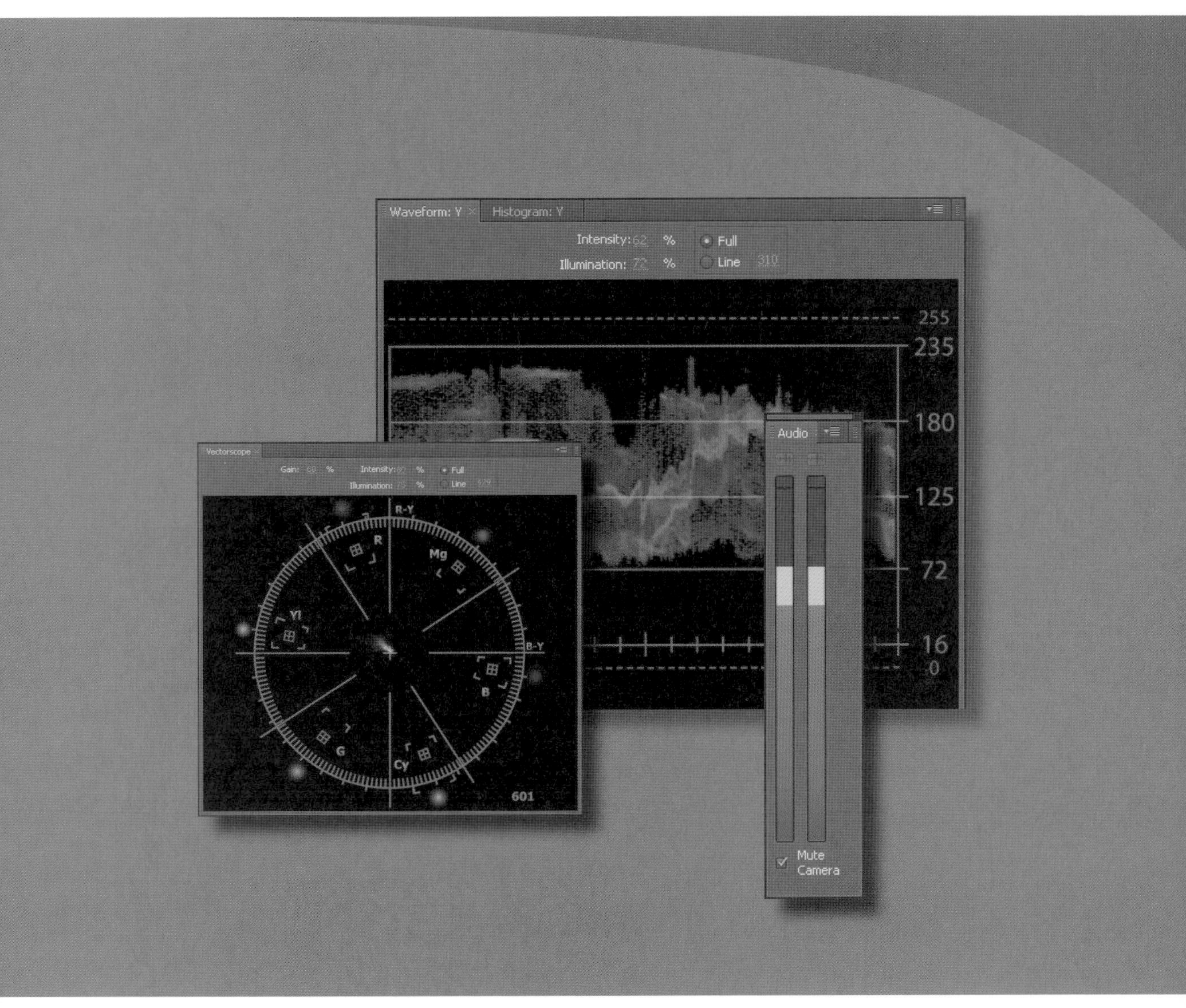

Adobe OnLocation allows you to bypass the time-consuming step of capturing video and also provides tools for ensuring your camera and lighting are set up perfectly, before you ever record a frame of video.

Getting started

Adobe OnLocation enables you to record video from your camcorder directly to disk, bypassing the slow process of recording to tape and then capturing. Because editors are often up against tight deadlines, this capability can deliver a huge boost in productivity. Adobe OnLocation can also save time and improve the quality of your shots by providing professional monitoring tools and scopes while you shoot. Adobe OnLocation is now available for Windows and Mac platforms.

Setting up Adobe OnLocation

Adobe OnLocation communicates with camcorders and other OHCI-compliant devices using the IEEE 1394 standard. You can connect your camera to your desktop or notebook computer, as described in the next chapter's lesson, via an IEEE 1394 cable, just as you would to capture video that you've already recorded to tape. However, instead of capturing video to Adobe Premiere Pro, you will be recording live video directly to your computer. This requires your computer to be "on location" with your camcorder. These are the basic steps to follow:

1 Connect the camcorder to your computer.

2 Turn on your camcorder and set it to camera mode.

3 In Windows XP, if the Digital Video Device message pops up, click Take No Action, select the Always Perform The Selected Action option, and click OK. (The next time you fire up your camcorder, you should not see this connection query.) In Windows Vista, an AutoPlay dialog box may appear. Click "Set AutoPlay defaults in Control Panel," as shown here. In Mac OS, if iMovie or another application starts, see that application's Help for information about which application to open when a camera is connected.

4. Start Adobe OnLocation.

5 Click New Project.

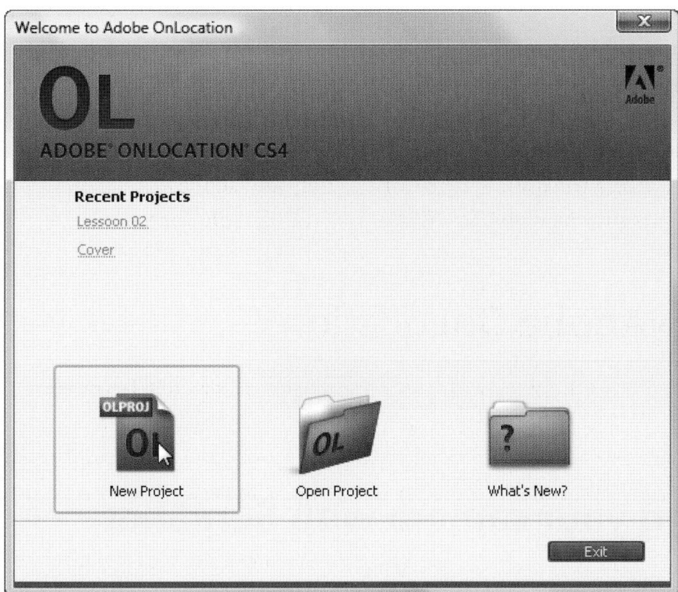

6 Name the project First_Project, and save it to a folder of your choice.

7 Choose Window > Workspace > Calibration to change to the Calibration workspace.

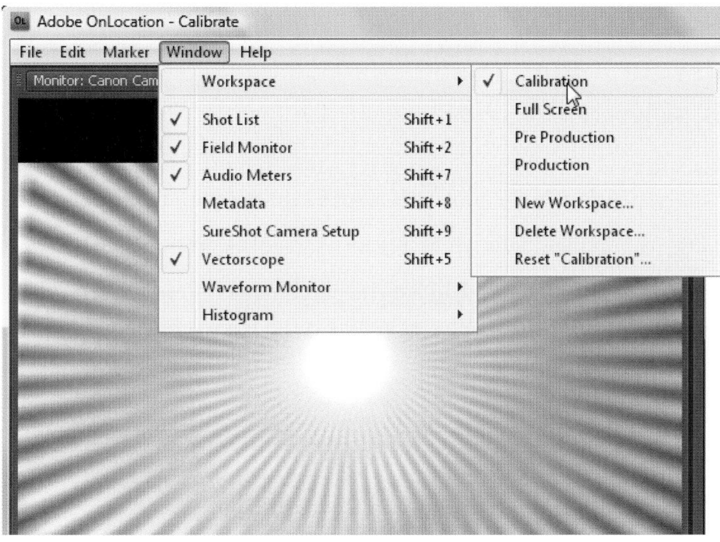

8 Click the SureShot tab near the bottom of the window.

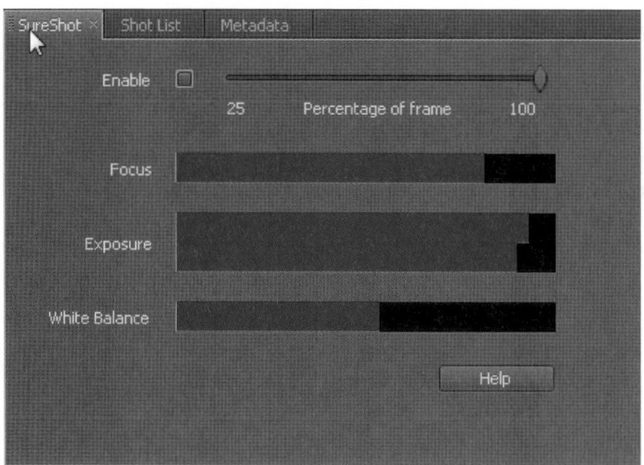

Calibrating your camera with SureShot

You can dramatically improve your videos by fine-tuning your camera setup before recording a single frame of video. The SureShot component in Adobe OnLocation is an excellent tool to help you calibrate your camera's focus, exposure, and white balance. To fine-tune your camera setup effectively, it will be helpful to set your camcorder to manual focus, manual exposure, and manual white balance so you have complete control over these attributes.

Setting up your frame

To set up your frame, follow these steps:

1 Point your camera at your subject, and place the SureShot Focus and exposure chart (which is included in the box with Adobe OnLocation) next to the subject.

2 Zoom in with your camera lens so the Focus chart takes up most of the frame.

3 If necessary, enable the slider and adjust the percentage of frame value on the SureShot panel to crop the frame to include just the Focus chart.

Setting your focus

To set up your focus, adjust the focus on your camcorder until the focus indicator in the SureShot component grows as large as possible. You will also notice the focus fine-tuning in the monitor window.

Setting your iris/exposure

To set up your iris/exposure, adjust the exposure on your camera so that the exposure meter in the SureShot panel grows as far to the right as possible but remains even. Achieving this exposure gives you the maximum range of darks to whites without overexposing the video. Note that the top exposure line indicates darks, and the bottom exposure line indicates lights.

About exposure

Exposure is determined by multiple factors: lighting, iris/aperature, shutter speed, and gain.

- Adjust the physical lighting of your scene (ambient or created) to achieve the best exposure.
- Adjust the aperture of your camera to let more or less light into the camera. (The wider your iris, the shallower your depth of field.)
- Adjust the shutter speed to allow light into the camera for shorter or longer periods of time. (Shutter speeds of 1/60 second are typical for shoots not involving very fast action.)
- Adjust the gain to set the level of electronic lighting enhancement.

Setting your white balance

White balancing your shot is important to help ensure that the camera records the correct colors. When properly white balanced, the recorded images will accurately reflect the real colors in the scene. By following these steps, you can ensure that your camera will record an optimally exposed and focused video.

1 Flip over the SureShot Focus and Exposure chart to reveal a blank white card.

2 Adjust the white balance on your camera until the white balance meter in the SureShot panel is maximized to the right. When properly set, the white card in the field monitor component will appear white rather than gray or a different hue.

White balance controls on camcorders

The white balance controls on most camcorders include manual settings, presets, and custom presets.

Manual: Some camcorders allow you to manually dial any color temperature. This is the most flexible method.

Presets: Some camcorders have white balance presets such as Indoors, Outdoors, and so on. Scroll through them to see which one best matches your scene.

Custom presets: Some camcorders can "learn" custom white balance settings by pointing the camera at a white card and pressing a button on the camcorder to "learn" the color temperature.

Review the documentation for your camcorder to learn how to set the white balance properly on your camera.

Recording live video

Recording live video from your camera to your computer can save you hours of time in capturing and logging tapes. Recording directly to your computer's hard drive happens in real time, and the clips recorded are available immediately for editing. You simply need to import them into Adobe Premiere Pro.

Now that your camera is set up and calibrated, record some video directly to your hard drive.

1 Choose Window > Workspace > Production to change to the Production workspace.

2 If your camera is on, you should see the live video displayed in the monitor.

3 Click the red Record button at the bottom of the monitor panel. Notice that a clip appears in the Shot List panel to indicate the recording activity. Press Stop when you are finished recording.

4 To immediately use the clip in Adobe Premiere Pro, open Adobe Premiere Pro, choose File > Import, and navigate to the folder where you created your Adobe OnLocation project. Inside that folder will be a folder called Clips. Select the file or files you want and click Open. Your video is immediately available to edit, with no capture time or clip logging.

Adobe OnLocation recording features

The digital recorder will actually start recording video 5 seconds before you click the Record button. This helps ensure you never miss a good scene. You can adjust the amount of time this "pre-roll" is buffered in the Premiere Pro > Preferences > Device Control (Mac) or Edit > Preferences > Device Control menu (Windows).

If you want to break up a scene into multiple clips, clicking the Record button while already recording will start a new clip.

You can record directly to your hard drive and to tape with Adobe OnLocation. Simply follow the instructions for recording directly to disk and also put a tape in your camcorder. The tape can become a backup or archive as needed.

Recording video to a shot list

Planning a video shoot well can save you hours of time. Adobe OnLocation allows you to create a shot list in advance of the shoot to help you plan and organize your shots. In this exercise, you will create a shot list of three shots:

1 Use the project that is already open.

2 Click the "Add shot placeholder" icon three times to create three new shots for the shot list.

3 The shot placeholders will be named based on your project name. Rename them as shown in the figure.

4 Make sure your camera is connected and powered on in camera mode.

5 Select the "Establishing shot" clip in the shot list.

6 Click the Record button near the bottom of the Monitor panel. Notice the video is being recorded into the "Establishing shot" placeholder clip. Click the Stop button when you are done recording.

7 Repeat this recording for the wide-shot and close-up placeholder clips.

Retakes

It is common to encounter problems when shooting a scene, so it is often necessary to record multiple takes of the same shot. If a second or third take is required when recording to a shot list, click the "Add Shot Placeholder" icon while the main shot is selected, and Adobe OnLocation will create a new take for the same shot.

Analyzing video with Adobe OnLocation

Earlier in this lesson, you calibrated your camera to ensure that focus, exposure, and white balance are correct. This is an important step, and the SureShot feature is a very helpful tool in accomplishing that. But changing conditions in the scene can alter color or exposure, so it's important to monitor your shoot continuously. Adobe OnLocation provides a powerful set of tools to help you monitor video.

1 Open a new Adobe OnLocation project by choosing File > Open Project.

2 Navigate to the Lesson 02 folder and open the project called Lesson 02.olproj.

Notice three clips were captured in this project. These clips have some metadata in the Comments fields to help the editor choose the best clips. These clips are of the same scene but recorded with different exposure and audio settings on the camera.

Waveform Monitor

The Waveform Monitor represents *luminance* (or brightness) in a graphical form in real time as the video plays. The brightness value of each pixel in the video frame is represented by the waveform graph. The higher the graph, the brighter the pixel.

A well-exposed scene has brightness values across the entire scale. It is easy to see that pixels that are all dark would make a dark video or that pixels that are all bright would make a bright video. But it is also important to understand that having brightness values across the entire scale gives a feeling of depth to the image. Having brightness values across the entire scale is called *range*. Let's take a look at some examples of good range and bad range using the Waveform Monitor as a tool:

1 Select the clip named normal.avi. Play it by clicking the Play icon near the bottom of the monitor.

2 Observe the Waveform Monitor.

   The luminance or brightness values have a nice range, from 16 (the normal low range for black) to about 200 (the normal high range for white). This clip is an example of a scene that is properly exposed.

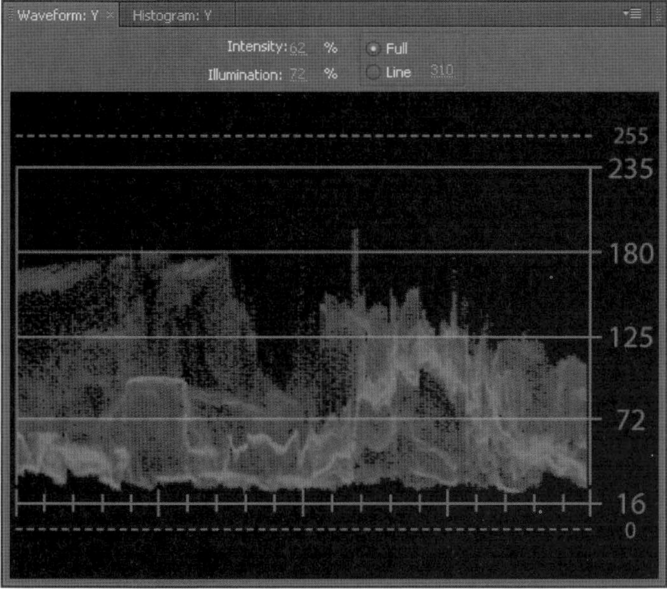

3 Select the clip named dark_loud.avi. When you play this clip, notice that the waveform does not extend to 200—all the brightness values are clumped at the bottom. Although the image is not overly dark, it is uninteresting because of the limited range of luminance values. When you see a waveform like this, you should consider adjusting the exposure on the camera or changing the lighting

to provide a greater range of luminance. Observing the Waveform Monitor while you make lighting changes is a good way to know when you have it right.

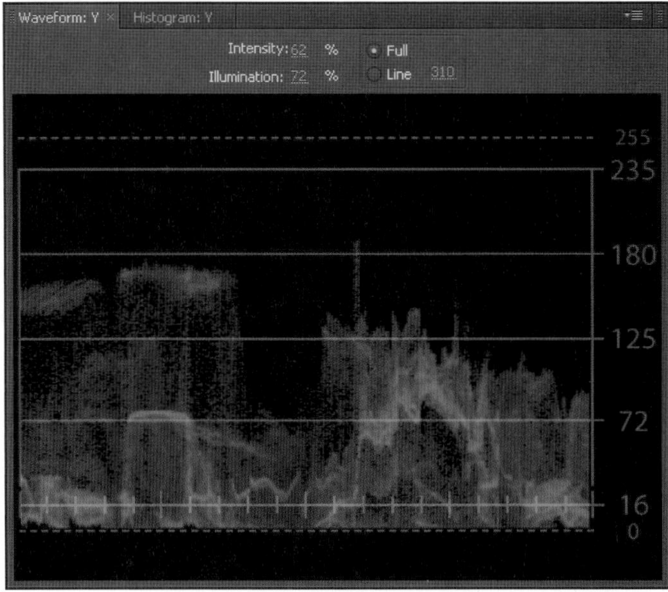

4 Select the clip named light_quiet.avi. When you play this clip, notice that the waveform is pushed to the top with very few dark values. Again, the limited range of luminance makes this image uninteresting. This is another case where adjusting the lighting or camera exposure would make a much nicer image.

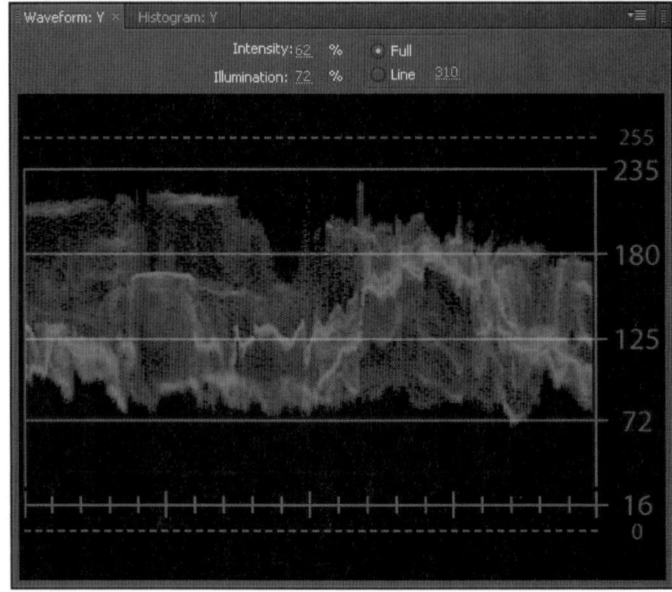

Vectorscope

Although the Waveform Monitor is helpful for analyzing brightness, the Vectorscope is useful for analyzing color. The Vectorscope is a round graph with "no color" represented in the center and a high value of color represented on the outer edge. The color wheel is represented in quadrants around the circle of the Vectorscope. Starting at 11 o'clock and going clockwise are Red, Magenta, Blue, Cyan, Green, and Yellow. The further the graph extends to the edge, the higher the saturation of that color.

The Vectorscope can be helpful in white balancing, since a shift in color is easy to see.

Play the sample clips that are included in the Lesson 2 Adobe OnLocation project. Notice that the Vectorscope shows a graph pointing between Yellow and Red. This is the predominant color in this scene.

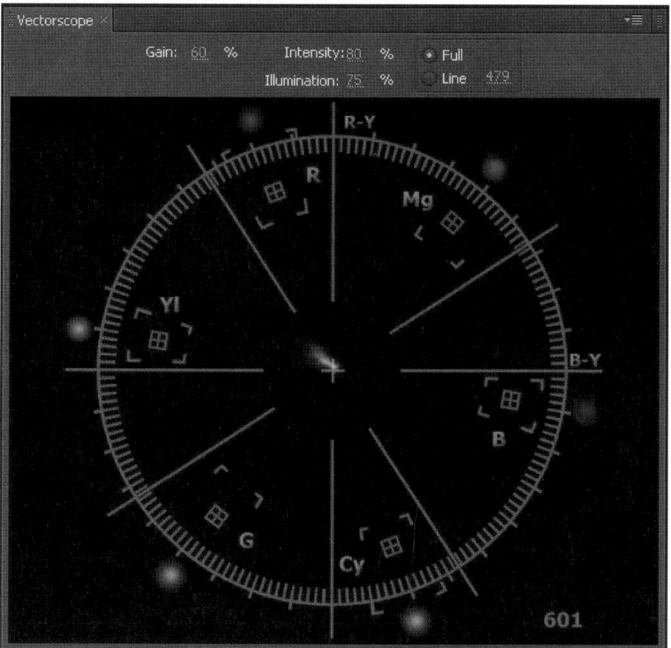

Analyzing audio with Adobe OnLocation

So far we have been focusing on Adobe OnLocation's video capabilities. But audio is half of any good production, so let's take a look at one of the audio tools included with Adobe OnLocation: the Audio Meter.

1 Play the clip named normal.avi and observe the levels represented by the green/yellow lines in the meter. Since this is a stereo clip, you can see the left and right channels represented as it plays. Notice that there are good levels across most of the frequency range, indicated by green and some yellow high points in the audio. This is an example of a good audio file. The meter did not peak (turn red) as you played this file. The overall volume is good—but it's not too loud.

2 Play the clip named dark_loud.avi. Notice this clip peaks, or clips, on the meter, as shown indicated by the red bars. This audio is too loud at some points, which causes clipping and makes the loud sections sound very flat. In this case, you should turn down the audio to the camera or reposition the microphone.

3 Play the clip named light_quiet.avi. Notice the overall level or volume is too low. This is represented visually by displaying only green levels, never peaking into yellow. This would be difficult to correct in postproduction. It is much easier to fix the problem at the scene when detected with the Audio Meter.

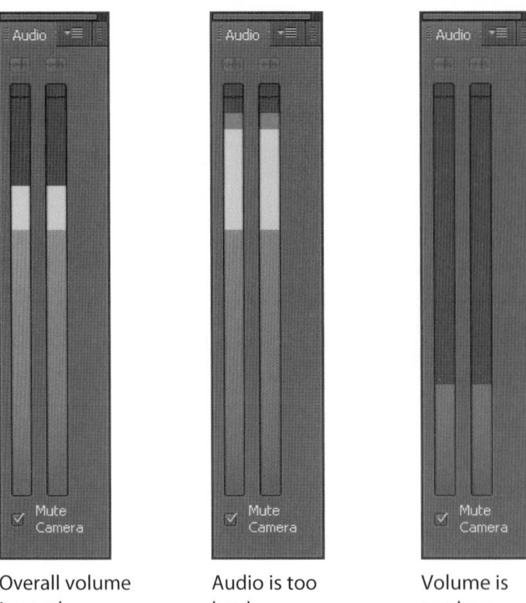

Overall volume is good | Audio is too loud | Volume is too low

Using these video- and audio-monitoring tools can save you hours in postproduction trying to correct problems. Adobe OnLocation can be a real time-saver in preventing problems and helping you produce high-quality video and audio.

Review Questions

1 Why should you take the time to white balance your camera?

2 What is the value of recording directly to disk?

3 Which does the Waveform Monitor indicate: color or brightness?

4 How is a shot list helpful?

5 What does it mean when the audio meters peak at red?

Review answers

1 You white balance your camera to make sure the color hue you are recording is accurate. It takes much longer to fix poorly white balanced video in postproduction than it does to correct it during a shoot.

2 Recording directly to disk saves a lot of time because you don't have to capture clips, which is a serial process.

3 The Waveform Monitor indicates luminance (or brightness).

4 The shot list lets you organize your shots prior to shooting a scene. This can save a lot of time during the actual shoot.

5 When the Audio Meter illuminates red at the high end of the scale, it's an indication that the volume of the audio is too loud. Red on the Audio Meter causes clipping in those sections of the audio.

3 SHOOTING AND CAPTURING GREAT VIDEO ASSETS

Topics covered in this lesson

- Shooting great video
- Capturing video clips
- Capturing an entire videotape
- Using batch capture and scene detection
- Capturing analog video
- Capturing HDV and other HD video

This lesson will take approximately 45 minutes.

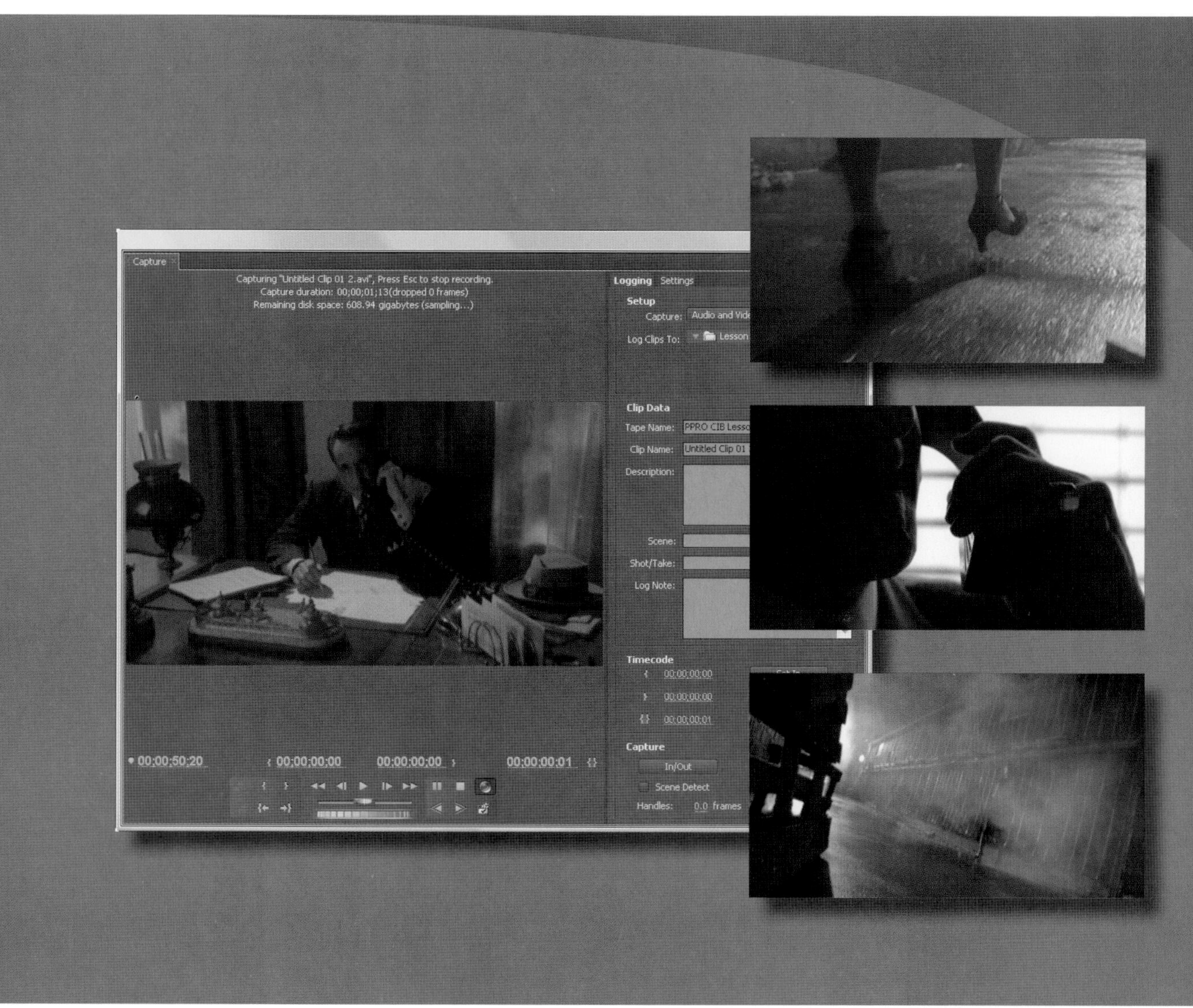

Your first task is to shoot some great-looking video. Then use Adobe Premiere Pro CS4 to capture that video—transfer it from your camcorder or VCR to your hard drive. Adobe Premiere Pro offers several ways to do that. Each is easy and fast.

Getting started

The purpose of this book is to help you use Adobe Premiere Pro to make professional-looking videos. To do that, you need to start with high-quality raw material. This lesson gives you tips for shooting great video and then describes how to get that video into Adobe Premiere Pro.

Tips for shooting great video

With your camcorder of choice in hand, it's time to venture out and shoot videos. If you're new to videography, following these tips will help you create better videos. If you're an old hand, think of this list of shooting axioms as a way to snap out of your routine and juice things up a bit:

- Get a closing shot.
- Get an establishing shot.
- Shoot plenty of video.
- Adhere to the rule of thirds.
- Keep your shots steady.
- Follow the action.
- Use trucking shots.
- Find unusual angles.
- Lean forward or backward.
- Get wide and tight shots.
- Shoot matched action.
- Get sequences.
- Avoid fast pans and snap zooms.
- Shoot cutaways.
- Use lights.
- Grab good sound bites.
- Get plenty of natural sound.
- Plan your shoot.

Get a closing shot

Your closing images are what stick in people's minds. You should be constantly on the lookout for that one shot or sequence that best wraps up your story.

Get an establishing shot

An establishing shot sets a scene in one image. Although superwide shots work well (aerials in particular), consider other points of view: a shot from the cockpit of a race car, a close-up of a scalpel with light glinting off its surface, or a shot of paddles dipping frantically in roaring white water. Each grabs the viewer's attention and helps tell your story.

The establishing shot sets the scene: It's a wide shot of the boss at his desk.

The close-up shot tells the story: He is talking to someone on the phone.

Shoot plenty of video

Videotape is cheap and expendable. Shoot a lot more raw footage than you'll put in your final production. Five times as much is not unusual. Giving yourself that latitude might help you grab shots you would have missed otherwise.

Adhere to the rule of thirds

It's called the rule of thirds, but it's more like the rule of four intersecting lines. When composing your shot, think of your viewfinder as being crisscrossed by two horizontal and two vertical lines. The center of interest should fall along those lines or near one of the four intersections, not the center of the image.

Consider all those family photos where the subject's eyes are smack dab in the center of the photo. Those are *not* examples of good composition.

Another way to follow the rule of thirds is to look around the viewfinder as you shoot, not just stare at its center. Check the edges to see whether you're filling the frame with interesting images. Avoid large areas of blank space.

Keep your shots steady

You want to give viewers the sense they're looking through a window or, better yet, are there with your subjects on location. A shaky camera shatters that illusion.

When possible, use a tripod. The best "sticks" have fluid heads that enable you to make smooth pans or tilts.

If it's impractical to use a tripod, try to find some way to stabilize the shot: Lean against a wall, put your elbows on a table, or place the camcorder on a solid object.

Follow the action

This might seem obvious, but keep your viewfinder on the ball (or sprinter, speeding police car, surfer, conveyor belt, and so on). Your viewers' eyes will want to follow the action, so give them what they want.

One nifty trick is to use directed movement as a pan motivator. That is, follow a leaf's progress as it floats down a stream, and then continue your camera motion past the leaf—*panning*—and widen out to show something unexpected: a waterfall, a huge industrial complex, or a fisherman.

Use trucking shots

Trucking or dolly shots move with the action. For example, hold the camera at arm's length right behind a toddler as she motors around the house, put the camera in a grocery cart as it winds through the aisles, or shoot out the window of a speeding train.

Find unusual angles

Getting your camcorder off your shoulder, away from eye level, leads to more interesting and enjoyable shots. Ground-level shots are great for gamboling lambs or cavorting puppies. Shoot up from a low angle and down from a high angle. Shoot through objects or people while keeping the focus on your subject.

Lean forward or backward

The zoom lens can be a crutch. A better way to move in close or away from a subject is simply to lean in or out. For example, start by leaning way in with a tight shot of someone's hands as he works on a wood carving; then, while still recording, lean way back (perhaps widening your zoom lens as well) to reveal that he is working in a sweatshop full of folks hunched over their handiwork.

Get wide and tight shots

Our eyes work like medium-angle lenses. So, we tend to shoot video that way. Instead, grab wide shots and tight shots of your subjects. If practical, get close to your subject to get the tight shot rather than use the zoom lens. Not only does it look better, but the proximity leads to clearer audio.

A close-up of walking through the mist.

Cutting to a wide shot showing she is alone.

Shoot matched action

Consider a shot from behind a pitcher as he throws a fastball. He releases it, and then it smacks into the catcher's glove. Instead of a single shot, grab two shots: a medium shot from behind the pitcher showing the pitch and the ball's flight toward the catcher, and a tight shot of the catcher's glove. It's the same concept for an artist: Get a wide shot of her applying a paint stroke to a canvas, and then move in for a close shot of the same action. You'll edit them together to match the action.

▶ **Tip:** Matched action keeps the story flowing smoothly while helping to illustrate a point.

Get sequences

Shooting repetitive action in a sequence is another way to tell a story, build interest, or create suspense. A bowler wipes his hands on a rosin bag, dries them over a blower, wipes the ball with a towel, picks up the ball, fixes his gaze on the pins, steps forward, swings the ball back, releases it, slides to the foul line, watches the ball's trajectory, and then reacts to the shot.

Instead of simply capturing all this in one long shot, piecing these actions together in a sequence of edits is much more compelling. You can easily combine wide and tight shots, trucking moves, and matched action to turn repetitive material into attention-grabbing sequences.

Avoid fast pans and snap zooms

Fast pans and zooms fall into MTV and amateur video territory. Few circumstances call for such stomach-churning camera work. In general, it's best to minimize all pans and zooms. As with a shaky camera, they remind viewers they're watching TV.

If you do zoom or pan, do it for a purpose: to reveal something, to follow someone's gaze from his or her eyes to the subject of interest, or to continue the flow of action (as in the floating leaf example earlier). A slow zoom in, with only a minimal change to the focal length, can add drama to a sound bite. Again, do it sparingly.

Keep on rolling along

Don't let this no-fast-moves admonition force you to stop rolling while you zoom or pan. If you see something that warrants a quick close-up shot or you need to suddenly pan to grab some possibly fleeting footage, keep rolling. You can always edit around that sudden movement later.

If you stop recording to make the pan or zoom or to adjust the focus, you might lose some or all of whatever it was you were trying so desperately to shoot. You will also miss any accompanying natural sound.

Shoot cutaways

Avoid jump cuts by shooting cutaways. A jump cut is an edit that creates a disconnect in the viewer's mind. A cutaway—literally, a shot that cuts away from the current shot—fixes jump cuts.

Cutaways are common in interviews where you might want to edit together two 10-second sound bites from the same person. Doing so would mean the interviewee would look like he suddenly moved. To avoid that jump cut—that sudden disconcerting shift—you make a cutaway of the interview. That could be a wide shot, a hand shot, or a reverse-angle shot of the interviewer over the interviewee's shoulder. You then edit in the cutaway over the juncture of the two sound bites to cover the jump cut.

The same holds true for a soccer game. It can be disconcerting to simply cut from one wide shot of players on the field to another. If you shoot some crowd reactions or the scoreboard, you can use those cutaways to cover up what would have been jump cuts.

Use lights

Lights add brilliance, dazzle, and depth to otherwise bland and flat scenes. Consider using an onboard camcorder fill light and, if you have the time, money, patience, or personnel, a full lighting kit with a few colored gels.

In a pinch, do whatever you can to increase available light. Open curtains, turn on all the lights, or bring a couple of desk lamps into the room. Keep in mind one caveat: Low-light situations can be dramatic, and flipping on a few desk lamps can destroy that mood in a moment.

Grab good sound bites

Your narrator presents the facts. The people in your story present the emotions, feelings, and opinions. Don't rely on interview sound bites to tell the who, what, where, when, and how. Let those bites explain the why.

In a corporate backgrounder, have the narrator say what a product does, and let the employees or customers say how enthusiastic they are about that product.

Your narrator should be the one to say, "It was opening night, and this was her first solo." Let the singer, who is recalling this dramatic moment, say, "My throat was tight, and my stomach was tied in knots."

In general, even though your interviews might take forever, use only short sound bites in your final production. Use those bites as punctuation marks, not paragraphs.

Exceptions for idiosyncratic characters

None of these admonitions is carved in stone. Some characters you'll videotape are so compelling, quirky, or humorous that your best bet is to let them be the primary narrator. Then you'll want to consider what scenes you can use to illustrate their commentary. You don't want to fill your entire video with a "talking head."

Get plenty of natural sound

Think beyond images. Sound is tremendously important. Listen for sounds you can use in your project. Even if the video quality is mediocre, grab that audio.

Your camcorder's onboard microphone is not much more than a fallback. Consider using additional microphones: shotgun mics to narrow the focus of your sound and avoid extraneous noise, lavalieres tucked out of sight for interviews, and wireless mics when your camera can't be close enough to get just what you need.

Plan your shoot

When you consider a video project, plan what you need to shoot to tell the story. Videotaping your kid's soccer championship match, a corporate backgrounder, or a medical procedure each requires planning to ensure success. Know what you want your final video project to say, and think of what you need to videotape to tell that story.

Even the best-laid plans and most carefully scripted projects might need some adjusting once you start recording in the field. No matter how you envision the finished project, be willing to make changes as the situation warrants.

Capturing video

Before you can edit your own video, you need to transfer it to your computer's hard drive. In NLE (non-linear editing) parlance, you need to *capture* it. This is a somewhat-misleading term used throughout the NLE world. All that Adobe Premiere Pro does during DV capture is to place the video data in a movie file "wrapper" without changing the original DV data.

The capture process in the analog world takes several steps: transfer, conversion, compression, and wrapping. Your camcorder transfers the video and audio as analog data to a video capture card. That card's built-in hardware converts the waveform signal to a digital form, compresses it using a codec (compression/decompression) process, and then wraps it in the AVI file format on Windows systems or in the QuickTime format for users working with Adobe Premiere Pro CS4 on the Mac.

Three DV-capturing scenarios

Adobe Premiere Pro offers tools to take some of the manual labor out of the capturing process. Three basic approaches exist:

- Capture your entire videotape as one long clip.
- Log each clip's In and Out points for automated batch capturing.
- Use the scene detection feature in Adobe Premiere Pro to automatically create separate clips whenever you press the Pause/Record button on your camcorder.

To do this exercise, you need a DV camcorder. Most DV camcorders have an IEEE 1394 cable that you hook up to your computer's IEEE 1394 connector. If your computer does not have an IEEE 1394 connector, it is recommended that you buy a IEEE 1394/USB combination card.

You can work with HDV or with a professional-level camcorder with a Serial Digital Interface (SDI) connector and a specialized video capture card.

Adobe Premiere Pro handles HDV and SDI capture with the same kind of software device controls used with a standard DV camcorder. SDI requires an extra setup procedure.

If you have an analog camcorder, you need a video capture card that supports S-Video or composite video connectors. The only option with most analog camcorders is to manually start and stop recording. Most analog capture cards do not work with remote device control or have timecode readout, so you can't log tapes, do batch capture, or use the scene detection feature.

Capturing an entire tape

To capture an entire tape, follow these steps:

1. Connect the camcorder to your computer.
2. Turn on your camcorder and set it to playback mode: VTR or VCR. Do not set it to camera mode.

Use AC, not a battery

When capturing video, power your camcorder from its AC adapter, not its battery. Here's why: When using a battery, camcorders can go into sleep mode, and the battery will often run out before you're done.

Note: Windows might note that you've powered up your camcorder by displaying a Digital Video Device connection message. Mac OS may start a default associated application, such as iMovie.

3 In Windows XP, if the Digital Video Device message pops up, click "Take no action," select the "Always perform the selected action" option, and click OK. (The next time you fire up your camcorder, you should not see this connection query.) In Mac OS, if iMovie or another application starts up, see that application's Help for information about which application to open when a camera is connected. In Windows Vista, an AutoPlay dialog box may pop up. Click "Set AutoPlay defaults in Control Panel."

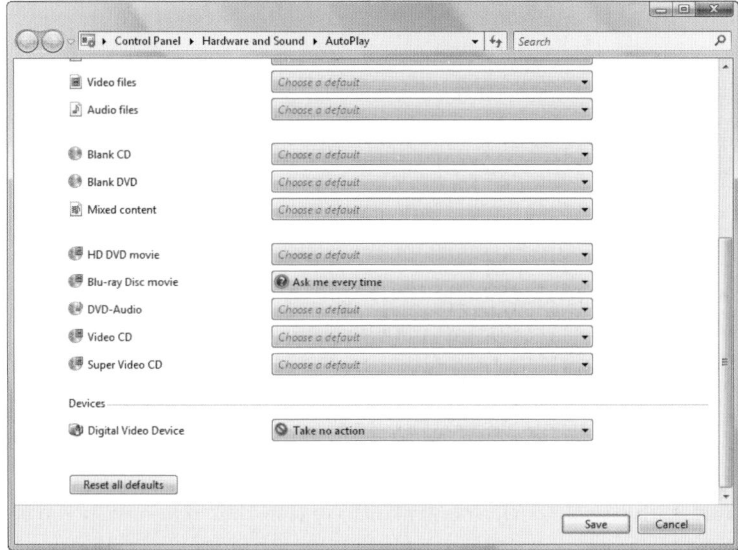

Project settings for SDI or HDV

This lesson assumes you are recording from a DV camcorder: standard 4:3 format or widescreen anamorphic 16:9 screen ratio. If you are working with SDI or HDV, you need to start Adobe Premiere Pro, click New Project, and select the preset project settings that match your camcorder.

4 Start Adobe Premiere Pro, click Open Project, navigate to the Lesson 03 folder, and double-click Lesson 03.prproj.

5 Choose File > Capture to open the Capture panel.

6 Look above the Capture panel preview pane to make sure your camcorder is connected properly.

7 Insert a tape into your camcorder. You will be prompted to give the tape a name.

8 Type a name for your tape in the text box. Be sure not to give two tapes the same name; Adobe Premiere Pro remembers clip in/out data based on tape names.

9 Use the VCR-style device controls in the Capture panel to play, fast-forward, rewind, pause, and stop your tape. If you have never used a computer to control a camcorder, this will seem pretty cool.

Note: If a message says "No Device Control" or "Capture Device Offline," you'll need to do some troubleshooting. The most obvious fix is to make sure the camcorder is turned on and the cables are connected. For more troubleshooting tips, refer to the Adobe Community Help web site.

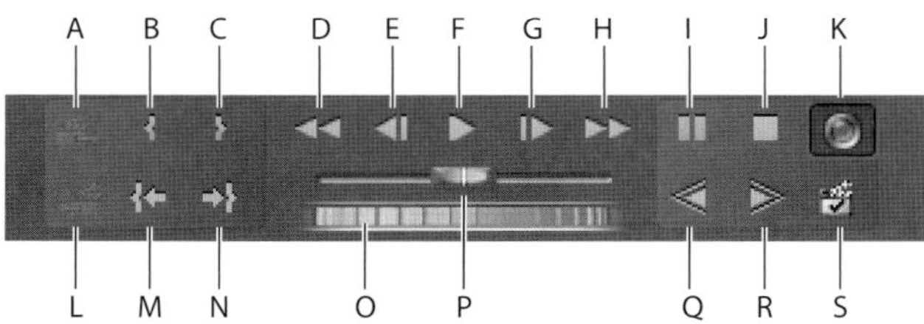

A. Next Scene **B.** Set In Point **C.** Set Out Point **D.** Rewind **E.** Step Back **F.** Play **G.** Step Forward **H.** Fast Forward **I.** Pause **J.** Stop **K.** Record **L.** Previous Scene **M.** Go To In Point **N.** Go To Out Point **O.** Jog **P.** Shuttle **Q.** Slow Reverse **R.** Slow Play **S.** Scene Detect

Note: To help you identify these buttons, move the pointer over them to see tool tips.

10 Try some of the other VCR-style buttons:

- Shuttle (the slider toward the bottom) enables you to move slowly or zip quickly—depending on how far you move the slider off center—forward or backward through your tape.
- Single-frame Jog control (below the shuttle slider)
- Step Forward and Step Back, one frame at a time
- Slow Reverse and Slow Play

11 Rewind the tape to its beginning or to wherever you want to start recording.

12 In the Setup area of the Logging tab, note that Audio and Video is the default setting. If you want to capture only audio or only video, change that setting.

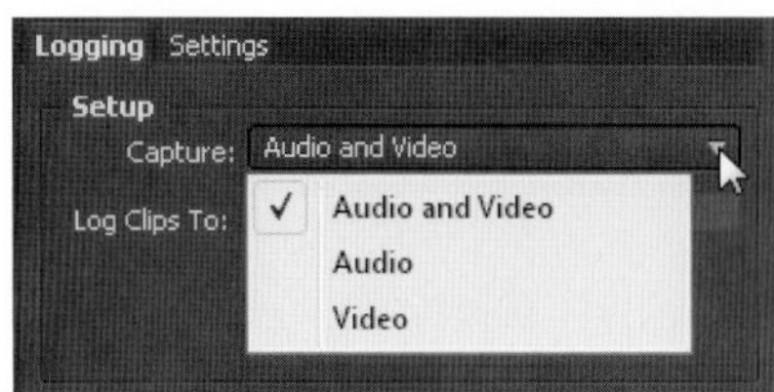

13 Click the Tape button in the Capture area of the Logging tab or the Record button in the Capture panel to start recording.

You'll see (and hear) the video in the Capture panel and on your camcorder. Since there is a slight delay during capture, you'll hear what sounds like an echo. Feel free to turn down the speaker on either your camcorder or your computer.

Note: If you are capturing HDV video, the video is not displayed in the Capture panel as it is being recorded.

14 Click the red Record button or the black Stop button when you want to stop recording.

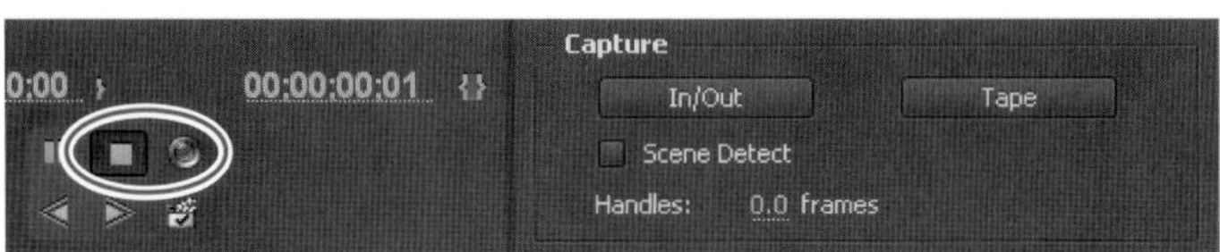

The Save Captured Clip dialog box appears.

15 Give your clip a name (add descriptive information if you want) and click OK.

Adobe Premiere Pro stores all the clips you capture during this lesson in the Lesson 03 folder on your hard drive. You can change the default location by choosing Project > Project Settings > Scratch Disks (Windows) or Premiere Pro > Project > Project Settings > Scratch Disks (Mac OS).

Using batch capture and scene detection

When you perform a batch capture, you log the In and Out points of a number of clips and then have Adobe Premiere Pro automatically transfer them to your computer.

Use the logging process to critically view your raw footage. You want to look for "keeper" video, the best interview sound bites, and any natural sound that will enhance your production.

The purpose of using a batch capture is threefold: to better manage your media assets, to speed up the video capture process, and to save hard disk space (one hour of DV consumes roughly 13 GB). If you batch capture all your clips, you may use the combination of the Adobe Premiere Pro project file (which is relatively small) and the MiniDV tapes as a backup of your project. To reedit the project, simply open the project file and recapture the clips.

Use a clip-naming convention

Think through how you're going to name your clips. You might end up with dozens of clips, and if you don't give them descriptive names, it'll slow down editing.

You might use a naming convention for sound bites such as "Bite-1," "Bite-2," and so forth. Adding a brief descriptive comment, such as "Bite-1 Laugh," will help.

Here are the steps to follow:

1 In the Capture panel, click the Logging tab.

2 Change the Handles setting (at the bottom of the Logging tab) to 30 frames.

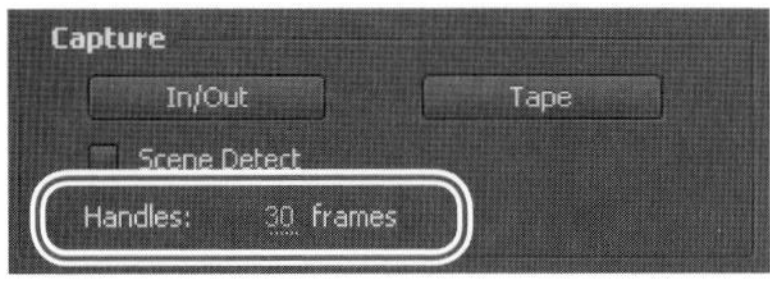

This adds 1 second to the start and finish of each captured clip, which will give you enough head and tail frames to add transitions without covering up important elements of the clip.

Using the click or drag method to change numeric values

When changing the Handles value, you can click the current number and type a new figure, or you can simply position your pointer over the Handles number and drag left or right to lower or raise the value. This method of changing a numeric value works throughout Adobe Premiere Pro.

3 In the Clip Data area of the Logging tab, give your tape a unique name.

4 Log your tape by rewinding and then playing it.

5 When you see the start of a segment you want to transfer to your computer, stop the tape, rewind to that spot, and click the Set In button in the Timecode area of the Logging tab.

6 When you get to the end of that segment (you can use Fast Forward or simply Play to get there), click Set Out. The in/out times and the clip length will appear.

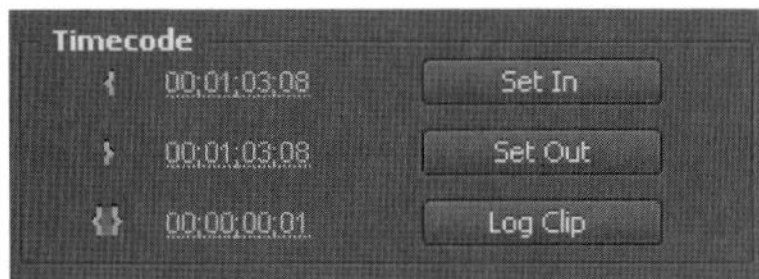

Three other ways to set In and Out points

You can use other means to set In points and Out points for selected clips: Click the brackets ({ or }) on the play controls, use the keyboard shortcuts (I for In and O for Out), or change the in/out time directly in the Timecode area by dragging left or right over the timecode.

7 Click Log Clip to open the Log Clip dialog box.

8 Change the clip name, if needed, and add appropriate notes if you want; then click OK.

That adds this clip's name with its in/out times and tape name information to the Project panel (with the word "Offline" next to it). You'll go there later to do the actual capture.

9 Log clips for the rest of your tape using the same method.

Each time you click Log Clip, Adobe Premiere Pro automatically adds a number to the end of your previous clip's name. You can accept or override this automated naming feature.

10 When you've finished logging your clips, close the Capture panel.

All your logged clips will be in the Project panel, with the offline icon next to each.

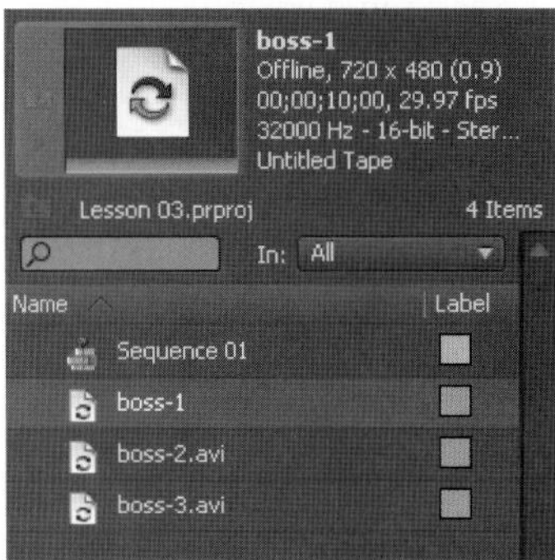

11 In the Project panel, select all the clips you want to capture (see the following tip for three methods to do that).

Three ways to select more than one item

There are usually three ways to select more than one file in a window. First, if the filenames are contiguous, click the top one, and then Shift-click the last one in the group. Second, you can click off to one side and above the top clip, and then drag down to the last one to marquee-select a group (the marquee-select method—creating the gray rectangle—was used in the previous figure). Finally, if the filenames are scattered about, click one first, and then Ctrl-click (Windows) or Command-click (Mac OS) each additional file in turn.

12 Choose File > Batch Capture.

Note: Handles are extra frames at the beginning and end of a clip. For example, adding 30 frames as handles would add 1 second of video to the start and end of your clips. This can be useful for transitions.

A very simple Batch Capture dialog box opens, allowing you to override the camcorder settings or add more handle frames.

13 Leave the Batch Capture options unselected and click OK.

The Capture panel opens, as does another little dialog box telling you to insert the proper tape (in this case, it's probably still in the camcorder).

14 Insert the tape and click OK.

Adobe Premiere Pro now takes control of your camcorder, cues up the tape to the first clip, and transfers that clip and all other clips to your hard drive.

15 When the process is complete, take a look at your Project panel to see the results. The offline icon is now a movie icon, and your footage is ready to be edited.

Use scene detection

Instead of manually logging In and Out points, you might want to use the scene detection feature. Scene detection analyzes your tape's time/date stamp, looking for breaks such as those caused when you press the camcorder's Pause button while recording.

When scene detection is on and you perform a capture, Adobe Premiere Pro automatically captures a separate file at each scene break it detects. Scene detection works whether you are capturing an entire tape or just a section between specific In and Out points.

To turn on scene detection, do either of the following:

- Click the Scene Detect button (below the Record button in the Capture panel).
- Select the Scene Detect option in the Capture area of the Logging tab.

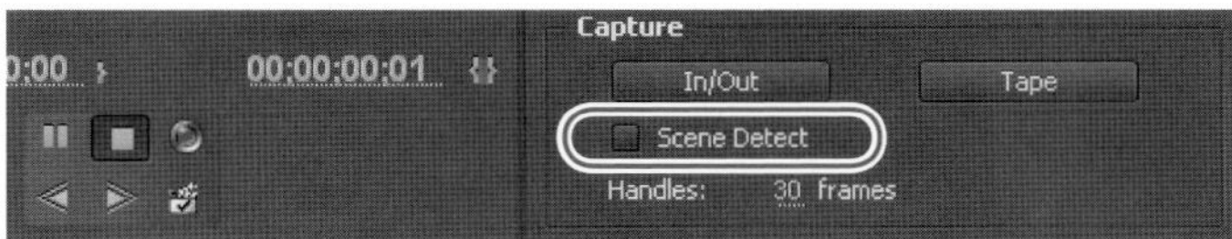

Then you can either set In and Out points and click Record or cue your tape to wherever you want to start capturing and click Record. In the latter case, click Stop when done.

Your clips will show up in the Project panel. You don't need to batch capture them—Adobe Premiere Pro captures each clip on the fly. Adobe Premiere Pro then names the first captured clip by putting a "01" after the name you put in the Clip Name box and increments the number in each new clip name by one.

Note: Automatic scene detection isn't available for HDV or HD assets.

Tackling manual analog movie capture

If you need to transfer analog video—consumer-level VHS, SVHS, Hi-8, or professional-grade video such as Beta SP—you need a video capture card with analog inputs. Most analog capture cards have consumer-quality composite connectors as well as S-Video and sometimes top-of-the-line component connections.

Check your card's documentation for setup and compatibility issues.

With analog video, you have only one capture option—to do it manually:

1 Open the Capture panel (File > Capture).

2 Use the controls on the camcorder to move the videotape to a point several seconds before the frame you want to begin capturing.

3 Press the Play button on the camcorder and then click the red Record button in the Capture panel.

4 When your clip has been captured, click the Stop button in the Capture panel and on the camcorder. Your clip will show up in the Project panel.

Capturing HDV and HD video

Note: HDV video is not displayed in the Capture panel while the video is being captured.

You can capture HDV video in the same way as DV video: by connecting the HDV camcorder or deck to your computer via IEEE 1394. When you start a new HDV project, select the appropriate HDV project preset and capture as described for DV video.

HD video requires an SDI card in your computer to connect the coaxial interface from the HD camcorder to your computer. The vendor that supplies the SDI card will typically install additional HD presets into Adobe Premiere Pro as part of its installation.

If you have ventured into tapeless camcorders such as the Panasonic P2 or Sony XDCAMs, the capture process is eliminated altogether. See the next chapter for working in this new tapeless environment.

Review questions

1 Why are cutaway shots so useful?

2 What should you check if you see "Capture Device Offline" at the top of the Capture panel?

3 What does scene detection do when selected?

4 What is one benefit of using batch capture rather than manual capture?

5 During the capture process, how do you add extra frames to ensure you have enough footage for transitions?

6 Is the actual media captured to your hard disk during a batch capture?

Review answers

1 Cutaway shots of a crowd, faces, or landscapes are often useful for covering up a bad shot or providing a pleasant transition to another scene.

2 Check that your camcorder or deck is connected to the computer, and that it is turned on and in VCR mode.

3 Enabling scene detection causes clips to be automatically logged at each point where the camcorder was stopped or paused.

4 If you batch capture all your clips, it is possible to save your Adobe Premiere Pro project file (which is relatively small), store your DV tapes, and be able to recapture the project easily if you ever need to reedit. This is a very efficient means of backup.

5 Type a number of frames in the Handles option in the Capture area of the Logging tab.

6 No. Only information about the clip is captured, such as tape name and In and Out points. The clip will be displayed as "Offline" in the Project panel.

4 SELECTING SETTINGS, ADJUSTING PREFERENCES, AND MANAGING ASSETS

Topics covered in this lesson

- Selecting project and sequence settings
- Setting scratch disk options
- Adjusting user preferences
- Importing assets
- Taking a closer look at images
- Managing media in bins
- Finding assets with the Media Browser

This lesson will take approximately 50 minutes.

Adobe Premiere Pro CS4 is eminently customizable and adaptable. All you need to do is adjust the sequence settings and preferences.

Getting started

In most of your Adobe Premiere Pro CS4 projects, you won't have to give more than a passing glance to project settings and preferences. Nevertheless, it's good to know the options available to you. You'll learn how to manage your assets from within the Project panel and delve into Adobe Bridge CS4—a full-scale asset browser that works with all products and file types in Adobe Creative Suite 4 Production Premium.

Selecting project settings by sequence

The basic rule of thumb when selecting project and sequence settings is to match the settings to your source material and not to the final output. Maintaining the original quality of source material means you'll have more options later. Even if your goal is to create a low-resolution video to play on the Internet, wait until you finish editing, and then reduce the output quality settings to make your video Internet-ready.

It's possible you might have a mix of source media—widescreen, standard, HDV, and P2, for example—among your project assets. With Adobe Premiere Pro CS4, you can create multiple sequences, each with a different media type or frame size, all in the same project.

Three types of settings

Adobe Premiere Pro CS4 has three types of settings:

- **Project settings**: These apply to the entire project, and most cannot be changed once the project is created.
- **Sequence settings**: You set these when you create a new sequence and deal with the type of media you will be using.
- **Preferences**: These generally apply to all projects, and you can change them at any time.

Project settings

To specify project settings for your Adobe Premiere Pro CS4 project, do the following:

1 Start Adobe Premiere Pro CS4.

The startup screen appears. The Recent Projects list should be populated with the projects you last opened. In this case, you will be starting fresh.

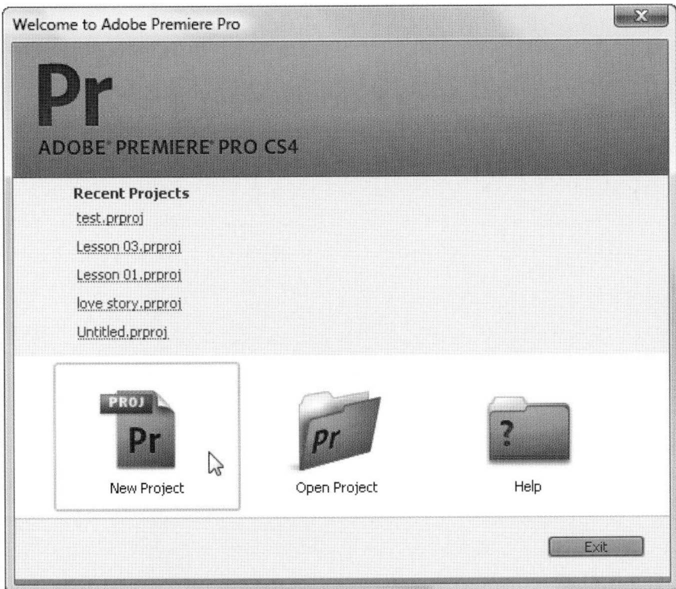

2 Click New Project to open the New Project dialog box.

This dialog box has two tabs: General and Scratch Disks.

General tab

The General tab contains these sections:

- **Action and Title Safe Areas**: It is recommended you leave the settings in this section at their default values. They do not affect the video in any way. They simply determine where guides are displayed on the Program Monitor and Source Monitor to help plan title placement and see where TV overlay molding may hide the edges of video.

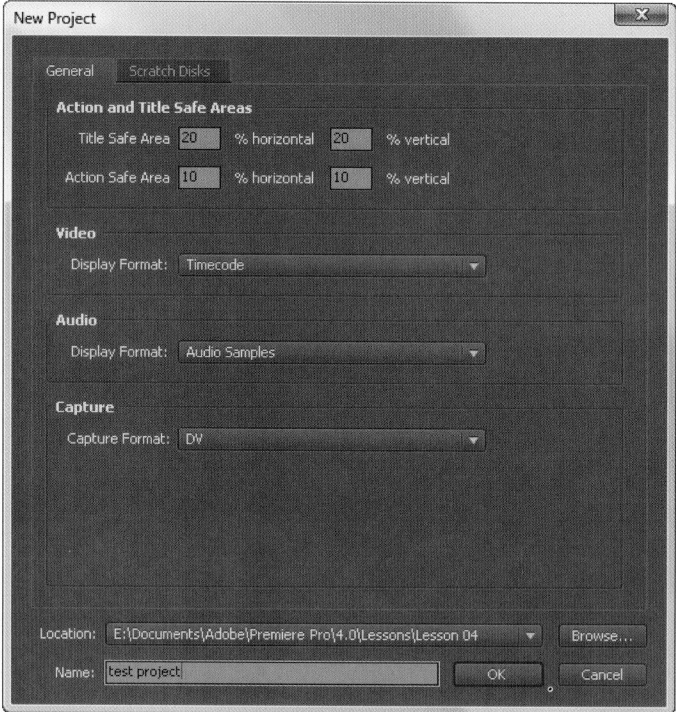

- **Video and Audio**: Again, it is recommended that you leave the Display Format settings at their defaults unless you need to display video increments in feet or frames rather than timecode, or need to display audio in milliseconds rather than sample rate.
- **Capture**: The only setting in this section, Capture Format, is important to set correctly based on the media you plan to capture. The choices are DV or HDV.

Scratch Disks tab

Scratch disks is a term used to describe the location on your computer hard drive where various files associated with video editing are stored. Scratch disks may be placed all on the same disk or on separate disks, depending on your hardware and workflow requirements.

The default for each type of file is Same as Project. This means all files will be stored in the same folder or subfolders of your project file. This is a very organized way to maintain your project; when you are finished with the project, deleting one folder will clean up the entire project.

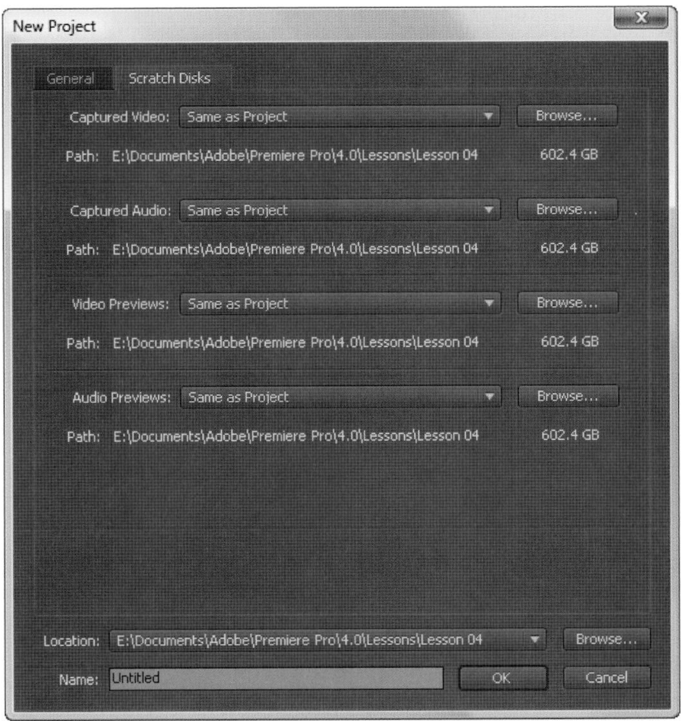

In some scenarios, you may have good reasons to specify different locations for different files (scratch disks). For example, you may have a really fast hard drive in a RAID 0 configuration. This would be the best place to store your captured video files because they require the most system input/output (I/O).

For the purposes of these lessons, it is recommended that you leave your scratch disks set to Same as Project. When you start capturing your own video clips, feel free to customize the scratch disks to your environment.

Typical drive setup

Although all files can exist on a single hard drive, a typical editing system will have three hard drives: drive 1 dedicated to the operating system and programs; drive 2 (the fastest drive) dedicated to captured video and video previews; and drive 3 dedicated to audio, miscellaneous still images, and exporting.

Note: Partitioning a single drive into multiple drives is not helpful for performance.

While on the Scratch Disks tab, set a location and filename for your new project, and click OK.

Sequence settings

You will be prompted to choose sequence settings every time you create a new sequence. This is because each sequence in Adobe Premiere Pro CS4 can have different settings. Since Adobe Premiere Pro assumes you need at least one sequence in your project, it prompts you for sequence settings when starting a new project.

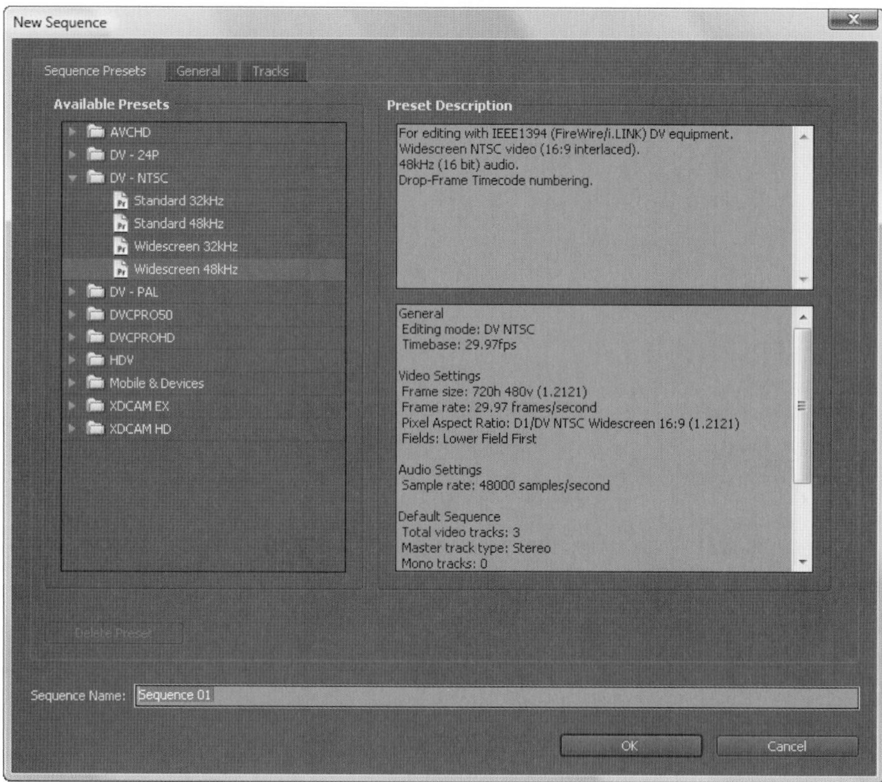

The New Sequence dialog box contains three tabs, which are as follows:

- **Sequence Presets**: This tab allows you to choose a preset for most commonly used and supported media types. The media used for these lessons is widescreen NTSC DV video, so choose the DV – NTSC/Widescreen 48kHz preset. When you capture your own video clips, choose the preset that matches your media.
- **General**: The General tab allows you to customize the individual settings of a preset. If your media matches one of the presets, it is not necessary to make any changes on the General tab. In fact, it is recommended that you do not. However, if you need to create a custom preset, choose the one that matches the closest on the Sequence Presets tab, and then make the customization on the General tab. You may save your custom preset by clicking the Save Preset button near the bottom of the General tab.

- **Tracks**: Here you can specify how many video and audio tracks will be added when the sequence is created. You can also add audio or video tracks later.

For this chapter's project, give your initial sequence a name on the Sequence Presets tab and click OK.

Custom preset for new projects

If you expect to use your modified project settings on multiple projects, you can save them for reuse by creating a customized new project preset. To do so, simply make your choices in the four categories and then click the Save Preset button on the General tab. Give your customized project settings preset a name on the Sequence Presets tab and click OK. The name will appear in the Custom folder under Available Presets.

If you are editing standard DV or native HDV, it is not necessary to use a custom preset. In this case, choose one of the standard presets on the Load Preset tab.

Adjusting user preferences

Preferences are different from sequence settings in that you typically set preferences once and have them apply to all your projects. You can change preferences and have them take immediate effect at any time.

Preferences include default transition times, timing and number of autosaves, Project panel clip label colors, and user interface brightness (you adjusted this in Lesson 1).

If you have been following along with this lesson, you should be sitting at the Adobe Premiere Pro blank workspace and can skip step 1. If you need to start fresh, load the Lesson 04 project from scratch.

Note: Unlike Lesson 01.prproj, this project has no media files imported. It is blank. That is because you will be importing assets into the project later in this lesson.

1 Start Adobe Premiere Pro, choose Open Project, navigate to the Lesson 04 folder, and choose Lesson 04.prproj.

2 Choose Edit > Preferences > General (Windows) or Premiere Pro > Preferences > General (Mac OS).

Note: You can select any of the Preferences submenus. All choices take you to the Preferences dialog box, with the appropriate category selected. You can easily move from one category to another by clicking a category name in the list on the left.

Preferences categories

The various preferences categories rarely come into play until you have used Adobe Premiere Pro for a while, and most are self-explanatory. Here's a brief run-through:

- **General**: This primarily sets default times for audio and video transitions, still-image duration, preroll/postroll for camcorders during capture, and bin behavior.

Default scale to frame size

An important preference to understand here is the "Default scale to frame size" setting. If this option is selected, any media you import will automatically scale to the frame size of the sequence. This may be desirable for importing a lot of still images. If you intend to do a lot of zooming or panning, you may not want stills to automatically scale. We will look closer at zooming and panning in Lesson 11.

- **Appearance**: This sets the interface brightness. You saw this in Lesson 1.
- **Audio**: The Automation Keyframe Optimization setting is relevant when you use the Audio Mixer to change volume or panning. Selecting Linear keyframe thinning and Minimum time interval thinning setting of greater than 30 ms makes it easier to edit the changes later.
- **Audio Hardware**: This sets the default audio hardware device.
- **Audio Output Mapping**: This specifies how each audio hardware device channel corresponds to an Adobe Premiere Pro audio output channel. Generally, the default settings will work fine.
- **Auto Save**: This sets the frequency and number of autosaves. To open an autosaved project, choose File > Open Project, navigate to the Premiere Pro Auto Save folder, and double-click a project.
- **Capture**: This sets four basic capture parameters.
- **Device Control**: The choices here are Preroll (which you can set in the General category in Preferences) and Timecode Offset (usually used only during analog video capture).
- **Label Colors**: This lets you change the default Project panel medialink label colors.
- **Label Defaults**: This assigns specific label colors to different media types.
- **Media**: This empties the cache folders.
- **Player Settings**: This is usually set to Adobe Media Player. However, some third-party capture cards may add their own video players, which you can choose to use here.
- **Titler**: This specifies the characters to be used for font and style samples in the Adobe Titler frame.
- **Trim**: This adjusts how many frames and Audio Time Units are trimmed if you select Large Trim Offset (a quick way to chop off chunks of video) in the Trim frame.

Note: When you finish reviewing the various options, click Cancel, or click OK if you made any changes you want to keep.

Any changes you make in Preferences take effect immediately and remain in effect the next time you start Adobe Premiere Pro. You can change them again at any time.

Importing assets

In Lesson 1, your project started with links to video clips (*assets*) that had already been placed in the Project panel. Adding those links to the Project panel—*importing assets*, in Adobe Premiere Pro parlance—is easy. But you should keep a few issues to keep in mind. This exercise will cover the how-tos of importing and the issues you're most likely to encounter.

You will import all four standard media types: video, audio, graphics, and still images. You will see two importing methods and take a look at the properties of audio and graphic files.

You can continue where you left off, or you can open Lesson 04.prproj from the Lesson 04 folder.

You should see the standard Adobe Premiere Pro opening workspace. All the frames should be empty except for the Sequence 01 item in the Project panel and in the Timeline.

1 Choose File > Import.

2 Navigate to the Lesson 04 folder and select the audio clip, the Illustrator image, the two JPEG images, and the two video AVIs, as shown here. Then click Open (Windows) or Import (Mac OS). This will import (create links from) these files to the Adobe Premiere Pro Project panel.

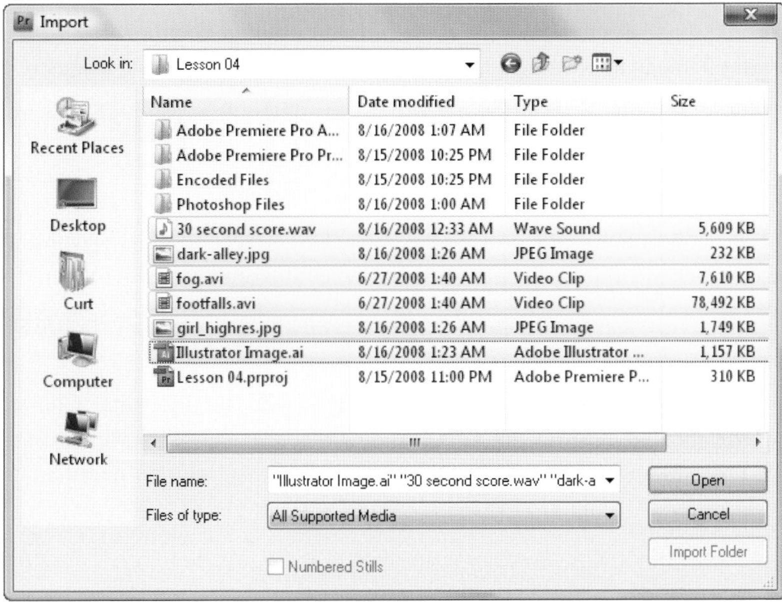

Note: This is a different and faster way to open the Import dialog box (Windows) or the Choose Object dialog box (Mac OS). You could also press the keyboard shortcut Ctrl+I (Windows) or Command+I (Mac OS).

3 In the Project panel, double-click in the empty space below the newly added clips.

   You will import files from a different file folder, demonstrating that you don't have to keep all your assets in the same place. The Project panel simply lists links to your assets, wherever they may be.

4 Navigate to the Lesson 04/Photoshop Files folder, select Layered Photoshop File.psd, and then click Open (Windows) or Import (Mac OS).

   For the Adobe Photoshop CS4 file, an Import Layered File dialog box appears.

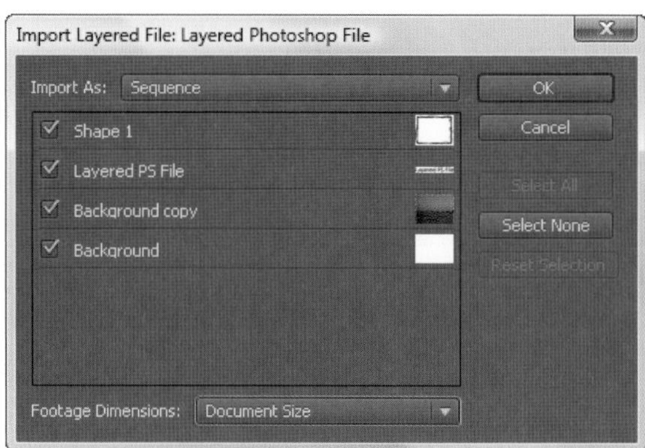

Note: Notice that when you choose to import the Photoshop file as a sequence, the dialog box shows the layers of the Photoshop image and allows you to turn on and off individual layers.

5 Choose Sequence from the Import As menu and click OK.

   You could have selected one of the Merge Layer options to import the Photoshop image into a single layer. Choosing Sequence does two things:

   - Adds a file folder to your Project panel with all the Photoshop CS4 layers listed as separate clips
   - Creates a new sequence with all the layers on separate video tracks

Note: The source audio format is 48000 Hz, 16-bit stereo, and the project audio format is 48000 Hz, 32-bit, floating-point stereo. Adobe Premiere Pro up-converts all audio to the project setting, thereby ensuring no quality is lost during editing. Floating-point data allows for even more precise and smoother edits.

6 Right-click (Windows) or Control-click (Mac OS) 30 second score.wav in the Project panel and choose Properties from the context menu to see information about the file.

7 Close the Properties dialog box.

8 Another way to see information about an asset is with the Info panel. Click the Info panel located in lower-left area of the workspace. Now click various assets in the Project panel to observe the properties being displayed in the Info panel.

Taking a closer look at images

Adobe Premiere Pro can import just about any image and graphic file type. You've already seen how it handles Photoshop CS4 layered files—giving you the option to import the layers as separate graphics within a sequence, import them as single layers, or merge the entire file into one graphic clip.

What's left to cover is how Adobe Premiere Pro handles Adobe Illustrator CS4 files and JPEG image files. You'll start this exercise where you left off. If you need to start fresh, just open Lesson 04-1.prproj from the Lesson 04 folder.

Note: You may be prompted with a dialog box asking where a particular file is. This will happen when the original files were saved on a hard drive other than the one you're using. You'll need to tell Adobe Premiere Pro where the file is. In this case, navigate to the Lesson 04 folder and select the file for which the dialog box is prompting you.

1 Right-click (Windows) or Control-click (Mac OS) Illustrator Image.ai in the Project panel and choose Properties from the context menu.

   This file type is Adobe Illustrator Art. Here's how Adobe Premiere Pro deals with Adobe Illustrator files:

   - Like the Photoshop CS4 file you imported in step 4 in the previous exercise, this is a layered graphic file. However, Adobe Premiere Pro doesn't give you the option to import Adobe Illustrator files in separate layers. It merges them.
   - It also uses a process called *rasterization* to convert the vector (path-based) Illustrator art into the pixel-based image format used by Adobe Premiere Pro.
   - Adobe Premiere Pro automatically anti-aliases, or smooths the edges of, the Illustrator art.
   - Adobe Premiere Pro converts all empty areas into a transparent alpha channel so that clips below those areas on the Timeline can show through if you choose.

2 Close the Properties dialog box.

Editing Illustrator files in Illustrator

If you right-click (Windows) or Control-click (Mac OS) IllustratorImage.ai again, you'll note that one option is Edit Original. If you have Illustrator installed on your computer, selecting Edit Original will open this graphic in Illustrator, ready to edit. So even though the layers are merged in Adobe Premiere Pro, you can return to Illustrator, edit the original layered file, and save it, and the changes will immediately show up in Adobe Premiere Pro.

3 To see more information in the Project panel, drag its right edge to the right as far as possible to reveal more columns.

4 Click one of the image assets again, and then press the Tab key to move from column to column. Note that you can enter text "spreadsheet style" into fields that are editable. This is another way to see properties of the assets.

Customizing the Project panel columns

While you have the Project panel stretched wide, try dragging the column headers around. You can move columns left or right to suit your style of work.

5 Drag the Project panel to its original size. If you have problems formatting the workspace the way it was originally, choose Window > Workspace > Reset current workspace.

6 Drag the two still images—dark-alley.jpg and girl_highres.jpg—to the Video 1 track in the Timeline.

7 Press the backslash (\) key. That is the keyboard shortcut for expanding the Timeline view to match the length of the clips in it.

Your Timeline should appear as shown here.

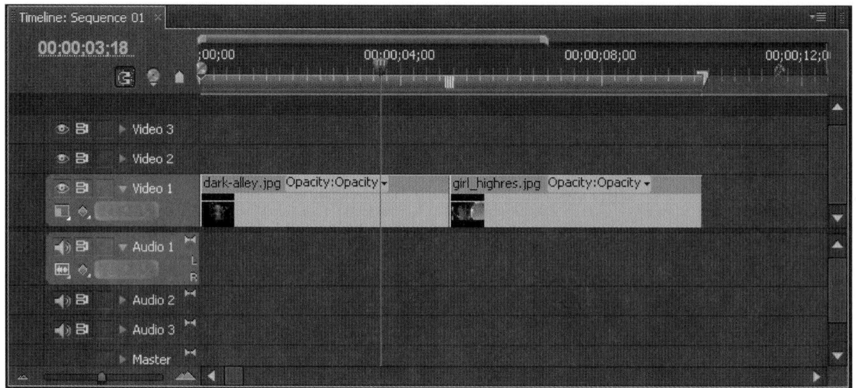

8 Drag the current-time indicator within the two clips.

9 Right-click (Windows) or Control-click (Mac OS) the first clip—dark-alley.jpg—in the Timeline and choose Scale to Frame Size to turn on that feature.

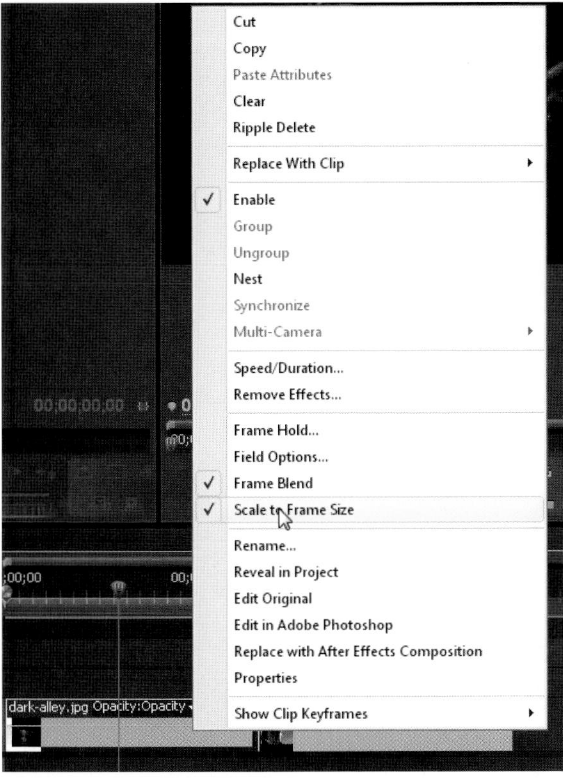

Note: As you drag the current-time indicator, look at the Program Monitor. You will see only a portion of each image because it is larger than the project preset dimensions. Both clips have resolutions that are much larger than the standard DV screen size. By default, Adobe Premiere Pro centers them in the screen and displays them in their original resolution. The next step explains how to view them in their entirety, without changing the aspect ratio of the images.

You should now see the entire image.

10 You can also manually scale the image from its full resolution using the Motion tool in the Effect Controls panel. The benefit of this method is that it allows you to pan or zoom up to the full image resolution. Move the current-time indicator over the girl_highres.jpg image so that it appears in the Program Monitor. Select the girl_highres image by clicking it once.

Note: If you want all your images to be automatically scaled to the project frame size, you can set that as a preference in the General category in Preferences by selecting "Default scale to frame size." You must set the option before you import the images for it to take effect.

11 Expand the Motion effect in the Effect Controls panel.

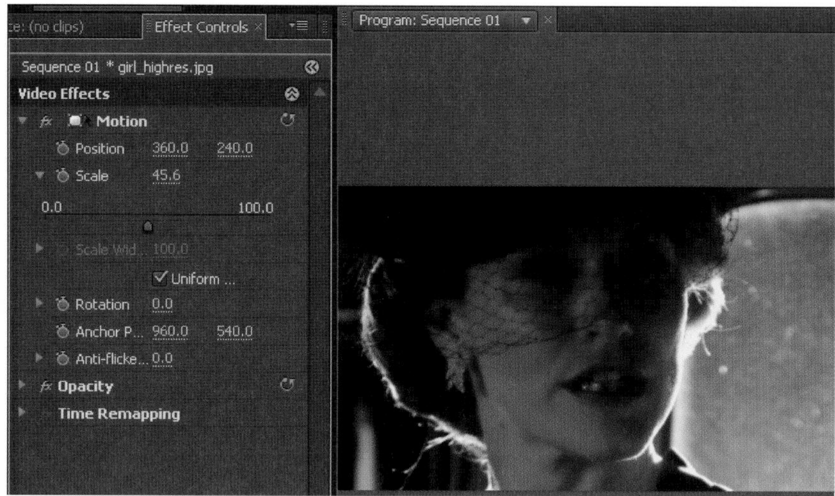

12 Expand the Scale parameter and adjust it larger or smaller. Watch the effect it has on the image. You can manually scale the image to any size you like. In a later lesson, we will look at keyframing this parameter to create animation.

Image tips

Here are a few tips for importing images:

- You can import images up to 16 megapixels in size (4096 x 4096).
- If you don't plan to zoom or pan, try to create files with a frame size at least as large as the frame size of the project—720 x 534 for NTSC DV (see the "Square versus rectangular pixels" tip). Otherwise you have to scale up the image, and it will lose some of its sharpness. Importing files overly large uses memory and can slow down your project.
- If you plan to zoom or pan, try to create images such that the zoomed or panned area has a frame size at least as large as the frame size of the project.

Square versus rectangular pixels

TV sets display rectangular pixels—slightly vertical rectangles (.9 aspect ratio) for NTSC and slightly horizontal rectangles for PAL. By contrast, computer monitors use square pixels. Images created in graphics software typically are square. Adobe Premiere Pro adjusts them to display properly by squashing and interpolating the square pixels to keep the images' original aspect ratios and to display them properly on TV sets. So when you create graphics or images with square pixels, create them with your TV standard in mind: 720 x 534 for NTSC (that resolution will become 720 x 480 after Premiere Pro squashes the square pixels into rectangles) and 768 x 576 for PAL.

Managing media in the bins

The Project panel provides a means of accessing and organizing your assets—video clips, audio files, still images, graphics, and sequences. Each listed media asset is a link. The files themselves remain in their file folders, while the assets are stored in *bins*. Bins behave like folders as a way to organize and categorize your assets visually within Adobe Premiere Pro.

Importing and logically arranging your assets in the Project panel is simple. You can create new bins and bins inside bins.

In this exercise, you will check out some of the Project panel options and then rearrange the clips you have been working with. If you need to start fresh, open Project 04-1.prproj.

1 Click the Icon View button in the lower-left corner of the Project panel.

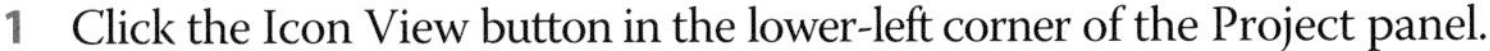

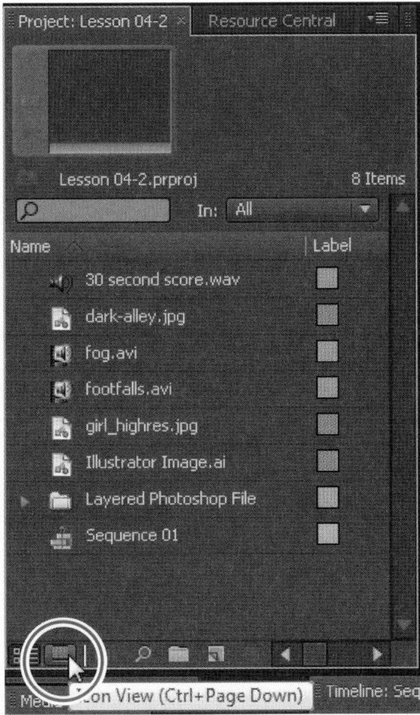

That changes the Project panel display from a list to thumbnails and icons.

2 Expand the Project panel by dragging its right edge to the right so you can see all the items.

3 Click 30 second score.wav to select it, and then click the Play-Stop Toggle button on the thumbnail viewer.

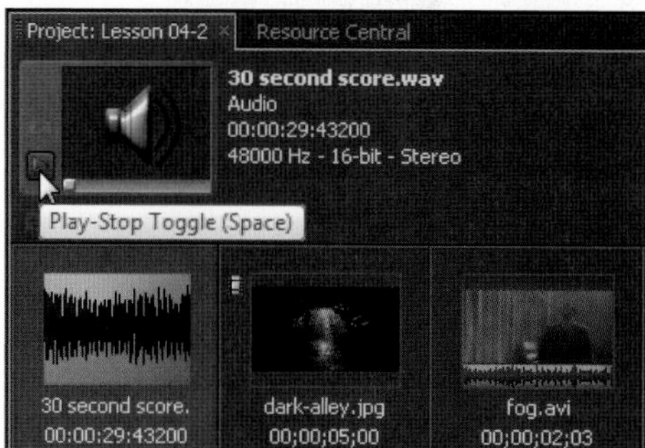

You can click any other asset and play it. The Play-Stop Toggle button will be unavailable (dimmed) for still images and graphics.

4 Click footfalls.avi and drag the slider under the thumbnail viewer a few seconds into the clip.

5 Click the Poster Frame button next to the preview to create a new thumbnail image for that clip.

Note: The new thumbnail appears immediately in the Project panel. The thumbnail image has an audio display in it, indicating this is a video clip with audio.

6 Click the New Bin button to create a new file folder.

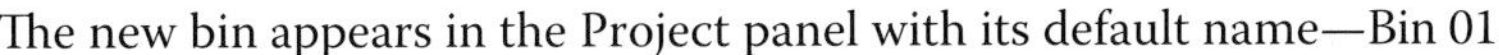

The new bin appears in the Project panel with its default name—Bin 01.

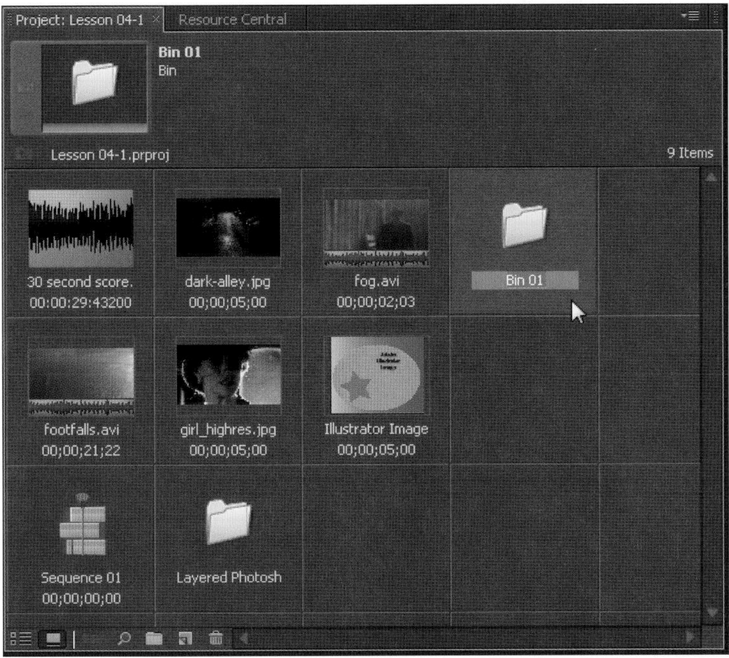

7 Change its name from Bin 01 to "audio" and press Enter (Windows) or Return (Mac).

8 Create another bin and name it "stills".

9 Drag the audio clip to the audio bin thumbnail.

10 Drag the two JPEG stills and the Illustrator file to the new stills bin.

11 Return to List view (click the List View button to the left of the Icon View button).

12 Click somewhere in the Project panel to deselect any bin that might be selected.

13 Click the New Bin button to create a new bin. Name it "sequences".

14 Open the Layered Photoshop File bin and drag the Layered Photoshop File sequence to the sequences bin.

15 Create one more bin named "movies" and drag the movie files to that bin.

16 Click somewhere in the Project panel to deselect any bin that might be selected.

Note: You need to deselect any bin at this point so that the bin you're about to add won't be a subfolder inside another folder. (Sometimes you might want to use subfolders to help organize the Project panel, but that's not what you're doing now.)

Note: It is useful to organize your project assets in this type of bin structure. You may come up with your own way of organizing, but organizing by asset type, as demonstrated here, is a good way to start.

17 Drag Sequence 01 to the movies bin as well.

18 Click Name at the top of the file link list in the Project panel twice to put all the asset links and bins in alphabetical order.

Your Project panel should appear as shown here.

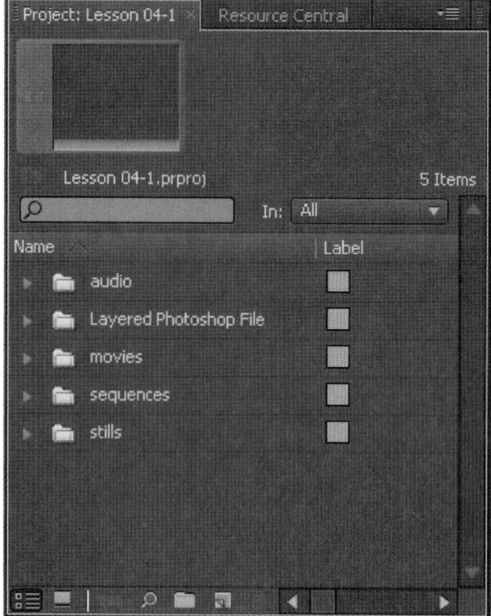

Exploring additional bin features

The bin feature in Adobe Premiere Pro CS4 is helpful when you have a lot of assets. It is possible to have thousands of assets (movie clips, image clips, audio clips, and so on) in your bins. Bins are very helpful in finding, moving, and organizing assets.

Having multiple bins open at once

In Adobe Premiere Pro CS4, you can open multiple bins at the same time in their own window or docked to a panel. This makes it easy to drag clips between two bins. Start this lesson where you left off in the previous section, or load Lesson 04-2.prproj from the Lesson 04 folder.

1 Double-click the stills bin you just created. Note that it opens in its own window.

2 Practice dragging clips from this new window to other bins and back.

3 Dock the new stills bin with another panel to try a different method of organizing your bins.

4 Close the stills bin by clicking the "x" on its tab. Note that the stills bin still exists in the main Project panel.

Finding assets

Adobe Premiere Pro CS4 has improved the searching capability within the Project panel. The Find tool is located near the top of the Project panel.

1 If your workspace has gotten messy, open the Lesson 04-2.prproj project.

2 Type the letters **fo** in the Search box. Notice that the movies bin automatically expands to reveal the movie clips with the letters fo in it.

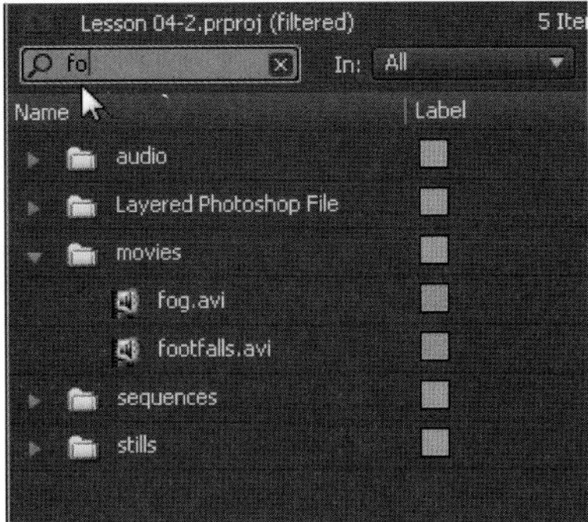

This feature is very simple yet is amazingly powerful in finding just the right clip quickly and easily.

3 When you're finished, clear all text in the Search box so all the files are visible.

4 Click the Find icon at the bottom of the Project panel to experiment with a more detailed, specific search tool. This tool is helpful when you have a lot of assets and the search tool is not specific enough.

Finding assets with the Media Browser

The Media Browser feature in Adobe Premiere Pro CS4 allows you to easily browse for files on your computer. Unlike the Import dialog box you used previously in this lesson, the Media Browser can stay open all the time and be docked where you find it convenient. In Lesson 5 you will learn how useful the Media Browser is for finding and importing file-based media such as P2 or XDCAM assets.

The Media Browser is pretty self-explanatory. You will learn to use it by importing the same assets you did earlier via the Import dialog box.

1 Open Lesson 04.prproj in the Lesson 04 folder. This project should have no assets imported yet.

2 Expand the Media Browser by dragging its right edge to the right.

3 Using the Media Browser, navigate to the Lesson 04 folder.

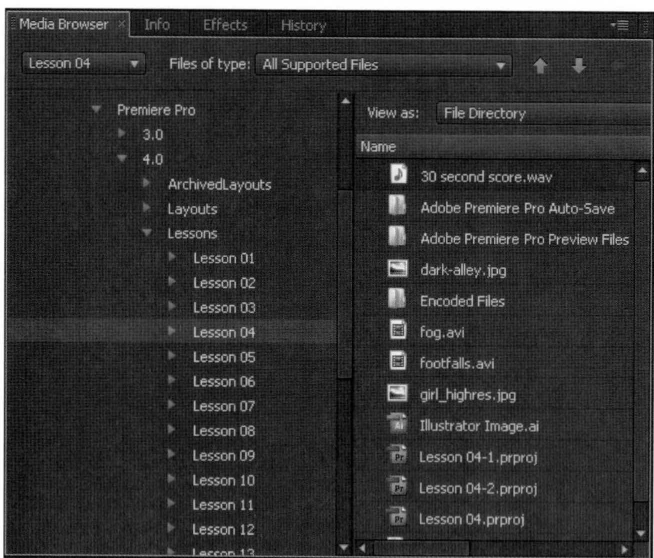

4 Select the same assets from the Lesson 04 folder as you did before and drag them to the Project panel.

Filter the assets you're looking for

Use the Files of Type menu in the Media Browser to filter the assets you want to find.

Review questions

1 What is the purpose of the General tab in the New Sequence dialog box?

2 How can you cause Adobe Premiere Pro to import all JPEGs so they are scaled to the dimensions of your current sequence?

3 Describe at least two ways to import assets.

4 Adobe Premiere Pro handles Photoshop CS4 and Illustrator CS4 layered graphic files differently. Explain the differences.

5 What is the advantage of importing high-resolution photos?

6 By default, what happens when you double-click a bin?

Review answers

1 The General tab is used to customize an existing preset or to create a new custom preset. If you are using a standard media type, the Sequence Preset option is all you should need to select.

2 In the General category of Preferences, check the "Default scale to frame size" box before importing the JPEGs.

3 Choose File > Import, double-click in an empty space in the Project panel, or drag assets from the Media Browser to the Project panel.

4 Adobe Premiere Pro lets you import Photoshop CS4 files in one of three ways: as a sequence with individual layers on separate video tracks, on an individual layer basis, or as a merged file. Adobe Premiere Pro imports Illustrator CS4 layered graphics only as merged files. It rasterizes and anti-aliases Illustrator vector-based art.

5 You can pan and zoom in on them and maintain a sharp-looking image. To see images at their full resolution, right-click (Windows) or Control-click (Mac OS) them in the Timeline and deselect Scale to Frame Size.

6 The bin will open in its own window.

5 IMPORTING TAPELESS MEDIA

Topics covered in this lesson

- Using a tapeless workflow
- Using Media Browser
- Importing P2, XDCAM, and AVCHD media
- Mixing media formats

This lesson will take approximately 30 minutes.

Many popular video cameras record to disk or flash memory rather than tape. The advantages of this "tapeless" workflow include reliability, ingest speed, and flexibility in frame rates. Adobe Premiere Pro CS4 allows you to edit these new formats natively without time-consuming conversions.

Getting started

All the lessons in this book, with the exception of this one, use standard-definition (SD) widescreen clips as examples in the lesson folders. This lesson uses high-definition (HD) video clips taken from a Panasonic P2 camera. This will allow you to experience the ease of editing P2 video natively in Adobe Premiere Pro even if you don't have a P2 camera.

Using a tapeless workflow

A tapeless workflow (also known as a *file-based workflow*) is simply the process of importing video from a tapeless camera, editing it, and exporting it. Adobe Premiere Pro CS4 makes this especially easy because, unlike many competing nonlinear editing systems, Adobe Premiere Pro CS4 does not require the media from these tapeless formats to be converted. Adobe Premiere Pro CS4 can edit P2, XDCAM, and AVCHD footage natively with no conversions.

Though P2, XDCAM, and AVCHD are all tapeless formats, they do have their differences. Let's review the basics of each format.

Panasonic P2

P2 is the video format recorded onto a P2 card by Panasonic P2 cameras. A P2 card is a PCMCIA flash memory card that is inserted into the camera for recording or into a PCMCIA slot in a workstation. Though Adobe Premiere Pro can read and edit directly from the P2 card, it is recommended that you copy the contents of the card to your local hard drive for best performance.

P2 cameras also have USB ports that allow the video to be transferred to an editing workstation via USB.

Notice that whether you move the files via the P2 card or transfer them via USB, the video does not need to be serially captured. It is transferred to the editing workstation at the speed allowed by the transfer I/O.

Several variants of the P2 format exist that specify different frame sizes and frame rates. Adobe Premiere Pro supports all the standard P2 variants.

A typical workflow for P2 media is as follows:

1 Shoot onto the P2 card in the camera.

2 Move the P2 card to your workstation and copy the files to your local hard drive.

3 Edit the files natively in Adobe Premiere Pro.

4 Export the project to Blu-ray Disc, to DVD, to the Web, or even back to the P2 native format.

Sony XDCAM

Sony XDCAM refers to a family of cameras that record to optical disc or SxS flash memory cards. Most of the cameras in the XDCAM and XDCAM HD lines record to optical disc. The XDCAM EX1 and EX3 models record to SxS flash memory cards.

You can remove the optical disc from your camera and place it in a deck attached to your workstation. Or you can insert the SxS flash memory card into a PCI Express card slot in your workstation and read it as a flash drive. In either case, it is recommended that you copy the files from the optical disc or SxS flash card to your local hard drive for best performance rather than attempting to edit directly from the source media.

Adobe Premiere Pro offers native support for optical disc XDCAM content recorded as standard-definition DVCAM and for all high-definition XDCAM HD formats recorded at 18 Mbps, 25 Mbps, and 35 Mbps. Adobe Premiere Pro does not currently provide native support for standard-definition IMX and the new high-definition MPEG HD422 50 Mbps codec. However, you can play content in those formats in an XDCAM or XDCAM HD player with SDI or HD-SDI I/O and bring it into Adobe Premiere Pro through a compatible third-party capture card.

Adobe Premiere Pro supports every XDCAM EX format variation except for 1440x1080/23.98p SP mode with 3:2 pulldown. As an alternative, Adobe Premiere Pro offers native support for 1920x1080/23.98 HQ.

A typical workflow for XDCAM EX media is as follows:

1 Shoot onto the SxS card in the camera.

2 Move the SxS card to your workstation and copy the files to your local hard drive.

3 Edit the files natively in Adobe Premiere Pro.

4 Export the project to Blu-ray Disc, DVD, or the Web.

AVCHD

AVCHD is a recording format generally used in consumer cameras to record high-definition video to a tapeless format. AVCHD is not limited to a single vendor's camera or family of cameras; it is used in many brands of consumer high-definition cameras including various models from Sony and Panasonic. Compared to HDV cameras, which are based on the MPEG-2 codec, AVCHD achieves higher compression and lower data rates using the H.264 codec.

Cameras using the AVCHD record onto one of three types of media:

- **DVD**: The camera burns video as it is recorded directly to a DVD in the camera using the AVCHD recording format.
- **Hard drive**: The camera records video directly to a hard drive inside the camera using the AVCHD recording format.
- **Flash memory**: The camera records video directly to a flash memory card inside the camera using the AVCHD format.

The AVCHD format is a good format to record and view video, but it has proven a challenge to edit because of its highly compressed nature. Adobe Premiere Pro CS4 has the ability to edit AVCHD video in its native format without converting it to an intermediate or alternate codec, but how smoothly the AVCHD edit process goes will depend largely on the power of the editing system you are using.

A typical workflow for AVCHD media is as follows:

1. Shoot the AVCHD video to DVD, flash media, or hard drive. The media will vary depending on the type of AVCHD camera you are using.
2. Copy the AVCHD video clips to your workstation by placing the capture disc in your DVD drive, moving the flash card, or copying from your camera's internal hard drive to your workstation via USB.
3. Edit the files natively in Adobe Premiere Pro.
4. Export the project to Blu-ray Disc, DVD, or the Web.

Using Media Browser

If you are an experienced Adobe Premiere Pro user, you will tend to want to use the traditional method of importing clips through the Project panel. You were introduced to Media Browser in Lesson 4, and you will be using it in this lesson to locate and import the P2 example clips. Although it is possible to import all the P2 clips using the Import menu in the Project panel, using Media Browser has advantages, especially for P2 media, as you will explore in this lesson.

Importing P2 and XDCAM media

If you were shooting P2 video using a Panasonic P2 camera, you would remove the P2 card from the camera, connect a P2 reader to your editing workstation, and copy the video clips to your local hard drive. Since many readers of this book do not have a P2 high-definition camera, I have completed this step for you and placed the P2 files in the Lesson 05 folder.

P2 folder structure

A typical Panasonic P2 file structure contains a folder called CONTENTS. Within this folder are subfolders containing the essence (the actual audio and video media) and the metadata. The essence is split into components, each sorted into corresponding subfolders, as follows:

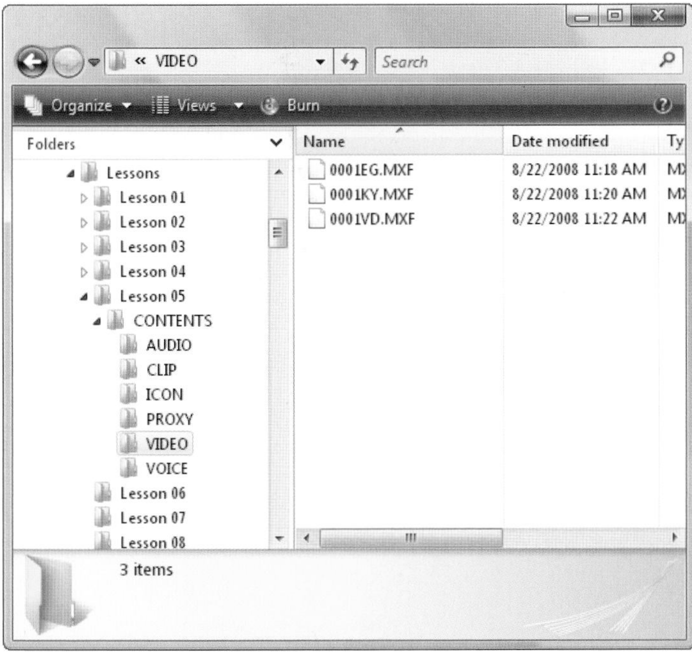

- **AUDIO folder**: This folder contains up to 16 independent mono audio MXF files for each clip, using the video clip's filename with the channel number appended.
- **CLIP folder**: This folder contains clip metadata, stored as [filename].xml.
- **ICON folder**: This folder contains a thumbnail icon or poster frame, stored as a BMP file.
- **PROXY folder**: This folder contains proxy files, stored as .mp4 files and containing quarter-resolution MPEG-4 video at around 200 Kbps and one mono AAC audio track, along with a BIN file. Adobe Premiere Pro does not support these proxies.
- **VIDEO folder**: This folder contains video MXF files.
- **VOICE folder**: This folder contains voice annotations added after capture in .wav format.

This folder structure may seem overly complex, because the audio, video, metadata, and thumbnails are all in separate folders, and long clips will often be split into multiple files. Adobe Premiere Pro handles this complexity very well. Using Media Browser makes it easy to browse and select your media:

1 After launching Adobe Premiere Pro, click New Project.

2 Name the new project P2 Test and save it in the Lesson 05 folder.

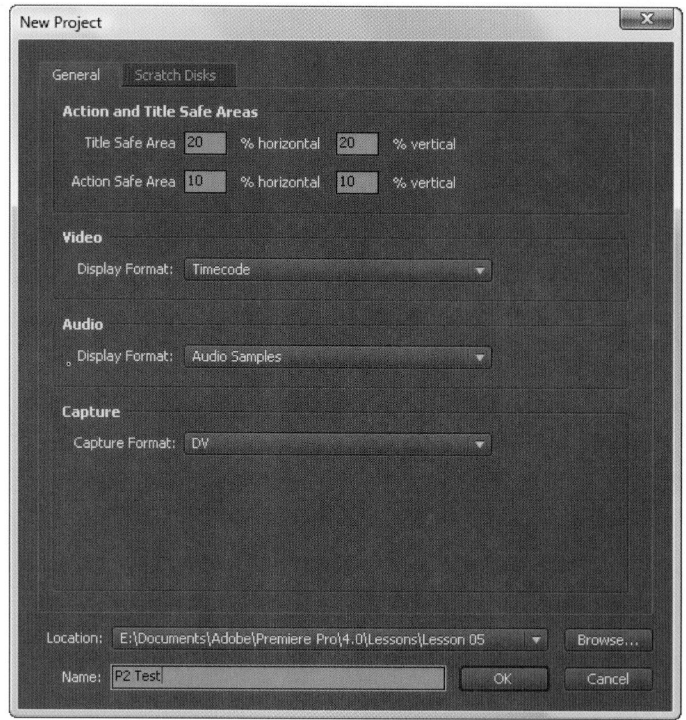

3 Since you will be importing P2 media, you need to choose the correct preset in the New Sequence dialog box. In our case, the video was shot at 960x720 1.33 PAR at 24p. So choose the DVCPROHD 720p 24p preset and click OK.

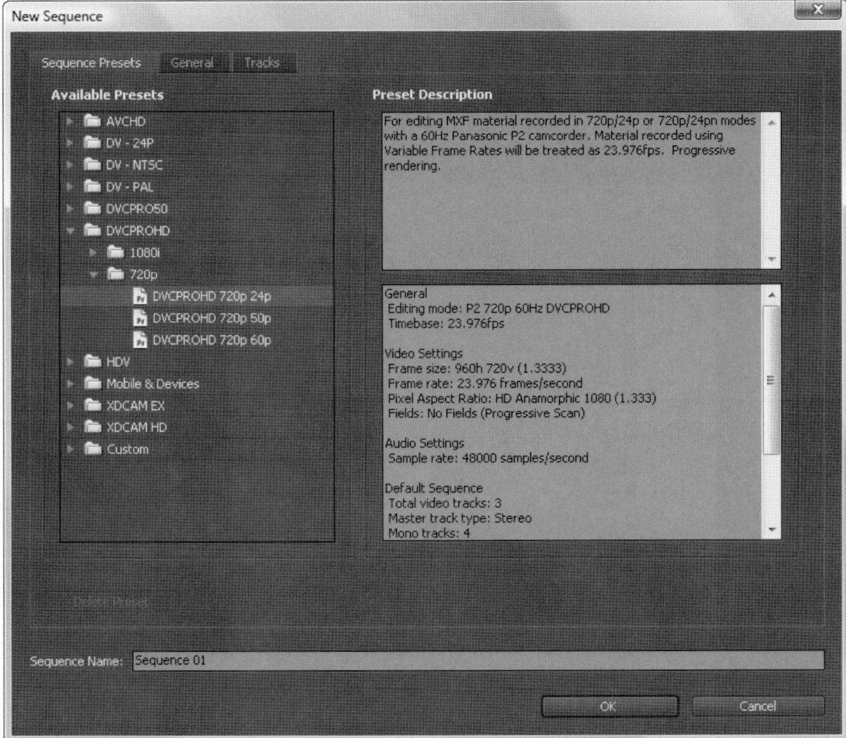

● **Note:** If you have problems creating the project, you can open Lesson 05.prproj in the Lesson 05 folder to start at this point.

4 Click the Media Browser tab if it is not already selected. You may also want to make the Media Browser window wider by dragging the right edge of the panel to the right.

5 Using Media Browser, navigate to the Lesson 05 folder.

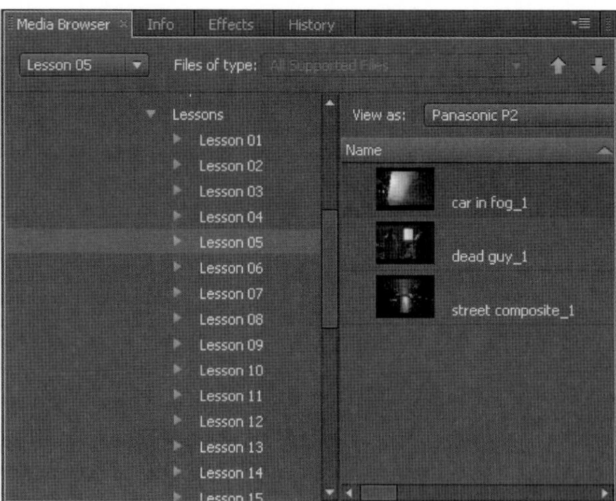

Notice that Media Browser has detected the P2 folder structure and is displaying P2 clips in a user-friendly way. It has retrieved the video, audio, metadata, and thumbnail from the four different folders for you and presented them as three simple video clips. The clip name appears rather than the P2 filename.

6 Double-click the car in fog_1 clip. It opens and plays in the Source Monitor but will not be imported into the Project panel. This feature allows you to preview the file easily before importing.

7 Right-click the car in fog_1 clip and choose Import. The clip is now imported and added to the Project panel.

8 Select both of the other clips by Shift-clicking them; then right-click and choose Import to add them both to the Project panel.

9 Drag the three clips to the Timeline and notice that no red render line appears. The clips will play and preview in real time with no rendering or conversion.

A word about P2 audio

The P2 format allows up to 16 independent mono audio files for each video clip depending on the setup and preferences set in the camera. Adobe Premiere Pro CS4 keeps track of what audio goes with what video clip and assembles them for you on the Timeline. The example P2 video clips used in this lesson include two audio channels.

XDCAM and AVCHD media

In the example you just completed, you used actual P2 media. XDCAM or AVCHD media is imported and used in a similar way. The difference comes in choosing the correct preset when starting the new sequence. The XDCAM folder structure is different from the P2 folder structure, but if you use Media Browser as we recommend here, the workflow will be identical.

Performance of AVCHD media

AVCHD media is a highly compressed format that creates a challenge when performing frame-accurate nonlinear editing. Adobe Premiere Pro CS4 is designed to handle native AVCHD media but does require a fast processor and a lot of memory to handle it efficiently. If you will be working with high-definition video, including AVCHD, it is recommended that you scale your hardware to the high end of the Adobe hardware recommendations.

Mixing media formats

It is not unusual to work on a project and end up with video clips from different cameras at different resolutions. This is no problem for Adobe Premiere Pro because you can mix different resolution clips on the same Timeline. In this exercise, you will do just that. You will add a standard-definition video clip to the Timeline with other P2 high-definition clips.

1 Start where you left off, or open Lesson 05-1.prproj from the Lesson 05 folder.

2 Using Media Browser, navigate to the Lesson 05 folder.

   There is an SD clip in the Lesson 05 folder, but Media Browser is not displaying it. Media Browser has detected that the folder contains a P2 folder structure, so it's displaying only P2 media. Notice that the "View as" field has automatically set itself to Panasonic P2. You can manually change it so it looks at all files.

3 Change the "View as" field in Media Browser from Panasonic P2 to File Directory. Now all files will be revealed, not just the P2 files.

4 Right-click the file named sd clip_pursuit.avi and choose Import.

5 Drag the sd clip_pursuit.avi file to the end of the Timeline and then play the Timeline.

   Notice the SD clip is much smaller than the P2 clips. This is because the SD clip is lower resolution than the P2 clips. You can deal with this in a couple of ways. One is to enlarge the SD clip, which will make it a little soft or fuzzy. Another solution is to use the SD clip as a picture-in-picture (PIP) over a P2 clip. You will try both methods in the following steps.

6 Select the sd clip_pursuit.avi clip by clicking it once in the Timeline. If it is too thin to click, zoom into the Timeline by pressing the = key on your keyboard.

7 Drag the current-time indicator over the clip so it appears in the Program Monitor.

8 Right-click the sd clip_pursuit.avi and choose Scale to Frame Size. Play the Timeline to see the SD clip expanded to fill the frame.

9 Drag another copy of the sd clip_pursuit.avi from the Project panel and position it on top of the first P2 clip, in the Video 2 track. Play the Timeline, and notice the SD clip is already a picture-in-picture because of its lower resolution.

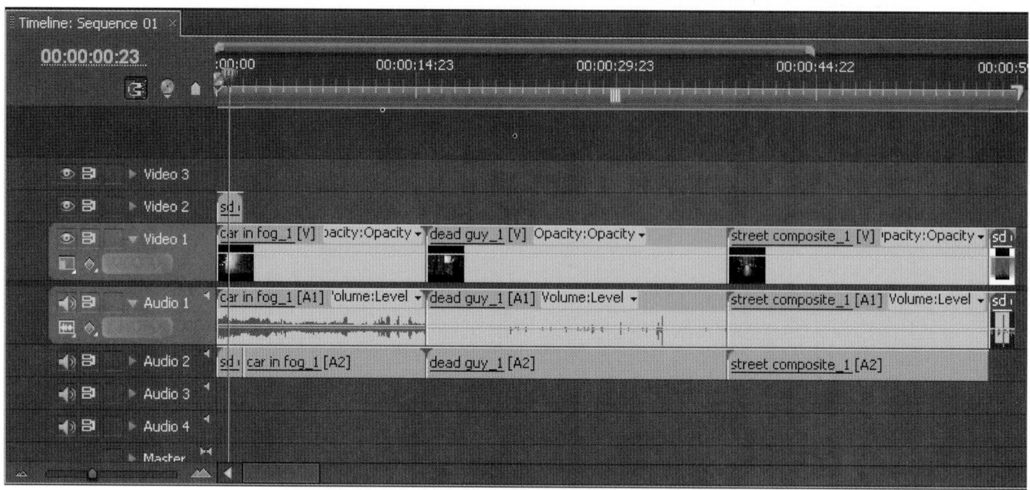

Note: The SD clips have a red line over them on the Timeline, which means they have to be rendered to export. They may still preview in real time. The reason they have a red line is that they do not match the frame size and frame rate set for that sequence. That sequence was optimized for P2 media. This is not a problem; it just means rendering will take place for the SD clips in this case when you export. So choose sequence settings that match the majority of your source clips.

Review questions

1 Does Adobe Premiere Pro CS4 need to convert P2, XDCAM, or AVCHD footage when it is imported?

2 What are two advantages of tapeless or file-based workflows?

3 What is one advantage of using Media Browser to import tapeless media over the File > Import method?

4 Can different media types be added to the same sequence, or must separate sequences be created?

5 Name two of the three media types to which consumer AVCHD cameras record.

Review answers

1 No. Adobe Premiere Pro CS4 can edit P2, XDCAM, and AVCHD natively.

2 Speed (no serial capture), reliability (fewer moving parts to store the video), and flexibility (clips do not have to be captured or searched serially) are advantages of a tapeless workflow.

3 Media Browser understands the P2 and XDCAM folder structures and shows you the clips in a friendly way.

4 Different media types can be added to the same sequence.

5 Consumer AVCHD cameras record to DVDs, hard drives, and flash memory cards.

6 CREATING CUTS-ONLY VIDEOS

Topics covered in this lesson

- Using a storyboard to build a rough cut
- Editing clips on the Timeline
- Moving clips to, from, and within the Timeline
- Working with Source Monitor editing tools
- Adjusting clips in the Trim panel
- Using other editing tools

This lesson will take approximately 80 minutes.

Watch any TV news program, and virtually every edit is a straight cut with no transitions. There's an art to creating cuts-only videos, and Adobe Premiere Pro CS4 gives you a full palette of cut edit tools and techniques.

Getting started

The first thing you do when you're creating a video is to lay down a cuts-only version. Later, you can apply transitions, effects, titles, and motion, as well as work on compositing. Whether or not you use these extra effects, building a cuts-only video is an art. You want to create a logical flow to your clips, make matching edits, and avoid jump cuts.

Adobe Premiere Pro offers several ways of achieving those ends. Depending on your circumstances, you might work in the Trim panel, use the Ripple Edit tool, or move clips on the Timeline using the Source Monitor or keyboard modifiers. You will use all those techniques in this lesson.

Using a storyboard to build a rough cut

Film directors and animators frequently use walls of photos and sketches to visualize story flow and camera angles. These are known as *storyboards*, and they can be very useful in planning a project and making sure you get the shots or material you need.

Storyboards also help after the fact. In the case of Adobe Premiere Pro, you can arrange clip thumbnails in the Project panel to get a basic feel for how your finished video will work. Then you can move all those clips to the Timeline for more precise editing.

This approach is useful in revealing gaps in your story. It's also a way to note redundancy and to quickly place a whole bunch of ordered clips on a sequence. When you are confronted with a Project panel loaded with clips, storyboards can help you see the big picture.

After creating your storyboard, you can place several clips in a sequence on the Timeline at one time. To begin, do the following:

1 Open Adobe Premiere Pro.

2 Click Open Project, navigate to the Lesson 06 folder, and double-click Lesson 06-1.prproj.

Note: This is a DV-NTSC wide 48 kHz project.

3 Using Media Browser, navigate to the Lesson 06 folder and import the five .avi files by dragging them to the Project panel.

4 Click the New Bin button in the Project panel and name your new bin Storyboard.

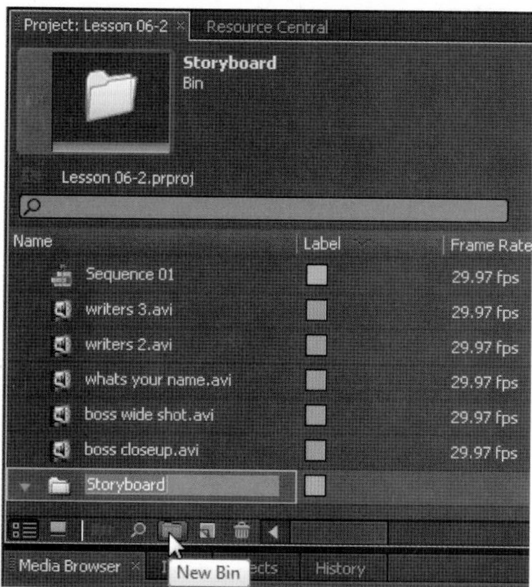

5 Double-click the new Storyboard bin icon to open it in its own window. This makes it easy to move clips into this bin.

6 In the main bin, select the five .avi movie clips (do not select Sequence 01).

7 Right-click (Windows) or Ctrl-click (Mac OS) one of the selected clips to open the context menu, and choose Copy. Note that you need to click the clip name, or you will deselect all the clips.

8 Select the Storyboard bin to make it the active window, and choose Edit > Paste.

All five video files now appear in the Storyboard bin. They remain in the main Project panel as well, because you copied them rather than dragged them.

9 Click the Icon View button in the Storyboard bin to switch to icon view.

Note: Choosing Copy when you've highlighted multiple clips will copy the entire collection of clips.

Note: The reason you have copied and pasted the video files into the separate Storyboard bin is because you will delete some of them during this lesson. This approach will allow you to remove them from the Storyboard bin without deleting them from the Project panel.

10 Click the panel menu icon and then choose Thumbnails > Large.

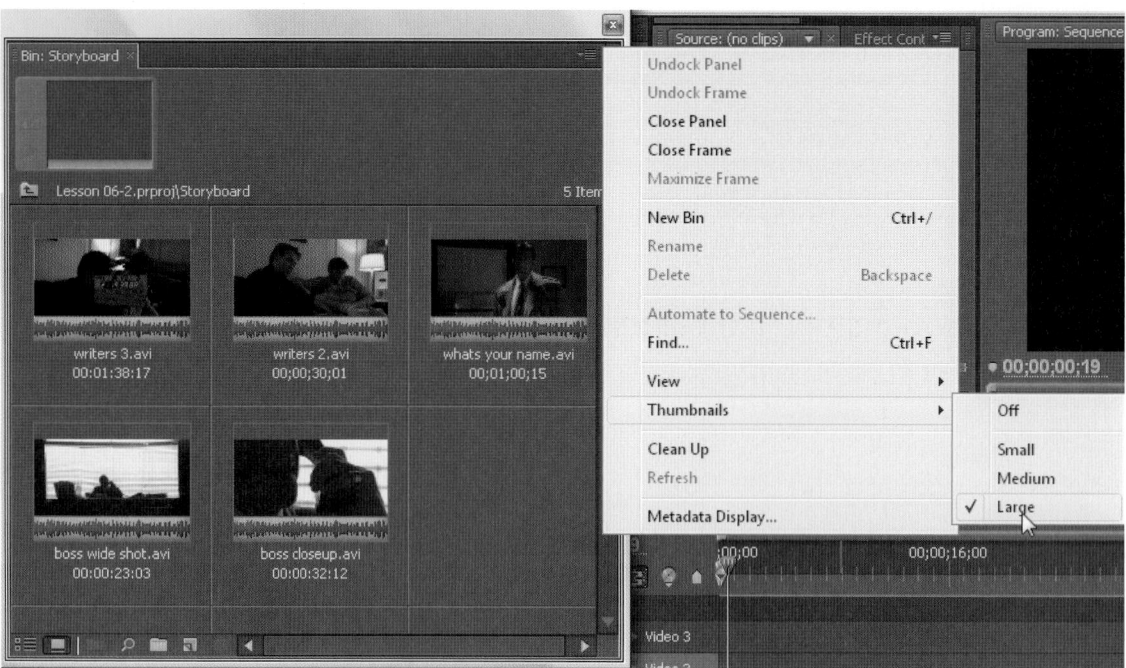

11 Resize the Storyboard bin so you can see all the thumbnails.

Thumbnail cleanup

When you resize a bin window while it is displaying in icon view, the thumbnails do not always wrap or flow with the resizing of the window. To correct this, click the panel menu icon and choose Clean Up from the menu. This will clean up the thumbnails for you.

Arranging your storyboard

In this section, you will learn how to arrange thumbnails into a logical order. Keep in mind that you will trim the clips later to make the edits work more smoothly.

Note: Some of the videos are a little dark and can be hard to view critically in the Project panel Preview Monitor. In those cases, double-click a clip and view it in the Source Monitor.

In turn, view each clip in the Preview Monitor by clicking the clip to select it and then clicking the Play button in the Preview Monitor.

After viewing the clips, decide what order you would like them to run in your project.

Here's how to create the sequence after you have decided the order in which the clips should run:

1 Continue where you left off in the previous section, or load Lesson 06-2.prproj from the Lesson 06 folder.

2 Drag the thumbnails within the bin to position them in the order you want them to play.

To move a clip, simply drag it to a new location. The pointer changes, and a black vertical line indicates the new location for placement.

Tip: As you drag clips, you will leave gaps. Use Clean Up to remove those gaps. If needed, stretch the size of the Bin panel to see all the clips at once.

Automating your storyboard to a sequence

Now you're going to move your storyboard clips to the Timeline, placing them there contiguously, in sequential order. Adobe Premiere Pro calls this process *Automate to Sequence*. Here's how you do it:

1 Make sure the current-time indicator is at the beginning of the Timeline. Automate to Sequence places the clips starting at the current-time indicator location.

2 With the Storyboard bin window active, choose Edit > Select All to highlight all the clips (you can also marquee-select or use the Shift-click method).

3 Click the Automate to Sequence button in the lower-left corner of the Project panel.

Note: You can also choose Automate to Sequence from the panel menu.

4 The newly opened Automate To Sequence dialog box has several options. Choose the settings shown in the following image. The options include the following:

- **Ordering**: Sort Order puts clips on a sequence in the order you established in the storyboard. Selection Order places them in the order you selected them if you Ctrl-clicked (Windows) or Command-clicked (Mac OS) individual clips.
- **Placement**: This places clips sequentially on the Timeline.
- **Method**: The choices here are Insert Edit and Overlay Edit, both of which will be discussed later in this lesson. Because in this instance you are placing the clips on an empty sequence, both methods will do the same thing.

- **Clip Overlap**: Overlap presumes you'll put a transition such as a cross-dissolve between all clips. The goal in this lesson is to create a cuts-only video—that is,
a video with no transitions—so you'll set Clip Overlap to 0.
- **Transitions**: Because you'll opt for no transitions, make sure these two options (Apply Default Audio Transition and Apply Default Video Transition) are deselected.
- **Ignore Options**: Check Ignore Audio to exclude the audio portion of the selected clips.

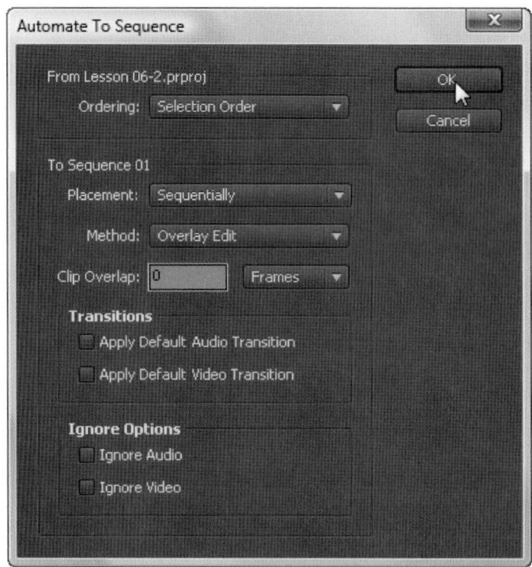

5 Click OK. This places your clips in the order you selected in Sequence 01.

6 Drag the Project panel out of the way, click inside the Timeline to activate it, and press the spacebar to play your sequence.

View this sequence critically. Several edits are jump cuts or feel awkward. Some clips are too long. The next task is to fix those flaws.

Editing clips on the Timeline

You will use a variety of editing tools to improve this storyboard rough cut, including the following:

- You'll trim a clip by dragging its end.
- You'll use the Ripple Delete command to remove a gap between clips.
- You'll use the Ripple Edit tool to save a step when you lengthen or shorten a clip.

Trimming a clip

To trim a clip, follow these steps:

1 Open Lesson 06-3.prproj from the Lesson 06 folder. The clips in this project may be in a different order than the order you selected. That's OK because you're going to edit the clips into a short movie that has some kind of plot.

2 Notice the Timeline now has two sequences, Sequence 01 and Complete. You may have as many sequences in a project as you like. Click the Complete sequence tab and play the completed project.

   The video in the Complete sequence is the final cuts-only video you will make using the edit tools available in Adobe Premiere Pro. It is amazing how some well-timed cuts can transform your footage from a bunch of confusing clips into a short movie with a plot.

3 Practice zooming in and out of the Timeline by pressing the equal sign (=) to zoom in and the minus sign (-) to zoom out. Press the backslash (\) to make the whole sequence fit on the screen.

4 Click the Sequence 01 tab to switch to Sequence 01. You will start editing this rough sequence so it looks like the Complete sequence.

5 Hover the pointer over the right edge of the first clip (whats your name.avi) until you see the left-facing Trim bracket.

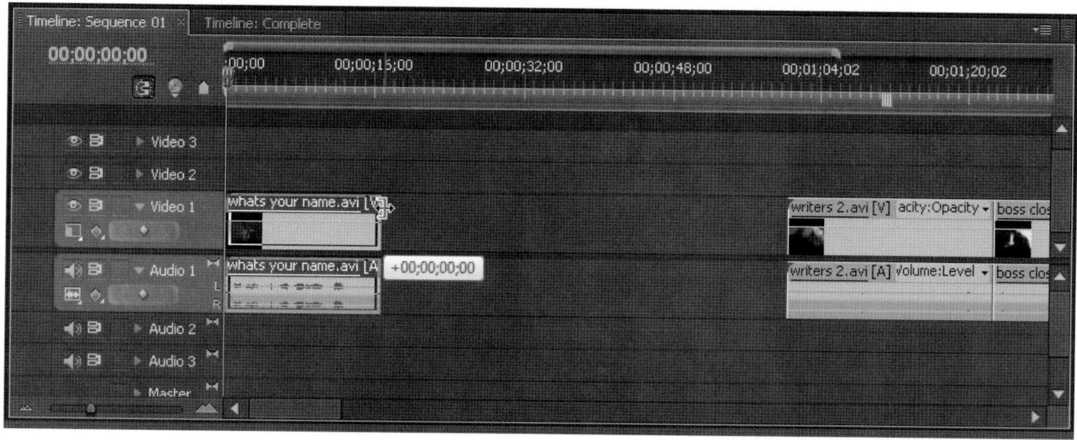

Note: As you move your pointer, you might notice that it changes into a Pen Keyframe tool. That happens when you hover the pointer over the thin yellow Opacity line. You'll work with the Opacity effect in upcoming lessons on compositing.

6 Drag the bracket to the left until just after the actor says, "What's your name?" Use the timecode in the Program Monitor display for reference. The edit point is at 00;00;16;25.

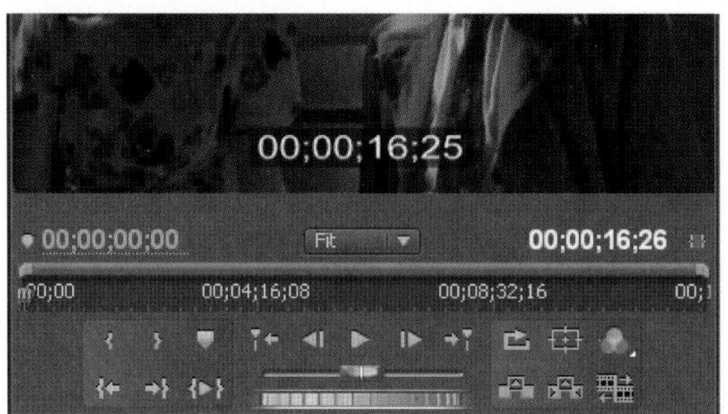

● **Note:** Editing the length of this clip on the Timeline does not delete the video to the right. It's still there, just edited from the Timeline.

This trim edit leaves a gap between the two clips on the Timeline. You'll remove this gap later.

7 Release the mouse button. This will remove the extra time after the actor says, "What's your name?"

8 The second clip, writers 2.avi, needs to have the beginning and end trimmed, and to be slid to the left to play right after the first clip. To do so, hover the pointer over the left edge of the clip until the Trim bracket appears, and drag it to the right until the timecode in the Program Monitor reads 00;00;10;00. Drag the right edge of the clip to the left until the timecode in the Program Monitor reads 00;00;18;24. Use the - and = keys to adjust the displayed area as needed.

Step further back using History

When working on most editing projects in Adobe Premiere Pro, you'll make multiple edits and, inevitably, a few mistakes. You can back up one step at a time by pressing Ctrl+Z (Windows) or Command+Z (Mac OS) or by choosing Edit > Undo. You can also use the History panel to move back several steps at once.

Frame-specific editing with Snap

Adobe Premiere Pro has a tremendously useful feature called Snap. It's a default setting, and in only a few instances will you want to turn it off. With Snap turned on, as you drag a clip toward another clip, it will jump to the edge of the adjacent clip to make a clean, unbroken edit. With Snap turned off, you'd have to slide the new clip very carefully next to the other clip to ensure there is no gap.

Snap is also useful when making precise edits. Using the Selection tool to trim a clip can be a bit clumsy, as you might have noted in step 6 in this section. Snap allows you to trim to the current-time indicator easily.

Locate the frame you want to trim by dragging the current-time indicator through your sequence to that frame's location (use the right arrow and left arrow keys to move to the specific frame). Use the Selection tool to drag the edge of the clip toward the current-time indicator line. When it gets near the line, it will snap to the current-time indicator, and you'll have made a frame-specific edit. You can use this technique in all sorts of circumstances.

If you want to toggle the Snap feature off or on, click the Snap button in the top-left corner of the Timeline (shown here).

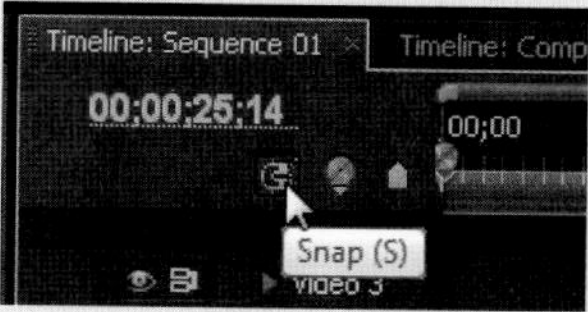

Closing the gaps using Ripple Delete

Trimming the two clips has left a gap in the sequence. You'll remove them using the Ripple Delete command:

1 Right-click (Windows) or Control-click (Mac OS) the gap between the first and second clips.

2 Choose Ripple Delete.

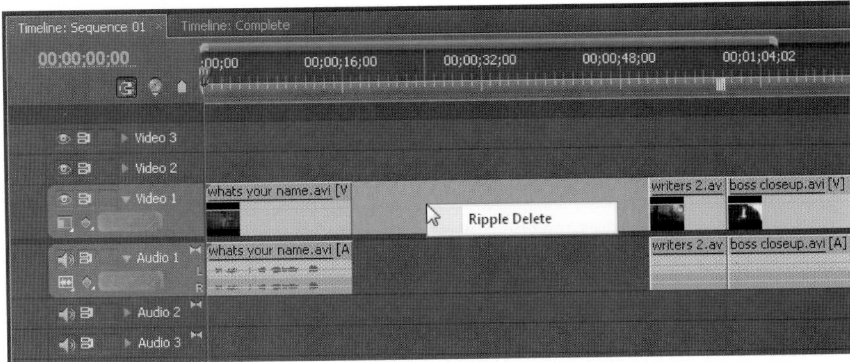

The Ripple Delete command removes the gap by sliding all the material after the gap to the left.

Using the Ripple Edit tool

A way to avoid creating gaps in the first place is to use the Ripple Edit tool. It's one of the many tools in the Tools panel.

Use the Ripple Edit tool to trim a clip in the same way you used the Selection tool in Trim mode. The two differences are that the Ripple Edit tool does not leave a gap on the sequence and the display in the Program Monitor gives a clearer representation of how the edit will work.

When you use the Ripple Edit tool to lengthen or shorten a clip, your action ripples through the sequence. That is, all clips after that edit slide to the left to fill the gap or slide to the right to accommodate a longer clip.

You'll perform the same edit to the first clip as you just did using the Selection tool, but this time you'll use the Ripple Edit tool so no space is left behind:

1 Press Ctrl+Z (Windows) or Command+Z (Mac OS) to return in your edit history to before you edited the first clip. Or, if you prefer, reopen Lesson 06-3.prproj without saving it.

2 Click the Ripple Edit tool (or press B on your keyboard).

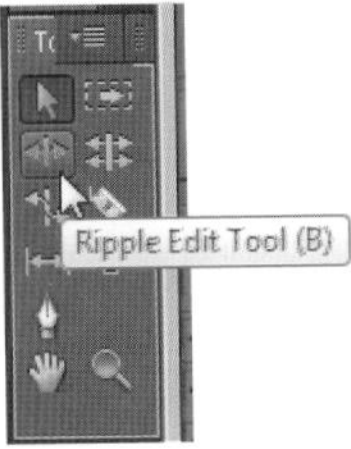

3 Hover the tool over the right edge of the first clip until it turns into a large, left-facing square bracket.

4 Drag to the left until just after the actor says, "What's your name?" Use the timecode in the Program Monitor display for reference. The edit point is at 00;00;16;25.

Notice that when you're using the Ripple Edit tool, the Program Monitor displays the last frame of the first clip on the left and the first frame of the second clip on the right. Watch the moving edit position on the left half of the Program Monitor. Your goal is to move that clip until the timecode reads 00;00;16;25.

5 Release the mouse button to complete the edit. The remaining part of the clip moves left to fill the gap, and the clips to its right slide along with it. Play that portion of the sequence to see whether the edit works smoothly.

6 Trim the second clip to the same points as you did earlier using the Ripple Edit tool.

You have several more edits to make to the rest of the sequence, but first I'll cover some editing terminology.

Note: The Ripple Edit pointer is larger than the Selection tool's Trim pointer.

Moving clips to, from, and within the Timeline

One of the beauties of Adobe Premiere Pro is how easy it is to add clips anywhere in the project, move them around, and remove them altogether.

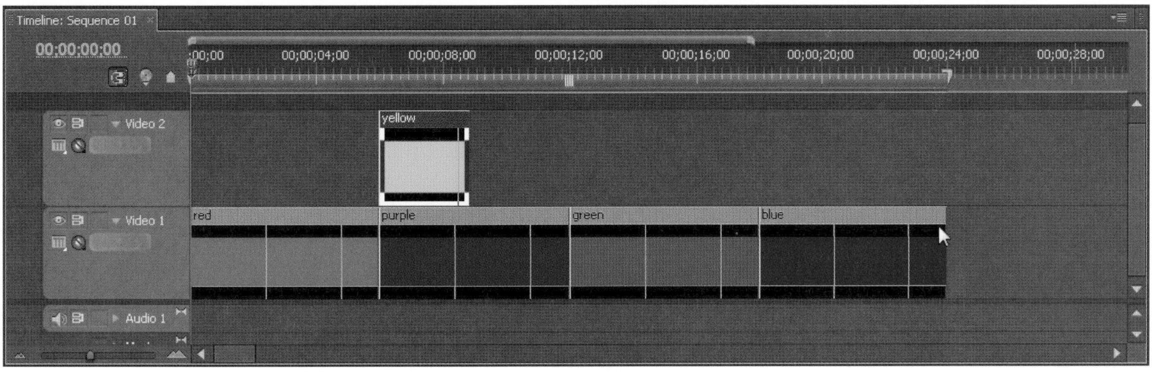

You can place a clip in the Timeline in two ways (whether you drag it from the Project panel or from another location in the Timeline). In the exercise in the next section, you will move the yellow clip to the Video 1 track in two different ways:

- **Overlay**: The newly placed clip and its audio (if applicable) replace what was in the sequence at the point in the Timeline at which the clip is placed.

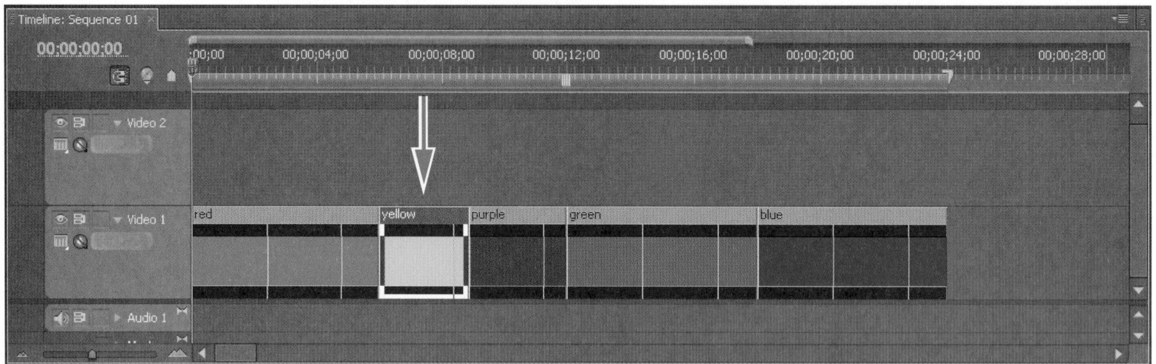

- **Insert**: The first frame of the newly placed clip cuts the current clip and, without covering up anything, slides the cut segment and all clips after it to the right. This process requires using a keyboard modifier—in this case, the Ctrl (Windows) or Command (Mac OS) key.

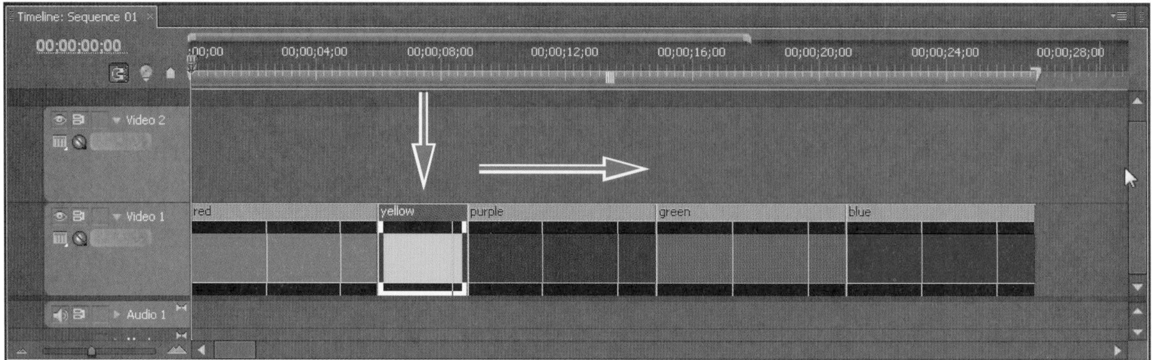

You can move a clip from a location in the Timeline in two ways:

- **Lift**: This leaves a gap where the clip used to be.

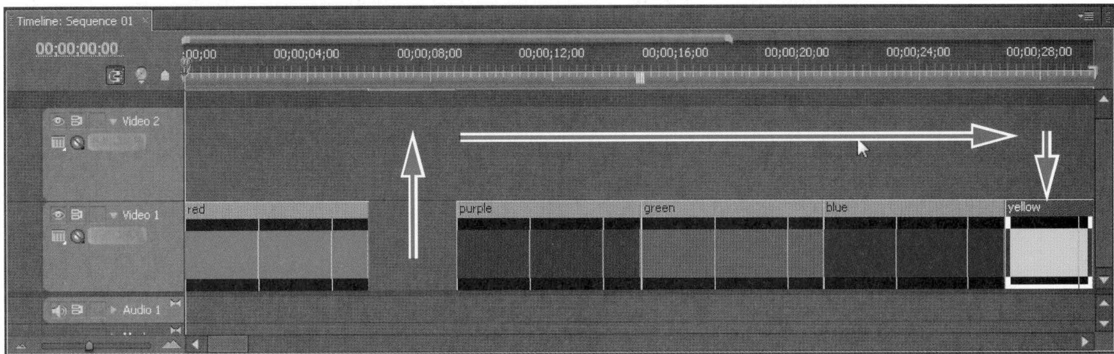

- **Extract**: This works like using the Ripple Edit tool in that other clips move over to fill the gap. This move also requires a keyboard modifier—holding down Ctrl (Windows) or Command (Mac OS) before clicking the clip to be removed.

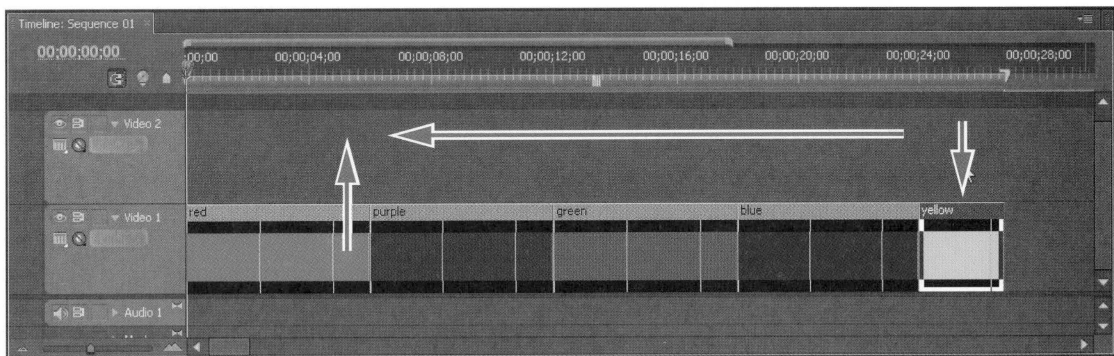

Adding and moving clips on the Timeline

Now that you've edited the first two clips, you need to edit the rest of the sequence to make it look and sound like the Complete sequence.

Let's start with an overlay edit. You may have noticed in the Complete sequence the same clip is used multiple times but different sections of the clip play. You'll make that happen here:

1 To begin, open Lesson 06-4.prproj to make sure you are starting from the same point as this portion of the lesson.

2 Drag the movie clip whats your name.avi from the Project panel to the Timeline, but don't release it yet—let it hover over the Video 2 track. Locate it at the beginning of the third clip, as shown on the next page. You will see that this clip

is longer than the last three clips in the Video 2 track. Do not release the mouse button yet, because you are not leaving the clip in track 2.

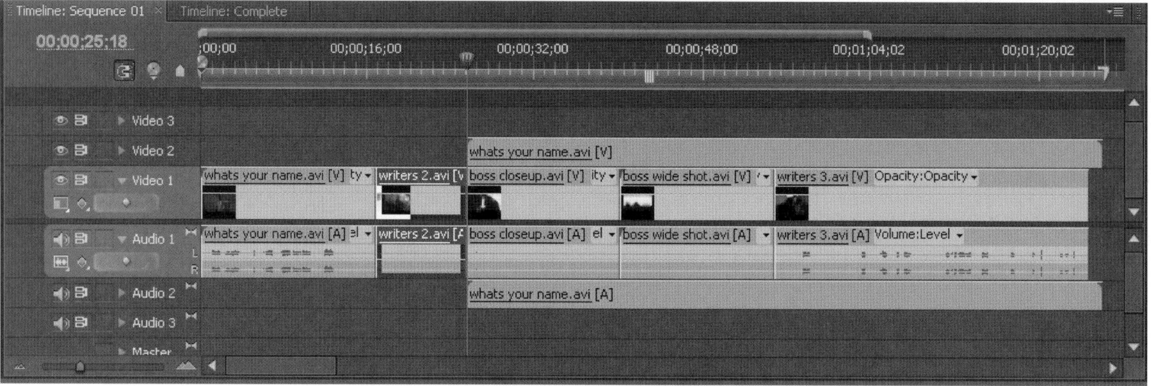

3 You need to replace the three last clips in the Video 1 track, so you are going to overlay the clip in the Video 2 track on top of them. Drag the whats your name.avi clip over the last three clips in the Video 1 track, and release.

The overlay edit you've just completed covers the video and audio that was there before. It does not change the length of the sequence.

4 Use the Ripple Edit tool to drag the left edge of the third clip to the right to timecode 00;00;18;03, just before she says "Dixie."

5 Now let's do an insert edit. To begin, mark the point where you want to insert the next clip with the current-time indicator.

6 Scrub the current-time indicator over the third clip to the point where the actors kiss. Leave the current-time indicator at that point in the clip.

When you drag a new clip to the sequence to insert, the current-time indicator will act as a guide of where to insert the new clip.

7 Drag the writers 2.avi clip to the Timeline using the current-time indicator as a guide for the left edge of the clip. Hold down the Ctrl key (Windows) or the Command key (Mac OS) to perform an insert edit rather than an overlay edit. The new clip will be inserted and existing clips will move to the right.

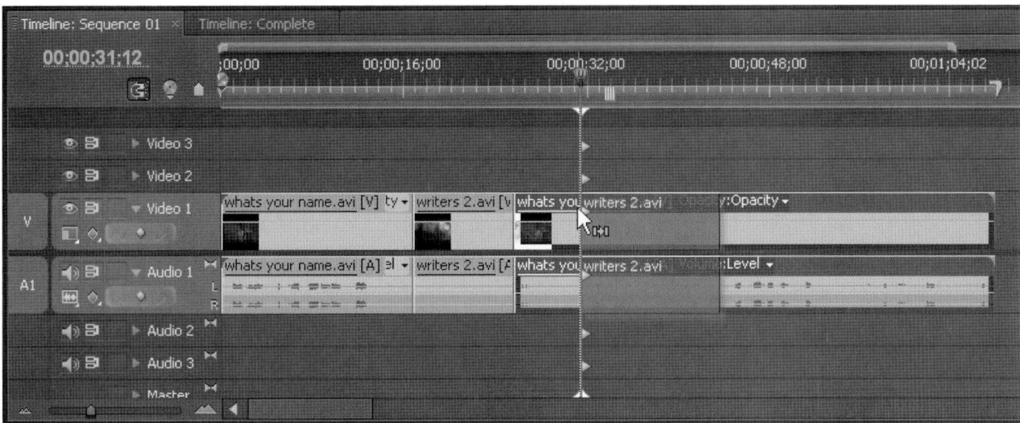

Your sequence is now longer.

8 Use the Ripple Edit tool on the fourth clip (writers.avi) so it starts at timecode 00;0018;25 and ends at 00;00;22;22 to show the writer's reaction to Dixie's name.

You don't need to do a lift or extract edit in this sequence, but you will practice it anyway.

9 Press the backslash key (\) and then the minus key (-) to give you a little room to drag things around the Timeline.

10 Drag the second clip from its current position to the end of the sequence.

Now there is a gap where the second clip used to be, and the end of the sequence extends beyond its former length.

Next let's try an extract edit, which differs from a lift edit in that it will not leave a gap.

Note: No keyboard modifier is needed as you place the clip at the end of the sequence, because nothing comes after it.

11 Press Ctrl+Z (Windows) or Command+Z (Mac OS) to return to the original position.

12 Press Ctrl (Windows) or Command (Mac OS), and then drag the second clip to the end of the sequence.

Because you held down Ctrl (Windows) or Command (Mac OS) while removing the clip from its former position, you created the equivalent of a ripple delete. The sequence length does not change.

Next let's do an extract-and-overlay edit. Clips slide over to fill the gap left by the removed clip (the keyboard modifier turned what would have been a lift into an extract). The sequence length is shorter.

13 Press Ctrl+Z (Windows) or Command+Z (Mac OS) to return to the original position.

Note: If you had not used the keyboard modifier when removing the clip from its original location, that would have left a gap there—a lift-and-overlay edit.

14 Press Ctrl (Windows) or Command (Mac OS), drag the first clip to the beginning of the third clip, release Ctrl or Command, and finally drop the clip there.

Now we'll do an extract-and-insert edit. Clips slide over to fill the gap left by the removed first clip, and the clips after the insert edit point slide to the right. The sequence length remains unchanged.

15 Press Ctrl+Z (Windows) or Command+Z (Mac OS) to return to the original position.

16 Press Ctrl (Windows) or Command (Mac OS), and drag the first clip to the beginning of the third clip. Continue holding down Ctrl or Command, and drop the clip there.

Modifier-key feedback

As you drag a clip from the Project panel to a sequence, or from one place on a sequence track to another, Adobe Premiere Pro displays a text message at the bottom of the user interface reminding you of modifier-key options.

Working with Source Monitor editing tools

In the beginning of this lesson, you assembled clips on the Timeline by creating a storyboard and then automating the storyboard to the Timeline. You also practiced dragging clips from a bin directly to the Timeline. Both of these methods (or workflows) are valid. Now you will look at one of the most common workflows for assembling clips onto the Timeline. It may seem awkward at first, but if you practice this method, you may find it to be the fastest, most efficient way to edit. It's helpful to trim clips before moving them from the Project panel to the Timeline. Do that by double-clicking a clip in the bin to open it in the Source Monitor.

1 Open Lesson 06-5.prproj to ensure you are at the same point.

You need to edit the fifth clip on the Timeline (whats your name.avi), but instead of editing it on the Timeline as you have been doing, you are going to edit it in the Source Monitor.

2 Select the fifth clip on the Timeline, and press the Delete key to remove it from the Timeline.

3 Press the End key to cause the current-time indicator to move to the right edge of the last clip.

4 To edit the whats your name.avi clip in the Source Monitor, double-click it in the Project panel.

5 Play the clip in the Source Monitor using the Play button (or the spacebar while the Source Monitor is active). Stop playback a second before Dixie says, "You gonna answer that?"

Note: You also can drag the clip from the Project panel and drop it on the Source Monitor.

6 Click the Set In Point button.

7 You need to trim extra footage off the end of this clip as well. Move the Source Monitor playhead until just after Dixie says, "You gonna answer that?"

8 Click the Set Out Point button.

9 Navigate back and forth between the In and Out points by clicking Go to In Point (or pressing Q) and Go to Out Point (or pressing W). Play that entire segment by clicking the Play In to Out button. Notice that the portion of the clip you want to keep is identified in blue under the Source Monitor.

   Clicking the Insert button on the Source Monitor will insert the portion of the clip you selected (between the In and Out points) at the current-time indicator on the main Timeline. This is why you parked the current-time indicator at the end of the last clip in step 3.

10 Check to see that the Video 1 and Audio 1 track headers (as shown here) are selected (or targeted, in Adobe Premiere Pro parlance). If not, click one or both to highlight them (their corners also become rounded).

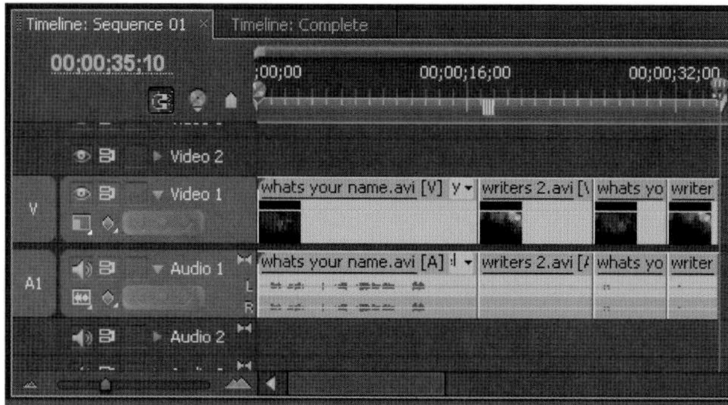

● **Note:** Clicking either Insert or Overlay will place the clip at the Timeline current-time indicator. Notice that the clip is sent to the Timeline with the beginning and ends trimmed because of the In and Out points you set in the Source Monitor for this clip. Also note that the sequence current-time indicator is automatically moved to the end of the clip on the Timeline. This is so that when you send the next clip from the Source Monitor, it will be placed right after the first clip.

You can use the Source Monitor to drag just the video or just the audio to the Timeline. Use the Audio Drag and Video Drag icons in the lower right of the Source Monitor to control this.

11 Click the Source Monitor Insert button to place this clip at the current-time indicator in Sequence 01.

You will finish this sequence using the insert edit method to insert clips.

12 Double-click the clip writers 3.avi in the Project panel to open that clip in the Source Monitor.

13 Click the Source Monitor pop-up menu to display a list of currently open clips.

All clips viewed in the Source Monitor show up in this list. You can access them here and remove them all or one at a time by choosing Close All or Close, respectively.

14 Play the writers 3.avi clip in the Source Monitor and look for edit points. Click the Complete sequence for help seeing where the edit points should be. This clip should start just before he answers the phone and ends just after he says, "Hello."

15 With the Timeline current-time indicator at the end of the last clip (it goes there automatically after either an insert edit or an overlay edit), click the Insert button on the Source Monitor to send this clip to the Timeline. The keyboard shortcut for this insertion is the comma (,) key.

16 Use the Source Monitor to create In and Out points for the rest of the clips using the Complete sequence as your model. When you're done, play Sequence 01 and make any fine adjustments by zooming into the Timeline and tweaking edit points with the Ripple Edit tool.

The more you practice this method, the more natural it will be. Practice using keyboard shortcuts for setting In and Out points and sending them to the Timeline (insert or overlay), and you will get faster and faster at editing. This is the preferred workflow for many professional editors.

Adjusting clips in the Trim panel

The Trim panel is a useful tool. Its value is its large preview monitors, precise controls, and informative timecode displays.

Rolling-edit and rippling-edit behaviors

You apply the Ripple Edit tool to only one clip. It changes the length of your project, because the rest of the project slides over to accommodate the change. A rolling edit does not change the length of your project. It takes place at an edit point between two clips, shortening one and lengthening the other.

1 Continue with the Lesson 06-5.prproj project.

2 Place the current-time indicator at the edit point between the first two clips in Sequence 01.

3 Click the Trim Monitor button (shortcut: T) in the lower-right corner of the Program Monitor.

The Trim Monitor opens.

4 Hover the pointer over the left preview screen until it turns into a left-facing Ripple Edit pointer.

5 Trim the right edge of clip (the Out point) by dragging it left to about 1 second (watch the Out Shift timecode below the center of the left preview screen).

6 Use the same method to trim the right clip's In point to the right to about 1 second (use the In Shift timecode beneath the center of the right preview screen).

7 Click the precision trimming tools—the –1 and +1 numbers—to trim or lengthen the clips one frame at a time until you have the exact edit point you want.

Trim Monitor editing tools

Click in the left or right preview screen to make it active so that the precision trimming tools apply to it. You can tell which preview screen is active by the thin blue line beneath it.

8 Click the Play Edit button in the Trim Monitor to review your work.

9 Hover the pointer between the two preview screens. It turns into the Rolling Edit tool (shown in the figure in the next section).

10 Drag the Rolling Edit tool left and right to change the Out and In points of the left and right clips, respectively. Notice how both clips move and the clips are in sync.

11 Close the Trim panel by clicking the Close button in its upper-right corner.

Using other editing tools

The Tools panel appears by default in the lower-right corner of the Adobe Premiere Pro workspace. Like with any other panel, you can dock it or make it its own floating window. Generally, editors like to keep the tools near the Timeline, because that is where they are used most often.

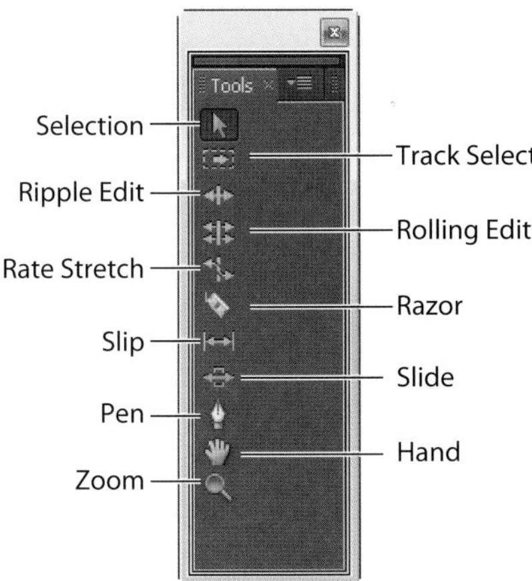

Here's a brief rundown of the Tools panel's editing tools (the keyboard shortcut letters are shown in parentheses):

- **Selection (V)**: This is a multipurpose, all-around aid. You use it frequently to drag, drop, select, and trim clips.
- **Track Select (A)**: Not to be confused with the Selection tool, the Track Select tool enables you to select all clips to the right of wherever you position it on a video or audio track. You can Shift-click to select other tracks. After you've selected them, you can slide them, delete them, cut/paste them, or copy/paste them.
- **Ripple Edit (B)**: You've worked with this many times already. A ripple edit trims a clip and shifts subsequent clips in the track by the amount you trimmed.
- **Rolling Edit (N)**: A rolling edit trims adjacent Out and In points simultaneously and by the same number of frames. This effectively moves the edit point between clips, preserving other clips' positions in time and maintaining the total duration of the sequence. You did this in the Trim panel in a previous exercise in this lesson.

- **Rate Stretch (X)**: You can stretch or shrink a clip, putting it in slow motion or speeding up the action.
- **Razor (C)**: The Razor slices a clip or clips in two. It can be useful when you want to use different effects that can't both be applied to a single clip.
- **Slip (Y)**: By dragging with the Slip tool, you can change a clip's starting and ending frames without changing its duration or affecting adjacent clips.
- **Slide (U)**: A slide edit shifts a clip along the Timeline while trimming adjacent clips to compensate for the move. As you drag a clip left or right with the Slide tool, the Out point of the preceding clip and the In point of the following clip are trimmed by the number of frames you move the clip. The clip's In and Out points (and, hence, its duration) remain unchanged. We'll cover the Slide tool, along with the Slip tool, in Lesson 9.
- **Pen (P)**: Use the Pen tool to add, select, move, delete, or adjust keyframes on a sequence as well as create and adjust curves in the Titler, Effect Controls panel, and Program Monitor. You use the keyframes to change audio volume levels and panning, alter clip opacity, and change video and audio effects over time.
- **Hand (H)**: Use the Hand tool to scroll an entire sequence by grabbing a clip and sliding it and the rest of the sequence to one side. It works the same as moving the scroll bar at the bottom of the Timeline.
- **Zoom (Z)**: This works like the Zoom In and Zoom Out buttons in the lower-left corner of the Timeline and the viewing area bar at the top of the sequence above the time ruler. The default is Zoom In (🔍). Hold down Alt (Windows) or Option (Mac OS) to change that to Zoom Out (🔍). When you want to expand the view of a set of clips in the sequence, drag the Zoom tool around those clips.

Review questions

1 How can storyboards help you create your project?

2 What is the difference between a trim and a ripple edit?

3 What effect does holding the Ctrl key (Windows) or Command key (Mac OS) have when dragging a clip to an edit point?

4 How do you move a clip from one position on a sequence to another without covering up other clips and at the same time automatically filling the gap left by the removed clip?

5 What is the keyboard shortcut to set the In and Out points of a clip in the Source Monitor?

6 What can you accomplish using the Trim panel's Rolling Edit tool?

Review answers

1 Storyboards can give you an overall feel for the flow of your project, reveal gaps, help you weed out weaker shots, and avoid redundancy.

2 Trims leave gaps where the trimmed video used to be (or, if you lengthen a clip using the Trim tool, they cover that portion of the next clip). Ripple edits automatically fill gaps by sliding the clips following the edit to the left (filling the space left by the edit) or to the right (to compensate for a lengthened clip).

3 It changes the edit from an overlay to an insert edit.

4 Hold down Ctrl (Windows) or Command (Mac OS) as you extract the clip, and hold down Ctrl (Windows) or Command (Mac OS) again as you place the clip in its new position.

5 I is the shortcut for an In point, and O is the shortcut for an Out point.

6 Once you find a matching edit between two clips, you can fine-tune that edit using the Rolling Edit tool. It'll help you find just the right place to make a seamless edit.

7 ADDING VIDEO TRANSITIONS

Topics covered in this lesson

- Using transitions with restraint
- Trying some transitions
- Changing parameters in the Effect Controls panel
- Fine-tuning transitions
- Applying transitions to multiple clips at once
- Using audio transitions

This lesson will take approximately 60 minutes.

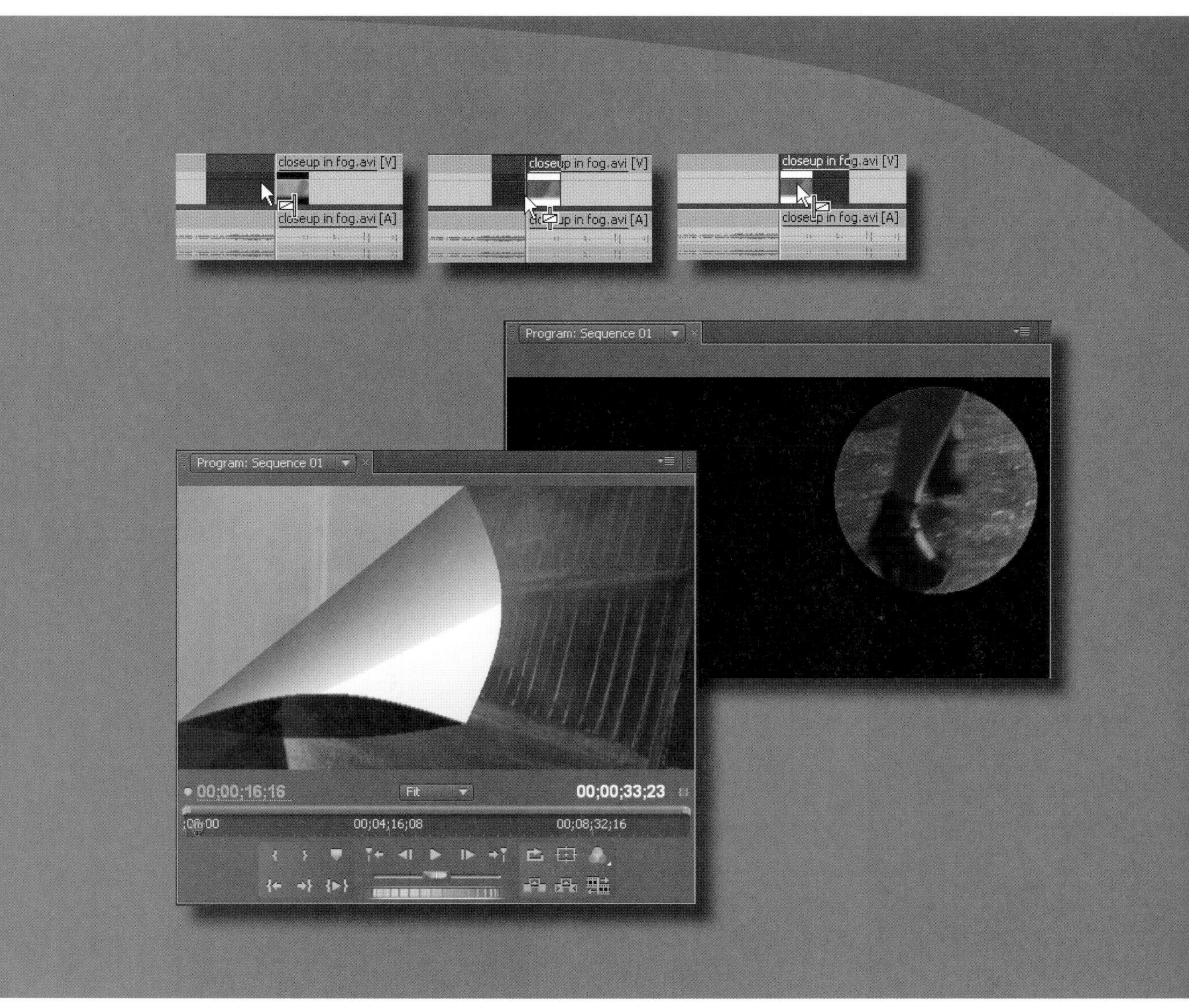

Transitions can make a video move more smoothly or snap the audience to attention. Adobe Premiere Pro CS4 has nearly 80 transitions that are easy to use and customize. Fun stuff—but try to use restraint.

Getting started

Bridging your clips with transitions—dissolves, page wipes, spinning screens, and many more—is a nice way to ease viewers from one scene to the next or to grab their attention.

Adding transitions to your project is an art, though. Applying them starts simply enough; it's a mere drag-and-drop process. The art comes in their placement, length, and parameters, such as colored borders, motion, and start/end locations.

Most transition work takes place in the Effect Controls panel. In addition to the various options unique to each transition, that panel displays something called an *A/B timeline*. This feature makes it easy to move transitions relative to the edit point, change the transition duration, and apply transitions to clips that don't have sufficient head or tail frames. With Adobe Premiere Pro, you can also apply a transition to a group of clips.

Using transitions with restraint

Once you discover the cornucopia of transition possibilities that Adobe Premiere Pro offers, you will be tempted to use them for every edit. They can be great fun. That said, it is highly recommended that you exercise restraint.

Watch some TV news stories. Most use cuts-only edits. It's unlikely you'll see any transitions. Why? Time is a factor, but more and more stations these days have ready access to nonlinear editors (NLEs) such as Adobe Premiere Pro, and it takes almost no time to add a transition when using an NLE.

The principal reason for the dearth of transitions is that they can be distracting. If a TV news editor uses one, it's for a purpose. Their most frequent use in newsroom editing bays is to take what would have been a jarring edit—such as a major jump cut—and make it more palatable. An oft-heard newsroom phrase applies: "If you can't solve it, dissolve it."

That's not to say transitions don't have their place in carefully planned stories. Consider the Star Wars movies with all their highly stylized transitions, such as obvious, slow wipes. Each of those transitions has a purpose. George Lucas purposely created a look reminiscent of old serialized movies and TV shows. Specifically, they send a clear message to the audience: "Pay attention. We're transitioning across space and time."

Adding whimsy

Transitions can lighten up a story. Here are a few examples:

- Start on a tight shot of someone's hands cutting a deck of cards, and make a Swap transition—one image slides to one side and another slides over it—to another card-related shot.
- Start with a tight shot of a clock (analog, not digital) and use the aptly named Clock Wipe—a line centered on the screen sweeps around to reveal another image—to move to another setting and time.
- Get that James Bond, through-the-bloody-eye effect with the Iris Round transition.
- Take a medium shot of a garage door and use a Push—one image moves off the top while another replaces it from below—to transition to the next shot of the garage interior.
- With some planning and experimentation, you can videotape someone pushing against a wall while walking in place and use that same Push transition (after applying a horizontal direction to it) to have that person "slide" the old scene offscreen.

Adding visual interest

Transitions can give your video some pizzazz:

- Take a shot of a car driving through the frame and use a Wipe, synchronized with the speed of the car, to move to the next scene.
- Transition from a shot of driving rain or a waterfall by using the Slash Slide transition, in which streaks, such as driving rain, slice through an image, revealing another image behind it.
- Use the Venetian Blinds transition to move from an interior to an exterior.
- A Page Peel transition works well with a piece of parchment.

During this lesson, feel free to experiment with all that Adobe Premiere Pro has to offer.

Trying some transitions

Adobe Premiere Pro contains nearly 80 video transitions (plus three audio transitions, covered in Lesson 13). Some are subtle, and some are "in your face." The more you experiment with them, the more likely you are to use them well.

Applying a transition between two clips starts with a simple drag-and-drop process. That might be enough for many transitions, but Adobe Premiere Pro gives you a wide variety of options for fine-tuning transitions. Some transitions have a Custom button that opens a separate dialog box with sets of options unique to each. And most offer tools that allow you to position the transition precisely.

First, you'll be introduced to some of the transitions in Adobe Premiere Pro. Then you'll see some others that offer extra options.

1 Start Adobe Premiere Pro and open Lesson 07-1.prproj.

2 Choose Window > Workspace > Effects.

   This changes the workspace to the preset that the Adobe Premiere Pro development team created to make it easier to work with transitions and effects.

Note: You'll see little triangles in the upper-right and -left corners of the clips (shown here). They indicate the clips are at their original, full length. For transitions to work smoothly, you need handles—some unused head and tail frames to overlap between the clips. Trimming both clips will give you those handles.

3 Drag the three .avi video clips from the Project panel to the Video 1 track, and press the backslash key (\) to expand the view.

4 Select the Ripple Edit tool (or press B on your keyboard) and drag the end of the first clip to the left to shorten it by about 4 seconds (note the time in the pop-up menu).

5 Use the Ripple Edit tool to drag the beginning of the second clip to the right about 4 seconds into the clip.

Note: Since you used the Ripple Edit tool, these two trims should have no gap. If there is a gap, right-click (Windows) or Ctrl-click (Mac OS), and choose Ripple Delete.

6 Press the backslash key (\) to expand the Timeline.

7 Create handles at the end of the second clip and beginning of the third clip in the same way. Use the Ripple Edit tool to drag the end of the second clip 4 seconds to the left, and drag the beginning of the third clip 4 seconds to the right.

8 The Effects panel should be docked with the Project panel. Select the Effects panel by clicking it, and then open the Video Transitions > Dissolve bin.

Note: Cross Dissolve has a red box around it, indicating it's the default transition.

9 Drag Cross Dissolve to the edit between the first two clips on the sequence, but don't release the mouse button just yet.

10 While still holding down the mouse button, move the pointer to the left and right, and note how the pointer and the highlighted rectangle on the clips change (shown here). You can place the transition such that it ends at the edit point, is centered on the edit point, or starts there.

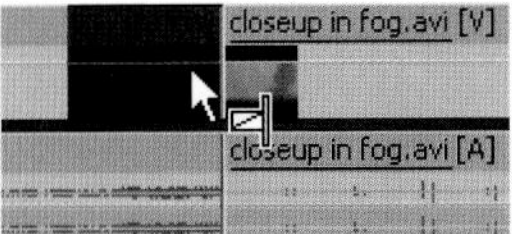

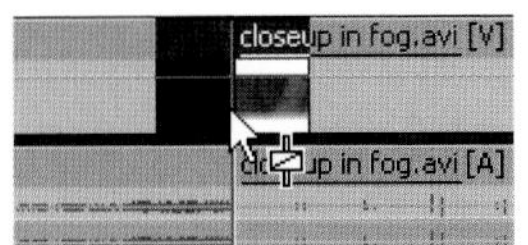

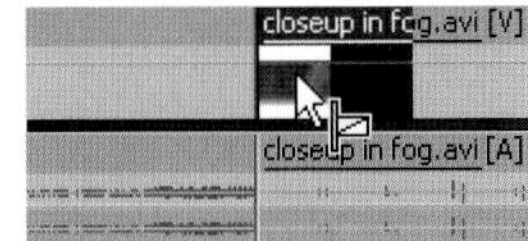

11 Place the transition at the middle of the edit point and drop the transition there.

12 Put the current-time indicator ahead of the transition and press the spacebar to play it.

The transition has a 1-second duration by default.

Changing the default transition and duration

The default transition has two primary uses: it's used when automating a storyboard to a sequence or as a quick means to add a transition by using the keyboard shortcut, which is Ctrl+D (Windows) or Command+D (Mac OS). To set a different default transition, select the transition you want to use, open the Effects panel menu, and choose Set Selected As Default Transition. A red box will appear around that transition. You can change the default duration by choosing Default Transition Duration, which opens the Preferences dialog box.

13 Open the 3D Motion bin under the video transitions and drag Flip Over to the beginning of the first clip. Note that the only placement option is to have the transition start at the edit point.

One very cool characteristic of transitions in Adobe Premiere Pro is that you can use them at the beginning or end of a clip. This is called a *single-sided transition* (*double-sided transitions* go between clips).

14 Press Home to move the current-time indicator to the beginning of the Timeline and play the transition. This is an interesting way to start a video.

Transitions on any track

Adobe Premiere Pro lets you place transitions between two clips (or at the beginnings or ends of clips) on any track in a sequence. A cool use of single-sided transitions is to put them in clips on higher tracks so they gradually reveal or cover up what's below them in the Timeline. You're using only a single track in these lessons to simplify things and because transition behavior on the Video 1 track is the same as on any other track.

15 Drag the Flip Over transition to the end of the third clip.

16 If it's not already open, click the Effect Controls tab to open the Effect Controls panel.

17 Click the Flip Over transition rectangle at the end of the clip in the Timeline to switch on the display of its parameters in the Effect Controls panel.

18 Select the Reverse option (shown here) to have the Flip Over transition flip in the opposite direction at the end of the clip.

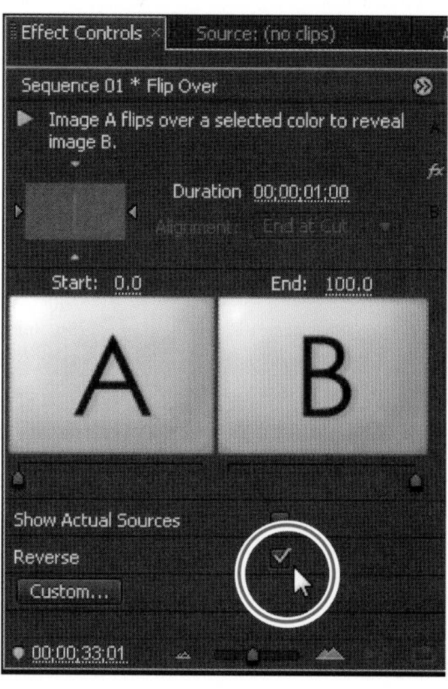

● **Note:** The next step calls for the use of a graphics processor unit (GPU). If your computer does not have a GPU with enough horsepower to handle the GPU effects in Adobe Premiere Pro, the effects will not show up in the Effects panel. In that case, skip the next step. Note that GPU transitions are not currently available for the Mac OS version of Adobe Premiere Pro.

19 Open the Page Peel bin, and drag the Page Peel transition over the Cross Dissolve transition between the first and second clips. That replaces Cross Dissolve with Page Peel. Play that transition.

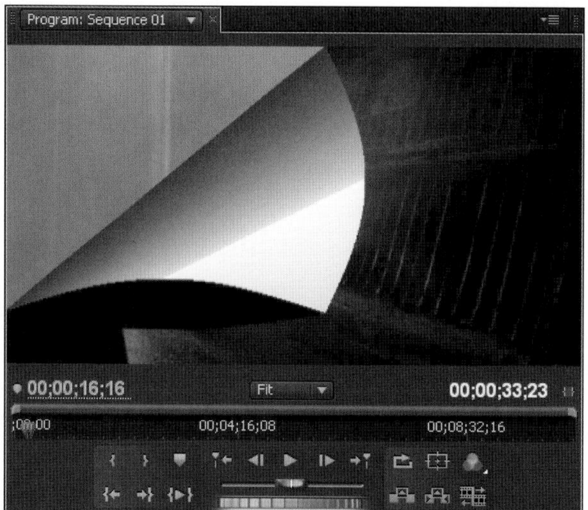

20 If you are running the Windows version of Adobe Premiere Pro CS4, open the GPU Transitions bin and drag the Center Peel transition on top of the Page Peel transition already on the Timeline. Play that transition.

21 Test some other transitions. It's a good idea to try at least one from every bin.

Note: You'll also see a Center Peel transition in the Page Peel folder in the Windows version. They behave very differently.

Sequence display changes

Note: You can choose from dozens of transitions. If you know the name of a transition, you can type the beginning of that name in the search field in the Effects panel to find a single transition quickly.

When you add a transition to a sequence, a short red horizontal line appears above that transition (shown here). The red line means that this portion of the sequence must be rendered before you can record it back to tape or create a file of your finished project.

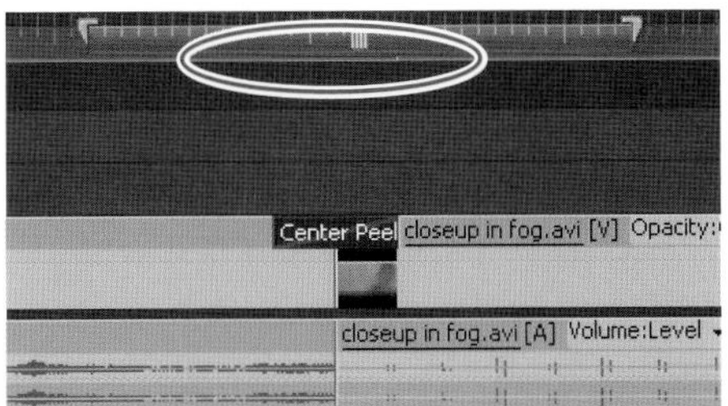

Rendering happens automatically when you export your project, but you can choose to render selected portions of your sequence to make those sections display more smoothly on slower computers. To do that, slide the handles of the Viewing Area bar (shown here) to the ends of the red rendering line (they will snap to those points), and press Enter (Windows) or Return (Mac OS). Adobe Premiere Pro will create a video clip of that segment (tucked away in the Preview Files folder with an indecipherable filename) and will change the line from red to green.

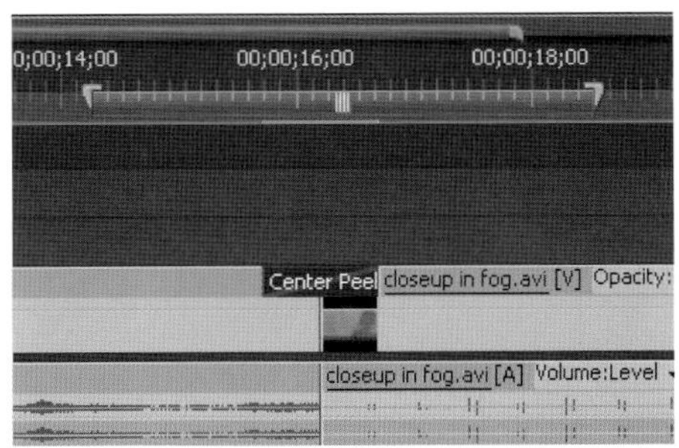

Note: The Viewing Area bar may cover all clips on the Timeline by default. Pressing Enter (Windows) or Return (Mac OS) will render any areas that require rendering that are between the In and Out points of the Viewing area bar. By adjusting the length of the Viewing Area bar, you can control what areas of the project are rendered.

Changing parameters in the Effect Controls panel

Up to this point you've seen the default action of each transition you've tested. That just scratches the surface of their possibilities. Tucked away in the Effect Controls panel is a passel of parameters, unique to each transition.

You'll start with the Cross Dissolve transition and then move on to most of the transitions that you used earlier in this lesson. Here's how you adjust transition characteristics:

1 Continue where you left off or open Lesson 07-2.prproj.

2 Drag the Cross Dissolve transition from the Effects > Video Transitions > Dissolve bin to the beginning of the first clip.

3 Click the transition rectangle in the upper-left corner of the clip in the sequence to display its parameters in the Effect Controls panel.

4 Select the Show Actual Sources option (shown here), and drag the sliders beneath the Start and End preview screens.

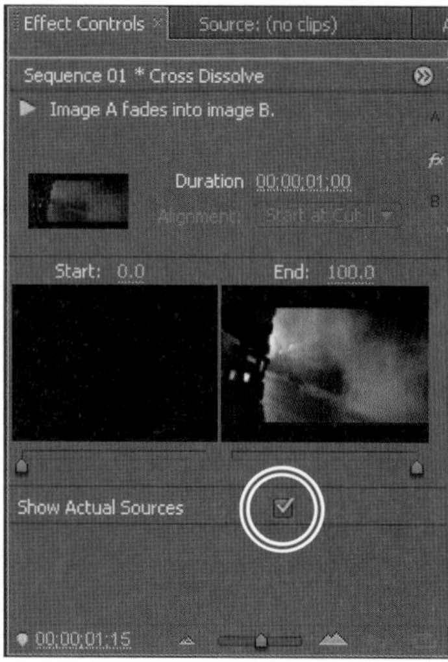

You can use those sliders to have the transition start partially faded up and end less than completely faded up.

5 Change the duration in the Effect Controls panel to 2 seconds and play the transition in the Timeline.

6 Play the transition at different lengths to see the effect.

Note: Another way to change the duration of the transition is to drag the edge of the transition on the Timeline. With the Video track expanded, drag the right edge of the transition left and right with the standard Selection tool to adjust its length.

7 Drag the Push transition from the Slide Transitions bin to the edit between the first and second clips. Play it in the Timeline and notice the direction it pushes.

8 Change the direction to go from the top to bottom by selecting the transition by clicking it and then clicking the north-to-south triangle in the Effect Controls panel (shown here).

9 Apply the Wipe transition (Wipe bin) between the second and third clips.

Three new options appear: Border Width, Border Color, and Anti-aliasing Quality.

10 Change Border Width to 20.

11 Click the upper-left direction triangle to change the direction to northwest to southeast.

12 Select the Eyedropper tool, located next to the Border Color swatch, and click the mist in the sky to choose a light gray.

13 Set Anti-aliasing Quality to High. Play that transition. Anti-aliasing adjusts the smoothness of the edges of the transition.

14 Select the Iris Round transition in the Iris bin and apply it at the end of the last clip. Notice that when you drop a new transition on top of an old transition, it replaces the old transition.

This transition has a new option: a small positioning circle.

15 Select the Reverse option to make the iris closed rather than open.

16 On the End Preview screen, move the End slider to the left so you can see how the transition will look as it finishes.

Note: You can also watch the end position in the Program Monitor. You need to drag the Timeline current-time indicator through the transition to view it.

17 On the Start screen, move the positioning circle to make the transition finish on the woman's feet (watch the position of the transition change on the End screen).

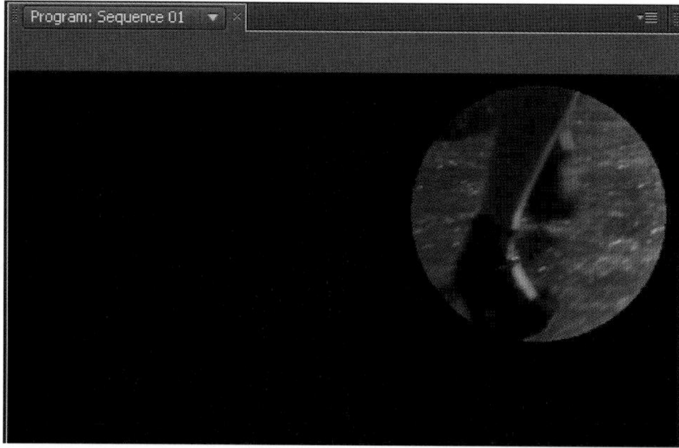

18 When you settle on a location, return the End slider all the way back to the right. Play the transition.

Using A/B mode to fine-tune a transition

Because the developers of Adobe Premiere Pro initially created it from the ground up, they had the opportunity to make some fundamental decisions. One was to no longer include A/B editing in the Timeline.

A/B editing is old-school, linear, film-style editing. Film editors frequently use two reels of film—an A-roll and a B-roll—which are usually duplicates made from the same original. The two-reel approach permits cross-dissolves from the A track to the B track.

The advantage of A/B editing in older versions of Premiere was that it let you modify transition positioning and start and end points more easily than you could using single-track NLEs.

Here's the good news for both the A/B and single-track editing camps: Adobe Premiere Pro includes all that functionality in its Effect Controls panel.

Working with the Effect Controls panel's A/B feature

The Effect Controls panel's A/B editing mode splits a single video track into two subtracks. What would normally be two consecutive and contiguous clips on a single track are now displayed as individual clips on separate subtracks, giving you the option to apply a transition between them, to manipulate their head and tail frames (or handles), and to change other transition elements.

1 Continue where you left off in the previous exercise or open Lesson 07-3.prproj.

2 Click the Push transition that is applied between the first and second clips to display its parameters in the Effect Controls panel.

3 Open the A/B timeline in the Effect Controls panel by clicking the Show/Hide Timeline View button (⊙) in the upper-right corner.

Note: You might need to expand the width of the Effect Controls panel to make the Show/Hide Timeline View button available. Also, the Effect Controls Timeline may already be visible. Clicking the Show/Hide Timeline View button in the Effect Controls panel toggles it on and off.

4 Drag the border (as shown below) between the A/B timeline and the transition parameters section to expand the view of the timeline.

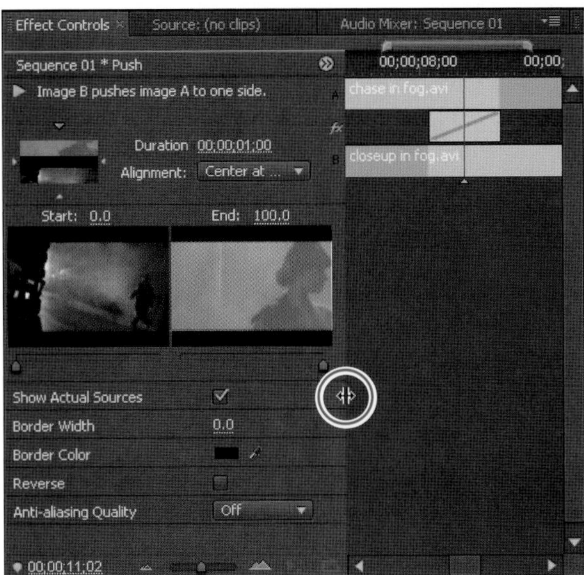

5 Hover the pointer over the edit line at the center of the transition rectangle (as shown on the left).

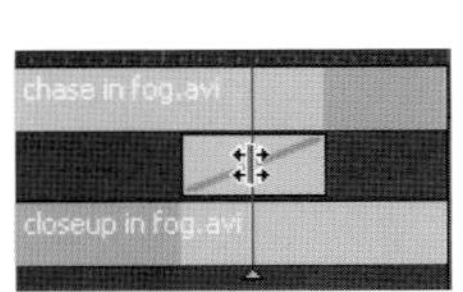

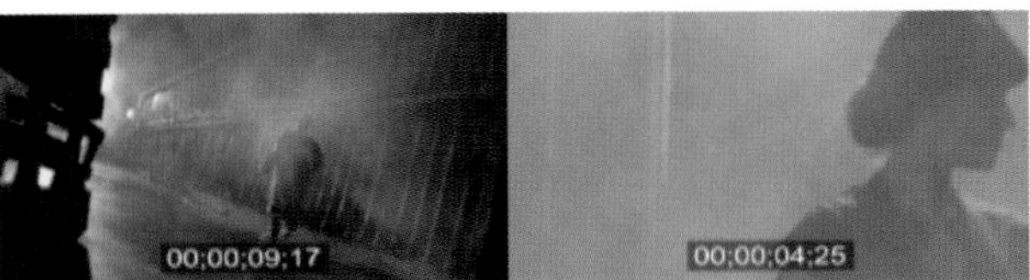

That's the edit point between the two clips, and the pointer that appears there is the Rolling Edit tool (⇼)—the same Rolling Edit tool you encountered in the Trim panel in Lesson 6.

6 Drag the Rolling Edit tool left and right, and note how the changing Out point of the left clip and the changing In point of the right clip show up in the Program Monitor.

Note: As was the case when you used the Rolling Edit tool in the Trim panel, moving it left or right does not change the overall length of the sequence.

7 Move the pointer slightly to the left or right of the edit line, and notice that it changes to the Slide tool (⇔).

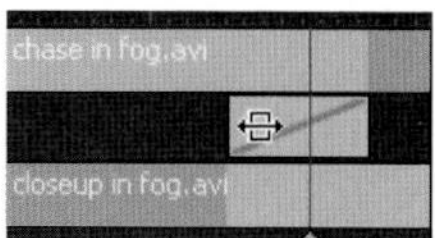

Note: Using the Slide tool changes the start and end points of the transition without changing its overall length (the default duration is 1 second). The new start and end points show up in the Program Monitor, but unlike using the Rolling Edit tool, moving the transition rectangle by using the Slide tool does not change the edit point between the two clips.

8 Use the Slide tool to drag the transition rectangle left and right.

9 Click the Alignment menu and click through the three available options: Center At Cut, Start At Cut, and End At Cut.

The transition rectangle moves to a new location as you make each change. These three locations mimic the options when you drag a transition to the Timeline. Also, if you manually change the transition location, the Custom Start alignment option becomes available.

10 Drag an end (it doesn't matter which end) of the viewing area bar to the edge of the A/B timeline.

This expands your view of the two adjacent clips so you can see the beginning of the left clip and the end of the right clip.

11 Drag the right and left edges of the transition to lengthen it.

Two other ways to change transition duration

You can also change the duration value by typing a new time or by clicking the duration time and dragging left or right to decrease or increase its value.

Note that as you lengthen the transition, the viewing area bar shrinks, thereby allowing you to drag its ends yet again to expand the area viewed in the A/B timeline.

Dealing with inadequate (or no) head or tail handles

Eventually you will want to place transitions at edit points where you don't have adequate head or tail handles (footage beyond the In or Out point of your clip). This might be because you paused the camcorder too soon or didn't get it started fast enough. You might want to add a transition to ease what would be an abrupt cut edit. Adobe Premiere Pro deals elegantly with that:

1 Open Lesson 07-4.prproj. Notice that the two clips on the Timeline have no "heads or tails." You can tell this because of the little triangles in the corners of the clips; the triangles indicate the very ends of the clips.

2 Using the standard Selection tool, drag the right edge of the last clip to the left, and release. Notice that the little triangle at the end of that clip is no longer visible. Stretch the clip back to its full length.

3 Drag the Cross Dissolve transition to that edit point between the two clips.

   The "Insufficient Media" alert appears. Click OK.

4 Click the transition to display it in the Effect Controls panel, and note that the transition rectangle has parallel diagonal lines running through it, indicating the lack of head or tail frames.

5 Lengthen the transition to about 3 seconds by dragging the right and left edges of the transition rectangle. You may need to zoom in the Timeline by pressing the equal sign (=) to be able to grab the edge of the transition.

6 Drag the current-time indicator slowly through the entire transition and watch how it works:

   - For the first half of the transition (up to the edit point), the B clip is a freeze frame while the A clip continues to play.
   - At the edit point, the A clip becomes a freeze frame and the B clip starts to play.
   - When played at regular speed (at the default 1-second duration), few viewers would notice the freeze frames.

Note: In this lesson's example, both the A and B clips have no head or tail handle frames. Frequently only one clip has no head or tail room. In those cases, Adobe Premiere Pro forces the placement of the transition to start or end at the edit point, depending on which clip lacks extra frames for the overlap.

Applying transitions to multiple clips at once

So far you have been applying transitions to video clips. However, you can also apply transitions to still images, graphics, color mattes, and even audio, as you will see in the next section of this lesson.

A common project that editors encounter is the photo montage. Often these montages look nice with transitions between photos. Applying transitions one at a time for 100 images would not be fun. Adobe Premiere Pro makes it easy to automate this process by allowing the default transition (that you define) to be added to any group of contiguous or noncontiguous clips:

1 Open Lesson 07-5.prproj. Notice there are 40 JPEG images of sunsets already imported into the Project panel.

2 Select all 40 JPEG images in the Project panel and drag them to Sequence 01.

3 Play the Timeline by pressing the spacebar. You will notice the JPEG clips are all 5 seconds long.

4 Press the backslash key (\) to zoom out the Timeline to make the whole sequence visible.

5 With the Selection tool, draw a marquee around all the clips to select them.

6 Click the Sequence menu and choose Apply Default Transition To Selection. This will apply the default transition between any clips currently selected.

7 Play the Timeline and notice the difference a Cross Dissolve transition makes between images in a photo montage.

Note: The selection of clips does not have to be contiguous. You can Shift-click clips to select only a portion of the clips on the Timeline.

More than one way to batch transitions

The method described in this exercise is the most flexible way to add the default transition to multiple clips. However, Adobe Premiere Pro provides another method via the storyboard feature: Automate To Timeline. You explored this feature in Lesson 6 but did not apply the transitions. Feel free to repeat that exercise, and this time apply the default transition to all clips when you automate to the Timeline.

Adding audio transitions

Transitions are not just for video. Adding a crossfade transition to the end of an audio clip is a really fast way to add a fade-in or fade-out to an audio clip:

1 Open Lesson 07-6.prproj, play the Timeline, and notice the abrupt start and end volume of the soundtrack.

2 In the Audio Transitions bin in the Effects panel, click the Crossfade bin.

3 Drag the Constant Power transition to the beginning of the audio clip in the Audio 1 track. Play the Timeline and notice the transition has created a fade-in to the car sounds.

4 Position the current-time indicator on the Timeline at the edit point between the two clips, and press Shift+Ctrl+D (Windows) or Shift+Command+D (Mac OS).

   This is the keyboard shortcut to add the default audio transition to the edit point near the current-time indicator—a very fast way to add a fade-in or fade-out to an audio track. Placed between audio clips, the Constant Power transition will blend the two very different audio clips together to make the audio transition less harsh.

5 Drag the length of the audio transition to be longer or shorter, and listen to the effect when you play the Timeline.

6 To polish the project, add a Cross Dissolve transition to the beginning and end of the sequence by moving the current-time indicator near the beginning and pressing Ctrl+D (Windows) or Command+D (Mac OS) to add the default video transition. Repeat this for the end of the clip. This will create a fade from black at the beginning and a fade to black at the end.

Transitions are fun and interesting to add to your project. However, overusing them is the giveaway of an amateur video. When choosing a transition, make sure it adds meaning to your project rather than showing off how many editing tricks you know. Watch your favorite movies and TV shows to learn how the pros use transitions.

Review questions

1. Describe two ways to apply the default transition to multiple clips.
2. How do you track down a transition by name?
3. How do you replace a transition with another one?
4. Some transitions start as small squares, circles, or other geometric shapes and then grow to reveal the next clip. How do you get those transitions to start with large geometric shapes that shrink to reveal the next clip?
5. Explain three ways to change the duration of a transition.
6. What is an easy way to fade audio at the beginning or end of a clip?

Review answers

1. Use the Automate To Sequence feature, or select clips already on the Timeline and choose Sequence > Apply Default Transition To Selection.
2. Start typing the transition name in the Contains text box in the Effects panel. As you type, Adobe Premiere Pro displays all effects and transitions (audio and video) that have that letter combination anywhere in their names. Type more letters to narrow down your search.
3. Drag the replacement transition on top of the transition you're rejecting. The new one automatically replaces the old one.
4. Select the Reverse option in the Effect Controls panel. That switches the movement from starting small and ending full-screen to starting full-screen and ending small.
5. Drag the edge of the transition rectangle in the Timeline, do the same thing in the Effect Controls panel's A/B timeline, or change the Duration value in the Effect Controls panel.
6. An easy way to fade audio in or out is to apply an audio crossfade transition to the beginning or end of a clip.

8 CREATING DYNAMIC TITLES

Topics covered in this lesson

- Strengthening your project with titles
- Changing text parameters
- Building text from scratch
- Putting text on a path
- Creating shapes
- Making text roll and crawl
- Applying text effects such as sheens, strokes, shadows, and fills
- Copying titles to other Adobe applications

This lesson will take approximately 90 minutes.

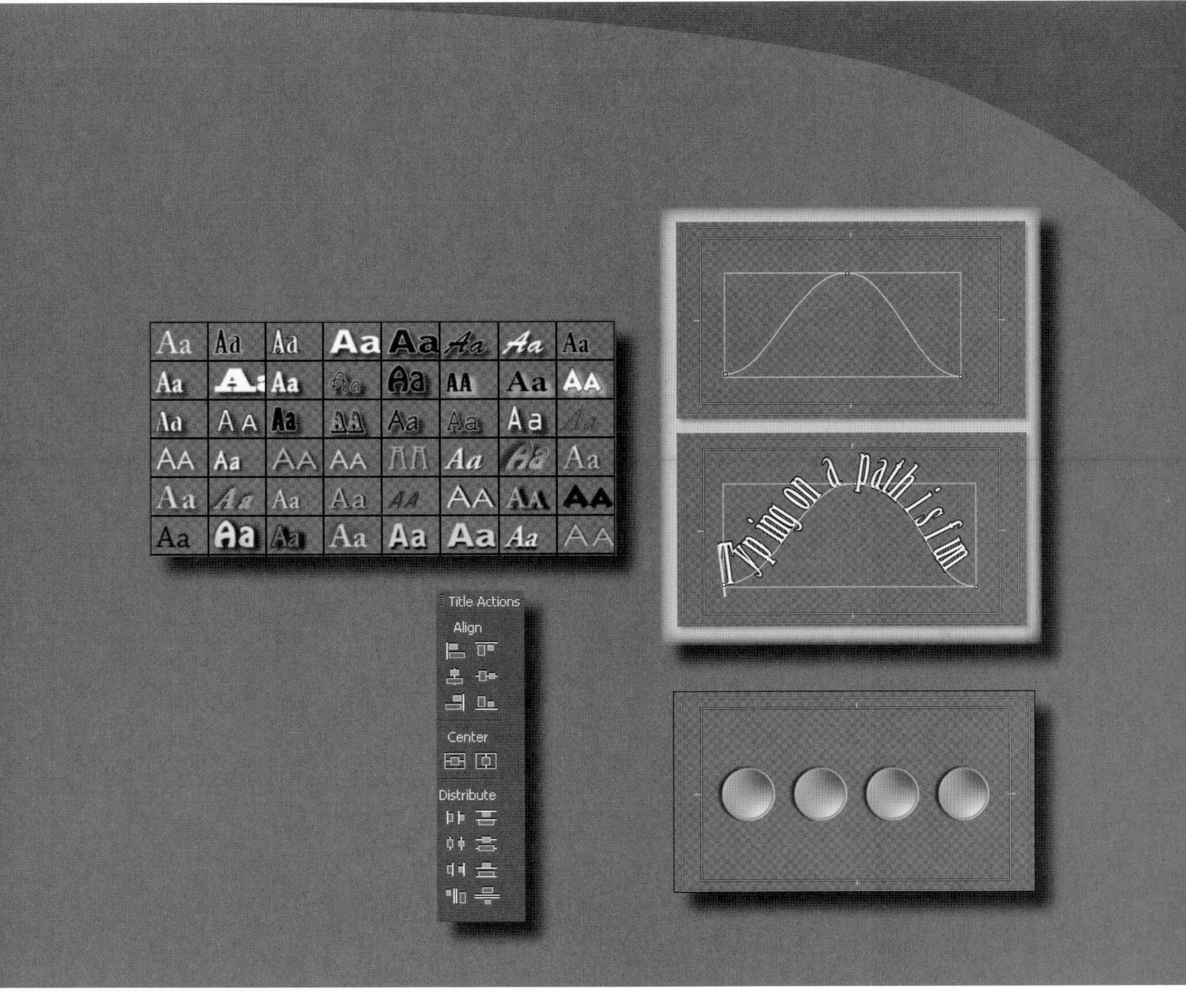

The Adobe Premiere Pro CS4 Titler is a multifaceted, feature-rich text- and shape-creation tool. Your Titler-designed text and objects can run superimposed over video as static titles, as rolling credits, or as stand-alone clips.

Getting started

Onscreen text helps tell your story. You can reinforce your message by using superimposed text (aka *supers*) to give a location or an interviewee's name and title, to show onscreen bulleted points, and to display opening titles and closing credits.

Text can present information much more succinctly and clearly than narration. It can also reinforce narrated and visual information by reminding viewers about the people in your piece and the message you're trying to convey.

The Adobe Premiere Pro CS4 Titler offers you a full range of text- and shape-creation options. You can use any font on your computer. Your text and objects can be any color (or multiple colors), any degree of transparency, and a variety of shapes. Using the Path tool, you can place your text on the most convoluted curved line you can imagine. The Titler is an engaging and powerful tool.

Its infinite customizability makes it possible for you to create a look unique to your productions.

Strengthening your project with titles

Consider this opening sequence: a telephoto shot of scorched desert sand with rippling heat distorting the scene. Dry, desiccated, lifeless sagebrush. A lizard slowly seeking shade beneath a small stone. And a small plume of dust in the distance. That's attention-getting stuff.

Now a narrator intones, "The summer heat beats down on the Bonneville Salt Flats." That's effective, but even better is a title: "Bonneville Salt Flats." Then, as the plume of dust moves toward the camera, another super displays this text: "Speed Trials—Summer 2005." Then a rocket-shaped vehicle screams through the scene.

Rather than interrupt the building suspense with a sonorous narrator, save him for later. Instead, use titles to set up your story.

Here are other instances in which text can be an effective alternative to voice-overs:

- Instead of using a voice-over to say, "Sue Smith, vice president of manufacturing for Acme Industries," put that information in a super at the bottom of the screen. This type of title is also known as a *lower third*, because it's positioned in the lower third of the screen.
- Instead of narrating a collection of statistics, use bulleted points that pop up onscreen with each new item.

Text strengthens your project.

Changing text parameters

In this lesson, you'll start with some formatted text and then change its parameters. This approach is a good way to get a quick overview of the powerful features of the Adobe Premiere Pro CS4 Titler. Later in this lesson you'll build basic text from scratch.

1 Start Adobe Premiere Pro CS4 and open Lesson 08-1.prproj.

2 Double-click Title Start in the Project panel.

The Titler opens with a title already loaded over a video frame. Here's a quick rundown on the Titler's panels:

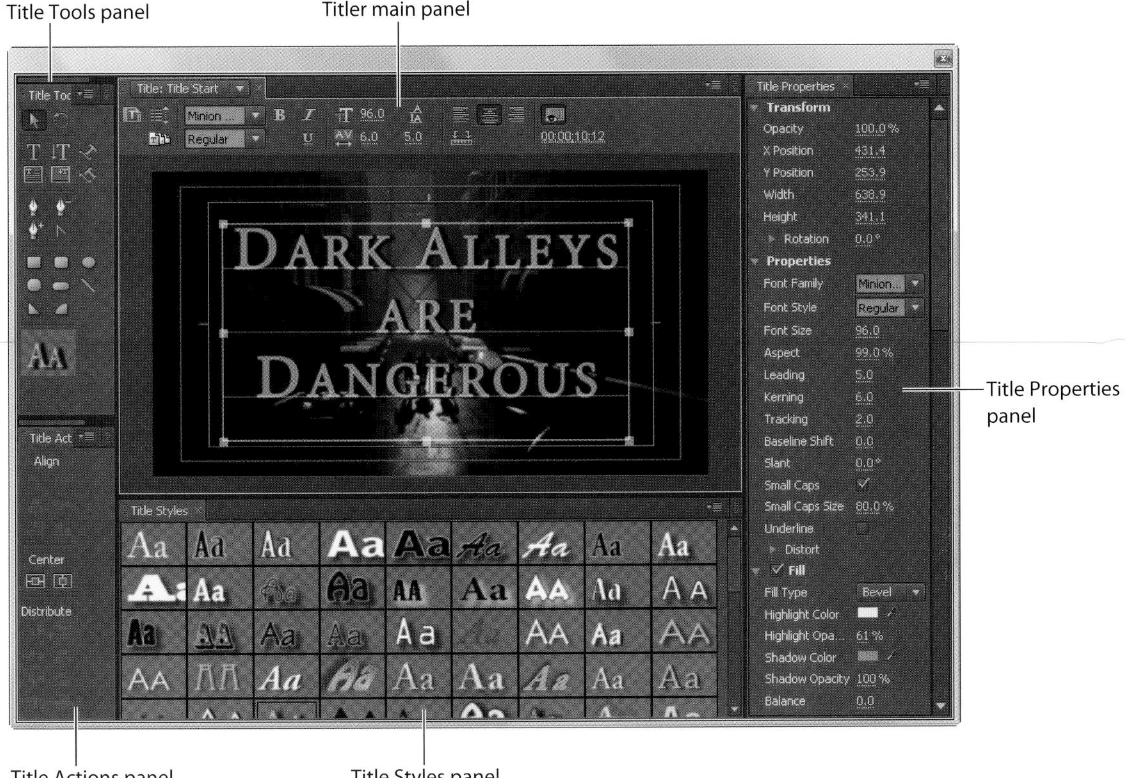

- **Title Tools panel**: These tools define text boundaries, set text paths, and select geometric shapes.
- **Titler main panel**: This is where you build and view text and graphics.
- **Title Properties panel**: Here you'll find text and graphic options such as font characteristics and effects.
- **Title Actions panel**: You'll use these to align, center, or distribute text and groups of objects.

- **Title Styles panel**: Here you'll find preset text styles. You can choose from several libraries of styles.

3 Click several different thumbnails in the Title Styles panel to acquaint yourself with the styles available.

Each time you click a new style, Adobe Premiere Pro instantly changes the active or selected text to that style. When you're finished checking out some of the styles, choose the style EccentricStd Gold 45 (shown here). This style more closely matches the mood of the scene in the video.

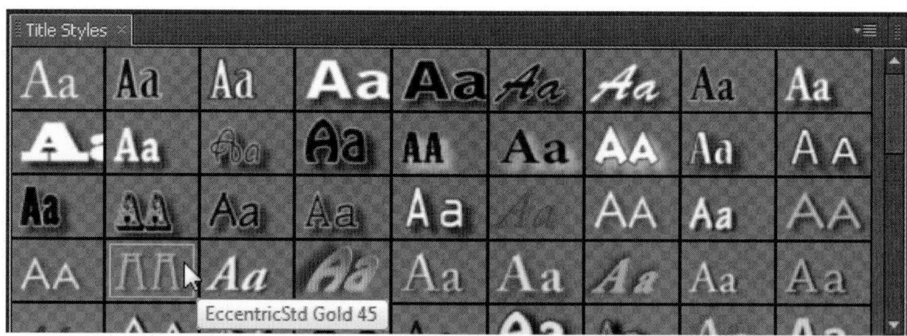

4 Click the Font Browser menu in the Titler. Note that the current font is EccentricStd.

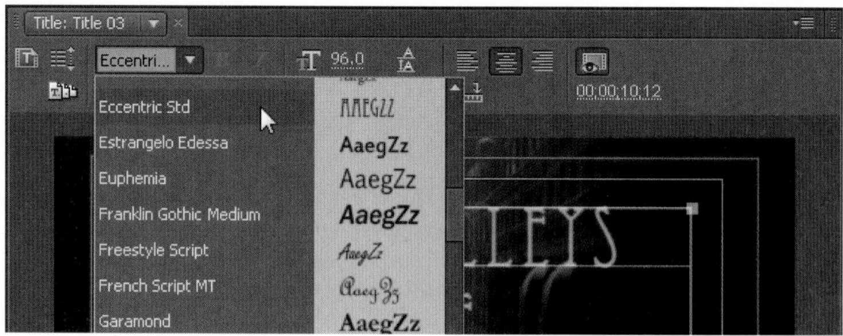

5 Scroll through the fonts and note that as you select a new font, you see immediately how it will work with your text.

Note: With all the clicking and testing, you might have deselected the text. If there is no bounding box with handles around the text, select the text by clicking the Selection tool (in the upper-left corner of the Titler) and clicking anywhere in the text.

6 Click the Font Family menu in the Title Properties panel on the right of the Titler. This is another way to change fonts in the Titler. Experiment with changing the font through this panel.

7 After you're done experimenting, change back to the EccentricStd Gold 45 style.

The changes show up immediately in the Titler panel.

8 Change the font size to 110 by typing the new value or by dragging the Size number until it reaches 110.

9 Deselect Small Caps if it is selected.

10 Change Leading to 5. Leading changes the vertical distance between lines of text.

11 Change Kerning to 5. Kerning changes the amount of space between characters horizontally.

12 Change Slant to 13.

13 Change Shadow Distance to 10, Shadow Size to 25, and Shadow Spread to 25.

14 Click the Horizontal Center and Vertical Center buttons in the Title Actions panel.

Note: Small Caps puts all selected objects into uppercase. Any size less than 100 percent shrinks all but the first character of each word.

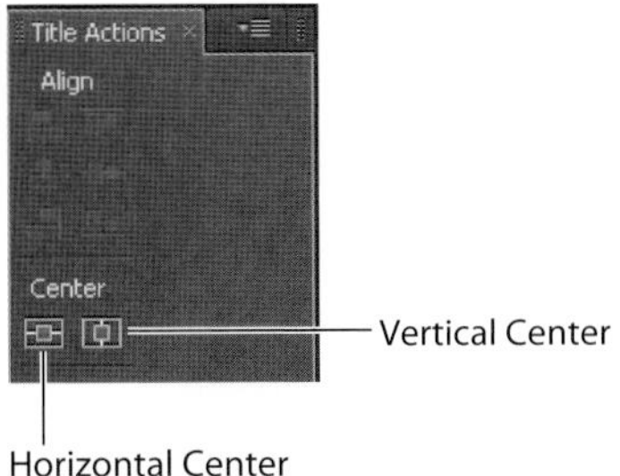

Note: NTSC-TV sets cut off the edges of a video signal. Keeping text within the title-safe margin (also called the title-safe zone), as shown by the rectangular fields in the title display area below, ensures viewers will see all your text.

Your screen should look like the one shown here.

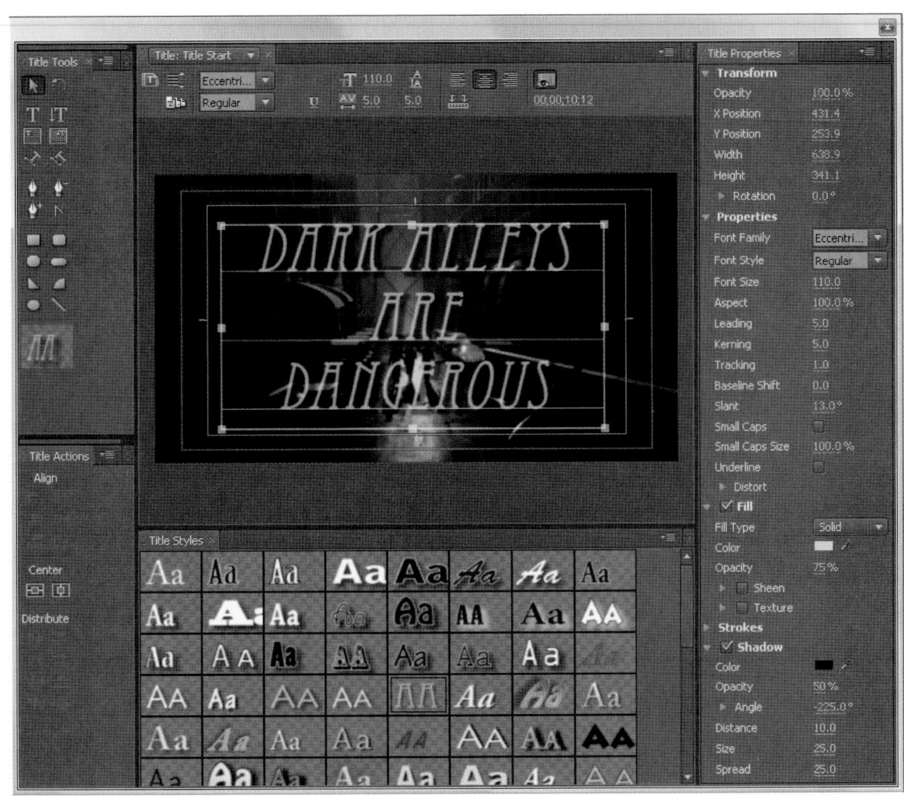

15 Drag the Titler floating window to the right—far enough to be able to see the Project panel.

16 In the Project panel, double-click Title Finished to load it in the Titler.

17 Toggle between the two titles by using the panel menu in the Titler main panel.

Your text should look similar to the Title Finished text.

Note: Adobe Premiere Pro CS4 automatically saves your updated title in the project file. It does not show up as a separate file on your hard drive.

18 Close the Titler by clicking the little x in the upper-right corner (Windows) or the close button (Mac OS).

19 Drag Title Start from the Project panel to the Video 2 track on the Timeline, trim it so it fits above the video clip, and drag the current-time indicator through it to see how it looks over that video clip.

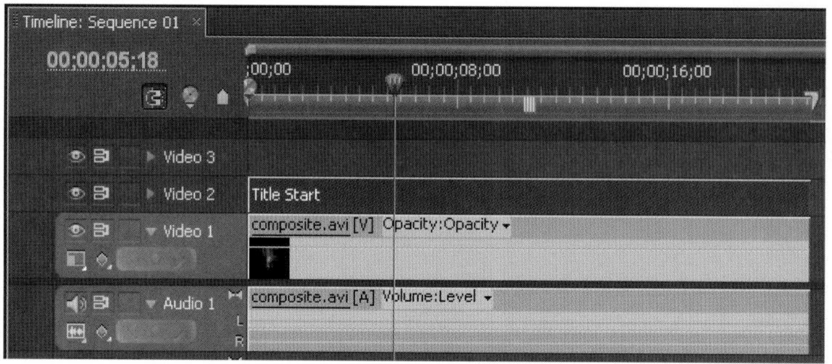

Note: You can apply transitions to titles to fade them up or move them on or off the screen.

20 Delete the Title Start title from the Timeline.

Using titles in other projects

You are likely to create title templates for location names and supers of interviewee names that you can use in multiple projects. However, Adobe Premiere Pro does not automatically save titles as separate files. To make a title available for use in another project, select the title in the Project panel, choose File > Export > Title, give your title a name, choose a location, and click Save. Later, you can simply import that title file the same way you would import any other asset.

Building text from scratch

The Titler offers three approaches to creating text, each offering both horizontal and vertical text-direction options:

- **Point text**: This approach builds a text bounding box as you type. The text runs on one line until you press Enter (Windows) or Return (Mac OS), or until you choose Title > Word Wrap. Changing the shape and size of the box changes the shape and size of the text.
- **Paragraph (area) text**: You set the size and shape of the text box before entering text. Changing the box size later displays more or less text but does not change the shape or size of the text.
- **Text on a path**: You build a path for the text to follow by clicking points in the text screen to create curves and then adjusting the shape and direction of those curves.

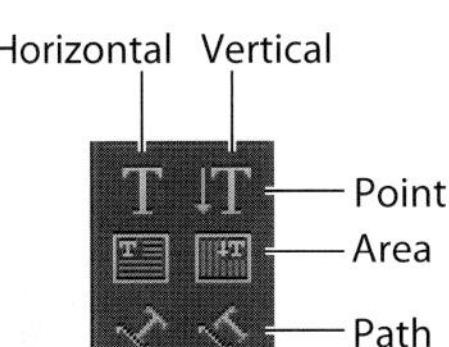

Selecting a tool from the left or right side determines whether the text will orient horizontally or vertically.

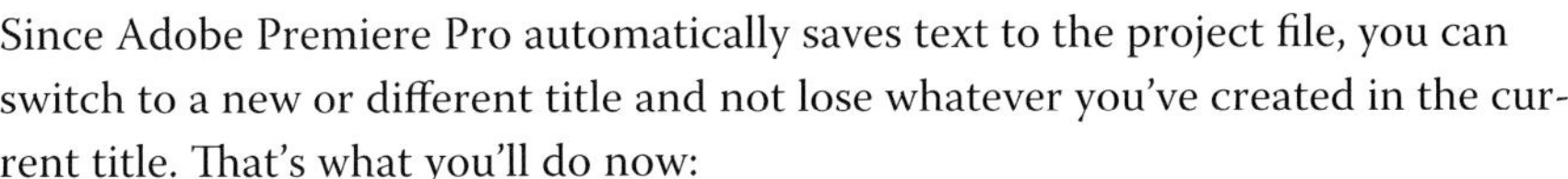
Since Adobe Premiere Pro automatically saves text to the project file, you can switch to a new or different title and not lose whatever you've created in the current title. That's what you'll do now:

1 If the Titler is open, move the Titler floating window so you can see the main menu.

2 To open the New Title dialog box, choose File > New > Title or press Ctrl+T (Windows) or Command+T (Mac OS).

   Adobe Premiere Pro CS4 allows you to have sequences with different video attributes, so the New Title dialog box allows you to create the title with different frame sizes and aspect ratios. It defaults to the settings of the active sequence. Because the settings you want to use for use for the title are the same as the active sequence, leave these settings at the defaults.

3 Type Dark Alley in the Name box and click OK.

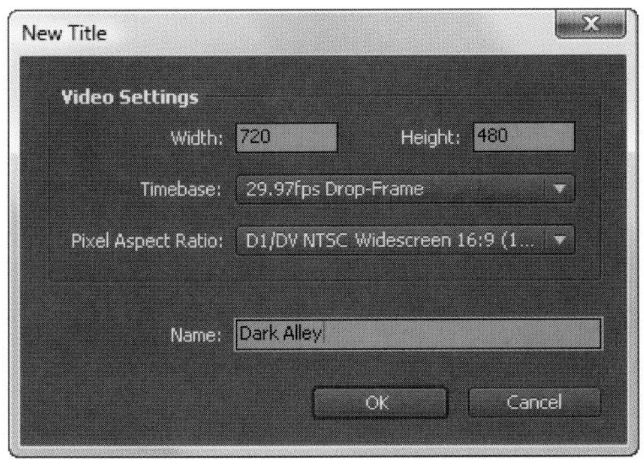

Tip: Dragging the timecode with the text screen displayed can come in handy if you want to position text relative to the video contents or check how the text looks over your video.

4 Drag the timecode (directly below the Show Video button) to change the video frame displayed on the text screen.

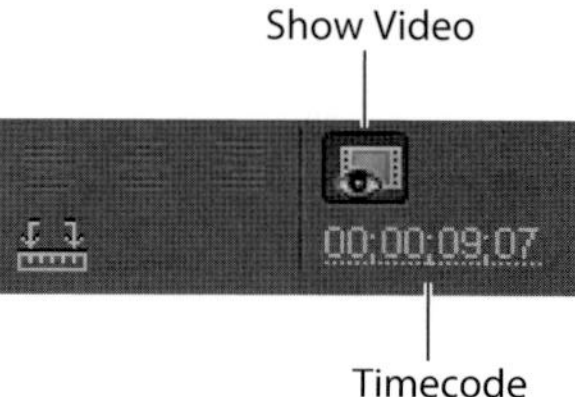

Note: The video frame displayed behind the title is not saved with the title. It is there as a reference for positioning and styling your title.

5 Click the Show Background Video button to hide the video clip.

Checkerboard pattern signifies transparency

The background now consists of a grayscale checkerboard, which signifies transparency. That is, if you place text created in the Titler on a video track above other video clips, the video on lower tracks will be visible wherever you see that checkerboard. You can also create text or geometric objects with some transparency. In that case, you'll see the checkerboard through an object, which means the video will show through but will appear as if it's covered with smoked or tinted glass.

6 Click the Birch White 80 style (the third style of the style group shown here).

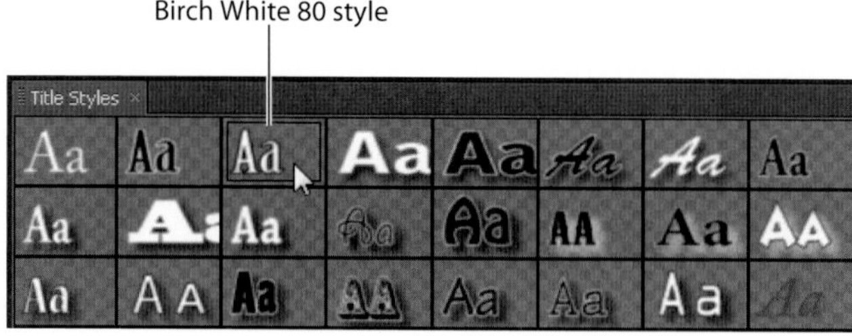

7 Click the Type tool (shortcut T) and click anywhere in the Titler panel.

The Type tool creates point text.

8 Type **Dark Alley**.

Note: If you continue typing, you will note that point text does not wrap. Your text will run off the screen to the right. To make it wrap when it reaches the title-safe margin, choose Title > Word Wrap. To begin a new line, press Enter (Windows) or Return (Mac OS).

9 Click the Selection tool (the black arrow in the upper-left corner of the Title Tools panel). That puts handles on the text bounding box.

Note: In this case, the Selection tool keyboard shortcut, V, won't work, because you are typing inside a text bounding box.

10 Drag the corners and edges of the text bounding box, and note how the text changes size and shape accordingly.

11 Hover the pointer just outside a corner of the text bounding box until a curved line pointer appears. Then drag to rotate the bounding box off its horizontal orientation.

More than one way to move a box

Instead of dragging bounding box handles, you can change values in the Transform settings in the Title Properties panel. Either type new values or position your pointer on a value and drag left or right. Your changes show up immediately in the bounding box.

12 After making sure the Selection tool is still active, click anywhere within the bounding box, and drag the angled text and its bounding box somewhere else on the Titler panel.

13 Edit that text by double-clicking anywhere in the text and typing.

You can drag to select text you want to remove or replace.

14 Delete all the text by clicking the Selection tool, which puts handles on the text bounding box indicating the entire frame is selected, and pressing Delete.

15 Click the Area Type tool and drag a text bounding box into the Titler panel that nearly fills the title-safe zone.

The Area Type tool creates paragraph text.

Turning off safe margins

You can turn off the title-safe margins or action-safe margins by opening the Titler panel menu (or choosing Title > View) and then choosing Safe Title Margin or Safe Action Margin, respectively.

16 Start typing. This time, type enough characters to go beyond the end of the bounding box.

Unlike point text, area text remains within the confines of the bounding box you defined. It wraps at the bounding box borders.

17 Press Enter (Windows) or Return (Mac) to go down a line.

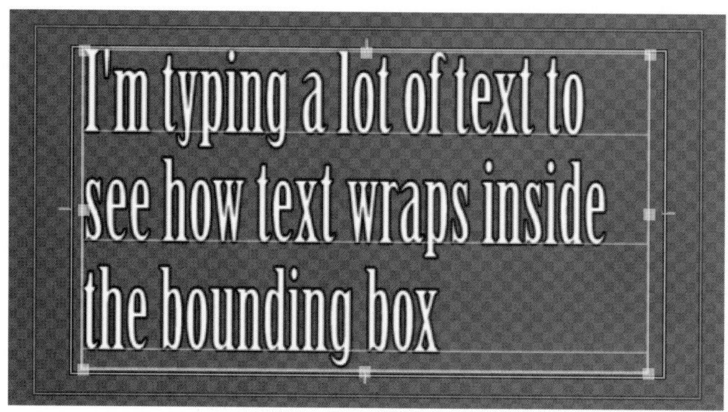

18 Click the Selection tool, and change the size and shape of the bounding box.

The text does not change size. Instead, it adjusts its position on the bounding box baselines. If you make the box too small for all your text, the extra text scrolls below the bottom edge of the bounding box. In that case, a small plus sign (+) appears near the lower-right corner outside the bounding box.

19 Double-click within the text to edit it.

20 Switch to the Selection tool, click anywhere in the text bounding box, and press Delete to remove the text.

Vertical text

While you're testing your text, try the vertically oriented Vertical Type tool and Vertical Area Type tool. They create text with each character standing on top of the next one.

Putting text on a path

The Path Type tool is both elegant and tricky. It enables you to build paths that are simple or complex, or straight or curved, for your text to follow.

If you've worked with the Pen tool in Adobe Photoshop or Adobe Illustrator, you know how to use the Path Type tool. You define a path by creating a number of points in the Titler panel and dragging handles at each point to define curves. Here's how it works in Adobe Premiere Pro:

1 Continue with the same title opened for the previous exercise, or start a new title. Select the Path Type tool.

2 Click and drag a short path horizontally anywhere in the Titler panel.

That creates an anchor point with handles. You'll use those handles to define the curve's characteristics. If you click without dragging, you won't add handles. It's tricky to add them later.

3 Click and drag a short path horizontally to two other places to create three points that will be joined together in a curve.

The Titler automatically creates a curved path between the three anchor points.

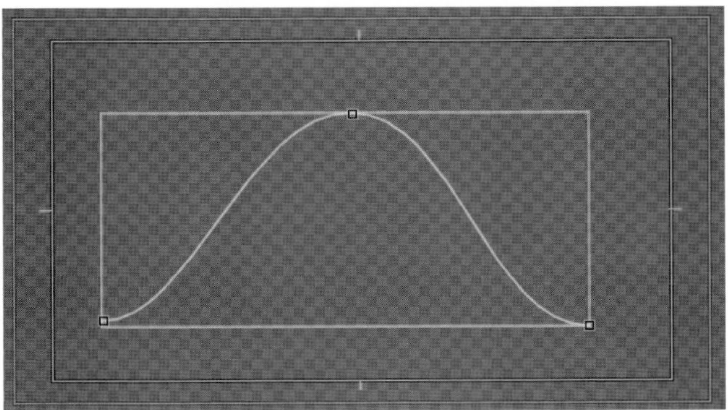

4 Click the Pen tool.

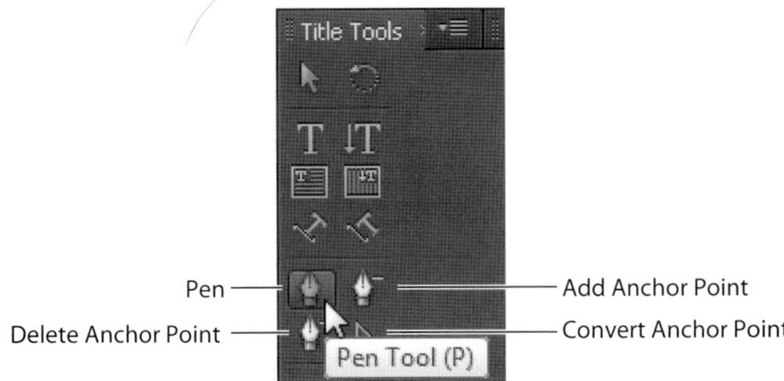

5 Hover the pointer over the handles (your pointer changes to a black arrow) and drag the handles.

Try making the handles longer or shorter, or just move them around to see how they work.

6 Drag the anchor points to lengthen or shorten the path.

7 Click anywhere inside the newly created bounding box.

A blinking text insertion point appears at the beginning of the curved line.

8 Type some text.

Your Titler panel should look something like the one shown here.

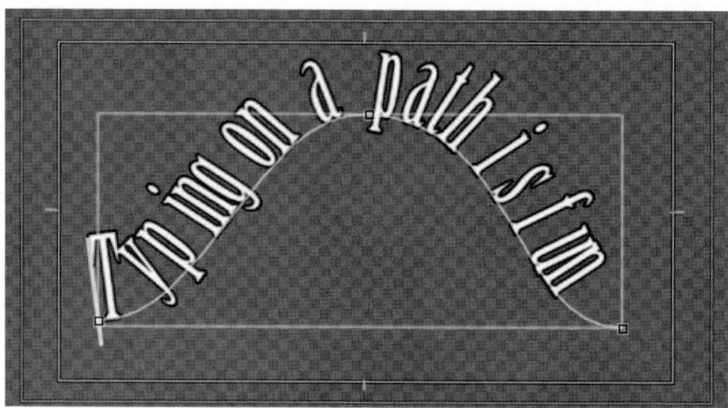

If you're having trouble with the Pen tool, double-click "Type on Path title" in the Project panel and work with it.

You will want to practice creating path text if you want to master the technique, but for now just try to get a basic idea of how it works.

Creating shapes

If you've created shapes in graphics-editing software such as Adobe Photoshop or Adobe Illustrator, you know how to create geometric objects in Adobe Premiere Pro. Simply select from the various shapes in the Title Tools panel, drag and draw the outline, and release the mouse button.

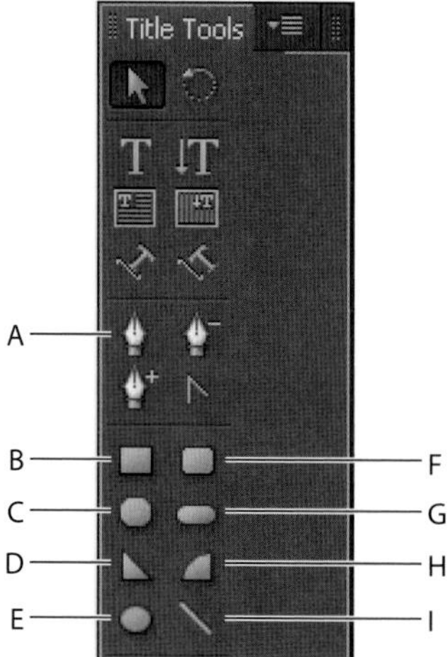

Shape drawing tools. **A.** Pen **B.** Rectangle **C.** Rounded Corner Rectangle **D.** Wedge **E.** Ellipse **F.** Clipped Corner Rectangle **G.** Rounded Rectangle **H.** Arc **I.** Line

Follow these step to draw shapes in Premiere Pro:

1 Press Ctrl+T (Windows) or Command+T (Mac OS) to open a new title. Type **Shapes** in the Name box in the New Title dialog box and click OK.

2 Select the Rectangle tool (R) and drag in the Titler panel to create a rectangle.

Note: Not all shape tools have keyboard shortcuts.

3 Click different title styles while the rectangle is still selected. Notice that title styles affect shapes as well as text. Click the first style (Caslon Pro 68) for a simple style with no shading, outlines, or shadows.

4 Shift-drag in another location to create a square.

Note: Pressing Shift creates shapes with symmetrical properties: circles, squares, and equilateral triangles. To maintain the original aspect ratio while resizing a shape you've already made, hold down the Shift key before making the change.

5 Click the Selection tool, drag it in the Titler panel to marquee-select the two objects, and press Delete to make a clean slate.

6 Select the Rounded Corner Rectangle tool, and Alt-drag (Windows) or Option-drag (Mac OS) to draw from the center of the shape.

The center remains in the spot where you first clicked, and the figure changes shape and size around that point as you drag.

7 Choose the Clipped Corner Rectangle tool, and Shift+Alt-drag (Windows) or Shift+Option-drag (Mac OS) to constrain the aspect ratio and draw from the center.

8 Select the Arc tool (A) and drag diagonally across the corner points to flip the shape diagonally as you draw.

Note: To flip the shape after you've drawn it, use the Selection tool to drag a corner point in the direction you want it to flip.

9 Click the Wedge tool (W) and drag across, up, or down to flip the shape horizontally or vertically as you draw.

10 Marquee-select those four objects and press Delete to make another clean slate.

11 Select the Line tool (L) and drag to create a single line.

12 Select the Pen tool and click in a blank area of the title canvas to create an anchor point (don't drag to create handles).

13 Click the Titler panel again where you want the segment to end (or Shift-click to constrain the segment's angle to a multiple of 45 degrees). This creates another anchor point.

14 Continue clicking the Pen tool to create additional straight segments. The last anchor point you add appears as a large square, indicating it is selected.

15 Complete the path by doing one of the following:

- To close the path, move the Pen tool to the initial anchor point. When it is directly over the initial anchor point, a square appears underneath the Pen pointer (as shown here). Click to make the connection.
- To leave the path open, Control-click (Windows) or Command-click (Mac OS) anywhere away from all objects, or select a different tool in the Title Tools panel

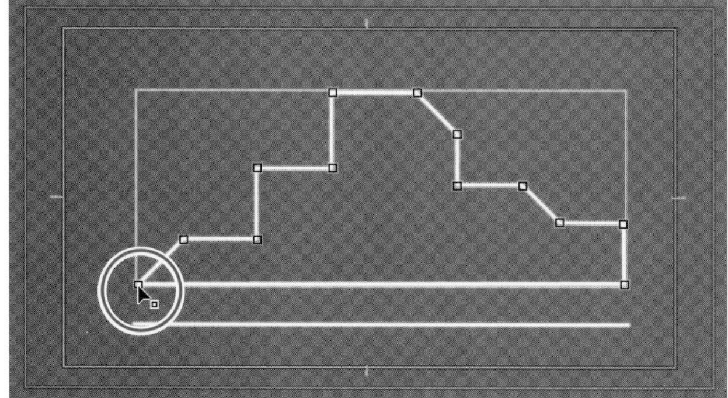

Experiment with the different shape options. Try overlapping them and using different styles. The possibilities are endless.

Aligning shapes

Sometimes you may need to create multiple shapes or titles and align them on the screen. The Titler has several alignment tools to make this job easy. You will explore a few here:

1 Delete your test shapes to create a blank Titler panel, or start a new title.

2 Draw a small circle using the Ellipse tool. You can constrain it to be a circle by holding down the Shift key while you drag the shape.

3 Style the circle by clicking the style HoboStd Slant Gold 80.

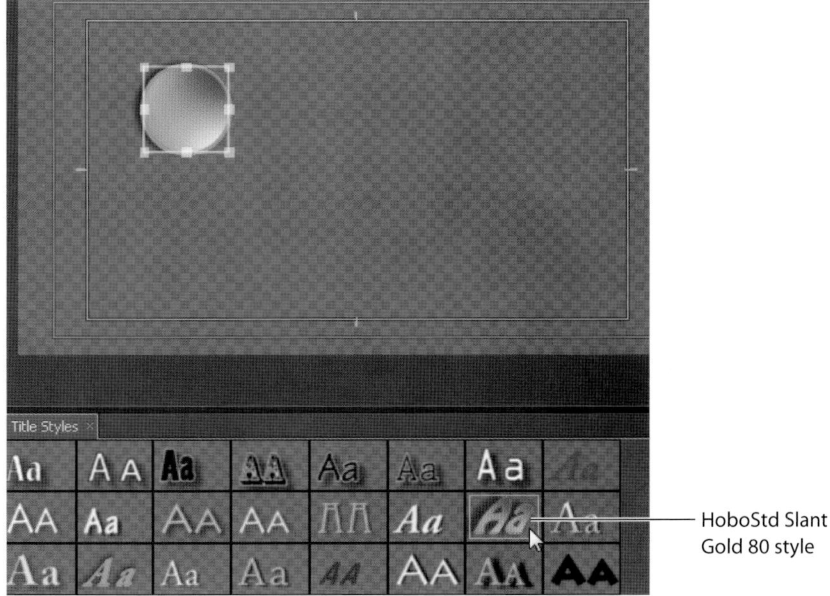

4 Make three exact copies by Alt-dragging the circle to three other locations within the title-safe area, roughly in a line horizontally.

5 Select all four circles by Shift-clicking each one.

Notice that when more than one object is selected, the Align tools become active.

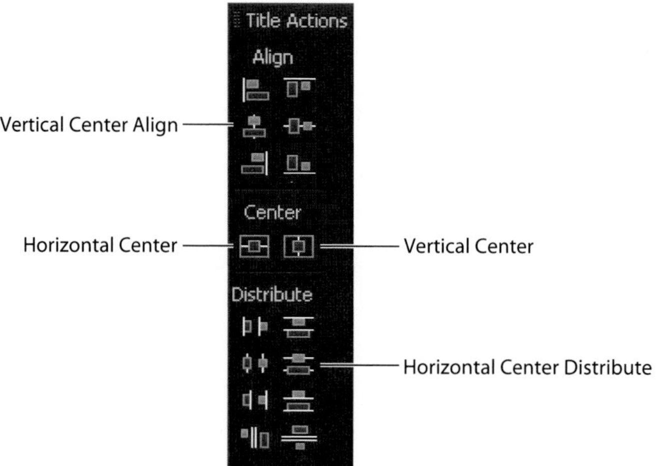

6 Click the Vertical Center Align tool.

7 Click the Horizontal Center Distribute tool.

8 Click both the Horizontal Center and Vertical Center tools.

You should have four perfectly aligned circles centered in the title area.

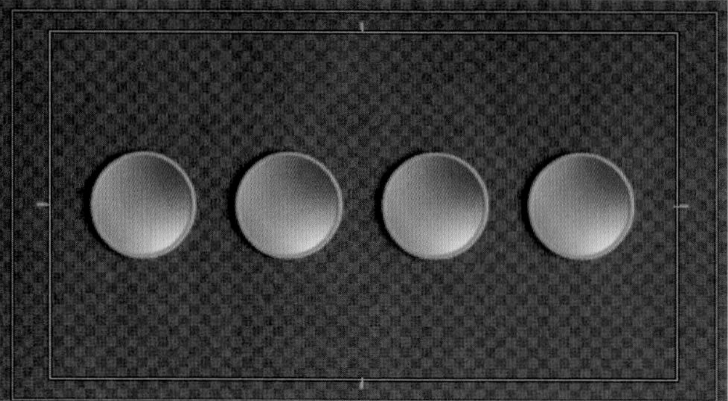

Making text roll and crawl

Using the Titler, you can make rolling text for opening and closing credits and crawling text for items such as headline bulletins.

1 Choose Title > New Title > Default Roll.

2 Name your title Rolling Credits and click OK.

3 Type some text with the Orca White 80 style.

Create placeholder credits as shown here, pressing Enter (Windows) or Return (Mac OS) after each line. Type enough text to more than fill the screen vertically.

Roll/Crawl Options

Note: With rolling text selected, the Titler automatically adds a scroll bar along the right side that enables you to view your text as it runs off the bottom of the screen (shown here). If you select one of the crawl options, that scroll bar will appear at the bottom to enable you to view text running off the right or left edge of the screen.

4 Click the Roll/Crawl Options button.

You have the following options:

- **Still**: This changes the credits to a still title.
- **Roll**: (Scroll text vertically) This should be selected already, because this title was created as rolling credits.
- **Crawl Left, Crawl Right**: These indicate the crawl direction (rolling text always moves up the screen).
- **Start Off Screen**: This controls whether the credits start completely off the screen and roll on or whether they begin with the uppermost text item at the top or side of the screen.
- **End Off Screen**: This indicates whether the credits roll completely off the screen.

- **Preroll**: This specifies the number of frames before the first words appear onscreen.
- **Ease-In**: This specifies the number of frames at the beginning to gradually increase the speed of the roll or crawl from zero to its full speed.
- **Ease-Out**: This specifies the number of frames to slow down the roll or crawl at its end.
- **Postroll**: This specifies the number of frames that play after the roll or crawl ends.

5 Select Start Off Screen and End Off Screen, and type **5** for Ease-In and Ease-Out.

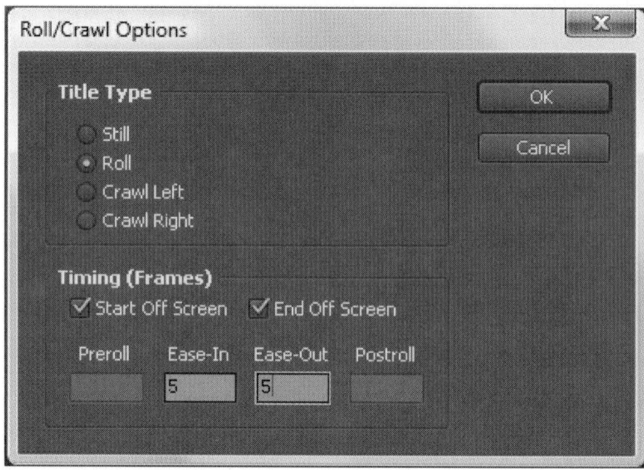

6 Close the Titler.

7 Drag your newly created Rolling Credits title to the Video 2 track of the Timeline above the video clip (if another title is there, drag this one directly on top of it to do an overlay edit).

8 With the sequence selected, press the spacebar to view your rolling credits.

Note: If you're having trouble with rolling or crawling text, open Lesson 08-2.prproj to work with the credits as described here.

Note: The default length of rolling or crawling credits is 5 seconds. If you change the length of the credits clip, that changes the speed. A longer clip length means slower rolling credits.

Adding text effects: sheens, strokes, shadows, and fills

Reverse engineering can be a good learning tool. So, in this exercise, you will deconstruct one of the many built-in templates that come with Adobe Premiere Pro to learn how to work with the Titler's effects.

Unlike styles, templates are a combination of background graphics, geometric shapes, and placeholder text. They are organized into themes with enough variety for just about any circumstance.

Templates are tremendously useful. You can easily customize graphic themes to suit your needs or build your own templates from scratch and save them for future projects. Let's begin:

1 Choose Title > New Title > Based on Template.

2 Open as many template folders, and click through as many templates, as you like.

3 Open the Lower Thirds folder, select Lower Third 1024, and click OK.

Note: You can also open the Titler and choose Title > Templates to get to the same Templates screen.

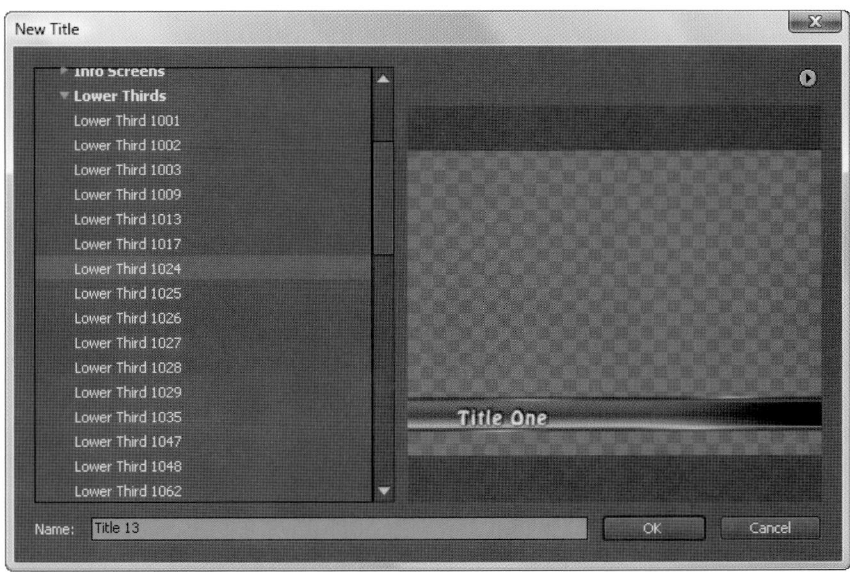

4 Click the Selection tool and move it over the template.

Bounding boxes appear, delineating the three components of this title: the *Title One* text, a brown and yellow rectangle, and a black rectangle with a gradient fill superimposed over the right side of the brown and yellow rectangle.

5 Drag each bounding box in turn up the screen so you can see the template's three components.

Your Titler panel should look something like the one shown here.

Note: This is a good template to experiment with because it has a full range of effects, including a four-color gradient, reduced opacity (transparency), a sheen, a stroke, and shadows.

6 Drag the top edge of the brown and yellow rectangle to expand it.

It is now selected, and its characteristics are displayed in the Titler Properties panel.

7 Collapse the Transform and Properties areas in the panel to make some room.

8 Expand Fill and then Sheen (shown here), Strokes, and Outer Strokes (no inner strokes are used in this template).

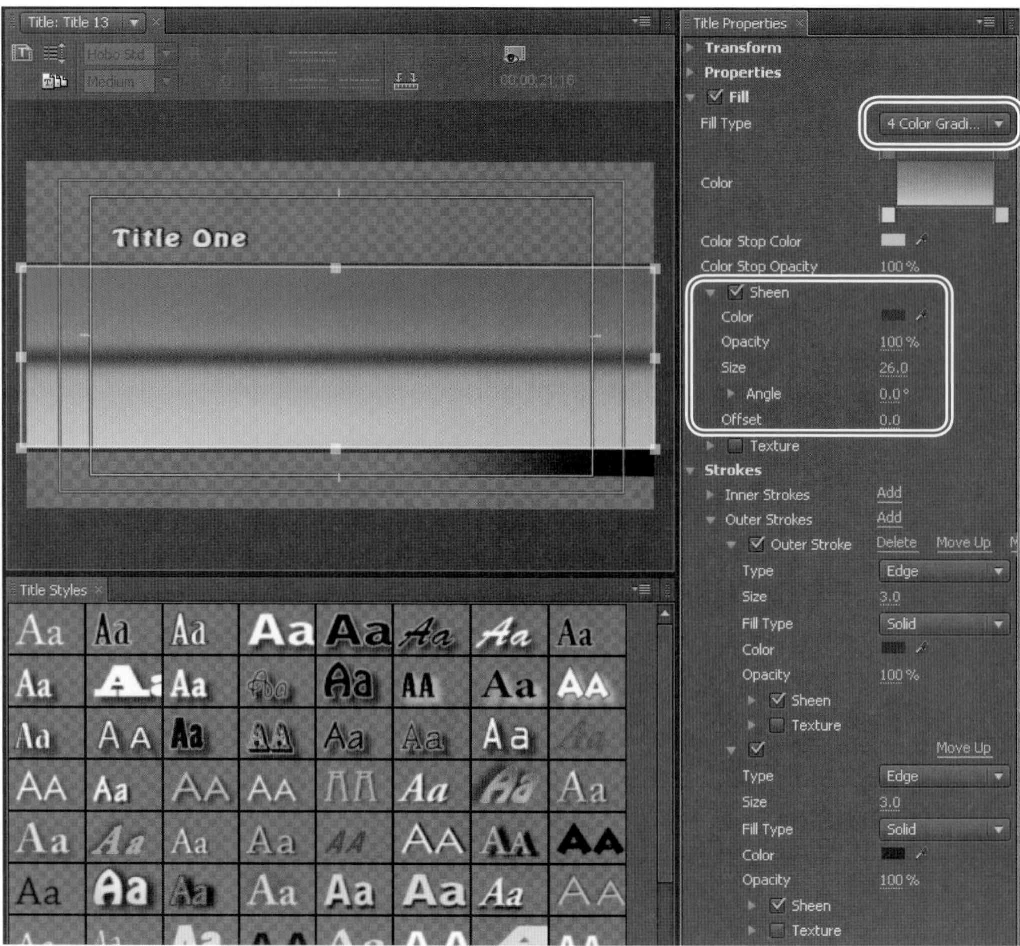

9 Open the Fill Type menu for Fill, and select each option in turn to see what they do. When done, return to 4 Color Gradient.

10 Double-click one or two of the four color-stop boxes around the 4 Color Gradient display to open the Color Picker. Select new colors.

Note: Each color is slightly different from the other three, and the colors at the top are slightly darker than the bottom colors. This gives this the rectangle extra depth.

Lift a color from your video

Instead of using the Color Picker to change the color-stop color, you can use the Eyedropper tool (located next to the color swatch) to select a color from your video. Click the Show Video button at the top of the Titler panel, move to a frame you want to use by dragging the timecode left or right, drag the Eyedropper tool into your video scene, and click a color that suits your needs.

11 Change the color-stop opacities by clicking each Color Stop box and changing its Opacity setting.

12 Click the Sheen color box and change its color, opacity, size, angle, and offset.

Note: *Sheen* is a soft-edged color that typically runs horizontally through shapes or text. In this case, it's the brown, horizontal line that runs through the entire rectangle.

13 Click the two Outer Stroke disclosure triangles to expand the parameters.

Strokes are outer or inner borders on text or graphic objects. They have the same collection of properties available for text and other Titler objects. In this case, both strokes are 3 points wide, and they fall adjacent to one another.

14 Change the size of the two outer strokes to 10 points each.

As shown here, that more clearly displays the sheen applied to these borders.

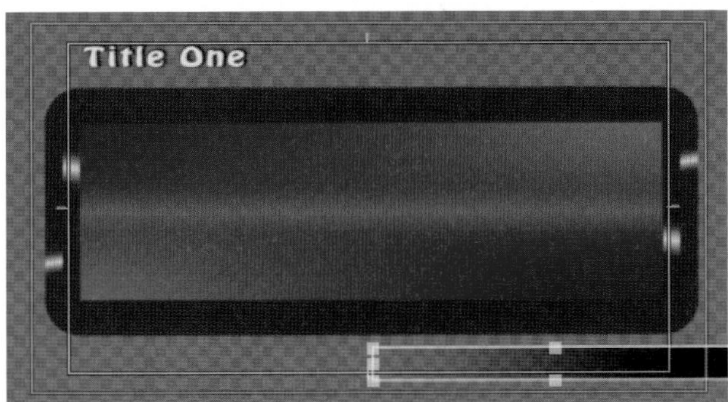

Note: You can change the opacity (transparency) of any color applied to any object or text, be it fill, sheen, or stroke. You can give a geometric shape or text a solid-color stroke border and convert its fill color to 0 percent opacity to display only its edges.

Sheen artistry

Take a look at the sheen properties for both outer strokes. Note that the angles are 191 degrees and 351 degrees (270 and 90 degrees are horizontal). That is, each sheen appears just a bit above the centerline on one side and a bit below the centerline on the other. If the sheens were to run through the entire box, they'd form an X. This is a clever bit of visual artistry. Before you expanded the rectangle, the sheens were on the top and bottom edges. In this taller mode, they appear along the sides. To see how that works, drag the rectangle's bounding box top edge up and down, and watch the sheens move along the edges.

15 Next to Inner Strokes, click Add.

The Inner Stroke properties box appears.

16 Select the Inner Stroke properties box to turn on the parameters, and experiment with this new stroke by changing its Size, Fill Type, Color, and Opacity settings.

Note: Adding a sheen or a shadow to an object is also easy. Just select the object in the Titler panel, select the appropriate properties box, and adjust the parameters.

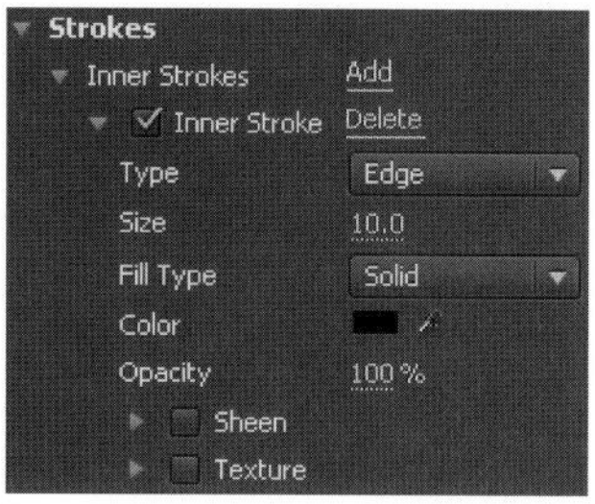

Strokes
Inner Strokes Add
Inner Stroke Delete
Type Edge
Size 10.0
Fill Type Solid
Color
Opacity 100 %
Sheen
Texture

17 Click the Title One text to select it, and then open its Shadow properties.

This text doesn't have an obvious shadow because the shadow size is only 2 points. It's more like an outer stroke.

Note: The Shadow settings are self-explanatory, with the exception of Spread. Increasing the Spread value softens the shadow.

18 Change all the characteristics to see how the Shadow feature works.

Experiment with effects

You can learn a lot by experimenting with effects. Open a new title, select a style, and draw an object. Do this with several distinctly different styles. Then open the Fill, Strokes, and Shadow properties, and make lots of changes to each object.

Create some new outer and inner strokes. Add sheens. Check a Texture box, and add any graphic image or Adobe Photoshop file to add some real pizzazz to your text and object.

The more you use the Titler, the more you'll come to appreciate its depth and creative possibilities.

Copy titles to other Adobe applications

Adobe Premiere Pro CS4 allows you to copy and paste formatted text objects from the Titler to other Adobe applications such as Adobe After Effects CS4, Adobe Photoshop CS4, Adobe Encore CS4, and Adobe Illustrator CS4. Simply copy the text object from the Titler and paste it into the destination application.

Review questions

1 What are the differences between point text and area (or paragraph) text?

2 Why display the title-safe margin?

3 What's the difference between a style and a template when using the Titler?

4 Why might the Align tools be dimmed?

5 How do you use the Ellipse tool to make a perfect circle?

6 How do you apply a stroke or a sheen?

Review answers

1 You create point text with the Type tool. Its bounding box expands as you type. Changing the box shape changes the text size and shape accordingly. When you use the Area Type tool, you define a bounding box, and the characters remain within its confines. Changing the box's shape displays more or fewer characters.

2 NTSC-TV sets cut off the edges of the TV signal. The amount lost varies from set to set. Keeping your text within the title-safe margin ensures that viewers will see all your title.

3 You can apply a style to characters or objects you create in the Titler. Templates give you a starting point for creating your own full-featured graphic or text backgrounds.

4 The Align tools become active if more than one object is selected in the Titler. The Distribute tools become active when more than two objects are selected.

5 To create a perfect circle, hold down the Shift key as you draw using the Ellipse tool.

6 To apply a stroke or sheen, select the text or object to edit, and select its Stroke (Outer or Inner) or Sheen box. Then start adjusting parameters, and they will show up on the object.

9 APPLYING SPECIALIZED EDITING TOOLS

Topics covered in this lesson

- Exploring the timesaving editing tools
- Slicing and moving clips
- Replacing a clip and replacing footage
- Using Sync Lock and Lock Track
- Creating sequence In and Out points
- Using subclips from the Source Monitor or a sequence
- Multicamera editing

This lesson will take approximately 60 minutes.

It's time to take a break from single-topic lessons and delve into some specialized editing tools and techniques. In this lesson, you'll use editing tools that can save you a lot of time.

Getting started

In this lesson, you'll try three specialized editing tools—Rolling Edit, Slide, and Slip—and two Program Monitor buttons—Lift and Extract. All of these can simplify certain tasks. Using the Track Select tool, you'll move entire Timelines or portions of Timelines with ease. You will learn about transitions that require the use of graphics.

You'll also explore some new ways to move and replace clips on the Timeline, and learn how to create subclips from long clips to help organize your project.

Then you'll dive into multicamera editing. If you ever have a multicamera video shoot, this feature will save you a lot of time switching between camera angles during the editing process.

Exploring the timesaving editing tools

You'll use the Rolling Edit, Slide, and Slip tools in a variety of situations, including when you want to preserve the overall length of your program while trimming and editing scenes within it. They come in handy for precisely timed projects such as 30-second advertisements. You've seen the Rolling Edit tool in action in the Trim Monitor.

You've worked with extract edits and lift edits by using the drag-and-drop method. In this lesson, you'll use the Program Monitor's Extract and Lift buttons to remove selected groups of frames—even when they're spread out over one or more clips.

In some cases, it can be easier to make individual edits and forgo these specialized tools, but it's good for any video editor to know how to use all of them. Here's a quick look at what they do and how they differ from one another:

- **Ripple edit**: A ripple edit trims a clip and shifts subsequent clips in the track by the amount you trim. You used this tool in the Lesson 6.

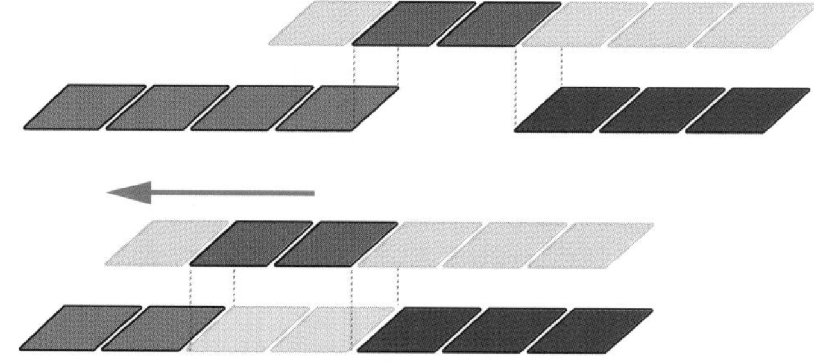

A ripple edit changes the overall length of the project.

- **Rolling edit**: A rolling edit rolls the cut point between two adjacent clips, shortening one and lengthening the other, thereby retaining the overall length of the project.

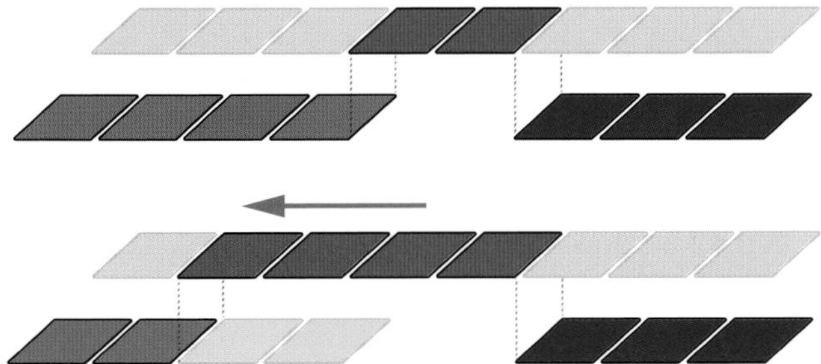

A Rolling edit retains the overall length of the project.

- **Slide edit**: A slide edit slides the entire clip over two adjacent clips, shortening and lengthening those adjacent clips without changing the selected clip's length or In and Out points.

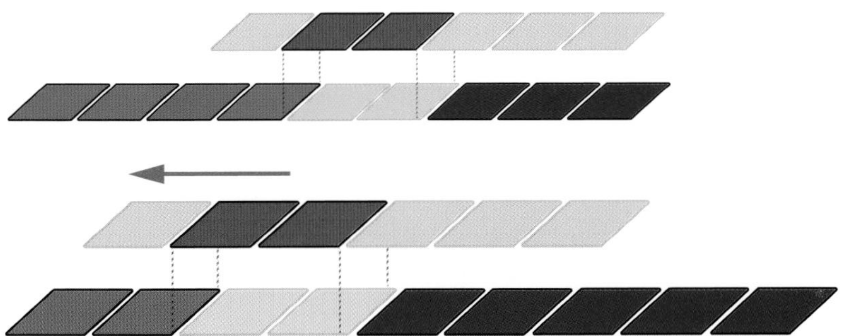

A slide edit changes the In and Out points of adjacent clips while retaining the original clip's edit points.

- **Slip edit**: A slip edit slips a clip under two adjacent clips. This changes the clip's starting and ending frames without changing its duration or affecting adjacent clips.

Note: Though the Slip and Slide tools are typically employed on the center clip of three adjacent clips, each tool functions normally even if the clip is adjacent to a clip on one side and a blank space on the other. For the Rolling Edit, Slip, and Slide tools to work as expected, you need to have sufficient unused head or tail frames to make the edits.

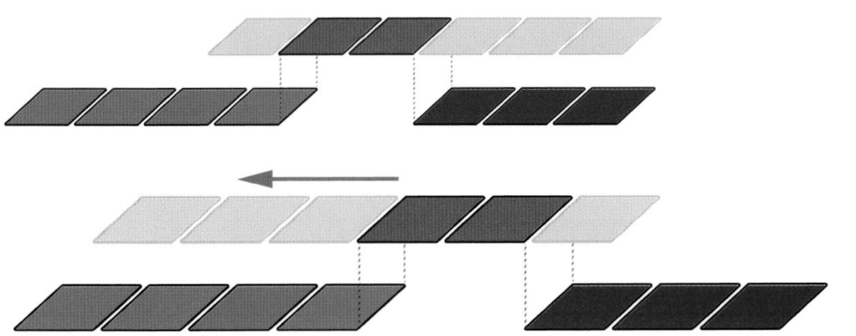

A slip edit changes the In and Out points of the selected clip while retaining the adjacent clip's edit points.

- **Extract edit**: An extract edit removes a selected range of frames and closes the gap by moving the following clips to the left.
- **Lift edit**: A lift edit removes a selected range of frames and leaves a gap.

Making rolling, slide, and slip edits

Let's begin with a rolling edit. To get started, do the following:

Note: This lesson uses NTSC-DV video in 4:3 format, rather than the 16:9 format in the other lessons.

1 Start Adobe Premiere Pro CS4 and open Lesson 09-1.prproj.

2 Open Sequence 01 in the Timeline, if it is not already open.

3 Set your workspace to Editing by choosing Window > Workspace > Editing.

Three clips already appear on the Timeline, with enough head and tail frames to allow the edits you're about to make.

4 Select the Rolling Edit tool (; keyboard shortcut N) in the Tools panel.

5 Drag the edit point between Clip A and Clip B (the first two clips on the Timeline), using the Program Monitor split screen to find a better matching edit.

Note: To ensure you'll be able to make a precise, frame-specific edit, expand the view of the Timeline by pressing the equal sign (=) key.

Try rolling the edit point to the right to 00;20 (20 frames). You can use the Program Monitor timecode or the pop-up timecode in the Timeline (shown here, respectively) to find that edit.

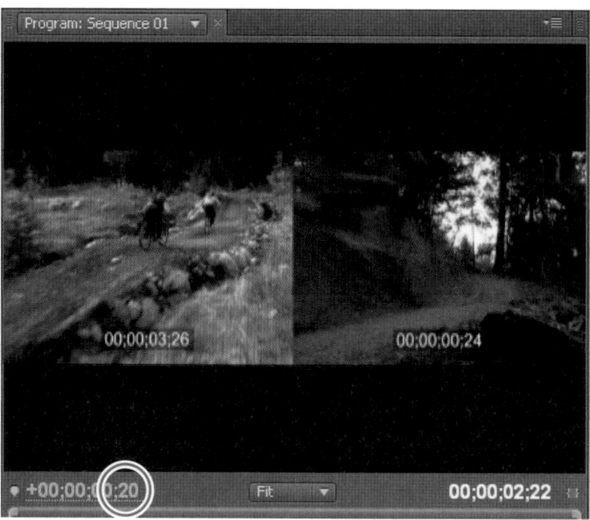

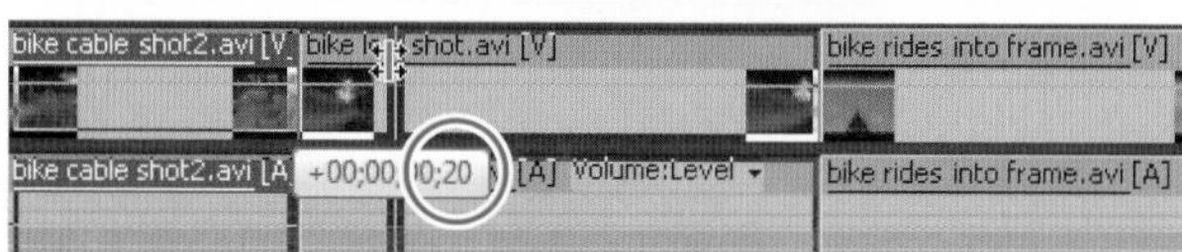

The Rolling Edit tool changes the Out and In points of adjacent clips.

6 Select the Slide tool (↤↦; keyboard shortcut U) and position it over the middle clip.

7 Drag the second clip left or right.

Take a look at the Program Monitor as you perform the slide edit. The two top images are the In point and Out point of Clip B. They do not change. The two larger images are the Out point and In point of the adjacent clips—Clip A and Clip C, respectively. These edit points change as you slide the selected clip over those adjacent clips.

Note: This is just to demonstrate the edit. You don't need to find a specific edit point.

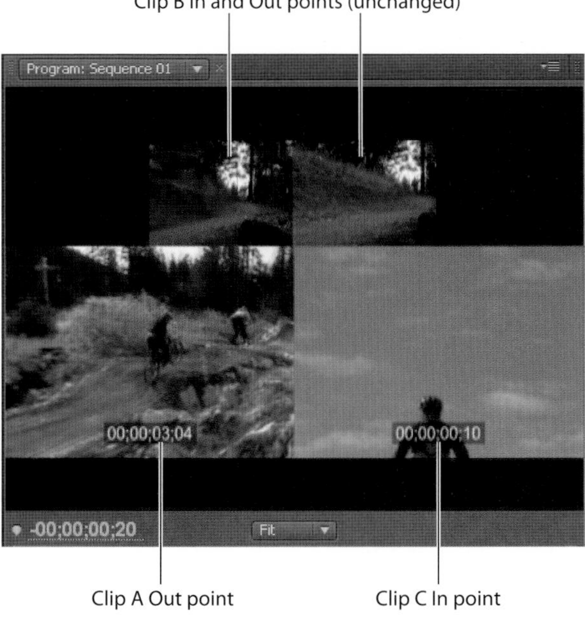

The Slide tool moves a clip over two adjacent clips.

Note: As you move the clip, you will eventually run out of head or tail frames, and the timecodes will stop changing in the Program Monitor.

8 Select the Slip tool (⟼⟻; keyboard shortcut Y) and drag Clip B left and right.

Note: Try both the Slide and Slip tools on Clips A and C. Both editing tools work on the first or last clips in a sequence.

Take a look at the Program Monitor as you perform the slip edit. The two top images are the Out point and In point of Clips A and C, respectively. They do not change. The two larger images are the In point and Out point of Clip B. These edit points change as you slip Clip B *under* Clips A and C.

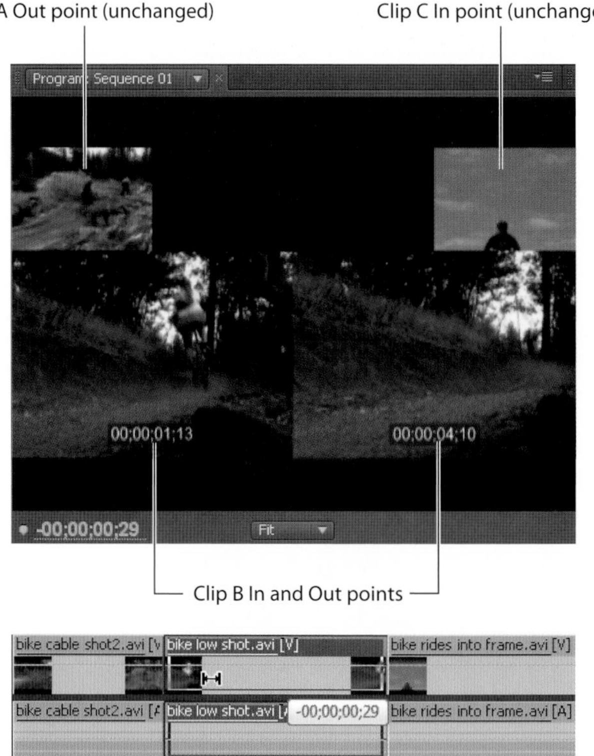

The Slip tool moves a clip under two adjacent clips.

Using the Program Monitor's Lift and Extract buttons

Next, you'll do a lift edit and then an extract edit:

1 Click the History tab and choose New > Open to undo all the rolling, slide, and slip edits you just made.

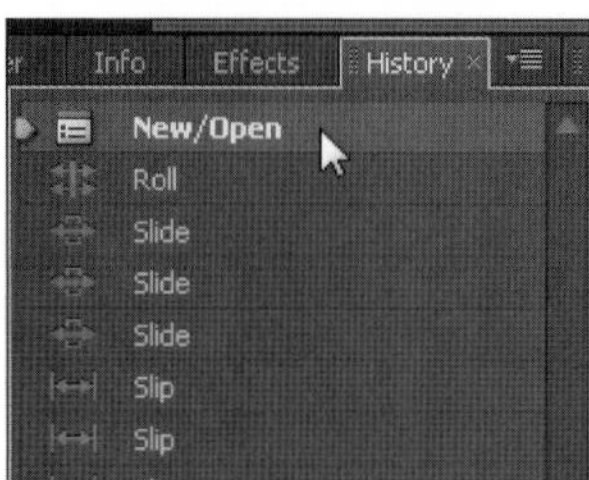

2 Move the Timeline current-time indicator to about midway on the first clip.

3 Drag a viewing area bar handle (shown here) in the Program Monitor so its current-time indicator is roughly centered. This makes it easier to set In and Out points.

4 Use the Jog, Step Forward, and Step Back controls in the Program Monitor to advance the current-time indicator to where the second bike lands after the jump. This should be at 00;00;02;00.

5 Click the Set In Point button (I) in the Program Monitor.

6 Drag the Program Monitor current-time indicator within the second clip to find a matching edit. You should end up at about 00;00;04;25.

7 Click the Set Out Point button (O).

As shown here, your Timeline now has a light blue highlighted zone between the In and Out points, as well as a gray area in the time ruler with In and Out point brackets at each end.

Note: The Lift and Extract buttons look the same until you get really close to the screen. As shown here, Extract has tiny triangles indicating that adjacent clips will fill the gap left by the edit.

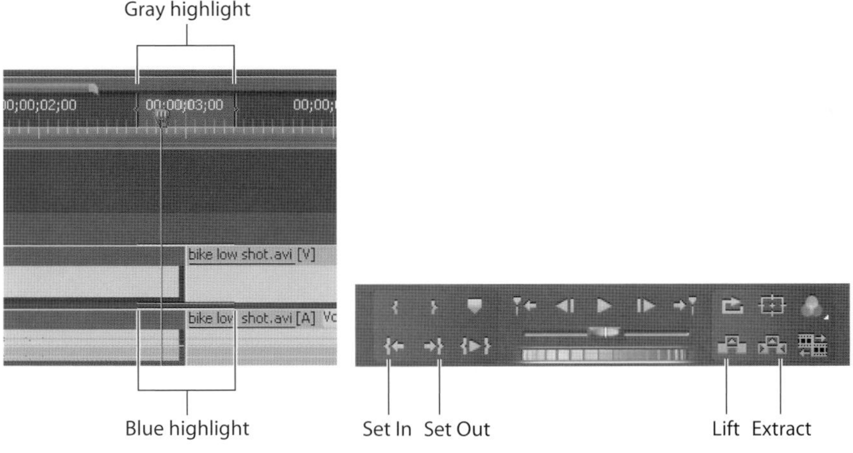

8 Click the Lift button.

That deletes the selected frames and leaves a gap.

9 Press Ctrl+Z (Windows) or Command+Z (Mac OS) to undo that edit.

10 Click the Extract button.

That performs the equivalent of a ripple delete. Play this edit to see how, by clicking only one button, you edited two clips.

Replacing a clip and replacing footage

Sometimes you may want to replace a clip with another clip and have the new clip fit in the same place and inherit all the effects of the original clip. For example, you may create an opening sequence for wedding videos that you use over and over for new projects. By replacing the clip with a new clip, you can save a lot of time by not having to rebuild the opening sequence from scratch.

Adobe Premiere Pro provides two ways to do this: Replace Clip and Replace Footage. You will explore them both.

Using the Replace Clip feature

Let's start with the Replace Clip feature:

1 Open Lesson 09-2.prproj.

2 Play the Timeline. Notice that the same clip is played twice as a picture-in-picture (PIP). The clip has some motion effects that cause it to spin onto the screen and then spin off. You will learn how to create these effects in a later lesson.

   You want to replace the first PIP clip (bike low shot.avi) in the Video 2 track with a new clip called multicam_03.avi. But you don't want to have to re-create all the effects and timing. This is a great scenario for using the Replace Clip feature.

3 Locate the multicam_03.avi clip and drag it on top of the first bike low shot.avi clip. Do not drop it yet. Notice that it is longer than the clip on the Timeline.

4 Press the Alt (Windows) or Option (Mac OS) key. Notice that the replacement clip now becomes the exact length of the clip it is replacing. Release the mouse button to complete the Replace Clip function.

5 Play the Timeline. Notice the first PIP clip has the same effects but is using the new footage. The second PIP clip remains unchanged.

Using the Replace Footage feature

The Adobe Premiere Pro Replace Footage feature replaces footage in the Project panel. This can be a huge benefit when you need to replace a clip that recurs several times in a sequence or multiple sequences. When you use Replace Footage, all instances of the clip you replace are changed anywhere the original clip was used in any sequence in the project.

1 Press Ctrl+Z (Windows) or Command+Z (Mac OS) to undo the Replace Clip function you just performed. Play the Timeline to see the original bike low shot.avi clip being used in both picture-in-picture instances.

2 Select the bike low shot.avi clip in the Project panel.

3 Right-click the bike low shot.avi clip and choose Replace Footage from the menu that appears.

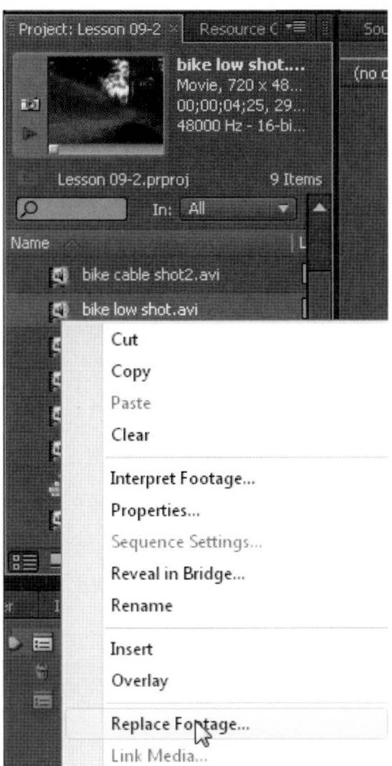

4 Navigate to the Lesson 09 folder, select the bike rides into frame.avi file, and click Select.

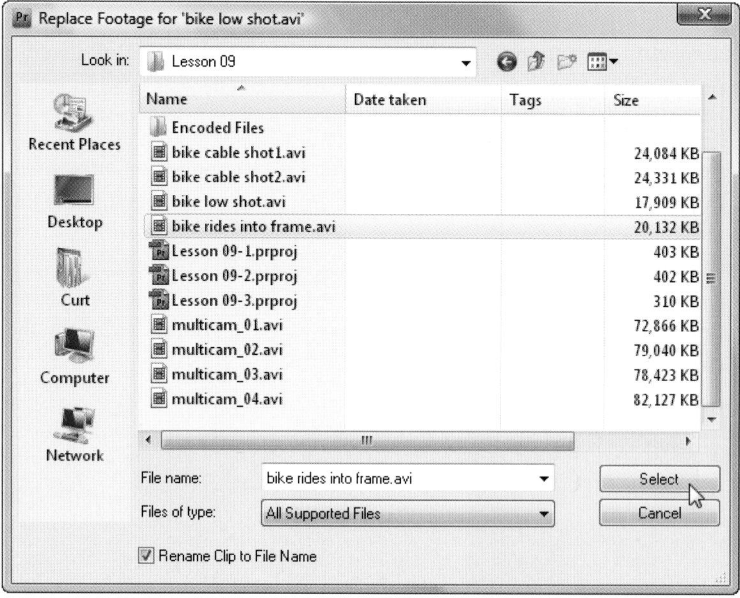

Note: You can use the Replace Clip and Replace Footage features with dissimilar media. For example, you can replace a video clip with a still image.

5 Play the Timeline, and notice that both PIP clips were replaced with the new footage while they maintained their timing and effects.

Using Sync Lock and Lock Track

In a typical editing project, you will have multiple layers of video clips. When you edit a sequence by doing ripple edits or inserts, you'll want all the video tracks to stay in sync. This means if one track moves, all the other tracks move the same amount.

However, sometimes you may want one track not to move when you're performing ripples or inserts. Adobe Premiere Pro provides two methods of protecting one or more tracks from being moved: Sync Lock and Lock Track.

Using Sync Lock

Let's start by trying the Sync Lock feature:

1 Open Lesson 09-3.prproj. Note that this sequence has four video tracks with a gap between clips.

2 Right-click the gap between clips on the Video 1 track and choose Ripple Delete.

   The clips on the right move left to close the gap.

3 Press Ctrl+Z (Windows) or Command+Z (Mac OS) to undo the ripple delete.

4 Switch the Toggle Sync Lock icon (▤) off on the Video 4 track. Notice that by default all tracks have Sync Lock enabled.

5 Right-click the gap between clips on the Video 1 track and choose Ripple Delete. All tracks stay in sync except the Video 4 track. This is because you toggled Sync Lock off on this track.

6 Press Ctrl+Z (Windows) or Command+Z (Mac OS) to undo the ripple delete.

7 Choose the Ripple Edit tool, grab the right edge of the first clip in the Video 1 track, and drag it an inch or so to the left. All tracks ripple except the clips in the Video 4 track.

8 Grab the right edge of the first clip in the Video 4 track and drag it to the left. Notice that the clips are still editable in this track. The Sync Lock toggled off does not prevent the clips in the track from being edited or deleted.

Using Lock Track

Now let's try editing with the Lock Track feature:

1 Press Ctrl+Z (Windows) or Command+Z (Mac OS) a few times until the project is back to the start point.

2 Make sure all tracks have Toggle Sync Lock on.

3 Click the Lock Track icon (🔒) in the Video 4 track. Diagonal lines appear through the track header.

4 Try doing a ripple delete as you did earlier, and notice the locked track is unaffected.

5 Try to edit or move clips in the Video 4 track. Notice that you cannot do anything to the clips in the Video 4 track.

Note: A locked track differs from a track with Toggle Sync Lock turned off in that a locked track cannot be changed.

Editing with In and Out points around a clip

In Lesson 6 you set In and Out points on a sequence to perform some lifts and extracts. You can use the same In and Out points in a sequence to identify the location to insert a source clip that also has In and Out points marked. This is called a *four-point edit.*

Adobe Premiere Pro has two features called In and Out Around Clip and In and Out Around Selection. In this exercise you will perform a four-point edit using In and Out Around Clip. This may seem like a complex edit, but once you get used to it, you may find it will save you a lot of time in certain editing situations. This is especially helpful when your start and end frame points are both important but you need to replace the frames in between. Let's begin:

1 Open Lesson 09-4.prproj.

2 Play the Timeline and then click the second clip to select it.

The second clip on the Timeline is going to be replaced with a clip of a different camera angle. You want to remove the second clip and replace it with the In and Out sections of a new clip you will specify.

3 Move the current-time indicator over the second clip. Right-click in the Timeline area.

4 Choose Set Sequence Marker > In and Out Around Clip. The Timeline is now shaded above the second clip.

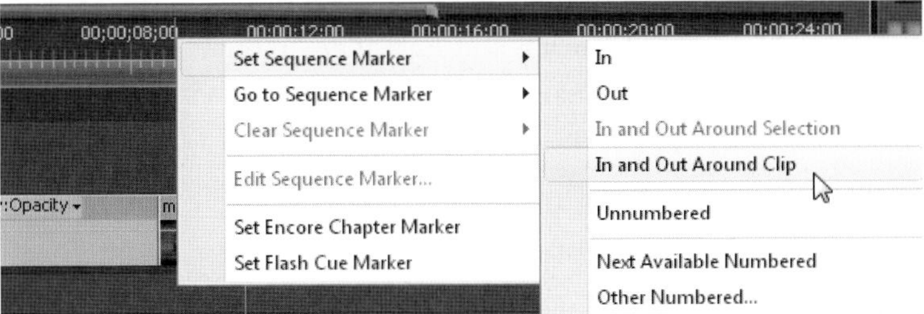

5 Double-click the multicam_02.avi clip in the Project panel to open it in the Source Monitor.

6 Drag the current-time indicator in the Source Monitor to 00;00;14;20 and set the In point by clicking the Set In Point bracket ({).

7 Drag the current-time indicator in the Source Monitor to 00;00;16;20 and set the Out point by clicking the Set Out Point bracket (}).

8 Click the Overlay icon in the Source Monitor (as shown here) to overlay the marked source clip on the clip you marked on the Timeline. A dialog box appears, warning that the marked source clip is shorter than the destination clip. Accept the default to allow Adobe Premiere Pro to adjust the speed of the source clip to make it match the length of the destination clip.

9 Play the Timeline.

Creating subclips from the Source Monitor

If you have a very long clip, it is often helpful to break it down into smaller clips (subclips). You can rename these subclips and store them in the Project panel in bins as you choose. Creating subclips can help you organize your project and make it easy to find just the clip you need.

1 Open Lesson 09-5.prproj.

2 Double-click multicam_01.avi to open it in the Source Monitor.

3 Set the In point at the beginning of the clip. Set the Out point at around 08;00 seconds. This will represent the race portion of the clip.

4 Drag the marked clip from the Source Monitor back to the Project panel while holding down Ctrl (Windows) or Command (Mac OS).

5 When you drop the clip in the Project panel, you will be prompted to give it a name. Name this subclip Race. Notice that subclips have a different icon than master clips.

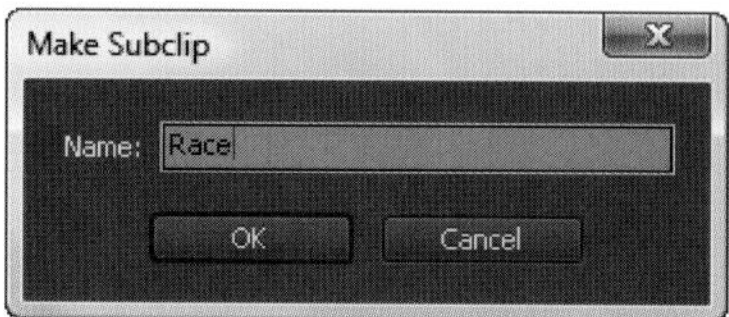

Now you will make a subclip from the Timeline rather than the Source Monitor.

6 Drag the master clip multicam_01.avi to the Timeline in the Video 1 track.

7 Drag the right edge of the multicam_01.avi clip out to its full length.

8 Using the Selection tool (↔), drag the left edge of the clip to the right until you see the bikers high-five each other in the Program Monitor. This will be the Hug section of the clip.

9 Drag the shortened clip from the Timeline to the Project panel while holding down Ctrl (Windows) or Command (Mac OS).

10 When you drop the clip in the Project panel, you will be prompted to give it a name. Call this subclip **Hug**.

Multicamera editing

The Adobe Premiere Pro multicam editing feature is a tremendous time-saver when you're editing footage captured from a shoot or event captured with multiple cameras. Here's how it works.

Creating the initial multicamera sequence

The first step is to create a multicamera sequence from your captured footage:

1 Open Lesson 09-6.prproj.

2 Double-click multicam_01.mov to open it in the Source Monitor.

3 Move the Source Monitor current-time indicator to where the bikers high-five after the race, which is at 00;00;16;16.

   You will use this as your clapper slate to set the sync point on all four clips.

4 Right-click (Windows) or Control-click (Mac OS) in the Source Monitor time ruler and choose Set Clip Marker > Next Available Numbered.

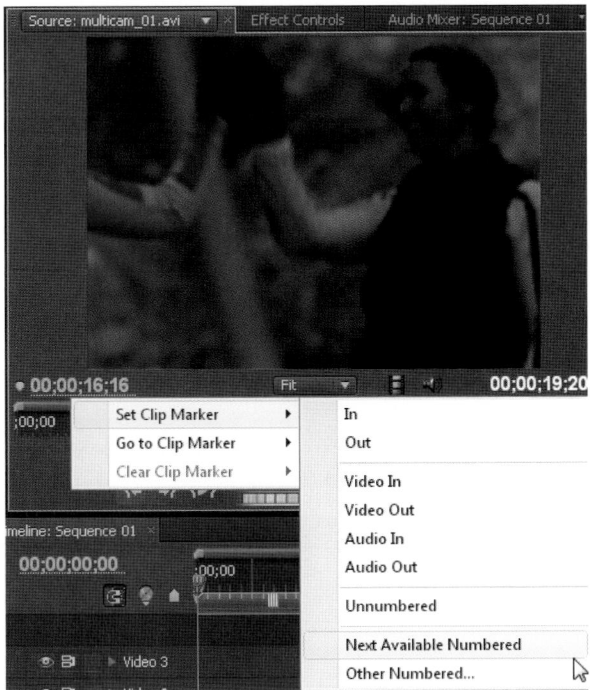

   This adds a little marker triangle behind the Source Monitor current-time indicator (you'll need to drag the current-time indicator out of the way to see that marker).

5 Check that the Video 1 track header is targeted (highlighted). If not, click it as needed to target the track, and move the current-time indicator to the beginning of the sequence.

Note: You can put markers on clips or sequences. You use markers for a variety of purposes, most frequently to mark DVD chapter points in sequences. In this case, you will have Adobe Premiere Pro move the four clips so the markers you place on their sync points all line up vertically.

Using track targeting

Adobe has enhanced track targeting in Adobe Premiere Pro by adding source track indicators. When dragging clips from the Source Monitor to the Timeline, you target the track by dragging the clip to it. If you are adding clips to the Timeline by using the Source Monitor Insert or Overlay button, it is necessary to target your selected tracks, or to tell Adobe Premiere Pro which track or tracks you want the clip to go to.

You must do two things to target the track or tracks you want to be the destination. Highlight (by selecting) the track or tracks you want to be the destination, and then target the track by dragging the source track indicator to the desired track. This may sound like a lot to do to target a single video or audio track, but this combination of tools can be very useful, such as when you have clips with multiple audio tracks attached.

Note: All four multicam clips were recorded at the same time, so using the high-five near the ends of the clips is a good way to sync them all up. Because they are at four different angles, you might have to look closely at some clips to see the exact frame where the bikers touch.

6 Click the Overlay button (Insert will work in this case too) in the Source Monitor to drop multicam_01.avi on the Video 1 track in the sequence.

7 Repeat the sync point location process, including adding the clip marker, for multicam_02.avi. I selected 00;00;16;29 as the sync point. Add the marker to this clip as you did on the first clip.

8 Click the Video 2 header to target that track, move the current-time indicator to the beginning of the sequence, and click the Overlay button in the Source Monitor.

Your sequence should look like the one shown here. Note the marker icons in the clips. You will line up those markers in a few steps.

9 Repeat this process for multicam_03.avi, marking it at 00;00;15;27, targeting the Video 3 track, and moving the Timeline current-time indicator to the beginning before clicking the Overlay button.

10 Repeat the marker setting and overlay process for multicam_04.avi, except there is no Video 4 track on the Timeline, so you can't target a track to overlay it to. Instead of moving the clip with the Overlay button, you can drag it to the Timeline. Click in the Source Monitor window, drag to the gray blank space above the Video 3 track, and drop it. Adobe Premiere Pro creates the Video 4 track.

Your sequence should look like the one shown here. Notice that the markers do not line up. That is OK; you'll take care of that next. If you had trouble marking your clips, open Lesson 09-7.prproj to start at this point.

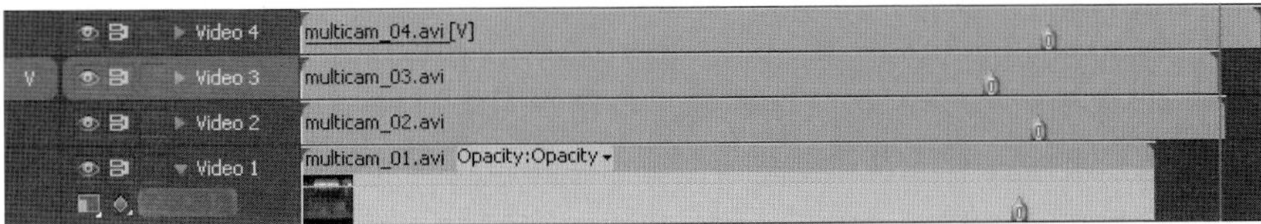

11 Marquee-select the four clips.

12 Check whether the Video 1 track is targeted (highlighted). If not, click its header to target it (it's not necessary, in this case, to target an audio track).

13 Choose Clip > Synchronize, select Numbered Clip Marker (Marker 0 is the only choice), and then click OK. The clips align to the marker on the clip in the Video 1 track.

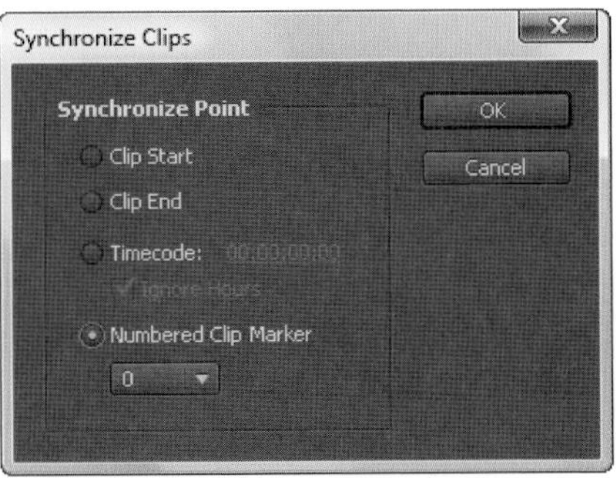

All the markers are lined up vertically. The beginning of the clips above the Video 1 track were trimmed because they all had more video before the sync point than the clip in the Video 1 track.

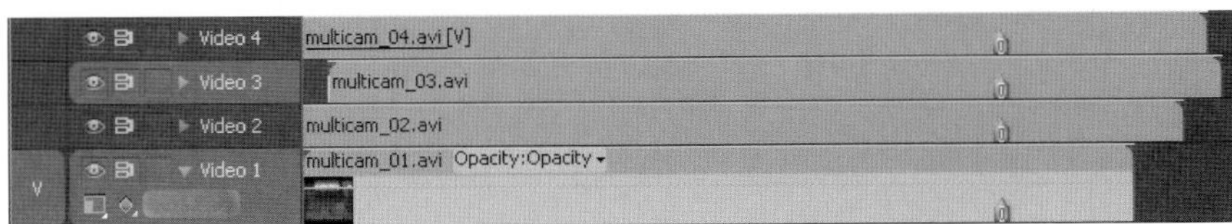

Switching multiple cameras

Now you will nest that synced and trimmed sequence in another sequence, switch on the multicamera function, and edit this four-camera shoot:

1 Choose File > New > Sequence and name it **Multi-cam**. Choose the Preset DV – NTSC Standard 48kHz to match your source media for this project.

2 Drag Sequence 01 from the Project panel to the beginning of the Video 1 track on the Multi-cam sequence. This is called nesting a sequence in a sequence.

3 Click the Video 1 track header to target it, click the nested sequence video clip to select it, and then choose Clip > Multi-Camera > Enable.

Note: The Multi-Camera > Enable command will be unavailable unless you have the video track selected.

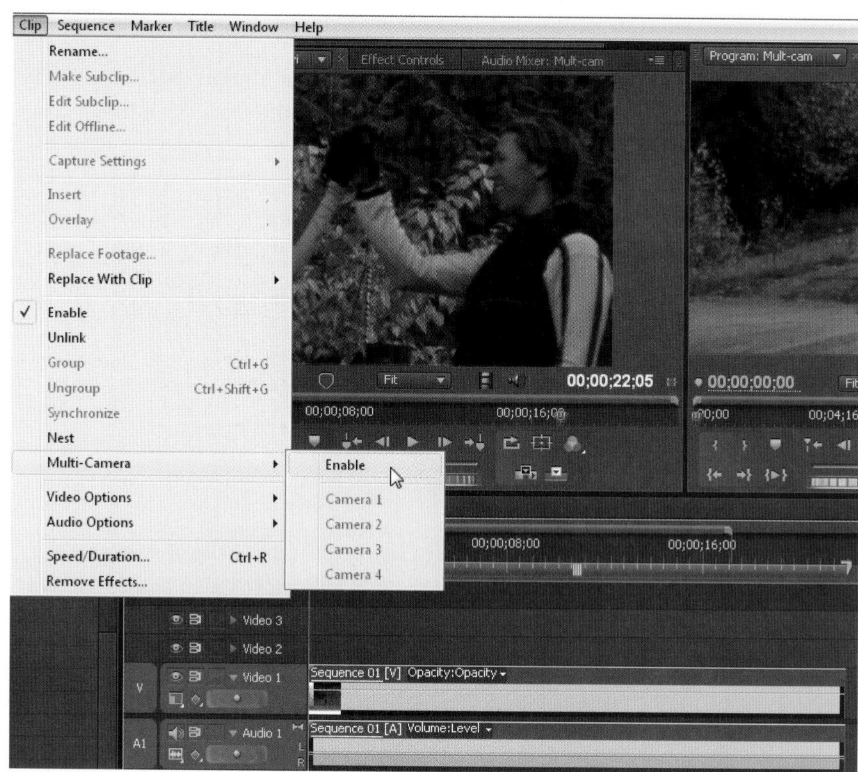

4 Choose Window > Multi-Camera Monitor.

The five-pane Multi-Camera Monitor opens.

5 Click the Play button and watch this video to get a feel for when to make your edits.

6 Move the current-time indicator to the beginning of the Timeline, click Play, and start clicking any of the four screens on the left side to switch among those cameras.

A red box appears around the selected camera each time you make an edit.

7 Use the playback controls to review your edited sequence.

Note that at each edit point, a yellow box appears on that camera shot.

8 Close the Multi-Camera Monitor. You can always return to it by selecting it from the Program Monitor panel menu.

9 Take a look at the sequence in the Timeline.

Note: After making your edits, you can always change them in the Multi-Camera Monitor or on the Timeline.

Note: You can also press the number keys 1–4 to switch among the four cameras.

As shown here, the sequence now has multiple cut edits. Each clip's label starts with [MC#]. The number represents the video track used for that edit.

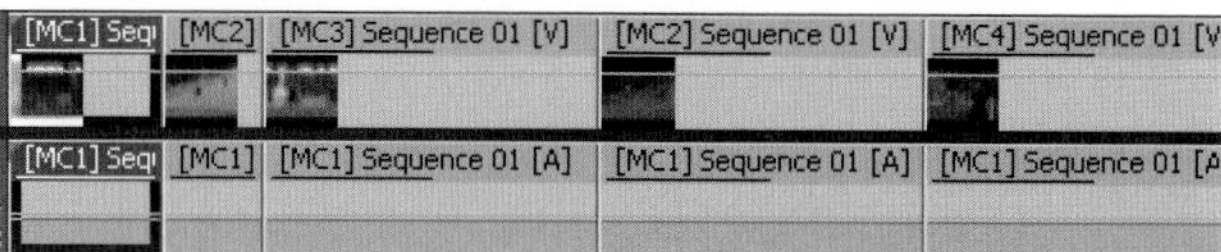

Finalizing multicamera editing

To change an edit in the Multi-Camera Monitor, do the following:

1 Open the Multi-Camera Monitor by choosing Window > Multi-Camera Monitor.

2 Click the Go To Previous (or Next) Edit Point buttons, or use the Page Up and Page Down keys to move to an edit.

3 Click a different camera to change that edit.

Changing an edit in the Timeline

To change a multicamera edit in the Timeline, do the following:

1 Right-click (Windows) or Control-click (Mac OS) the clip you want to change.

2 Choose Multi-Camera from the context menu and click the camera number.

Note: Open Lesson 09-8.prproj and play the Timeline if you want to see how we edited the multicam sequence.

Multicam tips

Here are a few helpful tips on multicam editing in Adobe Premiere Pro:

- You can use any of the Timeline editing tools to change the edit points of a multicam sequence.
- You can replay the multicam sequence with the Multi-Camera Monitor from any point to re-edit the project.
- You can switch back to the sequence where the original clip is and apply effects or color correction (you'll learn about color correction in Lesson 17), and the effect will ripple to the nested multicam sequence.

Note: This example of multicam footage did not include any audio.

- If you don't have a good visual clue in the video to sync multiple clips, look for a clap or loud noise in the audio track. It is often easier to sync video by looking for a common spike in the audio waveform.

Review questions

1 What's the basic difference between a slide edit and a slip edit?

2 What's going on when you use the Rolling Edit, Slip, or Slide tool and the clip frames stop moving in the Program Monitor and you can't move the edit point any further?

3 What is the difference between the Replace Clip feature and the Replace Footage feature?

4 What will happen to a subclip if you delete the master clip media from your hard drive?

5 Describe four ways to set sync points for multicamera clips.

Review answers

1 You *slide* a clip over adjacent clips, retaining the selected clip's original In and Out points. You *slip* a clip under adjacent clips, changing the selected clip's In and Out points.

2 You've reached the end of the line—the beginning or end of the original clip. There are no additional head or tail frames to enable you to move the edit any further.

3 Replace Clip replaces a single targeted clip on the Timeline with a new clip from the Project panel. Replace Footage replaces a clip in the Project panel with a new source clip. Any instance of the clip in any sequence in the project is replaced. In both cases, the effects of the replaced clip are maintained.

4 The subclip will go offline. Subclips do not copy the physical media of the master clip; they are references to it.

5 The four ways are clip start, clip end, timecode, and markers.

10 ADDING VIDEO EFFECTS

Topics covered in this lesson

- Sampling some basic video effects
- Applying effects to multiple clips
- Using keyframing effects
- Adding keyframe interpolation and velocity
- Applying lighting effects
- Creating custom presets

This lesson will take approximately 90 minutes.

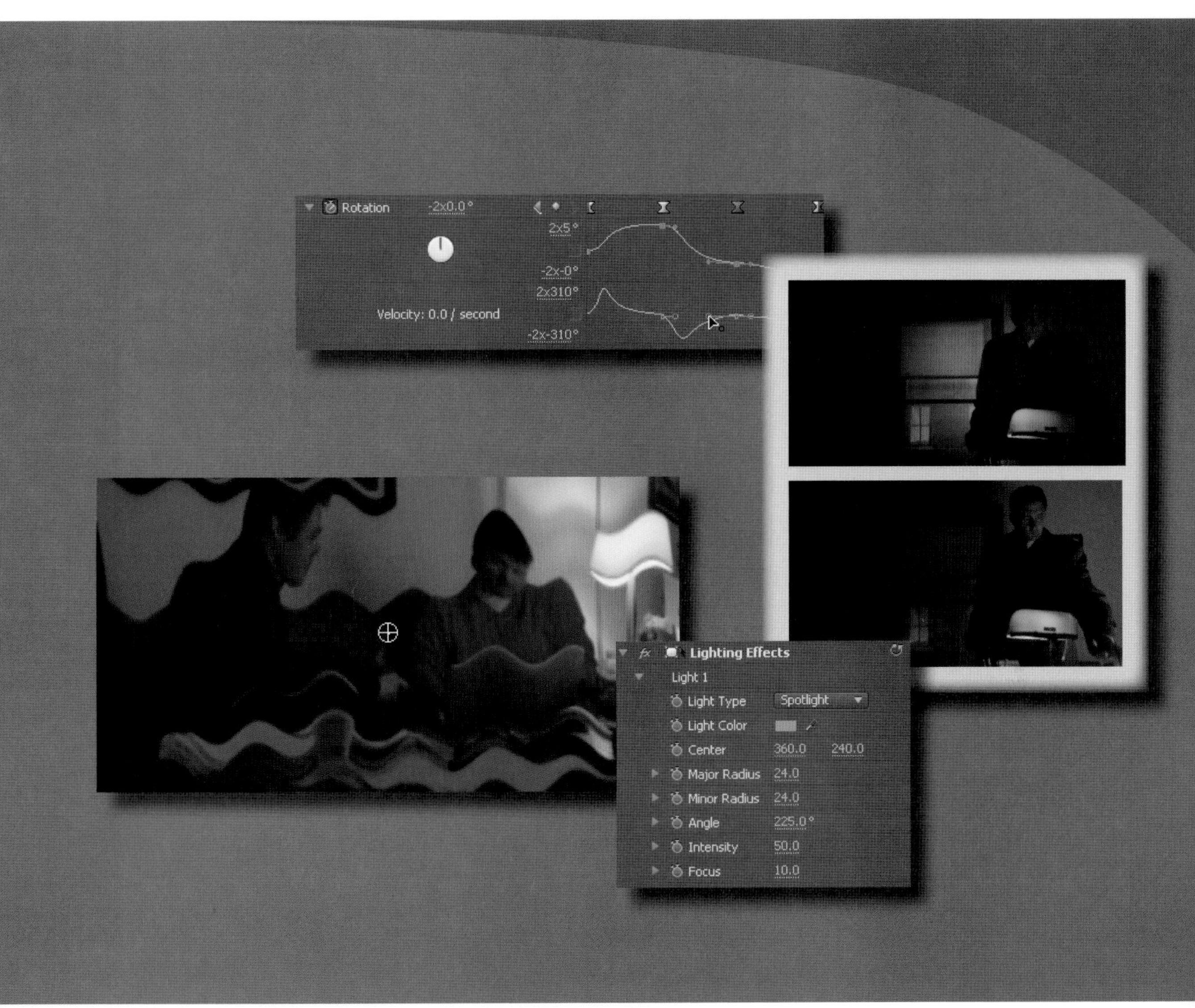

Adobe Premiere Pro CS4 features more than 140 video effects. Most effects come with an array of parameters, all of which you can animate—have them change over time—by using precise keyframe controls.

Getting started

Video effects let you add visual flair to your project or repair technical issues in your source footage. Video effects can alter the exposure or color of footage, distort images, or add artistic style. You can also use effects to rotate and animate a clip or adjust its size and position within the frame.

Adding video effects is easy: You can drag an effect to a clip, or you can select the clip and drag the effect to the Effect Controls panel. You can combine as many effects as you want on a single clip, which can produce surprising results. Moreover, you can use a nested sequence to add the same effects to a collection of clips.

Virtually all the video effect parameters are accessible within the Effect Controls panel, making it easy to set the behaviors and the intensity of those effects. You can add keyframes independently to every attribute listed in the Effect Controls panel to make those behaviors change over time. In addition, you can use Bezier curves to adjust the velocity and acceleration of those changes.

We don't have the space in this lesson to explain the more than 140 video effects included with Adobe Premiere Pro. Instead, you will look at a representative sample of what's available and learn how to use the various types of parameters you'll encounter. To really get a feel for the possibilities of Adobe Premiere Pro, you'll need to do some experimenting.

Sampling some basic video effects

In this lesson you will work with several effects, each offering something new in terms of its parameters or settings. Let's begin by creating a custom bin for your most frequently used effects:

1 Start Adobe Premiere Pro, open Lesson 10-1.prproj, and choose Window > Workspace > Effects to switch to the Effects workspace.

2 If necessary, click the Effects tab next to the Project panel to make it visible.

3 Open the Video Effects folder.

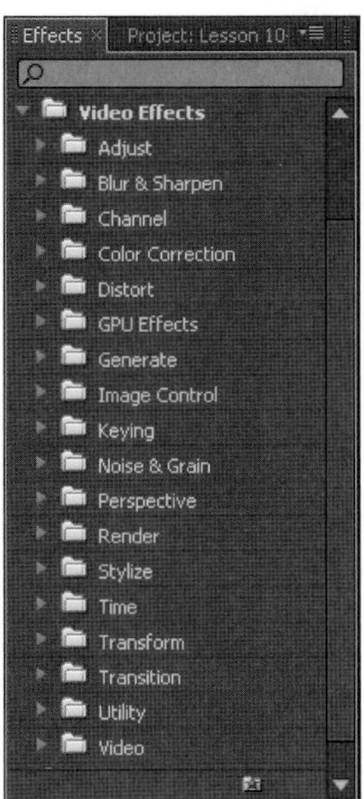

Note: You'll see many Video Effects categories. Some effects are difficult to categorize and could reside in multiple categories or in categories by themselves, but this taxonomy works reasonably well.

4 Click the Effects panel menu and choose New Custom Bin.

The New Custom bin/folder appears in the Effects panel below Video Transitions.

5 Highlight the bin and change its name to something like My Favorite Effects.

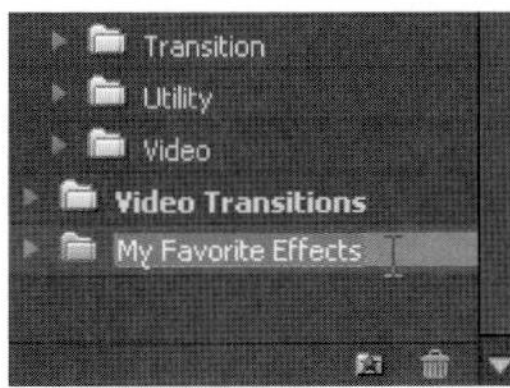

6 Open any Video Effects folder and drag a few effects into your custom bin.

Note: The effects remain in their original folder and also appear in yours. You can use custom folders to build effect categories that match your work style.

7 Choose Video Effects > Image Control > Black & White and drag the Black & White video effect to the writers 1.avi clip on the Timeline.

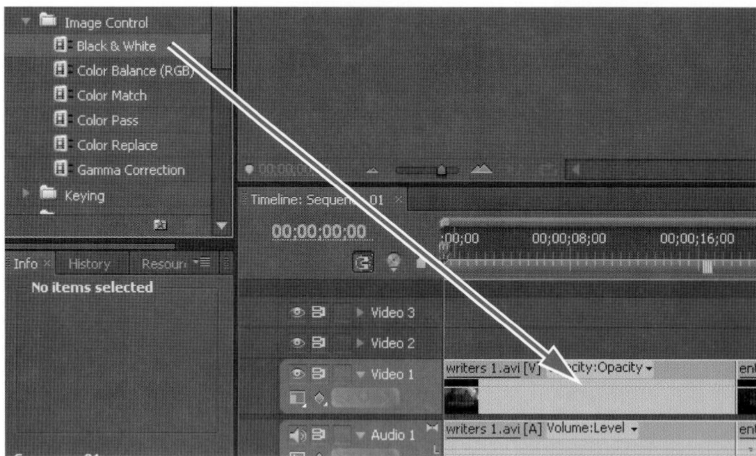

That immediately converts your full-color footage to black-and-white—or, more accurately, *grayscale*. It also puts that effect in the Effect Controls panel.

Note: The Effect Controls panel contains three other effects: Motion, Opacity, and Time Remapping. These are fixed effects. Adobe Premiere Pro automatically makes them available for all video clips. If the clip has audio, you will also see the Volume fixed effect.

8 If necessary, click the Effect Controls tab to open it. Toggle the Black & White effect off and on by using the button in the Effect Controls panel.

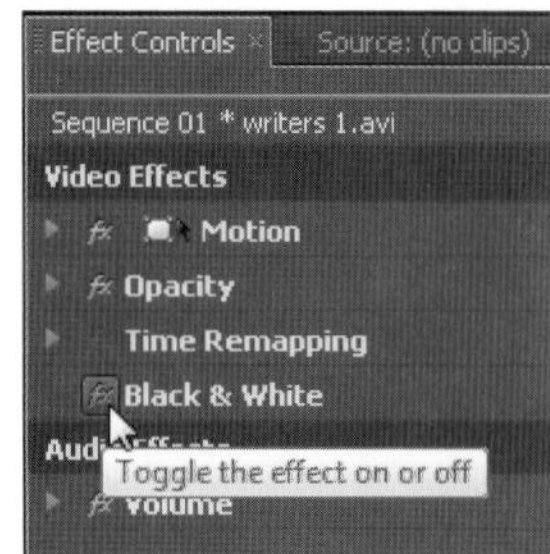

Toggling an effect on and off is a good way to see how an effect works with other effects. This toggle switch is the only parameter available with the Black & White effect. The effect is either on or off.

Resolve jarring shifts to grayscale

Moving between full-color and black-and-white clips can be jarring. So, here's a fix: Use a cross-dissolve between clips or within the grayscale clip. To put one within the clip in this lesson, select the Razor Edit tool (C), cut the clip in two places, drag the Cross Dissolve transition to those edit points, select the first and third clip segments in turn, and switch off the Black & White effect on both. Now your sequence shifts gradually from color to black-and-white and back to color. Undo those edits by clicking the History tab and clicking Apply Filter.

9 Check that the clip is selected so that its parameters are displayed in the Effect Controls panel, click Black & White to select it, and then press the Delete key.

10 Choose Video Effects > Blur & Sharpen > Directional Blur, and drag the Directional Blur effect to the Effect Controls panel.

This is the other way to apply a video effect: Select the clip in the Timeline to display it in the Effect Controls panel, and drag the effect to the Effect Controls panel.

Finding effects

With so many video effects folders, it's sometimes tricky to locate the effect you want. If you know part or all of an effect's name, start typing it in the Contains text box at the top of the Effects panel. Adobe Premiere Pro immediately displays all effects and transitions that contain that letter combination, narrowing the search as you type.

11 In the Effect Controls panel, expand the Directional Blur effect's filter and note there are options the Black & White effect did not have: Direction, Blur Length, and a stopwatch next to each option (the latter is to activate keyframing, which we will cover later in this lesson).

12 Set Direction to 90 degrees and Blur Length to 4 to simulate the scene being filmed with a slow shutter speed.

Note: The specific options available in each effect vary; however, they all operate in a similar manner.

13 Expand the Blur Length option and move the slider in the Effect Controls panel.

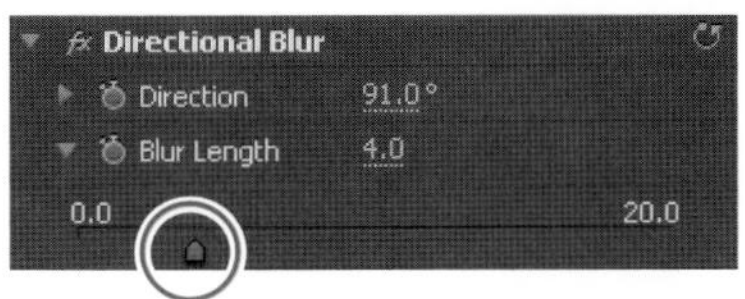

As you change that setting, it shows up in real time in the Program Monitor.

14 Open the Effect Controls panel menu and choose Remove Effects. Choose OK in the dialog box that pops up asking which effects you want to remove. You want to remove them all.

This is an easy way to start fresh.

15 Choose Video Effects > Distort and select the Spherize effect. Drag it to the Effect Controls panel and click its disclosure triangles to display its parameters.

Like the Motion fixed effect above it in the Effect Controls panel, Spherize has a Transform button that lets you directly control its location in the Program Monitor.

16 Move the Radius slider to about 170 so you can see the effect in the Program Monitor.

17 Click the word Spherize (the name of the effect) in the Effect Controls panel to switch on its Transform control crosshair in the Program Monitor, and drag the effect around in that screen.

● **Note:** Wave Warp has three menus. These are specific effect conditions that do not have numeric values associated with them, but even these can be keyframes; that is, you can switch from one discrete condition to another at any time in the clip's duration.

18 Delete Spherize and choose Video Effects > Distort >Wave Warp. Drag the Wave Warp effect to the Effect Controls panel and click its six disclosure triangles to display its eight parameters.

19 Make various selections from each of the three menus and then adjust some of the other parameters.

20 Play this clip.

This is one of the animated effects you'll find in Adobe Premiere Pro. Although virtually all Adobe Premiere Pro video effects let you animate them over time with keyframes, Wave Warp and a few others have built-in animations that operate independently of keyframes.

21 Reset the Wave Warp effect to its starting point by clicking the Reset button in its upper-right corner.

Applying effects to multiple clips

In this exercise, you will apply the same effect to two clips in the Timeline at the same time. Although you'll be using only two clips, you can use the technique to apply the same effect or effects to as many clips as you can select.

1 Remove any effects you have been testing from both clips on the Timeline.

2 Select both clips on the Timeline by holding down the Shift key and clicking each one. Another method of selecting clips is by dragging around them.

3 Choose Video Effects > Generate and drag the Lens Flare effect to either clip. The effect is applied to both selected clips.

Other ways to apply effects

You can also select an effect from the Effect Controls panel, choose Edit > Copy, select the Effects Controls panel of a destination clip, and choose Edit > Paste.

To copy all effects on one clip to paste to another clip, select the clip, choose Edit > Copy, select the destination clip, and choose Edit > Paste Attributes.

Adding keyframing effects

You can turn almost all parameters for all video effects into keyframes. That is, you can change the effect's behavior over time in myriad ways. For example, you can have an effect gradually change out of focus, change color, warp into a fun-house mirror, or lengthen its shadow.

1 Select the first clip on the Timeline.

2 Expand the display of the Effect Controls panel until its view is wide enough for the Show/Hide Timeline View button to become active, and click that button to open the effect's Timeline.

> **Tip:** Depending on your screen size, you might want to put the Effect Controls panel into a floating window.

3 Delete any effects on the clips, then choose Presets > Solarizes > Solarize In and drag the Solarize In preset to the Effect Controls panel.

4 Play the clip to see how this preset works. The clip starts at the maximum Solarize threshold value and reduces to 0 at the 1-second point.

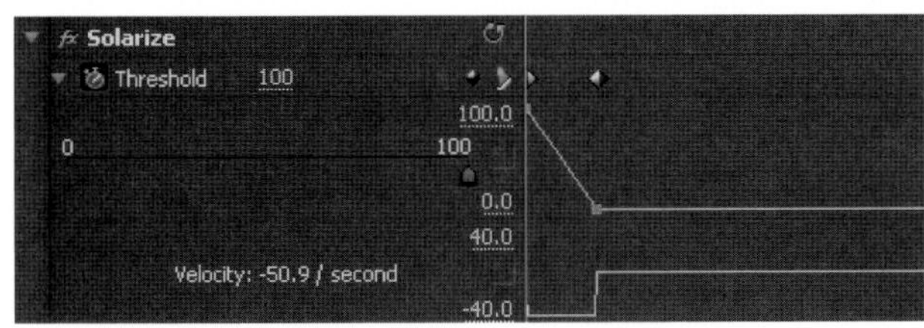

5 Drag the effect's second keyframe to the right and play the clip again.

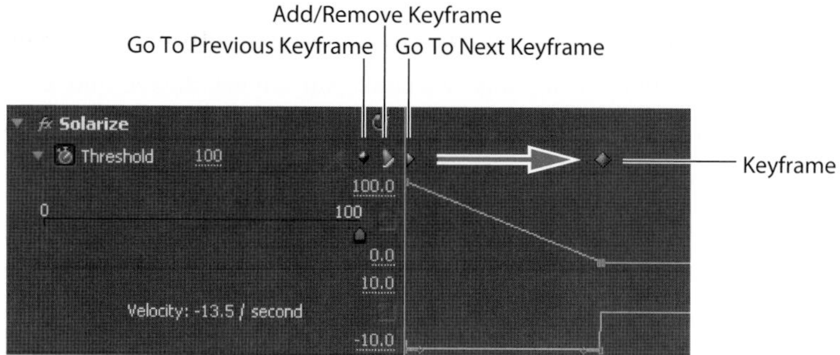

It takes longer for the Solarize effect to resolve to the normal image. Keyframes are not permanently fixed; you can change a keyframe's position without changing its value.

6 Delete the Solarize effect. Choose Video Effects > Stylize, select the Replicate effect, drag it to the Effect Controls panel, and click its single disclosure triangle to display its parameter.

7 With the Effect Controls panel active, press the Home or Page Up key to position the current-time indicator at the beginning of the clip.

8 Click the Toggle animation button, shown here.

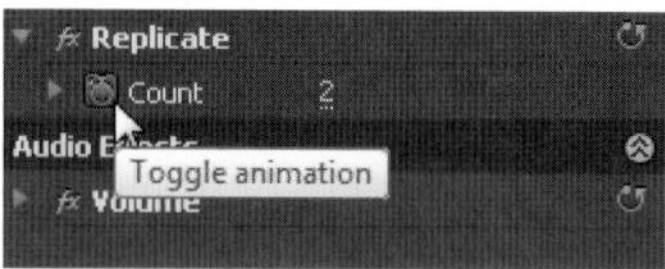

Clicking this button does three things:

- Activates keyframing for the Replicate effect's Count parameter
- Adds a keyframe at the current-time indicator location and gives it Replicate's default starting value of 2 (a 2x2 grid of replicated clips)
- Displays two thin black lines in the Effect Controls Timeline: the Value graph and the Velocity graph

Note: Changing the effect's Count parameter automatically adds another keyframe at the current-time indicator's position in the Effect Controls Timeline; changing a parameter at a location without a keyframe automatically adds a new keyframe.

9 Drag the current-time indicator to about the 1-second point. Locate the 1-second point by looking in the Program Monitor or the Timeline time ruler. It's generally not easy to see an exact time in the Effect Controls Timeline unless you really widen its viewing area.

10 Change the Replicate effect's Count parameter to 4.

11 Drag the current-time indicator to about the 3-second point.

12 Click the Add/Remove Keyframe button (between the two keyframe navigation buttons). Adobe Premiere Pro adds a keyframe with the same value as the previous keyframe. In this way, the effect will not change from the 1-second to the 3-second position.

13 Press Page Down and then press the left arrow key to go to the end of the clip. The last frame of the clip appears.

Note: Pressing Page Down takes you to the frame following the last frame in a selected clip. That is by design. You can use the keyboard shortcut Page Down to go to the start of the next clip, not the final frame of the current clip.

14 Change the Count value to 10.

Your Effect Controls panel should look like the one shown here.

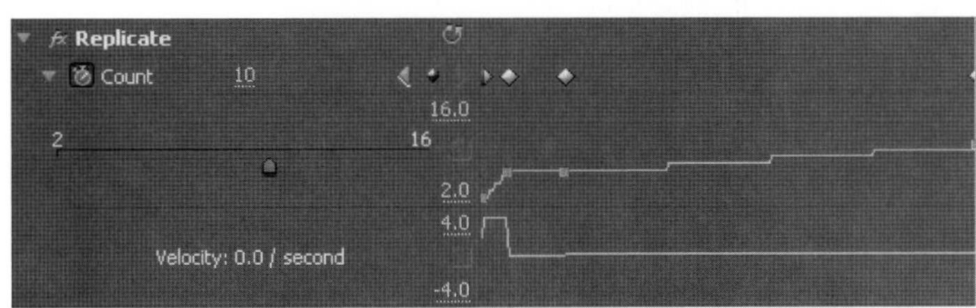

15 Play the clip, and note how the effect builds to a 6x6 grid, holds for 2 seconds, and then changes to a 16x16 grid at the end.

Now you'll use two methods to change two keyframe values.

16 Click the Go To Previous Keyframe button twice to move to the second keyframe.

17 Use the slider to change the Count value to 2. That's one simple way to change a keyframe's value.

18 Click the Go To Next Keyframe button to move to the third (of fourth) keyframe.

19 Hover the pointer over the corresponding keyframe on the Value graph (shown here). When it changes to the Selection tool, drag the keyframe as high as it will go to change its value to 16.

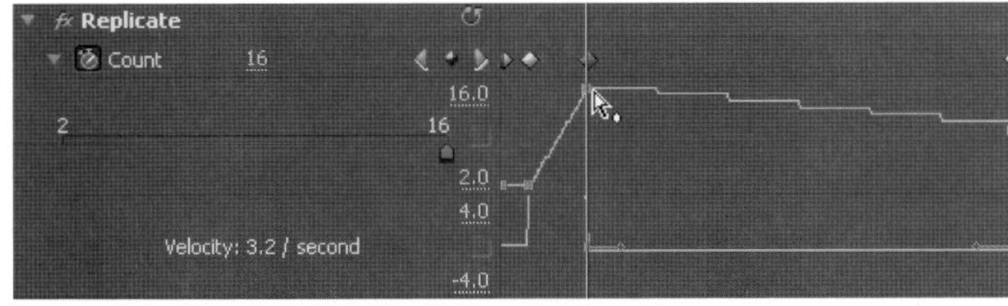

This is the other way to change a keyframe's value.

Note: If you don't move the current-time indicator to the clip you're applying an effect to, you won't see that clip or its effect in the Program Monitor. Selecting a clip does not move the current-time indicator to that clip.

20 Drag the title called The Writers from the Project panel to the track above the first video clip. Stretch the title clip to be the same length as the video clip beneath it.

21 Position the current-time indicator over the clip The Writers and select it to display its parameters in the Effect Controls panel.

22 Select the Magnify effect from the Video Effects > Distort menu and drag it to the title clip or to the Effect Controls panel.

23 Set a keyframe at the beginning of the clip, with the Center value set to 10, 240.

24 Set a keyframe near the middle of the clip, with the Center value set to 740, 240.

● **Note:** Make sure to activate keyframing in the Center option by clicking the Toggle animation button.

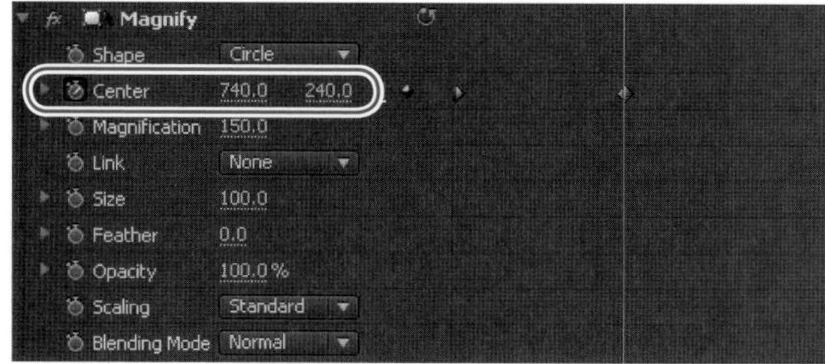

● **Note:** Effects are great ways to animate or move a graphic or text over a video clip.

25 Play this clip.

Extra credit: combining effects

Open Lesson 10-2.prproj to see multiple keyframed effects added to the title clip The Writers. Gaussian Blur, Lens Flare, and Basic 3D effects are applied to the same title clip so you can deconstruct the file. Each effect is keyframed over time.

- Gaussian Blur provides an interesting entrance and exit for the title.
- Lens Flare moves across the letters, giving the illusion of light and movement.
- Basic 3D gives the title a swivel movement that enhances the Lens Flare effect.

See whether you can re-create the effect from scratch.

Creating an effect preset

If you plan to reuse an effect with keyframes, save it as a preset. To do that, set your keyframes, parameters, and interpolation controls (these will be covered later); click the effect name in the Effect Controls panel; open the panel menu; choose Save Preset; give the preset a name; note whether to scale it to the clip length or anchor it to the clip In or Out point; and then click OK. It'll show up in the Presets folder.

Order counts

Clip-based (nonfixed) video effects work from bottom to top in the Effect Controls panel, with the most recently applied effect appearing at the bottom of the effect list. For example, if you apply the Tint effect and then apply Black & White, the clip will appear as grayscale. Black & White trumps Tint because it appears below Tint in the Effect Controls panel effect list. If you apply Black & White first and then apply Tint, the clip will have the color you select in the Tint effect. Opacity and Motion, which are fixed effects, are always the final two effects applied—even when, in this case, you used a Motion preset and applied it first. If you want Motion to be applied in a different order, then use a clip-based motion effect, such as Basic 3D. You can drag effects up and down within the Effect Controls panel to change their order.

Adding keyframe interpolation and velocity

Keyframe interpolation changes the behavior of an effect parameter as it moves toward or away from a keyframe. The default behavior you've seen so far is linear—in other words, you have a constant velocity between keyframes. What generally works better is something that mirrors your experience or exaggerates it, such as a gradual acceleration or deceleration, or super-fast changes.

Adobe Premiere Pro offers two ways to control those changes: keyframe interpolation and the Velocity graph. Keyframe interpolation is the easiest—basically two clicks—while tweaking the Velocity graph can become a full-time occupation. Getting a handle on this feature will take some time and practice on your part.

For this lesson, you'll use the Motion fixed effect. Its Position, Scale, and Rotation parameters all lend themselves to speed changes.

1 Open Lesson 10-3.prproj.

2 The title The Writers is over the writers 1.avi clip. Click the title clip to select it.

3 Stretch the Effect Controls panel as wide as you can without covering up other workspace elements you need to see. If you put it in a floating window, leave room to view the Program Monitor.

4 Open the Effect Controls panel's Timeline (click the Show/Hide Timeline View button).

   You will be adding four Rotation keyframes: the first frame, the last frame, and two more frames spaced in between.

5 Position the current-time indicator at the beginning of the clip, expand the Motion effect, and click the Rotation effect's Toggle animation button. This adds a keyframe at the beginning of the clip with the default parameter value of 0.

6 Drag the current-time indicator to the three other positions and click the Add/Remove Keyframe button in each spot.

Your Effect Controls panel should look like the one shown here.

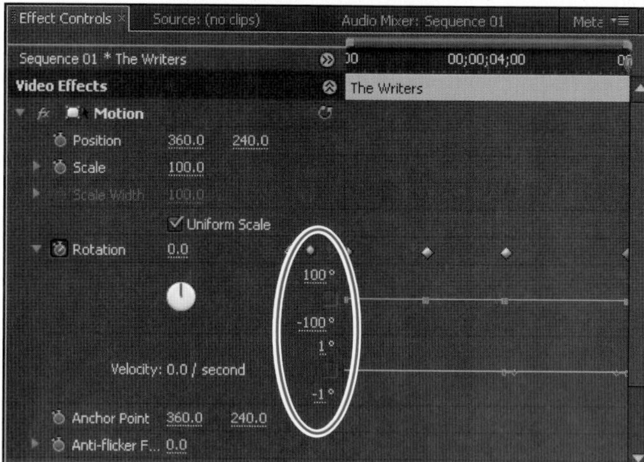

7 Look at the numbers highlighted in the previous figure. Expand the Rotation parameter if you haven't already.

- **100 and –100**: These are default values for the highest and lowest Rotation parameter settings. They will change to accommodate the actual high and low Rotation values once you change the keyframe settings.
- **1 and –1**: These are default relative velocity values. Since you have not changed any parameters, the velocity is a straight line with a value of 0.

8 Change the Rotation value for the second, third, and fourth keyframes by using three separate methods (navigate to the keyframes by using the Go To Next/Previous Keyframe buttons):

- **Second keyframe**: Click the Rotation value and type **2x** (two full clockwise rotations).
- **Third keyframe**: Drag the keyframe on the Value graph to –1x0.0 degrees.
- **Fourth keyframe**: Drag the Rotation wheel left until the value displayed is –2x0.0 degrees (it's difficult to get that exact figure, so it's OK if you end up at something like –2x0.0 degrees).

Once completed, your keyframes and graphs should look like the ones shown here. If the graph lines are clipped, click the "Toggle automatic range rescaling" button.

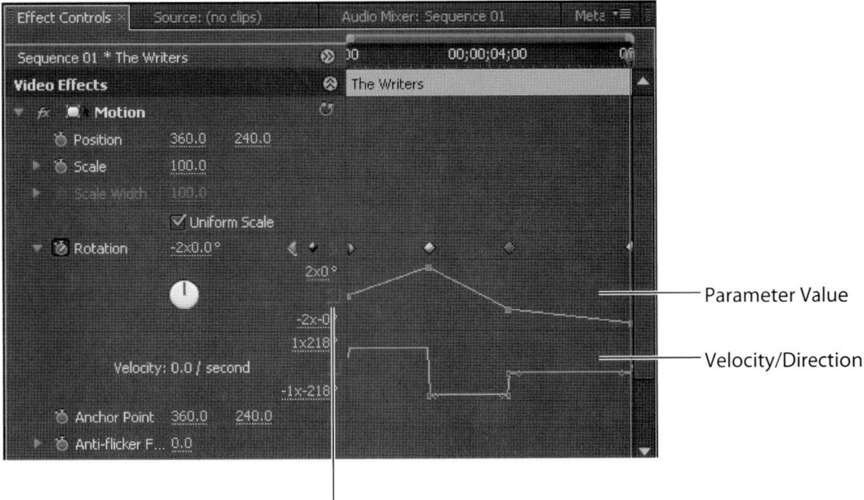

9 Drag the current-time indicator through the clip, and look at the Value and Velocity graphs and the numbers to the left of the graphs (shown in the previous figure). You should see the following:

- The top and bottom Value numbers have changed to 2x0 and –2x0 (two full rotations in both directions) to show the actual maximum and minimum parameter values. They remain unchanged as you move the current-time indicator.
- The Value graph shows the parameters' values at any given time.
- The top and bottom Velocity numbers on the left side of the graph indicate the spread of the parameters' velocity in degrees per second.
- The Velocity graph shows the velocity between keyframes. The sudden drops or jumps represent sudden changes in acceleration—*jerks,* in physics parlance. Points on the graph above the middle of the Velocity graph area represent positive (clockwise) speeds, and points below the center represent negative (counterclockwise) speeds. The farther the point or line is from the center, the greater the velocity (and you thought high school algebra was a waste of time).

10 Press Enter (Windows) or Return (Mac OS) to render the work area and play the clip.

The text spins clockwise twice, spins faster going counterclockwise three times, and then slows down for one last rotation.

11 Right-click (Windows) or Control-click (Mac OS) the first keyframe, and then choose Ease Out.

This does several things:

- The keyframe icon changes to an hourglass.
- The keyframe on the Value graph now has a Pen Tool handle, and the graph has a slight curve.
- The keyframe on the Velocity graph has a similar Pen Tool handle and a more obvious curve. That curve shows the velocity change over time—its acceleration.

12 Play that portion of the clip. The effect looks more realistic as the motion "eases."

13 Right-click (Windows) or Control-click (Mac OS) the next three keyframes, and apply (in this order) the Bezier, Auto Bezier, and Ease In interpolation methods.

Here's a rundown on the Adobe Premiere Pro keyframe interpolation methods:

- **Linear**: This method is the default behavior, which creates a uniform rate of change between keyframes.
- **Bezier**: This method lets you manually adjust the shape of the graph on either side of a keyframe. Beziers allow for sudden acceleration changes into or out of a keyframe.
- **Continuous Bezier**: This method creates a smooth rate of change through a keyframe. Unlike Bezier, if you adjust one handle, the handle on the other side of the keyframe moves in a complementary fashion to ensure a smooth transition through the keyframe.
- **Auto Bezier**: This method creates a smooth rate of change through a keyframe even if you change the keyframe parameter value. If you choose to manually adjust its handles, it changes to a Continuous Bezier point, retaining the smooth transition through the keyframe.
- **Hold**: This method changes a property value without a gradual transition (sudden effect change). The graph following a keyframe with the Hold interpolation applied appears as a horizontal straight line.
- **Ease In**: This method slows down the value changes entering a keyframe.
- **Ease Out**: This method gradually accelerates the value changes leaving a keyframe.

Your Effect Controls Timeline should look like the one shown here (the Value and Velocity graph-limit numbers might differ, depending on the size of your Effect Controls panel).

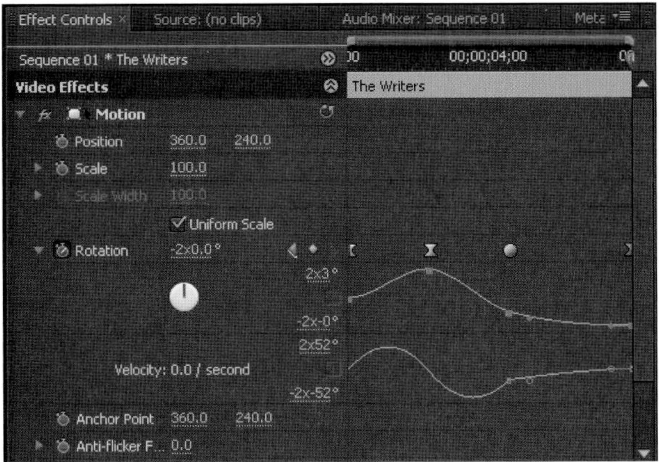

Note: By adding these smooth curves, the parameter values change over the course of the effect such that they sometimes might be greater than the highest keyframe parameter value or less than the lowest keyframe parameter you set.

14 Play the entire clip and marvel (really) at how slick it looks.

Simply by adding keyframe interpolation, you've made your Motion effect look much more realistic.

15 Select the second keyframe—the Bezier hourglass—to activate it.

Pen Tool handles appear on the Value and Velocity graph keyframes as well as on the two adjacent sets of keyframes. That's because changing one keyframe's interpolation handles can change the behavior of the keyframes next to it.

16 Drag the handle on the Velocity graph keyframe (shown here).

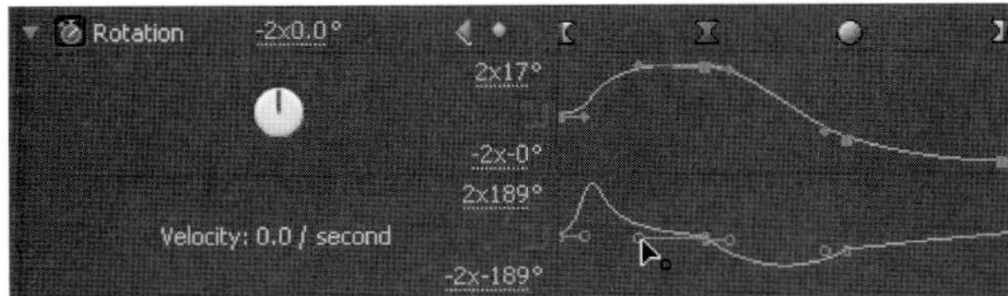

That creates a steep velocity curve, meaning the title will accelerate quickly, then decelerate quickly, but will still spin only twice between the first and second keyframes. You changed the velocity without changing the value.

16 Select the third keyframe—the Auto Bezier circle icon—to activate it.

17 Drag the handle and note that the circular keyframe icon immediately switches to an hourglass, because manually adjusting an Auto Bezier keyframe makes it a Continuous Bezier keyframe.

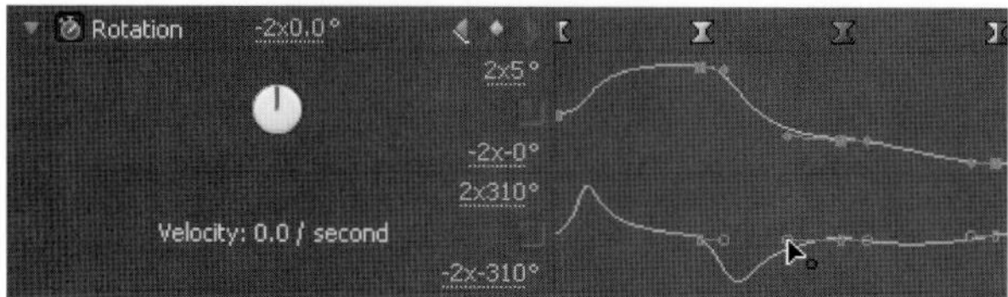

● **Note:** If you add another keyframe, it will have keyframe interpolation already applied to it. When you first add keyframes, you can grab their Value and Velocity graph handles and adjust the curves manually. Making any such adjustment will change the keyframe icon to the Bezier keyframe interpolation hourglass.

One additional velocity/interpolation issue

When working with position-related parameters, the context menu for a keyframe will offer two types of interpolation options: Spatial Interpolation (related to location) and Temporal Interpolation (related to time). You can make spatial adjustments in the Program Monitor as well as the Effect Controls panel. You can make temporal adjustments on the clip in the Timeline and in the Effect Controls panel.

Lesson 11 covers these Motion-related topics.

Adding lighting effects

This exercise combines hands-on, step-by-step tasks with experimentation. The purpose is to introduce you to a couple more advanced lighting effects and to encourage you to explore further.

1 Choose Help > Adobe Premiere Pro Help.

2 Type **Gallery of effects** in the Search field and press Enter.

   You will see examples of about a third of the video effects that come with Adobe Premiere Pro.

● **Note:** The other headings under Effect Reference match bin names in the Effects panel.

3 Search Premiere Pro Help for Lighting effect.

   This gives you an explanation of each parameter—25 in all!—in the Lighting effect. Every Adobe Premiere Pro video and audio effect has such a listing in Premiere Pro Help. This example illustrates how complete and useful Premiere Pro Help is.

4 Quit Help, return to the Adobe Premiere Pro workspace, and open Lesson 10-4.prproj.

5 Choose Video Effects > Adjust, select Lighting Effects, and drag it to the clip in the Video 1 track.

6 Expand the Lighting Effects, and also expand Light 1. You will leave off Lights 2 through 4.

7 Use the Color Picker under Light 1 to choose a light blue color from the desk light in the Program Monitor.

8 Set the Major Radius and Minor Radius values to 24. Set the Intensity value to 50 and the Focus value to 10.

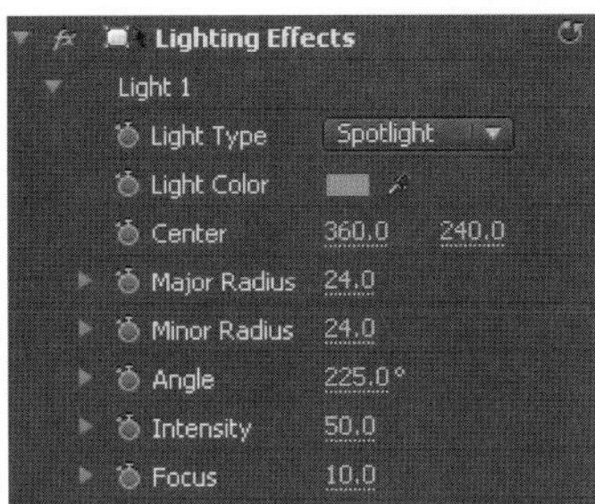

9 Toggle this effect on and off to see the significant difference it makes on the mood of the scene.

Lighting effects on

Lighting effects off

10 Remove all effects from the video clip and move the current-time indicator to the beginning of the clip.

11 Drag the Leave Color effect from the Color Correction folder to the video clip.

12 Use the eyedropper tool next to the Color To Leave field to sample the blue from the desk lamp.

13 Set the Amount to Decolor slider to 100 percent. This will decolor everything except the color you chose with the eyedropper.

14 Set the Tolerance slider to about 35 percent.

15 Render and play the clip to see the effect. The whole scene should be black-and-white, with the exception of the blue desk lamp.

Creating custom presets

Adobe Premiere Pro allows you to save your favorite effect settings to your own custom preset, so you don't have to re-create the settings every time. A preset may contain a single effect or multiple effects. Presets can be exported so you can share them with other editors, and of course you can import presets that have been exported from Adobe Premiere Pro.

In this exercise, you'll create a combination of effects and then save them as a custom preset:

1 Open Lesson 10-5.prproj.

2 Play the Timeline, and note that the title The Office is just a static title. You will animate it like you were challenged to try on your own earlier in the lesson as extra credit.

3 Drag the Basic 3D filter to the title clip. Set a keyframe at the beginning of the clip with Swivel set to –25. Set an end keyframe with Swivel set to 25.

4 Drag the Lens Flare filter to the title clip. Set a keyframe at the beginning of the clip with Flare Center set to 20, 192. Set an end keyframe with Flare Center set to 700, 192.

5 Drag the Gaussian Blur filter to the title clip The Office. Set a keyframe at the beginning of the clip with Blurriness set to 300. Set a second keyframe about 1 second in with Blurriness set to 0. Set a third keyframe about 1 second from the end with Blurriness set to 0, and finally set the end keyframe with Blurriness set to 700.

6 Play the clip. The title swivels slightly, the lens flare travels across the letters, and the whole title blurs in and out of existence. If you have problems setting up these filters, click the Finished sequence to see the completed effect.

Now that the combination of effects is working just how you want it to, you will save the combination of three effects as a single custom preset so you can use it again later.

7 Select the title clip so the three effects are visible in the Effect Controls panel. Collapse the three effects down so each occupies only one line.

8 Hold down the Ctrl key and click each of the three effects (Basic 3D, Lens Flare, Gaussian Blur) to select them all.

9 In the Effect Controls panel menu, choose Save Preset.

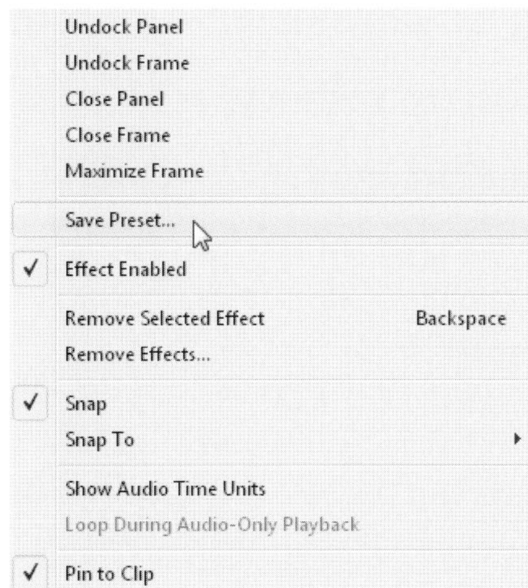

10 Name the preset and click OK.

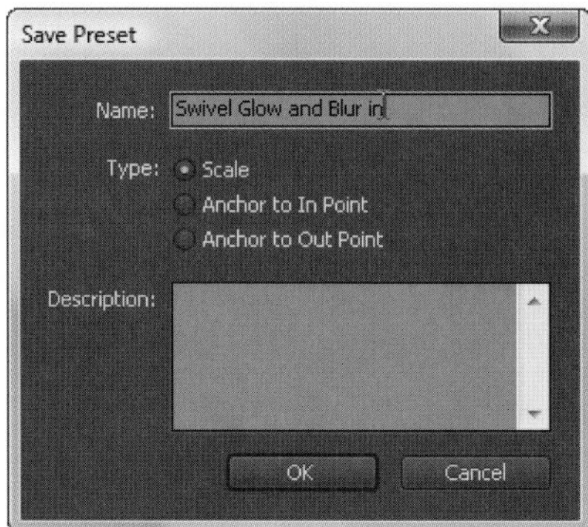

The preset appears in your Custom Preset folder.

11 Try dragging it to other titles to confirm that it works.

Review questions

1. What are the two ways to apply an effect to a clip?
2. List three ways to add a keyframe.
3. How do you make an effect start within a clip, rather than at the beginning?
4. Dragging an effect to a clip turns on its parameters in the Effect Controls panel, but you don't see the effect in the Program Monitor. Why not?
5. Describe how you can drag one effect to multiple clips.
6. Describe how to save multiple effects to a custom preset.

Review answers

1. Drag the effect to the clip, or select the clip and drag the effect to the Effect Controls panel.
2. Move the current-time indicator in the Effect Controls panel to where you want a keyframe, and activate keyframing by clicking the Toggle animation button; move the current-time indicator and click the Add/Remove Keyframe button; and with keyframing activated, move the current-time indicator to a position and change a parameter.
3. One of two ways, depending on the effect. Some effects, such as Fast Blur, have a 0 setting where they do not change the clip's appearance. In that case, add a keyframe where you want the effect to start, and then set it to 0. Other effects are always "on" to some degree. In those cases, use the Razor Edit tool to cut the clip where you want the effect to start, and then apply the effect to the segment on the right.
4. You need to move the Timeline current-time indicator to the selected clip to see it in the Program Monitor. Simply selecting a clip does not move the current-time indicator to that clip.
5. Select multiple clips on the Timeline by Shift-selecting or dragging a selection around them, and then drag the effect to the group of selected clips.
6. Ctrl-click (Windows) or Command-click (Mac OS) multiple effects in the Effect Controls panel, and then choose the Save Preset command from the menu that appears.

11 PUTTING CLIPS IN MOTION

Topics covered in this lesson

- Applying the Motion effect to clips
- Changing clip size and adding rotation
- Working with keyframe interpolation
- Creating a picture-in-picture (PIP) effect
- Enhancing motion with shadows and beveled edges
- Using other motion effects such as Transform and Basic 3D

This lesson will take approximately 50 minutes.

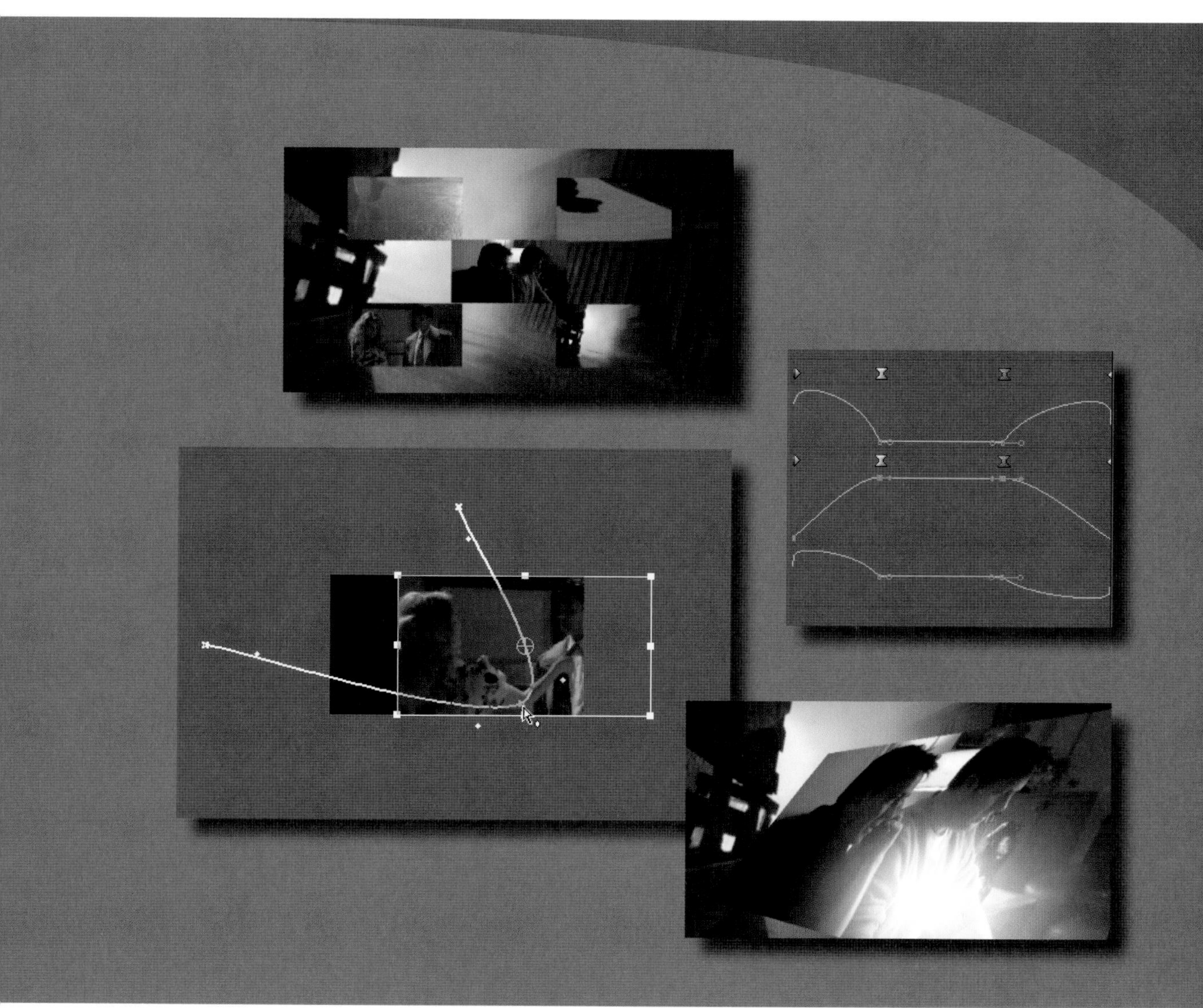

The Motion fixed effect adds drama to static images and lets you change image sizes, fly them anywhere on (and off) the screen, and rotate them. You can further enhance motion characteristics by adding drop shadows and frames and building pictures-in-picture.

Getting started

You've seen the Motion effect in action already in this book. You used its Rotation feature to test keyframe interpolation, and you saw how it can zoom and pan still images.

As you watch TV advertisements, you're bound to see videos with clips flying over other images or clips that rotate onscreen—starting as small dots and expanding to full-screen size. You can create those effects by using the Motion fixed effect or several clip-based effects with Motion settings.

You use the Motion effect to position, rotate, or scale a clip within the video frame. You can make those adjustments directly in the Program Monitor by dragging to change its position, or you can drag or rotate its handles to change its size, shape, or orientation.

You can also adjust Motion parameters in the Effect Controls panel and animate clips by using keyframes and Bezier controls.

Applying the Motion effect to clips

You adjust Motion effect parameters in the Program Monitor and the Effect Controls panel:

1 Open Lesson 11-1.prproj.

2 Choose Windows > Workspace > Effects to switch to the Effects workspace.

3 Open the View Zoom Level menu in the Program Monitor and change the zoom level to 25%.

This helps you see and work with the Motion effect's bounding box.

4 Expand the Program Monitor frame (if necessary) so there are no scroll bars in the screen.

Your Program Monitor should look like the previous figure.

5 Play the clip in the Timeline.

6 Click the Motion disclosure triangle in the Effect Controls panel to display its parameters.

7 Click the Position's "Toggle animation" stopwatch button to turn off its keyframes.

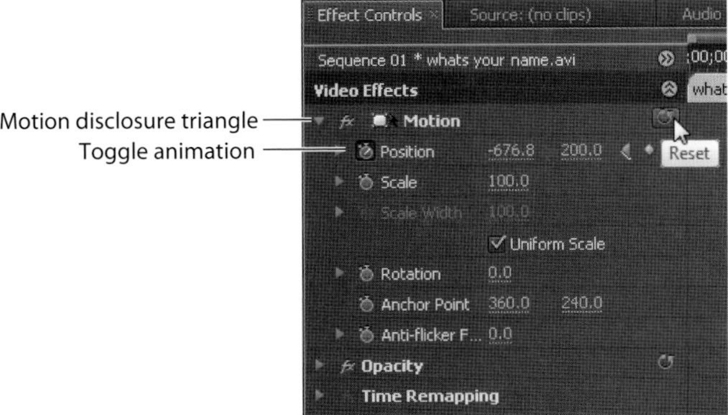

8 Click OK when prompted that all keyframes will be deleted if you apply the action.

9 Click the Reset button (to the right of Motion in the Effect Controls panel).

These two actions return Motion to its default settings.

Examining motion characteristics

To examine some Motion settings, follow these steps:

1 Drag the current-time indicator anywhere in the clip so you can see the video in the Program Monitor.

2 Click the image in the Program Monitor.

That puts a bounding box with a crosshair and handles around the clip (shown here) and activates the Motion effect in the Effect Controls panel. Clicking Motion or its Transform button in the Effect Controls panel will also activate the clip bounding box in the Program Monitor.

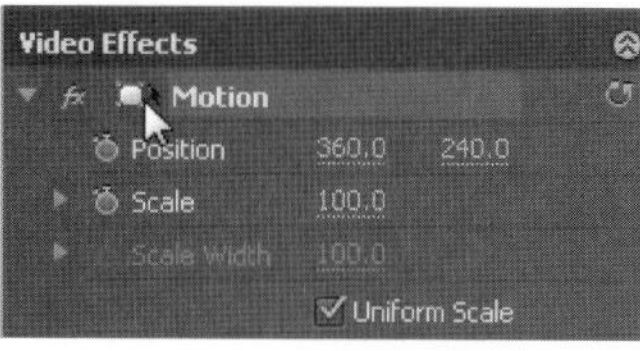

3 Click anywhere in the clip bounding box in the Program Monitor, drag this clip around, and note how the Position values in the Effect Controls panel change.

4 Drag the clip so its center is directly over the upper-left corner of the screen, and note that the Position values in the Effect Controls panel are 0, 0 (or close to that, depending on where you placed the center of the clip).

The lower-right corner of the screen is 720, 480—the standard NTSC-DV screen size.

Note: Adobe Premiere Pro uses something like an upside-down x/y coordinate system for screen location. That coordinate system is based on a methodology used in Windows for so long that to change it now would create numerous programming headaches. The upper-left corner of the screen is 0, 0. All x and y values respectively to the left of and above that point are negative. All x and y values respectively to the right of and below that point are positive.

5 Drag the clip completely off the screen to the left, as shown here.

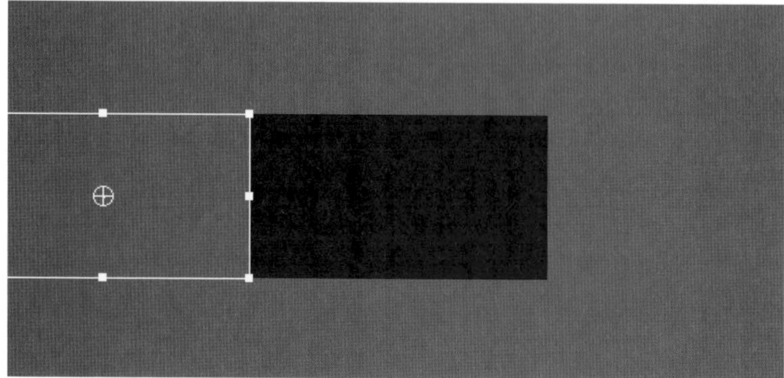

6 Fine-tune that adjustment by changing the Position values in the Effect Controls panel to -360, 240.

Since 360 is half of 720, this puts the right edge of the clip at the left edge of the screen frame.

7 Press Page Up or Home to put the current-time indicator at the beginning of the clip, and add a Position keyframe there by clicking Position's "Toggle animation" button.

8 Drag the current-time indicator to the center of the clip, and change the Position values to 360, 240 (the center of the screen).

Changing the Position parameters adds a keyframe at the current-time indicator.

9 Press Page Down and then the left arrow key to position the current-time indicator at the end of the clip.

10 Change the Position values to 360, -240.

This places the clip completely above the screen and adds a keyframe.

11 Play the clip.

It moves smoothly onscreen and then slides off the top. You have created a path (if you don't see the path, click the word *Motion* in the Effect Controls panel to switch on its display). Make note of a few things (shown below):

- It's a curved path. Adobe Premiere Pro automatically uses Bezier curves for motion.
- The little dots describe both the path and the velocity. Dots closer together represent a slower speed; dots farther apart represent a faster speed.
- The little four-point stars are keyframes.

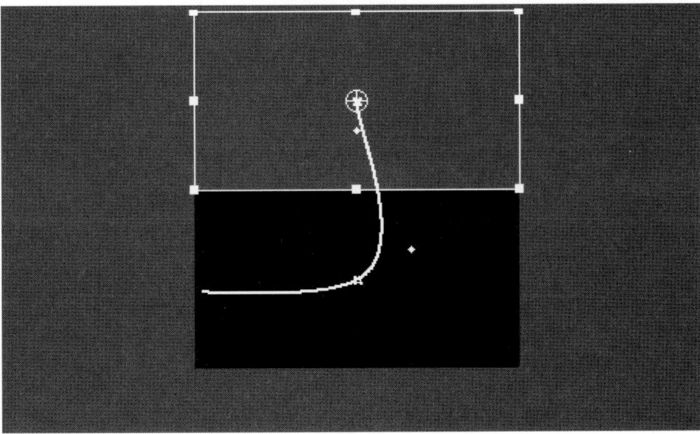

12 Drag the center keyframe in the Program Monitor (the four-point star/square) down and to the left.

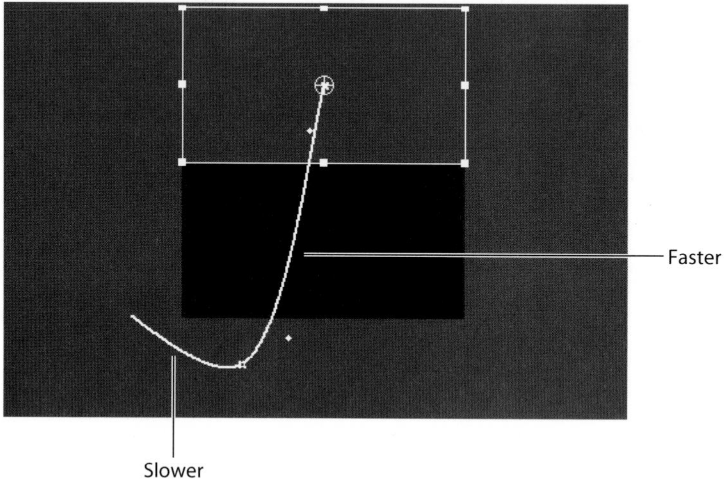

Notice that the dots get closer together to the left of the keyframe and farther apart to the right.

13 Play the clip. Note that it moves slowly until the first keyframe and then speeds up.

14 Drag the center keyframe again, this time down and to the right (use the figure shown here as a reference).

Note: By moving the center keyframe, you changed its location and thereby the distance the clip traveled between it and its adjacent keyframes. But you didn't change the time between keyframes. So, the clip moves faster between keyframes that are farther apart and slower for those closer to one another.

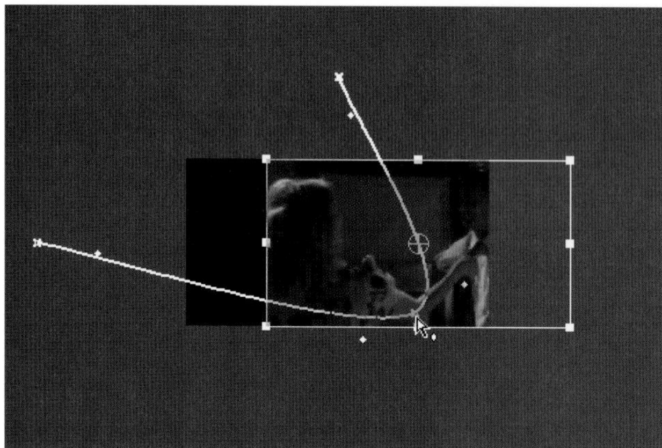

Note: Now you are changing the time between keyframes but not changing their physical location in the screen. The little path/velocity dots in the Program Monitor spread out or slide closer together, but the keyframes do not change locations.

Now you've created a parabola with evenly spaced dots on both sides, meaning the velocity will be the same on both arms of the parabola.

15 Drag the center keyframe in the Effect Controls panel first to the left and then most of the way to the right.

16 Play this clip, and note how much slower it goes at the beginning and how much faster at the end.

It should behave the same way it did when you opened the Lesson 11 project.

Changing clip size and adding rotation

Simply sliding a clip around only begins to exploit the possibilities of the Motion effect. What makes the Motion effect so useful is the capability to shrink or expand the clip and to spin it.

For example, you can start a clip full-screen (or zoom in even further) and then shrink it to reveal another clip. You can spin a clip onto the screen by having it start as a small dot and then spin it off the screen, having it grow as it moves away. You can also layer multiple clips, creating several pictures-in-picture (PIPs).

Before you dive into this exercise, look at Motion's six "keyframeable" options:

- **Position**: This is the screen location of the clip's anchor point (its center unless you change the anchor point).
- **Scale (Scale Height, when Uniform Scale is deselected)**: Scale refers the relative size of the clip. The slider has a range from 0 to 100 percent, but you can set the numerical representation to increase the clip size to 600 percent of its original size.
- **Scale Width**: You must deselect Uniform Scale to make Scale Width available. Doing so lets you change the clip's width and height independently.
- **Rotation**: You worked with this in Lesson 9-3.prproj. You can input degrees or number of rotations, for example 450° or 1 x 90. A positive number is clockwise, and a negative number is counterclockwise. The maximum number of rotations allowed in either direction is 90, meaning you can apply up to 180 full rotations to a clip.
- **Anchor Point**: The Anchor Point is the center of the rotation, as opposed to the center of the clip. You can set the clip to rotate around any point in the screen, including one of the clip's corners, or around a point outside the clip like a ball at the end of a rope.
- **Anti-flicker Filter**: This feature is useful for images that contain high-frequency detail, such as fine lines, hard edges, parallel lines (moiré problems), or rotation. Those characteristics can cause flickering during motion. The default setting (0.00) adds no blurring and has no effect on flicker. To add some blurring and eliminate flicker, use 1.00.

Note: The percent refers to the clip border perimeter, not the clip area. So, 50 percent is equal to 25 percent in terms of area, and 25 percent is equal to 6.25 percent in area.

1 Open Lesson 11-2.prproj and open the Finished sequence.

2 Play the clip to see the animation.

 This is how the Motion effect will look by the end of this exercise.

3 Open the Practice sequence to start with the same clip but with no effects.

4 Place the current-time indicator at the beginning of the clip, expand the Motion effect, click the Position's "Toggle animation" button to activate keyframing, and move the center of the clip to the upper-left corner (position 0,0).

5 Expand the Scale parameter, click the Scale button, and drag the slider to 0.

That sets the size to 0 for the beginning of the clip.

6 Drag the current-time indicator about a third of the way into the clip and click the Reset button. That creates two keyframes that use Motion's default settings: the clip at full size and centered in the screen.

7 Drag the current-time indicator about two thirds of the way into the clip, and click the Add/Remove Keyframe button for Position and for Scale.

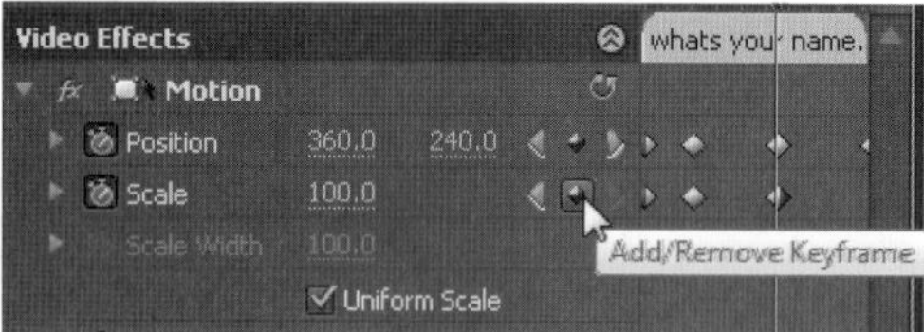

The clip will remain centered and at full screen for the time between the two keyframes. You could also have clicked Reset again to use those default parameters and achieve the same effect.

8 Press Page Down and the left arrow key with the Timeline active to move the current-time indicator to the end of the clip, and change the Position parameters to 720, 480 (lower-right corner).

9 In the Program Monitor, drag a bounding box corner handle to shrink the clip all the way down to the center crosshairs. That sets Scale back to 0.

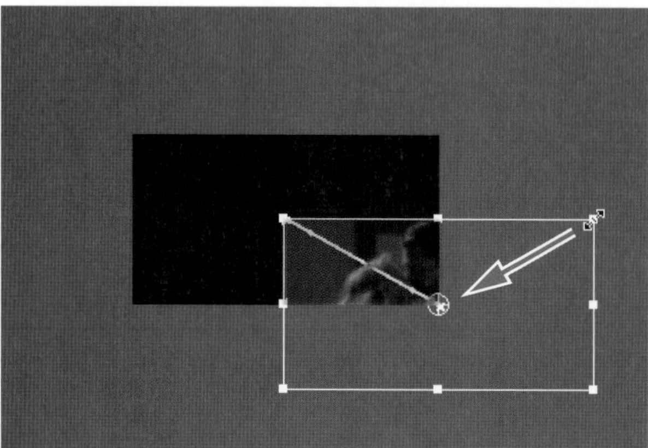

Changing clip size—like working with text

As you did in the Titler, you can change clip size by using the bounding box. Deselect Uniform Scale and then, to scale freely, drag a corner handle. To scale one dimension only, drag a side (not a corner) handle; to scale proportionally, Shift-drag any handle.

10 Play this clip.

   The clip should grow from a tiny dot in the upper left, move to full-screen in the center, hold there for a while, and then shrink to a dot while moving to the lower-right corner.

Adding rotation and changing the anchor point

Now you'll add some rotation to the clip:

1. With the Timeline active, press Page Up or Home to move the current-time indicator to the beginning of the clip, and click the Rotation's "Toggle animation" button.

   That sets a keyframe for Rotation with 0.0° as the starting point.

2. Click the Go To Next Keyframe button next to either Position or Scale to move the current-time indicator to the second keyframe.

3. Hover the pointer just outside a handle of the bounding box in the Program Monitor until it becomes a curved double-arrow pointer, and then drag the bounding box clockwise two full circles, as shown here.

Note: You can fine-tune this move in the Effect Controls panel by setting Rotation to 2x0.0°.

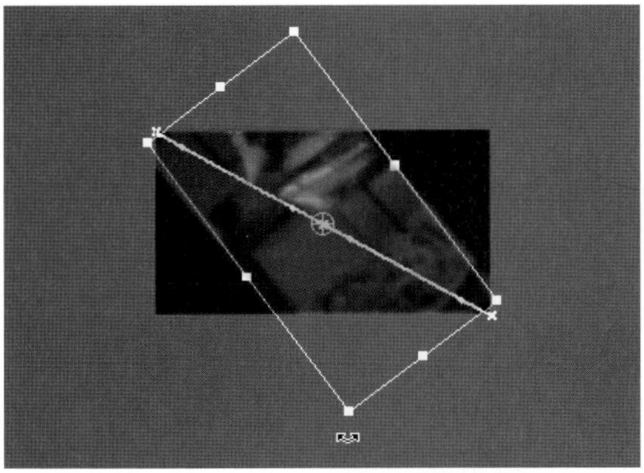

4. Move the current-time indicator to the third keyframe and click the Rotation Add/Remove Keyframe button. That adds a keyframe with the same value as the preceding keyframe.

5. Move the current-time indicator to the end of the clip.

6 Click the Rotation disclosure triangle to expand the Rotation parameter, and drag the Rotation circle counterclockwise twice. Note that you can't use the Program Monitor bounding box to adjust Rotation because the clip has been shrunk to a point.

That returns Rotation to its default setting of 0.0°. If you can't see the keyframe graphs, expand the Scale and Rotation parameters. Play this clip. It will rotate clockwise twice, hold, and then rotate counterclockwise.

7 Play this effect. It should look similar to the effect in the Finished sequence. A difference between this effect and what you see in the Finished sequence is that the rotation suddenly stops and starts. You'll fix that next.

If you like the effect, you can save it as a preset. Right-click (Windows) or Control-click (Mac OS) the Motion effect, and choose Save Preset.

Note: When you save a preset, you can choose for the preset to scale the length of any clip or anchor to a specific In or Out point. In many cases, setting the effect to scale to the length of the clip is most effective.

Working with keyframe interpolation

The Motion effect moves clips around the screen over a period of time. Adobe Premiere Pro offers keyframe interpolation methods that suit both aspects of that motion: spatial and temporal.

Spatial interpolation refers to the motion path—where the clip appears onscreen. *Temporal* interpolation refers to changes in velocity.

In this exercise, you will use an interpolation method called Ease In and Ease Out. Using Ease In and Ease Out is a quick way to set a Bezier curve on a keyframe without manually dragging the keyframe handles.

1 Continue with the Practice sequence where you left off.

2 To adjust the interpolation of scale, position, and rotation all at once, drag a selection box around the second set of keyframes, as shown here. The selected keyframes will be blue.

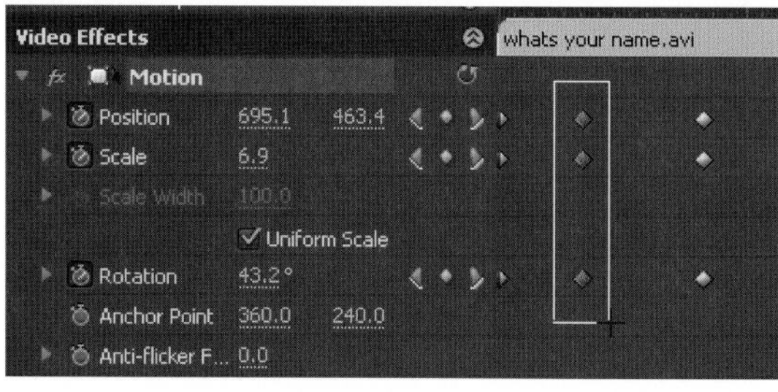

3 Right-click any of the selected keyframes and choose Ease In from the Temporal Interpolation menu.

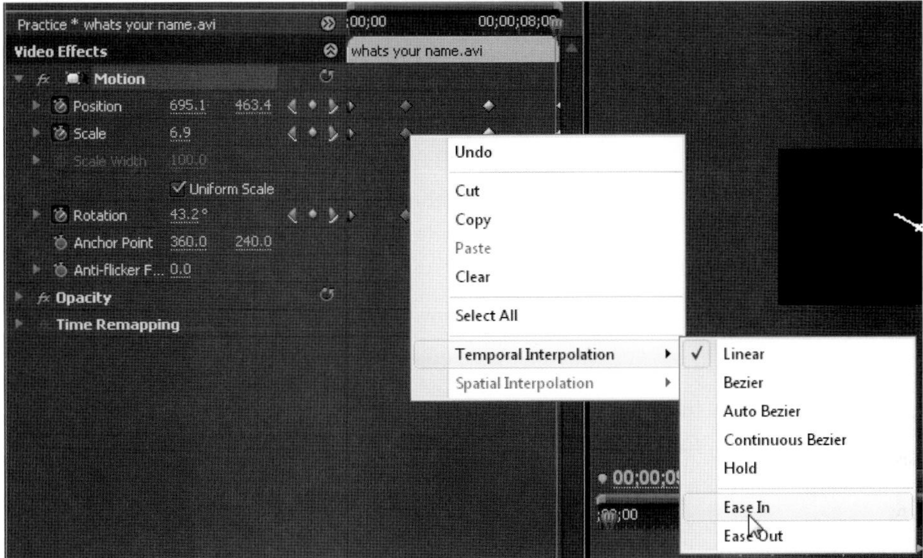

4 Using the same technique, select the third set of keyframes and choose Ease Out from the Temporal Interpolation menu.

5 Expand the Position, Scale, and Rotation parameters to display their graphs. You will see that choosing the Ease options changed the graph to a curve.

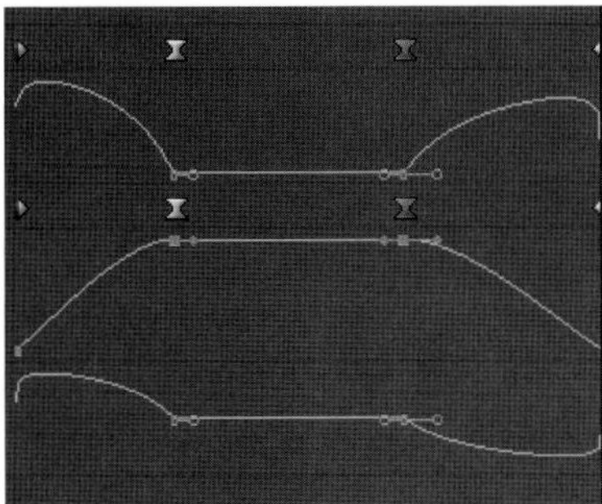

6 Play the clip, and note the subtle change to how motion starts and stops on the keyframes you changed.

Creating pictures-in-picture

The PIP technique is one of the most common uses of the Motion effect. It's also one of the easiest ways to see how you can *composite*, or layer, clips. You will begin formal work on compositing later in the book. This exercise will give you a taste.

To simplify things, you'll start with a sequence that has three layered clips in it, all ready to go. You will create PIPs and add drop shadows and beveled edges to the PIPs.

1 Open Lesson 11-3.prproj and open the Finished sequence by double-clicking it in the Project panel, if it is not already displayed. Render and play that sequence to get an idea of what you can do.

   It's five PIPs, each with a drop shadow and beveled edge.

2 Open the Practice sequence by double-clicking it in the Project panel.

   If you play this, you will see only the clip on the top track. It covers all the clips below it in the sequence.

3 In the Effects panel, expand Presets so you can see Effects > Presets > PIPs > 25% PIPs > 25% UL.

   Note the following:

   - All the PIP presets display clips at 1/16th their normal area (reminder: 25 percent refers to clip perimeter, not area).
   - LL, LR, UL, and UR refer to screen locations: Lower Left, Lower Right, Upper Left, and Upper Right.
   - Each PIP set offers different types of PIP moves.
   - Typically, you select a style and then adapt it to your needs. For example, you might change the preset start or end locations or the size.

Note: There is no 25% Center preset. You use one of the presets to create one. Simply change the start and end Position keyframes to 360, 240.

   The clip in the Video 1 track will remain as is; you want to use it as a background.

4 Drag the following PIP presets to the clips as follows:

   - **Clip in the Video 2 track**: Apply the preset PiP 25% LR Spin In.
   - **Clip in the Video 3 track**: Apply the preset PiP 25% UL Spin In.
   - **Clip in the Video 4 track**: Apply the preset PiP 25% UR Spin In.
   - **Clip in the Video 5 track**: Apply the preset PiP 25% LL Spin In.
   - **Clip in the Video 6 track**: Apply the preset PiP 25% LL Spin In.

Next, you need to customize this motion so that this PIP shows up in the center rather than the lower-left corner.

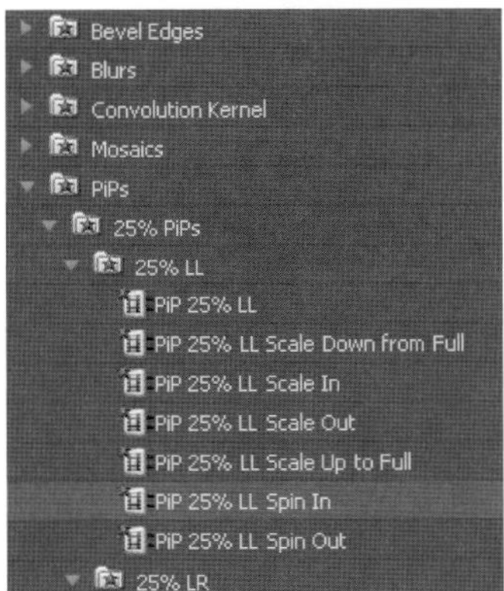

5 Select the video clip in the Video 6 track and expand its Motion settings in the Effect Controls panel.

6 Change the Position parameters to 360, 240. This centers the clip.

7 Play the clip to see the five PIPs you have added on top of a video background. If you have trouble with any of the steps, open the 5 pip sequence to see how it should look.

Enhancing motion with shadows and beveled edges

PIPs are more interesting when their shrunken clips have drop shadows, beveled edges, or some other kind of border. In this exercise, you'll add these enhancements to a clip:

1 Open the sequence called 5 PIP.

It has six layered clips (you might need to use the Timeline scroll bar to see them all). The top five all have 25 percent motion presets applied. The clip on the bottom of the sequence in the Video 1 track will serve as the PIP background.

2 Drag the current-time indicator past the 1-second point to display the five PIPs.

3 Choose Presets > Bevel Edges and drag the Bevel Edges Thin effect to the top clip in the sequence.

4 Zoom the Program Monitor view to 100 percent to get a better look at this effect.

The effect shows up in the center of the Program Monitor. After you adjust the Bevel Edges parameters, it will look as shown here.

5 Click the Bevel Edges disclosure triangles in the Effect Controls panel and change its parameters as follows:

- Increase Edge Thickness slightly.
- Change Light Angle to about 140° to illuminate the dark beveled edge at the bottom of the clip.
- Increase Light Intensity to about .4 to emphasize the beveled edges.

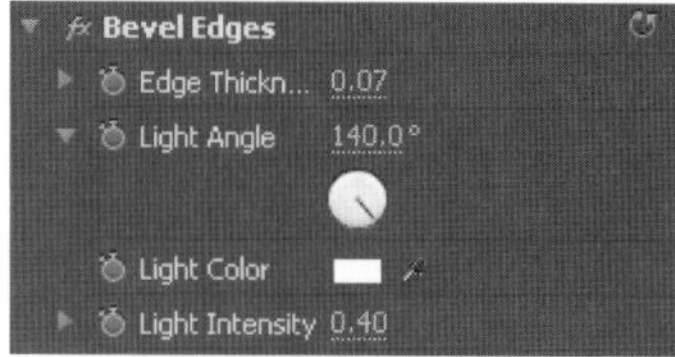

6 Click Bevel Edges in the Effect Controls panel to select the effect so you can create a preset with the parameters you just applied.

7 Open the Effect Controls panel, choose Save Preset, type **Lesson 11 Bevel Edges**, give it a description if you want, and click OK.

This new preset shows up immediately in the Presets folder.

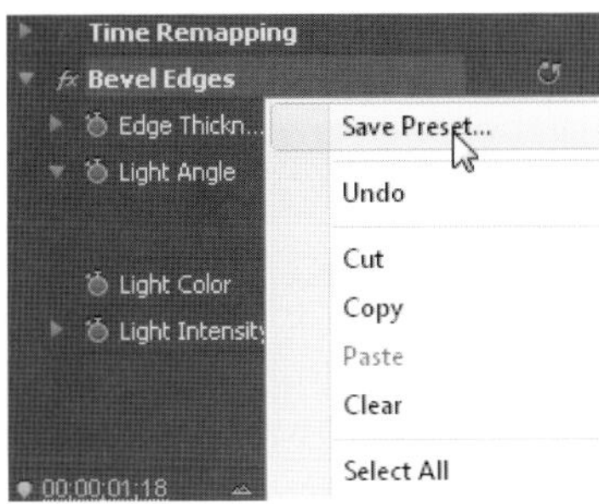

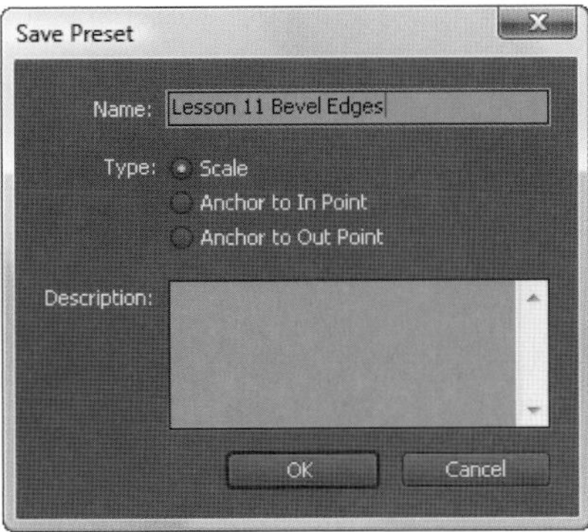

● **Note:** If you had used keyframes with this effect, selecting one of the three types as you're saving the preset—Scale, Anchor to In Point, or Anchor to Out Point—would have been of some value.

Saving presets for other projects

If you want to use this preset in other projects, export it. To do that, select the preset in the Effects > Presets folder, open the Effects panel menu, choose Export Preset, navigate to an appropriate file folder, give your preset a name (it doesn't have to be the same as its name in the Presets folder), and click Save.

8 Drag Lesson 11 Bevel Edges from the Presets bin to each clip in the Video 2–5 tracks (not to the clip in Video 1—that's the full-screen video you'll use as a background for the PIP).

9 Return the Program Monitor's View Zoom Level menu to Fit, and then play this sequence.

All five PIPs have the same beveled-edge look.

Adding a drop shadow

To add a drop shadow, follow these steps:

1 Choose Video Effects > Perspective to drag a drop shadow onto the top clip.

2 Change the Drop Shadow parameters in the Effect Controls panel as follows:

- Change Direction to about 320° or -40°.
- Increase Distance to 30 so you can see the shadow (you might need to adjust the View Zoom Level menu of the Program Monitor to see how this works).
- Change Opacity to 75 percent to darken the shadow (since the background clip is rather dark).

● **Note:** You want the shadow to fall away from any perceived light source. In this exercise, you set the light direction for bevel edges to about 140°. To make shadows fall away from a light source, add or subtract 180° from the light source direction to get the correct direction for the shadow to fall.

- Set Softness to 30 to soften the edges of the shadow. Generally, the greater the Distance parameter, the more softness you should apply.

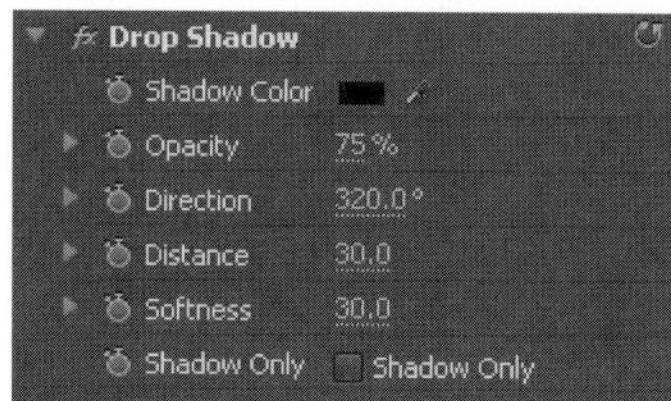

3 Apply these same values to the other four PIPs by using Copy and Paste. Right-click (Windows) or Control-click (Mac OS) the Drop Shadow effect in the Effect Controls panel, and choose Copy.

4 Select the clip in Video 2, right-click in a blank area of the Effect Controls panel and choose Paste. This will paste the shadow filter to the selected clip. Repeat this for the other PIP clips.

5 Render and play this sequence. It should look like the Finished sequence.

Using other motion effects: Transform and Basic 3D

If you use the Motion effect to apply rotation to your shadow and clip, the shadow will rotate with the clip as a single unit. That's unrealistic. It should always fall away from the rotating clip in the same direction. To get a realistic drop shadow with rotation applied to a clip, you can use the Transform or Basic 3D effect to perform rotation.

To *skew* your clips—tilt them to give them a 3D look—use Basic 3D:

1 Open Lesson 11-4.prproj and open the Practice sequence.

2 Click the writers 3 clip to select it, and view the effects already applied in the Effect Controls panel: Drop Shadow and Transform.

   The Transform filter has many of the same capabilities as the Motion fixed effect, but you can move the Transform effect to a lower position in the order of effects applied. You will soon see why this is important. In this case, the Transform effect is scaling the clip to a PIP, moving it left to right and rotating.

3 Play the sequence and observe the relationship of the shadow to the PIP as it rotates.

The shadow rotates with the PIP, which is unrealistic. It is behaving like that because the effects are applied from top to bottom. The shadow is being applied before the Transform effect.

4 In the Effect Controls panel, drag the Drop Shadow effect below the Transform effect. Play the sequence again.

Note: The shadow now remains on the same side while the PIP rotates for a more realistic effect.

Get a glint with Basic 3D

Basic 3D can swivel and tilt your clip to give the impression that it's moving through 3D space. What makes it even more fun is its specular highlight—a glint on the surface of the image that moves as you animate the clip.

1 Delete Transform and Drop Shadowfilters from the writers 3 clip.

2 Select Effects > Perspective > Basic 3D and drag the Basic 3D effect to the Effect Controls panel.

3 Expand the Basic 3D effect in the Effect Controls panel and select the Show Specular Highlight option.

4 Adjust Swivel and Tilt until you see the highlight moving across the clip.

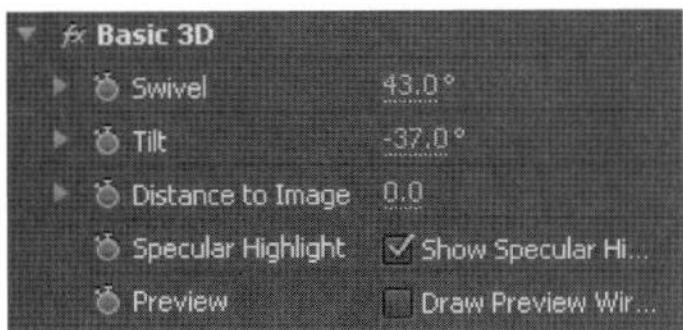

Note: The highlight gets very bright when centered on the clip. When using Basic 3D, it's best to swivel and tilt the clip in such a way that the specular highlight moves along the edge of the clip.

5 Render and play the sequence to see the effect play smoothly.

Review questions

1 What Motion parameter will create a PIP?

2 You start Rotation at its default setting, move the current-time indicator, add a Rotation keyframe with a value of 2x, and then give a value of –2x to the next keyframe. Describe what will happen.

3 You want a clip to appear full-screen for a few seconds and then spin away. How do you make the Motion effect's Rotation feature start within a clip rather than at the beginning?

4 How can you start a PIP rotating slowly and have it stop rotating slowly?

5 If you want to add a drop shadow to a spinning clip, why do you need to use some other motion-related effect besides the Motion fixed effect?

6 One way to apply the same customized effect to multiple clips is to use a preset. How do you make one?

Review answers

1 The Scale parameter will adjust the size of the clip larger or smaller.

2 It will spin clockwise twice as it approaches the first keyframe. Then it will spin counterclockwise four times as it moves to the next keyframe. The number of spins equals the difference between two keyframe rotation values. Set the Rotation value back to 0 (zero) to have it spin counterclockwise twice.

3 Position the current-time indicator where you want the Rotation to begin and click the Add/Remove Keyframe button. Then move to where you want the spinning to end and change the Rotation parameter; another keyframe will appear.

4 Use the Ease Out and Ease In parameters to change the keyframe interpolation to be gradual rather than sudden.

5 The Motion fixed effect is the last effect applied to a clip. Motion takes whatever effects you apply before it (including Drop Shadow) and spins the entire assemblage as a single unit. To create a realistic drop shadow on a spinning object, use Transform or Basic 3D, and then place Drop Shadow below one of those effects in the Effect Controls panel.

6 Adjust the effect parameters to your liking, click the effect name in the Effect Controls panel to select it, open the Effect Controls panel menu, choose Save Preset, give the preset a name, select one of the three parameters, and click OK.

12 CHANGING TIME

Topics covered in this lesson

- Using slow motion and reverse motion
- Enabling variable time changes with time remapping
- Performing time remapping with speed transitions
- Using time remapping with reverse motion
- Applying Timeline downstream effects for time changes
- Changing the speed of multiple clips simultaneously
- Changing the length of multiple stills simultaneously

This lesson will take approximately 30 minutes.

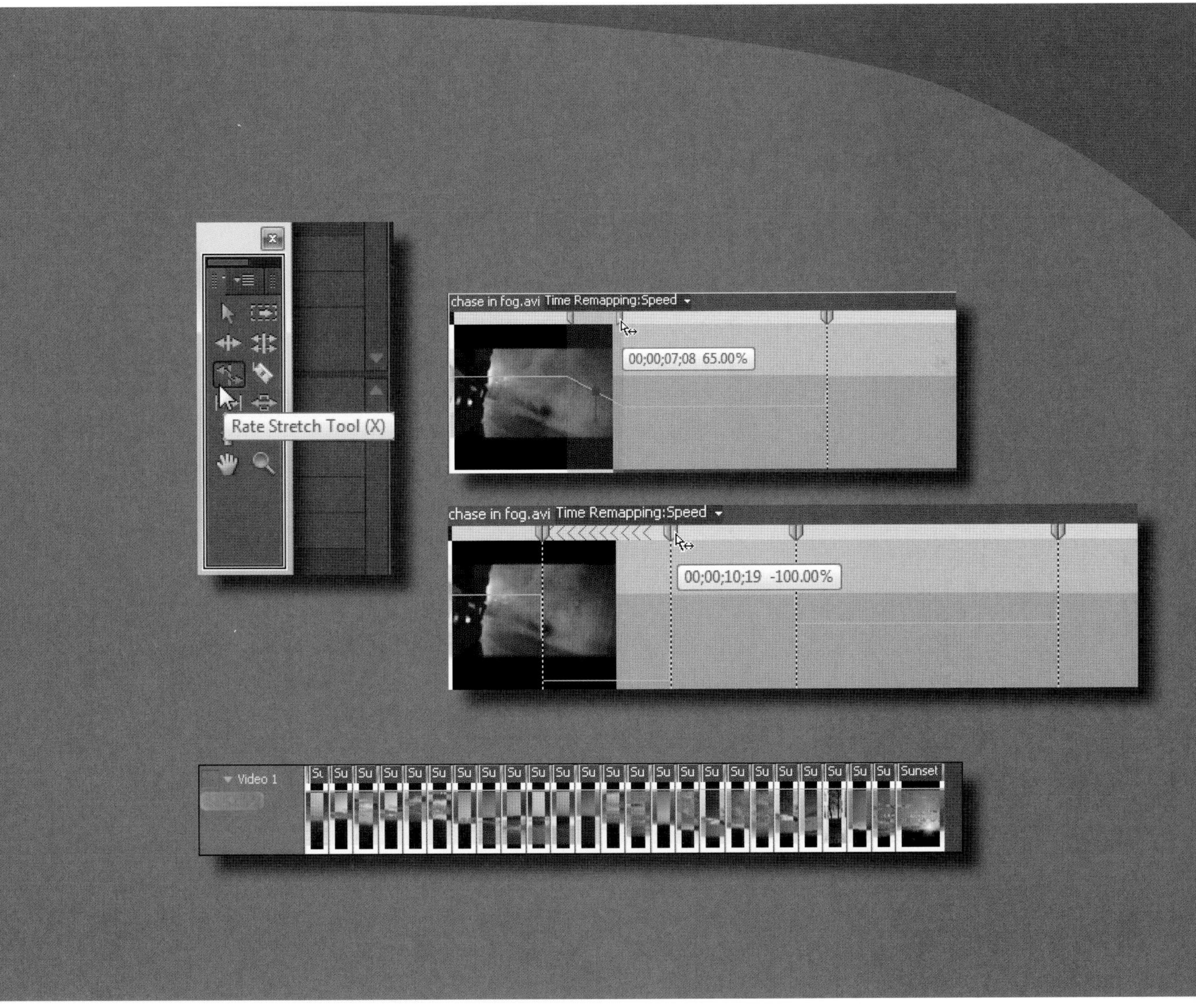

The slow-motion, reverse-motion, and time remapping features in Adobe Premiere Pro allow you to vary the speed of a clip with precise control.

Getting started

Slow motion is one of the most often used effects in video production. A simple slow-motion effect applied to a bride walking down the aisle or to an exciting sports clip can create a dramatic look. In this lesson, you will review the static speed changes, the time remapping feature, and some other tools that let you make time changes to multiple clips.

Using slow-motion and reverse-motion techniques

In this exercise, you will start by making a static speed change to a clip. You can speed up or slow down any clip on the Timeline.

1 Open Lesson 12-1.prproj. Notice that the chase in fog clip on the Timeline is 6 seconds long. It's important to remember that changing the speed of a clip will change its duration.

2 Right-click (Windows) or Control-click (Mac OS) the chase in fog clip and choose Speed/Duration from the context menu.

3 Change Speed to 50% and click OK.

4 Play the clip in the Timeline. Render the clip by pressing Enter (Windows) or Return (Mac OS) to see smooth playback.

Notice the clip is now 12 seconds long. This is because you slowed the clip to 50%, making it twice the original length.

5 Press Ctrl+Z (Windows) or Command+Z (Mac OS) to undo the speed change.

Sometimes you'll want to change the speed of a clip without changing the duration. This is impossible without trimming the clip as it is slowed down. Adobe Premiere Pro provides a tool that makes this easy to do.

6 Right-click (Windows) or Control-click (Mac OS) the clip and choose Speed/Duration from the context menu.

7 Click the link icon, which indicates that Speed and Duration are linked, so that the icon shows the settings unlinked (shown here). Then change Speed to 50%. Notice that with Speed and Duration unlinked, the duration remains 6 seconds.

8 Click OK and then play the clip.

Notice that the clip plays at 50% speed, but the last 6 seconds have automatically been trimmed to keep the clip at its original duration.

Occasionally you will need to reverse time. You can do this in the same Clip Speed/Duration dialog box.

9 Right-click (Windows) or Control-click (Mac OS) the clip and choose Speed/Duration from the context menu.

10 Leave Speed at 50%, but this time also select the Reverse Speed option, and then click OK.

11 Play the clip. Notice it plays in reverse at 50% slow motion.

Note: The Clip Speed/Duration dialog box shows an option called Maintain Audio Pitch if the clip has audio. Selecting this option keeps audio at the original pitch regardless of the speed at which the clip is running. This can be helpful when making small speed adjustments to clips when you want to maintain the pitch in the audio.

Speeding up a clip

Although slow motion is the most commonly used time change, speeding up clips is a useful effect as well.

1 Undo your changes until you have the clip at its original speed at 6 seconds. (If you get confused, reopen Lesson 12-1.prproj.)

2 Right-click (Windows) or Control-click (Mac OS) the chase in fog clip and choose Speed/Duration from the context menu.

3 Type 300% for Speed, click the lock icon so Speed and Duration are linked, and then click OK.

4 Play the clip. Notice its new length is 2 seconds. This is because Speed is set to 300%—or three times its normal speed.

Changing speed with the Rate Stretch tool

Sometimes you'll need to find a clip that's just the right length to fill a gap in your Timeline. You might be able to find the perfect clip, one that's exactly the right length, but most times you will find a clip you want to use that is just a little too short or a little too long. This is where the Rate Stretch tool comes in handy.

1 Open Lesson 12-2.prproj.

   The situation in this exercise is fairly common. The Timeline is synchronized to music and the clips contain the content you want, but two clips are just too short. You can guess, or "hunt and peck," to change the speed until you get it right, or you can use the Rate Stretch tool.

2 Select the Rate Stretch tool in the Tools panel.

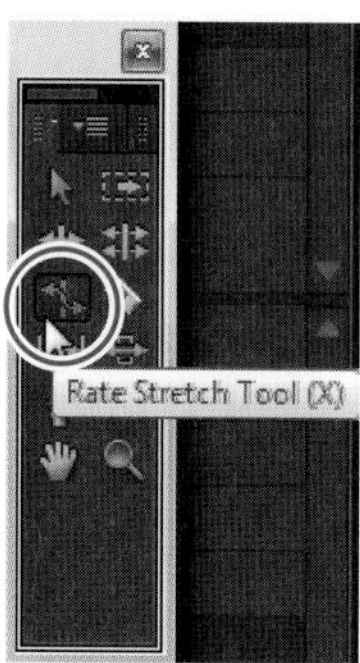

3 Move the Rate Stretch tool over the right edge of the first clip and drag it until it meets the second clip.

   Notice that the speed of the first clip changes to fill the space to which you stretched it.

4 Move the Rate Stretch tool over the right edge of the second clip and drag it until it meets the third clip.

5 Play the Timeline to view the speed change made using the Rate Stretch tool.

Enabling variable time change with time remapping

Time remapping lets you vary the speed of a clip by using keyframes. This means one portion of the same clip could be in slow motion while another portion of the clip is in fast motion. In addition to giving you this flexibility, variable-speed time remapping enables you to alter speed changes from fast to slow or from forward motion to reverse motion. Hang on—this is really fun.

1 Open Lesson 12-3.prproj.

2 Open the practice sequence.

   As you add time adjustments to the clip, it will change length.

3 Adjust the height of the Video 1 track by positioning the Selection tool over the Video 1 label and dragging the edge of the track up.

   Increasing the track height makes adjusting keyframes on the clip much easier.

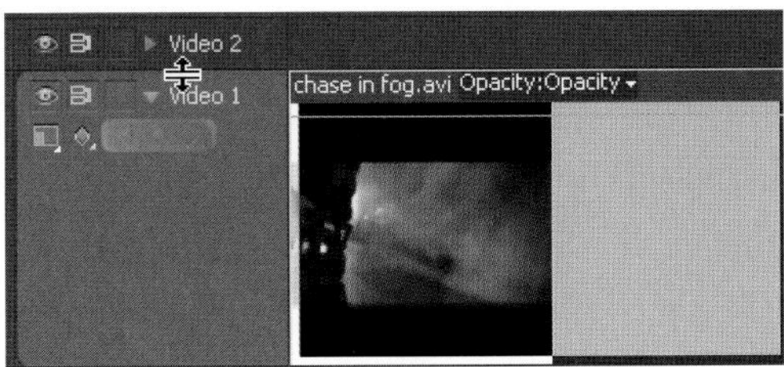

4 Choose Show Clip Keyframes > Time Remapping > Speed in the clip's menu. With this option selected, the yellow line across the clip represents the speed.

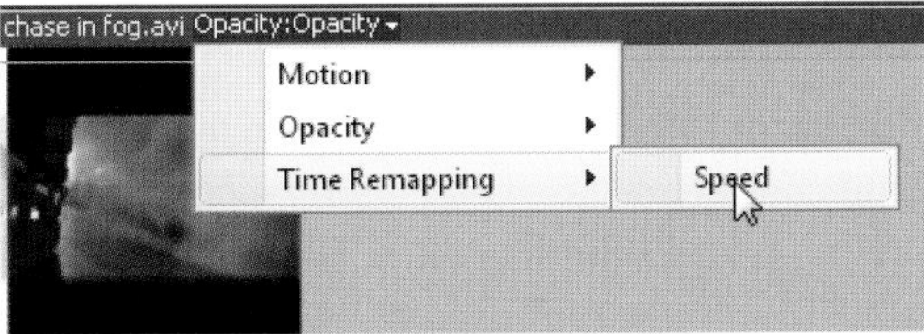

5 Scrub the Timeline to the point where the man following the woman enters the frame (about 00;00;03;00).

6 Ctrl-click (Windows) or Command-click (Mac OS) the yellow line to add a speed keyframe at this point. You are not yet changing the speed, just adding control keyframes.

7 Add another speed keyframe at 00;00;07;10, just as the car enters the frame. Notice that by adding two speed keyframes, the clip is now in three "speed sections." You will now set different speeds between keyframes.

8 Leave the first section, between the beginning of the clip and the first keyframe, set as is (100% speed). Position the Selection tool over the yellow line between the first and second keyframes, and drag it down to 18%. Notice the clip has stretched in length to accommodate the speed change of this section.

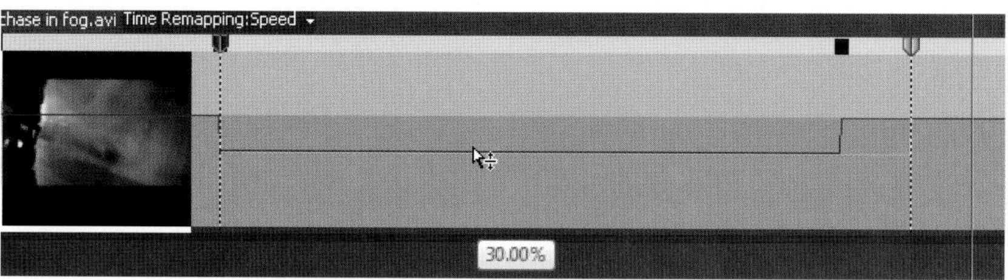

● **Note:** If you have problems setting the speed keyframes, open the complete sequence to see the completed process.

9 Play the clip. Notice the speed changes from 100% to 18% and back to 100% at the end. Render the clip for the smoothest playback.

Applying time remapping with speed transitions

Setting variable-speed changes on a clip can be a very dramatic effect. In the previous section, you changed from one speed to another, instantly. To create a more subtle speed change, it is possible to transition from one speed to another smoothly by using speed keyframe transitions.

1 Open Lesson 12-4.prproj.

● **Note:** The speed keyframes are actually two icons next to each other. You can drag these two icons apart to create a speed transition.

2 Select the practice sequence. You will recognize the clip and speed changes from Lesson 12-3.prproj. You will continue where you left off by creating a gradual speed transition where you changed the speed.

3 Drag the right half of the first speed keyframe to the right to create a speed transition. Notice the yellow line now ramps down, rather than making a sudden change from 100% to 30%.

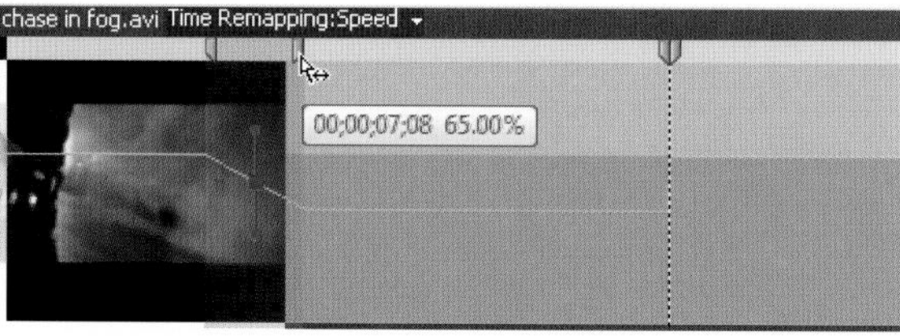

4 Repeat step 3 on the second speed keyframe to create a transition there as well.

5 Render and play the clip to see the effect.

Note: If you have problems creating these speed keyframe transitions, open the complete sequence to see the completed project.

Using time remapping with reverse motion

Reversing a clip can add comedy or drama to a sequence. Time remapping allows you to easily adjust variable-speed remapping and do reverse motion in the same clip.

1 Open Lesson 12-5.prproj.

2 Select the practice sequence.

As you add time adjustments to the clip, it will change length.

3 Ctrl+click-drag (Windows) or Command+click-drag (Mac OS) the right half of the first speed keyframe to the right until you reach timecode 00;00;00;00 (see the timecode in the Program Monitor). Notice the keyboard modifier creates a reverse speed keyframe; that is, when you drag to the right, you are dragging backward in time.

Note: After the reverse motion keyframe is created, Adobe Premiere Pro adds a keyframe to the right at the point in the clip where you started the reverse motion.

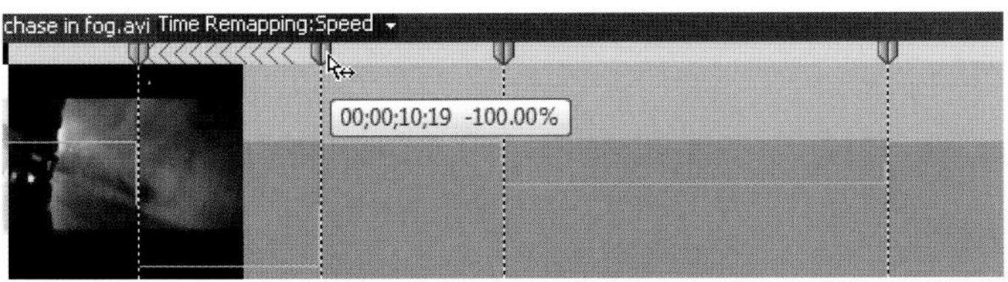

4 Play the clip to see the effect.

5 To make the reverse portion of the clip move in slow motion, drag the yellow line to -50% for that section of the clip. (-50% represents 50% slow motion in reverse.)

6 Drag the right half of the first keyframe to the right to make the transition from forward motion to reverse motion gradual.

Time remapping is a great feature in Adobe Premiere Pro CS4. The quality of the slow motion is very good. Experiment with slowing down and speeding up time, but always try to make the effect match the mood of your project or the story you are telling.

Recognizing Timeline downstream effects of changing time

You may decide to change the speed at the beginning of the Timeline after assembling many clips in your project. It is important to understand how changing the speed of a clip affects the rest of the clips "downstream."

1 Open Lesson 12-6.prproj. Notice that there are three clips on the Timeline in the Video 1 track, with one title clip, called footsteps title, positioned over the short footsteps movie clip. In this exercise, you'll change the speed of the first clip and see how the rest of the Timeline is affected.

2 Right-click (Windows) or Control-click (Mac OS) the chase in fog clip and choose Speed/Duration from the context menu. Change the speed to 50% and click OK.

   Notice that the rest of the Timeline was not affected, but the first clip plays at 50% speed. The clip could not expand because of being confined against another clip. The Out point of the clip was adjusted in order to allow it to play at 50% speed.

3 Press Ctrl+Z (Windows) or Command+Z (Mac OS) to undo the speed change.

4 Right-click (Windows) or Control-click (Mac OS) the chase in fog clip and choose Speed/Duration from the context menu. Change Speed to 50% and also select the Ripple Edit, Shifting Trailing Clips option; then click OK.

   Notice that now the first clips expands to play at 50% and the rest of the Timeline shifts to accommodate it.

Note: Since all the video tracks have Toggle Sync Lock enabled by default, all tracks shift (stay in sync), not just the track with its speed being adjusted.

Changing the speed of multiple clips simultaneously

A new feature of Adobe Premiere Pro CS4 is the ability to change the speed of multiple clips at the same time.

1 Continuing where you left off with Lesson 12-6.prproj, press Ctrl+Z (Windows) or Command+Z (Mac OS) to undo any speed changes.

2 Select all three video clips in the Video 1 track by Shift-clicking each one.

3 Right-click (Windows) or Control-click (Mac OS) any of the selected clips and choose Speed/Duration from the context menu. Change Speed to 50% and click OK.

   All three video clips now play at 50% speed, but only the last clip expanded in length. This is because the last clip was not constricted by any other clips.

4 Press Ctrl+Z (Windows) or Command+Z (Mac OS) to undo the speed change.

5 Select all three video clips again.

6 Right-click (Windows) or Control-click (Mac OS) any of the selected clips and choose Speed/Duration from the context menu. Change Speed to 50% and also select the Ripple Edit, Shifting Trailing Clips option; then click OK.

   All three clips expand to allow them to play at 50% speed.

Changing the length of multiple stills simultaneously

Although a still image does not really have a speed, it does have a duration. Adobe Premiere Pro CS4 allows you to adjust the duration of any group of selected still images.

1 Open Lesson 12-7.prproj. Notice that the Timeline is full of still images of sunsets. The duration of all the images is 5 seconds, and there is a Cross Dissolve transition between all of them.

2 Press the backslash key (\) to zoom the Timeline so all images are visible.

3 Marquee-select all the images by dragging the pointer around them.

4 Right-click (Windows) or Control-click (Mac OS) any of the selected images and choose Speed/Duration from the context menu. Change Duration to 10 seconds and then click OK.

You will notice that only the last image on the Timeline (shown here) expanded to 10 seconds. This is because the other images are bound by other trailing clips.

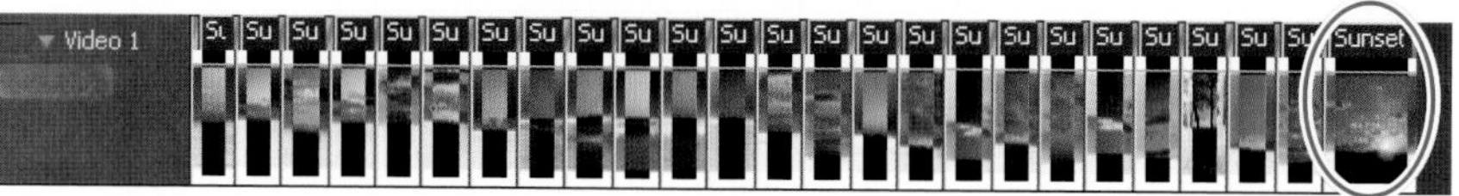

5 Press Ctrl+Z (Windows) or Command+Z (Mac OS) to undo the Duration change.

6 Select all the image clips again.

7 Right-click (Windows) or Control-click (Mac OS) any of the selected clips and choose Speed/Duration from the context menu. Change Duration to 10 seconds and select the Ripple Edit, Shifting Trailing Clips option; then click OK.

All clips expand to 10 seconds in duration, and the transitions between the clips remain in place.

Review questions

1 Changing the Speed parameter of a clip to 50% has what effect on the length of the clip?

2 What tool is useful in stretching a clip in time to fill a gap?

3 Where is the Time Remapping function located?

4 Can you make time remapping changes directly on the Timeline?

5 How do you create a smooth ramp-up from slow motion to normal speed?

6 Explain how you can adjust the duration of several still images after they are already on the Timeline.

Review answers

1 Slowing a clip's speed causes the clip to become longer, unless the Speed and Duration parameters have been unlinked in the Clip Speed/Duration dialog box or the clip is bound by another clip.

2 The Rate Stretch tool is useful for the common situation of needing to fill a small amount of time.

3 The time remapping feature is not found in the Effects folders. It is a common effect available on all clips by default.

4 Time remapping is best done on the Timeline; because it affects time, it is best (and most easily) used and seen within the Timeline sequence.

5 Add a speed keyframe and split it by dragging away half of the keyframe to create a transition between speeds.

6 Select the clips on the Timeline that you want to change and then adjust the duration, being careful to select the Ripple Edit, Shifting Trailing Clips option.

13 ACQUIRING AND EDITING AUDIO

Topics covered in this lesson

- Connecting microphones to your computer
- Setting up a basic voice-recording area
- Voicing professional narrations
- Using Adobe Premiere Pro audio features
- Examining audio characteristics
- Adjusting audio volume
- Adjusting audio gain
- Adding J-cuts and L-cuts

This lesson will take approximately 50 minutes.

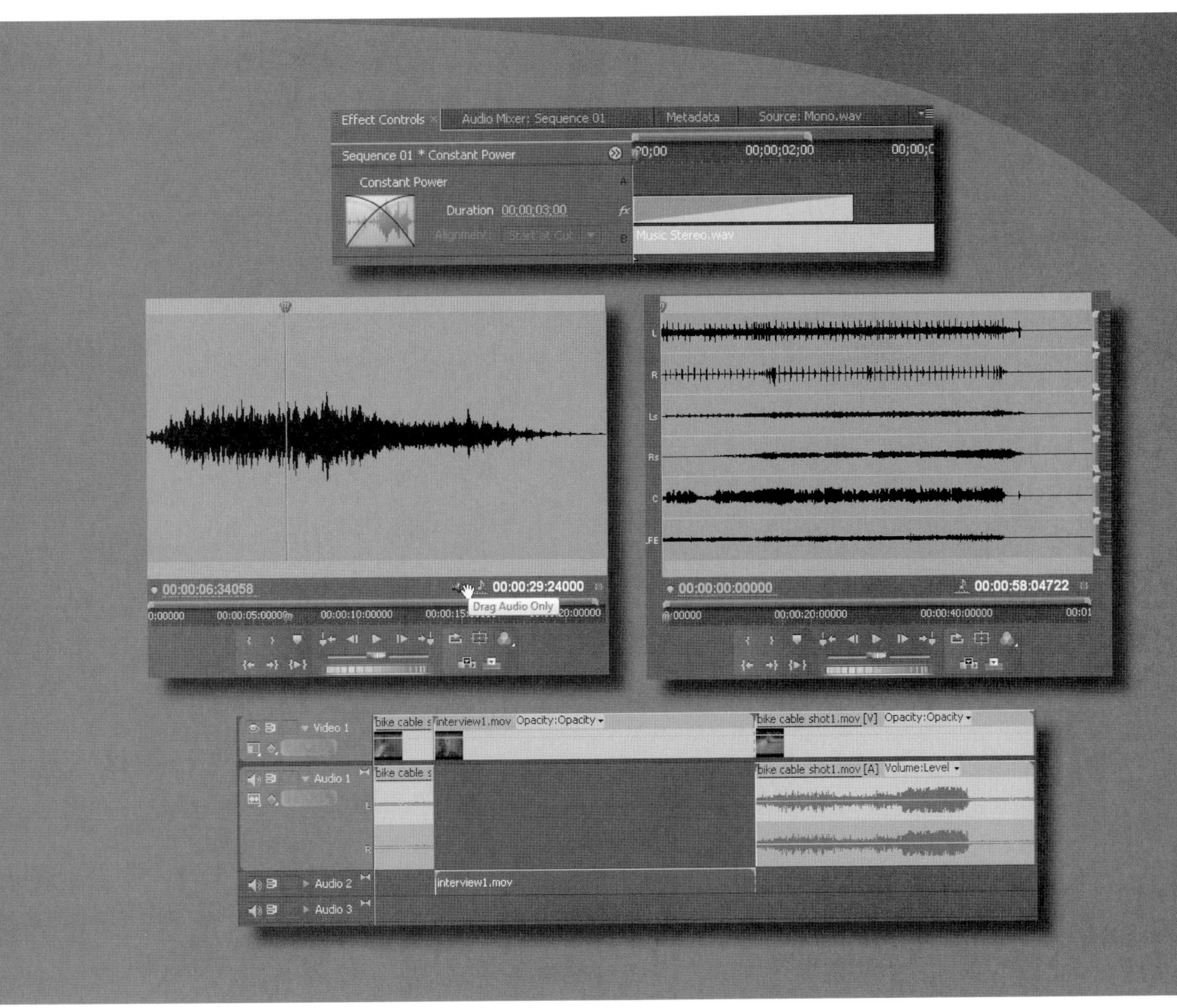

Audio is critical to good video, and Adobe Premiere Pro CS4 has the tools to take your audio editing to a higher level. It features industry-standard plug-ins, audio conforming, sample-specific editing, and multiple track types.

Getting started

Audio typically takes a backseat to video, but it shouldn't. Clear and well-edited audio is crucial to your projects. The best images lose their impact if their audio is mediocre. Your first goal is to acquire high-quality audio from the get-go, both in the field and when recording narration.

Adobe Premiere Pro gives video producers and audiophiles all they need to add top-notch aural quality to their productions. The software has a built-in Audio Mixer that rivals hardware found in production studios. The Audio Mixer lets you edit in mono, stereo, or 5.1 surround sound; has a built-in instrument and vocal recording feature; and offers several ways to mix selected tracks.

You can perform industry-standard edits such as J-cuts and L-cuts on the Timeline, as well as adjust audio volume levels, keyframes, and interpolation.

In addition, Adobe Premiere Pro is in compliance with two audio industry standards—ASIO (Audio Stream In/Out) and VST (Virtual Studio Technology)—which ensures that it works smoothly with a wide range of audio cards and dozens of audio effect plug-ins.

Making the connection

Adobe Premiere Pro lets you record narration directly to your project by using a microphone connected to your computer's sound card. Most sound cards have only a 1/8" (3.5 mm) stereo minijack outlet. Microphones built specifically for personal computers typically cost less than $25. When you visit your local electronics store, you'll have two basic options:

- **Dynamic microphones**: These are headsets or long-necked versions that sit on your desk.
- **Condenser microphones**: Typically lavaliere or clip-on microphones, these offer slightly better voice-over quality and require a battery.

Plug the microphone into the correct sound-card outlet (usually marked Mic or with a microphone icon), not the line-in jack used with amplified devices such as CD players and sound mixers.

Whichever microphone you choose, make sure you also get a good headset—one that covers your ears to block extraneous sound. Use that headset both when shooting your video and when voicing a narration. It's important to hear how the microphone hears you.

Setting up a basic voice-recording area

To create your voice-over narration, you'll need a quiet, sound-absorbing location. The easiest solution is to build a temporary recording area simply by hanging some thick blankets or fiberglass insulation on two adjoining walls. If you can create something like a four-sided blanketed cubicle, so much the better.

If you drape the blankets in a single corner, point the microphone *toward* that corner, place yourself between the microphone and the corner, and speak *away* from the blankets. It seems counterintuitive, but the microphone is sort of like a camera. It "sees" what's in front of it. In this case, it *sees* your face and the hanging, sound-absorbing blankets.

Voicing professional narrations

Review this checklist before recording your voice-over:

- **Practice reading your copy out loud**: Listen to your words. They should sound comfortable, conversational, even informal.
- **Avoid technical jargon**: Tech-speak demands extra effort from your listeners, and you might lose them.
- **Use short sentences**: If you find yourself stumbling over certain phrases, rewrite them.
- **Stress important words and phrases**: As you review your copy, underline important words. When you record your voice-over, you'll want to give those words extra emphasis with more volume and punch.
- **Mark pauses**: Mark logical breaks in narration with short parallel lines.
- **Avoid overly smooth and constant pacing**: Narration that lacks variation in tone or pacing is characteristic of a scripted delivery. You don't want to remind viewers that this is TV. It should sound conversational, like real life.
- **Punch up your voice**: Do not slip into a dull, monotone voice. Add some zest and enthusiasm to your narration.
- **Practice**: Record a couple of narrations and listen to them. Most first-time narrators mumble or swallow words. Have you made yourself clear?
- **Don't pop your p's and t's**: As you say *p*- and *t*-words, you project a small blast of wind. Avoid speaking directly into the microphone.
- **Wear a headset**: Hearing yourself helps you avoid popping p's or speaking with too much *sibilance* (an overemphasis on the "s" sound). It also helps minimize room noise and other extraneous sounds.

Creating a high-quality aural experience in Adobe Premiere Pro

Adobe Premiere Pro offers professional-quality audio-editing tools that rival many stand-alone audio-mixing and editing products. For example, it includes the following:

- **Sample-specific edits**: Video typically has between 24 and 30 frames per second. Edits fall between frames at intervals of roughly 1/30 second. Audio typically has thousands of samples per second; for example, CD audio is 44,100 samples per second (44.1 kHz). Adobe Premiere Pro lets you edit between audio samples.
- **Three types of audio tracks**: The three categories of audio tracks are mono, stereo, and 5.1 (six-channel surround). You can have any or all of these track types in a sequence.
- **Submix tracks**: You can assign selected audio tracks to a submix track. That lets you apply one instance of audio and effect settings to several tracks at once.
- **Channel editing**: You can split out individual audio channels from stereo and 5.1 surround sound files and apply effects only to them. For example, you can select the two rear channels in a 5.1 track and add reverb to them.
- **Recording studio**: Adobe Premiere Pro lets you record any instrument or microphone you can connect to an ASIO-compliant sound card. You can record directly to a track on an existing sequence or to a new sequence.
- **Audio conforming**: Adobe Premiere Pro up-converts audio to match your project's audio settings. It also converts so-called fixed-point (integer) data to 32-bit floating-point data. Floating-point data allows for much more realistic audio effects and transitions.

Note: Floating-point data has no fixed number of digits before and after the decimal point; that is, the decimal point can float. This leads to more accurate calculations.

Camcorder kHz and bit-rate settings

Many DV camcorders give you two audio quality options: 16-bit audio recorded at 48 kHz (16 bits of data per sample at 48,000 samples per second) or lower-quality 12-bit audio recorded at 32 kHz. The latter option lays down two stereo tracks on your DV tape: one with audio recorded by the on-camera microphone and the other giving you an option to insert narration or some other audio. If you recorded at 32 kHz and set your project to 48 kHz, that isn't a problem. Adobe Premiere Pro CS4 will up-convert your audio during the conforming process.

Examining audio characteristics

Audio editing is similar to video editing. It uses most of the same tools, and you apply transitions and effects in much the same way.

But audio has some characteristics that are different from video and that affect the way you approach editing. In this exercise, you will be introduced to the basics of audio editing. We'll explore more advanced audio-editing topics in Lesson 14.

1 Start Adobe Premiere Pro and open Lesson 13-1.prproj.

   This project has three music clips—one in mono, one in stereo, and one in 5.1 surround sound—as well as three movie clips.

2 Double-click Mono.wav to open it in the Source Monitor.

   A waveform appears in the Source Monitor. The peaks and valleys indicate volume levels.

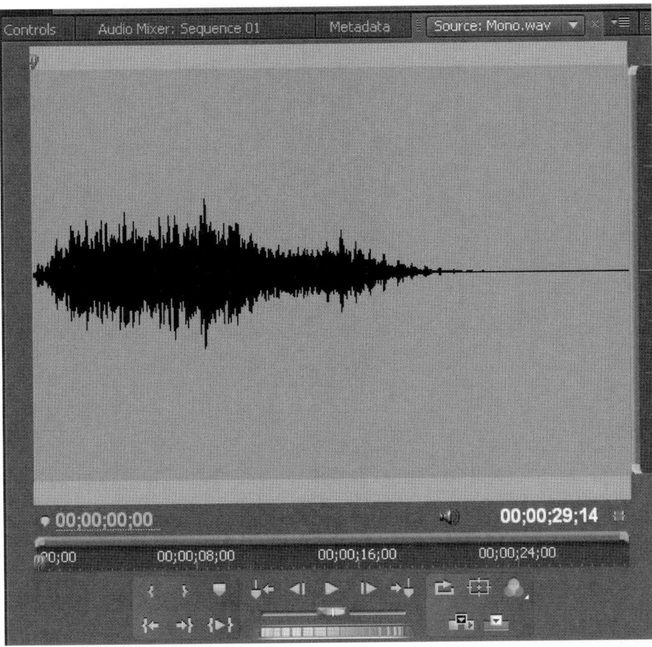

3 Play the audio by clicking the Play button at the bottom of the Source Monitor.

4 Scrub the audio by click-dragging your pointer across the waveform in the Source Monitor.

5 Experiment with zooming in and out on the waveform vertically (the amplitude) by dragging the vertical zoom bar located at the right edge of the Source Monitor. This is helpful for observing more detail in the amplitude of the waveform.

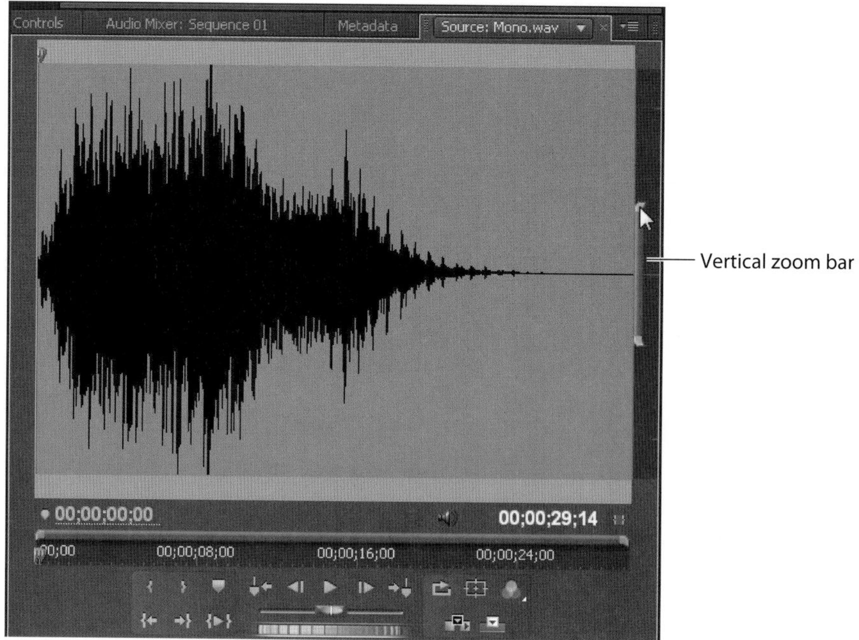

6 Open the Source Monitor panel menu and choose Show Audio Time Units.

The time ruler switches from the standard video-oriented time increments (seconds; frames) to audio samples.

7 Drag the left handle of the viewing area bar to the right to zoom in on the Source Monitor Timeline until the difference between numbered markers is 1,000 samples.

8 Type **1:0** in the current-time display and press Enter (Windows) or Return (Mac OS).

9 Press the left arrow key once and note that the sample preceding 1:0 is 0:47999.

This clip has 48,000 audio samples per second (48 kHz). Switching to audio units enables you to make sample-specific edits down to (in the case of this project's settings) 1/48,000 of a second. This might seem like splitting hairs, but when cutting audio this precision will come in handy.

Note: Audio units appear with colons (:) versus semicolons (;) for the video frame timecode.

10 Drag the center of the viewing area bar to the left and right to take a closer look at the audio peaks and valleys.

Note: You can drag the right or left handle of the viewing area bar to change the zoom level.

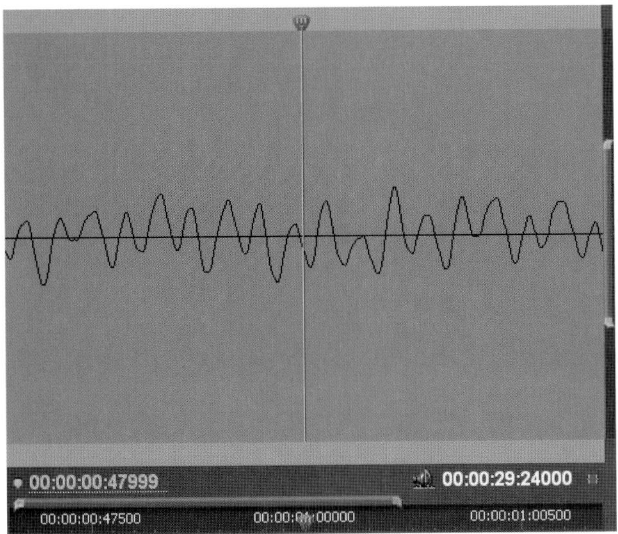

11 Double-click Music Stereo.wav and take a look at it in the Source Monitor.

This is how a stereo signal looks. The layout follows the industry standard: the left channel (L) on the top and the right (R) on the bottom, as shown here.

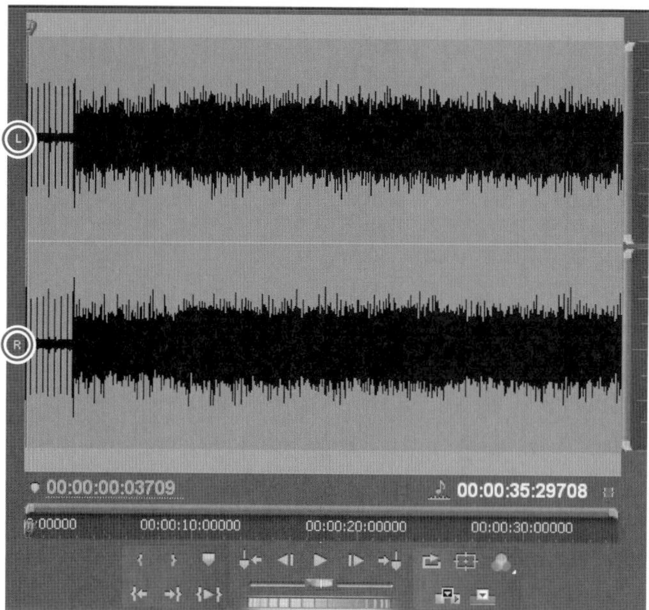

12 Choose Edit > Preferences > Audio (Windows) or Premiere Pro > Preferences > Audio (Mac OS), and make sure 5.1 Mixdown Type is set to Front + Rear + LFE.

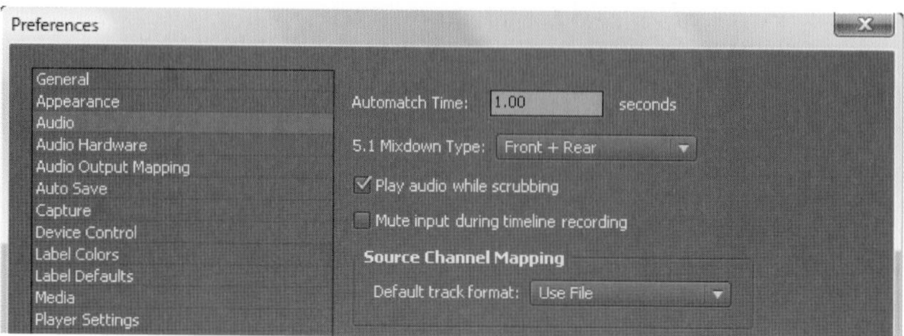

You need to use this setting to hear all six channels of the 5.1 clip in the next step.

13 Double-click Music 11 5.1.wav and take a look at it in the Source Monitor.

This is a 5.1 surround sound clip. It has six channels: right, left, center, right-surround (rear), left-surround (rear), and LFE (low-frequency effects—the subwoofer channel).

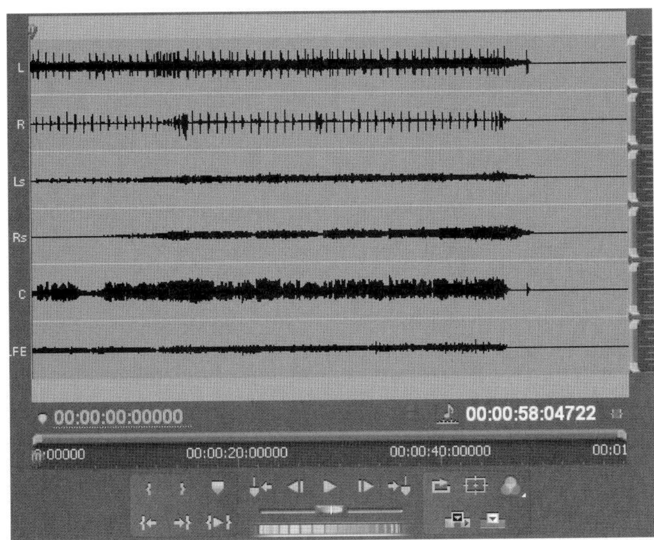

14 Click Music 11 5.1 in the Project panel to select it and then choose Clip > Audio Options > Breakout To Mono.

That creates six links, one for each channel (it does not create six new audio files). Using Breakout To Mono lets you edit individual channels of a stereo or 5.1 clip. For example, you might want to give the LFE channel a bass boost. That does not change the original 5.1 clip. You can link this edited channel to the other 5.1 mono channels and create another 5.1 clip.

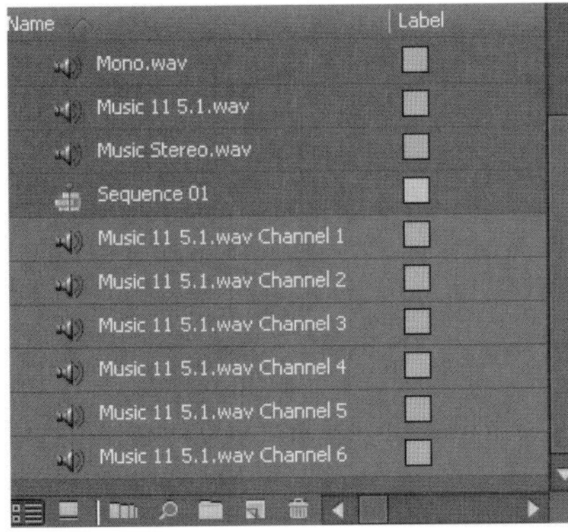

Waveforms are immutable

Adding an effect to a clip in Adobe Premiere Pro will not affect the original audio or video clip, or the visible audio waveform. If you change a clip's volume or apply audio effects to it, the waveform will always display the clip's original volume levels.

15 Drag Music 11 5.1 to the Timeline and notice that Adobe Premiere Pro will not let you drop it in the Audio 1 track.

Audio 1 is a stereo track. When you drag an audio clip to a sequence that does not have a track that matches the clip's type, Adobe Premiere Pro automatically creates a new track to suit that clip type. Even though Adobe Premiere Pro appears to move the new clip below the master audio track, the new track will appear above the master audio track once you release the mouse button.

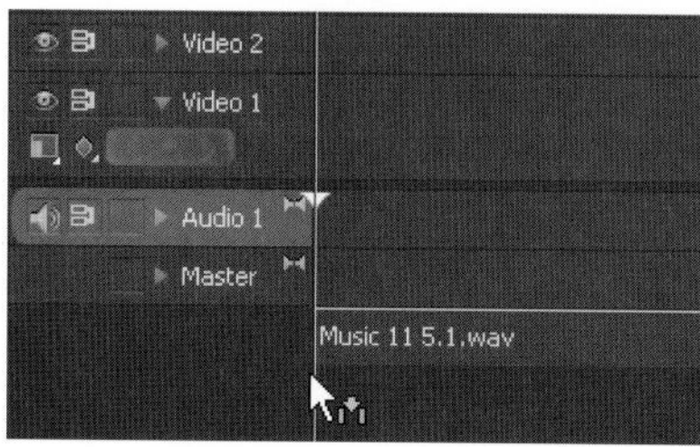

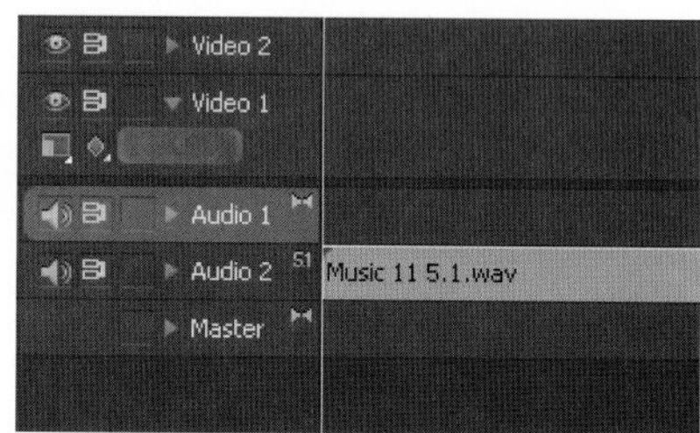

16 Expand the view of the newly added Audio 2 track by clicking its Collapse/Expand Track triangle (shown here) to open its waveform view. Drag the boundary between Video 1 and Audio 1 up the screen, and then drag the bottom of Audio 2 down.

Your sequence should look like the figure shown here. Note the labels for each of the six channels in this 5.1 surround sound clip.

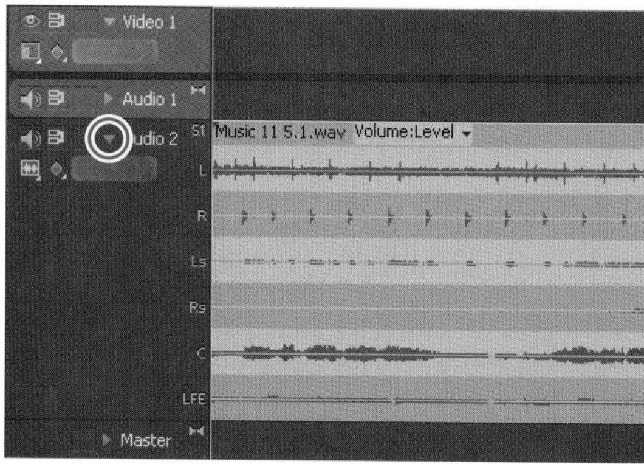

17 Click the menu of open clips in the Source Monitor and select Source: Mono.wav.

18 Drag the Drag Audio Only icon to the Timeline to bring the Mono.wav file into the Timeline. Note that Adobe Premiere Pro will not allow you to drop the mono clip in the Audio 1 track, because Audio 1 is a stereo track. Drop it below the master track, and Adobe Premiere Pro CS4 will create a new mono track above the master track.

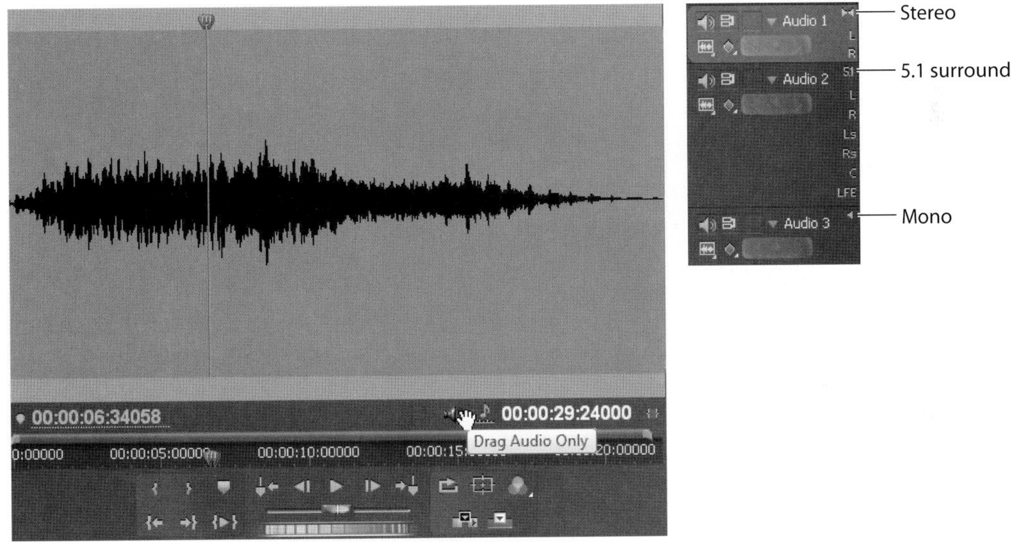

● **Note:** You can tell the audio track type by its icon: Mono is a single speaker, Stereo is a double speaker, and 5.1 says 5.1. The master audio track is stereo by default. This is set under the Track tab when you create a new sequence.

Adjusting audio volume

You might want to decrease or increase the volume of an entire clip or parts of a clip. For example, you might need to bring the natural sound on a video clip down by half while you narrate, gradually fade up the audio at the start or end of a clip, or fade up an interview just as the narrator completes a segment. The last example is part of a J-cut or L-cut. These will be explained later in the lesson. Let's adjust the volume on a clip:

1 Choose Window > Workspace > Reset Current Workspace to get your workspace back in order.

2 Delete the audio clips in the Timeline by marquee-selecting them and pressing Delete.

3 Next, right-click (Windows) or Control-click (Mac OS) an audio track header, select Delete Tracks, select the Delete Audio Tracks option in the Delete Tracks dialog box (shown here), and then click OK to delete all the added audio tracks.

Your sequence now has only two audio tracks: Audio 1 and Master (both are stereo).

4 Drag Music Stereo.wav from the Project panel to the Audio 1 track.

5 Expand the track view by clicking the Collapse/Expand Track triangle.

6 Click the Show Keyframes button and choose Show Clip Keyframes to ensure you are looking at clip keyframes.

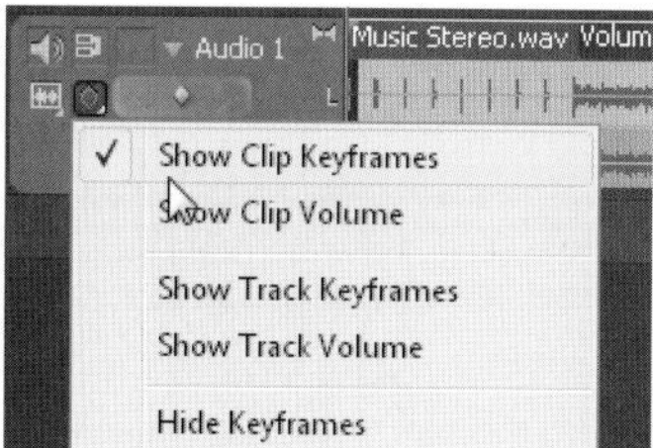

You can now edit a clip's volume in the Timeline rather than using the Volume effect in the Effect Controls panel.

7 Hover your pointer over the volume level graph—the thin, horizontal yellow line between the left and right channels—until it turns into the Vertical Adjustment tool pointer, and then drag that yellow line up and down.

● **Note:** A dB (decibel) level readout gives you feedback on the volume change (0 dB is the default starting point no matter the actual volume of the original clip). It's not easy to move to an exact setting. You use the Volume effect in the Effect Controls panel to do that.

8 Ctrl-click (Windows) or Command-click (Mac OS) the volume level graph in four places evenly spaced along the yellow line.

That adds four keyframes on the volume line.

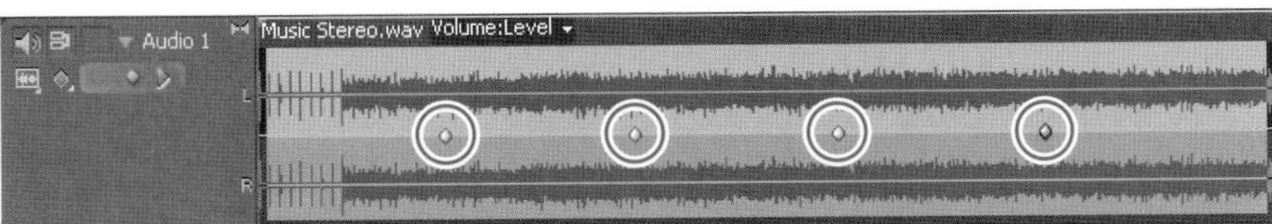

9 Drag the first and last keyframes all the way to the left and right, respectively, to place those keyframes on the first and last frames of the clip.

10 Drag the second and third keyframes left and right, respectively, to about 2 seconds from the beginning and 2 seconds from the end.

11 Drag the start and end keyframes all the way to the bottom of the clip view to create a fade-up and a fade-out.

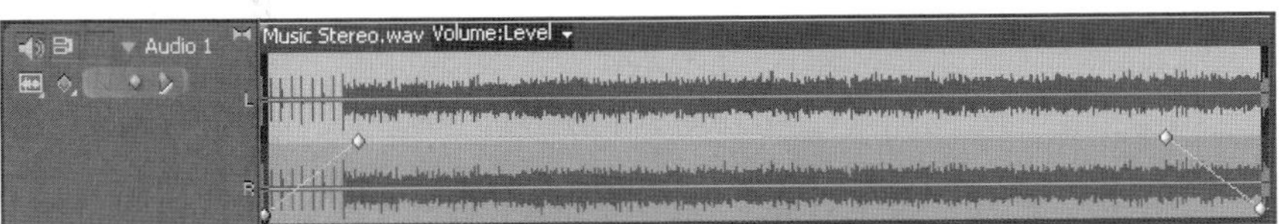

12 Play the beginning and end of the clip to see how this works.

● **Note:** As you slide keyframes around in the clip, you will invariably change their volume settings. Adjusting keyframes on the Timeline is quick and easy. You'll want to use the Volume effect in the Effect Controls panel to fine-tune those keyframe parameters.

13 Right-click (Windows) or Control-click (Mac OS) the second and third keyframes, and choose Ease In and Ease Out, respectively.

● **Note:** As you can see, you can apply keyframe interpolation in the Timeline. However, selecting one of the Bezier curve options would create a more pronounced curve in the middle. So stick with Ease In and Ease Out for most audio keyframes.

Adjusting audio in the Effect Controls panel

The Audio fixed effect works like any other effect in that you can use keyframes to change audio over time. You can also apply an audio transition (which changes audio volume levels over time) and adjust its settings in the Effect Controls panel.

1 Make sure the Music Stereo clip is selected on the Audio 1 track and open the Effect Controls panel. Click the Volume disclosure triangles to display the parameters and widen the Effect Controls panel so you can see its Timeline.

   If the Timeline is not open, click the Show/Hide Timeline View button. Make note of a few things:

   - **Bypass**: Bypass is something you haven't seen up to this point because only audio effects have this option. For the Volume effect, turning on Bypass at any point in the clip (Bypass is "keyframeable") switches back to the clip's original volume level. You can use Bypass to switch any audio effect off and on any number of times within a clip.
   - **Level**: This is the only adjustable parameter.
   - **Keyframes**: All the keyframes and keyframe interpolation methods (the hourglass icons) you applied to the clip in the Timeline show up in the Effect Controls Timeline.

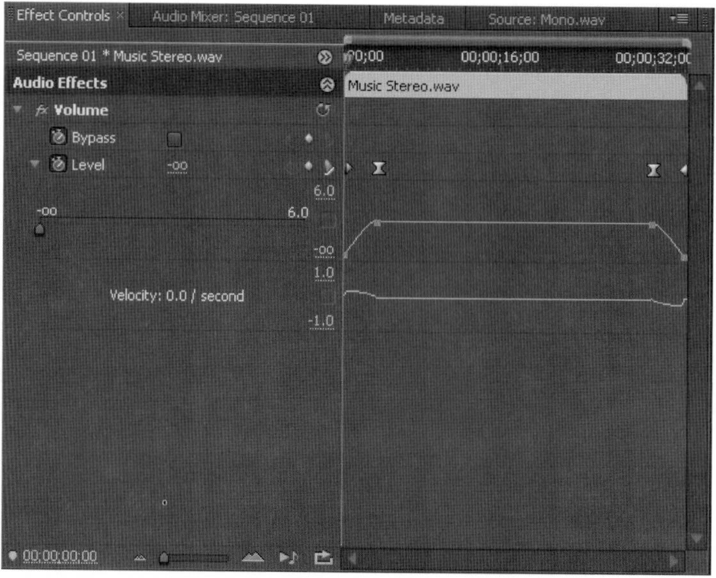

2 Add several keyframes and change the volume level on each one. Play the clip to hear the level adjustments. Click the box next to Bypass and notice the level adjustments you made are not used.

3 Marquee-select all the keyframes in the Effect Controls Timeline and press Delete.

4 Drag the Constant Power audio transition (Audio Transitions > Crossfade) to the beginning of the clip on the Timeline.

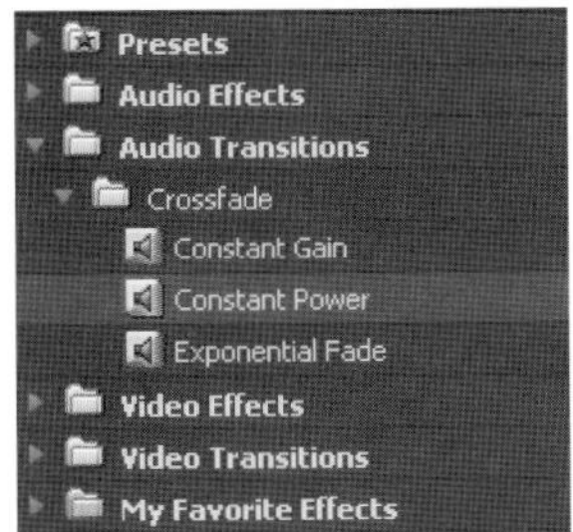

5 Click the transition rectangle on the clip to select it, and view its parameters in the Effect Controls panel.

6 Change the duration to 3 seconds.

This gives you a nice fade-in.

7 Drag the interview1.mov clip to the Timeline just after the Music Stereo clip.

8 Trim the end Music Stereo.wav back by 1 second. Then trim the beginning of interview1.mov to about 00;00;04;12.

This gives them both tails for a smooth transition.

9 Drag Constant Power to that edit point and listen to how that works.

10 Replace Constant Power with Constant Gain and listen to it.

Note: Open the completed sequence if you get confused or want to see the completed lesson up to this point.

Favor constant power

Constant Gain changes audio at a constant rate in and out as it transitions between clips. Sometimes this can sound abrupt. Constant Power creates a smooth, gradual transition, like a video cross-dissolve. It decreases audio for the first clip slowly at first and then quickly falls off at the end of the transition. For the second clip, this audio crossfade increases audio quickly at first and then more slowly as it reaches the end of the transition. Constant Power is the default audio transition. Rely on it for most transitions. But your ears are the best judge.

Adjusting audio gain

Sometimes the audio you acquire requires a gain adjustment to bring its overall levels up or down to meet the gain of other clips. This can be done by trial and error with manual volume adjustments, but Adobe Premiere Pro provides an Audio Gain tool that will help you do much of this automatically.

1 Continuing with the open project, click the Music Stereo.wav clip to select it.

2 Right-click the clip and choose Audio Gain. Notice the four options for adjusting the gain of the clip:

- **Set Gain to**: The default value is 0.0 dB. This option allows you to set the gain to a specific value. This value is always updated to the current gain, even when the radio button is not selected and the value appears dimmed.
- **Adjust Gain by**: The default value is 0.0 dB. This option allows you to adjust the gain by + or - dB. Entering a value other than zero in this field automatically updates the Set Gain to dB value to reflect the actual gain value applied to the clip.
- **Normalize Max Peak to**: The default value is 0.0 dB. You can set this to any value less than 0.0 dB. For example, this clip has a peak amplitude of -2.7 (as shown in the next figure). Normalizing this clip to 0 db will raise its gain by an adjustment of 2.7 db.
- **Normalize All Peaks to**: The default value is 0.0 dB. This is useful when selecting multiple clips at once. This feature will adjust all selected clips to a gain necessary for them all to peak at 0 db.

3 Set the Normalize Max Peak to option to 0 db and click OK. Notice that the waveform on the Timeline will expand to show the increased gain.

You can also normalize the entire audio track at once using the new Normalize Master Track option.

4 Play the Timeline and notice that the master audio meter plays between -6 and 0 db, which is generally a good level.

5 In the Sequence menu choose Normalize Master Track. The Normalize Track dialog box opens.

Sometimes you may want more "headroom" in your audio track, so you'll want to adjust the entire track down a bit. This feature is useful for performing that function.

6 Set the value to -3 and click OK.

7 Play the Timeline and notice that the levels on the master audio meter have been reduced by 3 db.

Adding J-cuts and L-cuts

Frequently you'll want to start a video clip by having its sound play under the previous video clip and then transition to its associated video. This is a great way to let your audience know that someone is about to say something or that a transition is coming. This is called a *J-cut,* so named because it looks vaguely like a *J* in the sequence.

Conversely, another slick editing technique is to let audio tail off under the next video clip. This is an *L-cut.*

Doing either of these cuts requires you to unlink the audio and video portions of a linked A/V clip so you can edit them separately. After you've unlinked them, you can move that audio segment to another audio track and then extend or shorten the audio portion to make the J- or L-cut. There are two unlinking methods—a context menu and a keyboard modifier.

1 Open Lesson 13-2.prproj and play the Complete sequence.

Note: In this case, the cutaway clips aren't being used as cutaways. They're B-roll—basic video used to piece together a project.

This is how your J- and L-cuts will look and sound by the end of this exercise. It has the sound bite and cutaway clips used in Lesson 8.

The cutaway *video* plays over the first few words of the sound-bite *audio,* and then the cutaway *video* dissolves to the interview clip while the cutaway *audio* fades out—a J-cut. That process is reversed for the end of the sound bite—an L-cut.

2 Open the Lesson 12-3 Working sequence.

3 Right-click (Windows) or Control-click (Mac OS) the second clip and choose Unlink.

4 Complete the unlinking process by clicking outside that clip in the Timeline to deselect it.

Now when you click either the audio or video portion of that clip, only that portion is selected. You'll relink these clips and then use a keyboard modifier to temporarily unlink them.

5 Shift-click both of those unlinked clips to select them (if one is already highlighted, you don't need to Shift-click it).

6 Right-click (Windows) or Control-click (Mac OS) one of them and choose Link.

Now you'll use the keyboard modifier unlinking method.

7 Alt-click (Windows) or Option-click (Mac OS) the audio portion of the second clip to unlink it and select it.

8 Drag the unlinked audio portion of the second clip straight down to the Audio 2 track and deselect it.

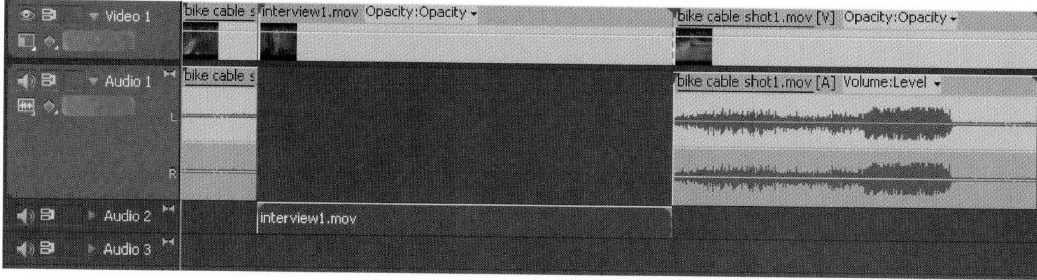

9 Use the Rolling Edit tool (⇹) to move to the right about 1 second the edit that is between the first and second video clips (not the audio clips).

Use the Program Monitor and the Timeline pop-up timecode displays to help make the edit.

10 Apply a fade-out using the Constant Power transition (you used this transition in the previous exercise) on the first audio clip to fade out the bike sound gradually as the subject starts to speak.

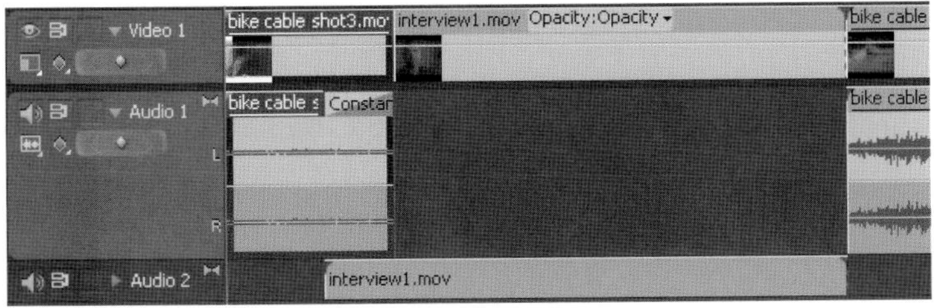

11 Play that J-cut. The bike sound should fade as the interviewer begins speaking.

Note: As you move the audio portions of your clips in the sequence, take care that you don't slide them left or right when you drag them; otherwise the audio and video will get out of sync. Adobe Premiere Pro gives you a visual cue to help you line up your clips: If you see a black line with a triangle, your clips are properly lined up. If that black line disappears, you have moved out of sync. In that case, move the clip around a bit until the black line reappears.

Adding an L-cut

Now that you've unlinked the center clip, adding an L-cut at the end of this segment will take only a few steps:

1 Trim the third clip by dragging the left end of the bike cable shot1 clip to the right about 1 second. This will shorten it a bit and give it head frames for a transition.

2 Drag the entire third clip (video and audio) to the left about 1 second so it overlaps the audio from clip 2. You've now created an L-cut.

3 Create a fade-in of the third audio clip to gradually fade in the bike audio over the end of the interview from the second clip.

4 Add a video Cross Dissolve effect between the video portions of these two clips.

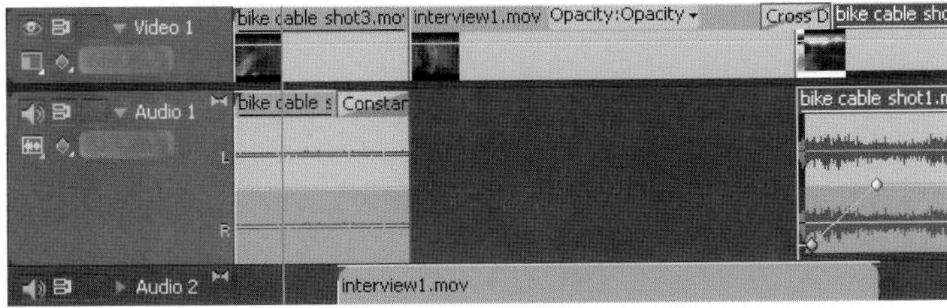

5 Play that L-cut.

The closing biker's natural sound should fade up quietly beneath the interviewer's closing comment.

Review questions

1 When you set up a voice-recording space in the corner of a room, which way do you face to voice the narration, and why?

2 When you videotape indoors, your audio has a "tin can" quality. What's going on?

3 Explain three ways to start your piece by fading up your audio.

4 How is applying the Normalize filter in Adobe Premiere Pro different from just raising the volume?

5 Why use a J-cut or an L-cut?

6 You have a quiet video clip, but in the middle someone honks a car horn. How could you remove that sound and replace it with the original quiet background of the original clip?

Review answers

1 As counterintuitive as it seems, you face away from the sound-absorbing material. The microphone picks up sound from the direction it's facing. The absorbing material minimizes the reflections the microphone picks up.

2 The microphone is probably too far from your subject, and you're in a room with reflective surfaces such as flat walls and an uncarpeted floor.

3 Drag an audio crossfade transition (Constant Power or Constant Gain) to the beginning of the clip. Or use the volume level graph in the Timeline clip display with two keyframes, dragging the first keyframe to the first frame and dragging that keyframe to the bottom of the clip. Or use the Volume audio effect and two keyframes to fade up the audio. Use interpolation controls to smooth what would otherwise be a straight-line fade-in.

4 Raising the gain or volume increases the amplitude of the waveform. Normalizing the audio examines it for peak values and allows you to adjust gain based on the peaks.

5 You use these cuts either to ease into a clip such as a sound bite or to let it fade out. A J-cut starts audio under the preceding video (which also has associated audio or a narration) and then fades up as you transition or cut to the video portion of that clip. An L-cut fades audio under the next clip as a way to ease out of that audio/video clip.

6 Use keyframes to silence that portion of the audio. Then add part of the original audio to another audio track and fade that up to fill the audio gap you created in the original clip.

14 SWEETENING YOUR SOUND AND MIXING AUDIO

Topics covered in this lesson

- Sweetening sound with audio effects
- Trying stereo and 5.1 surround sound effects
- Working with the Audio Mixer
- Outputting tracks to submixes
- Recording voice-overs
- Creating a 5.1 surround sound mix
- Integrating with Soundbooth
- Working with multiple tracks and Adobe Dynamic Link in Soundbooth

This lesson will take approximately 90 minutes.

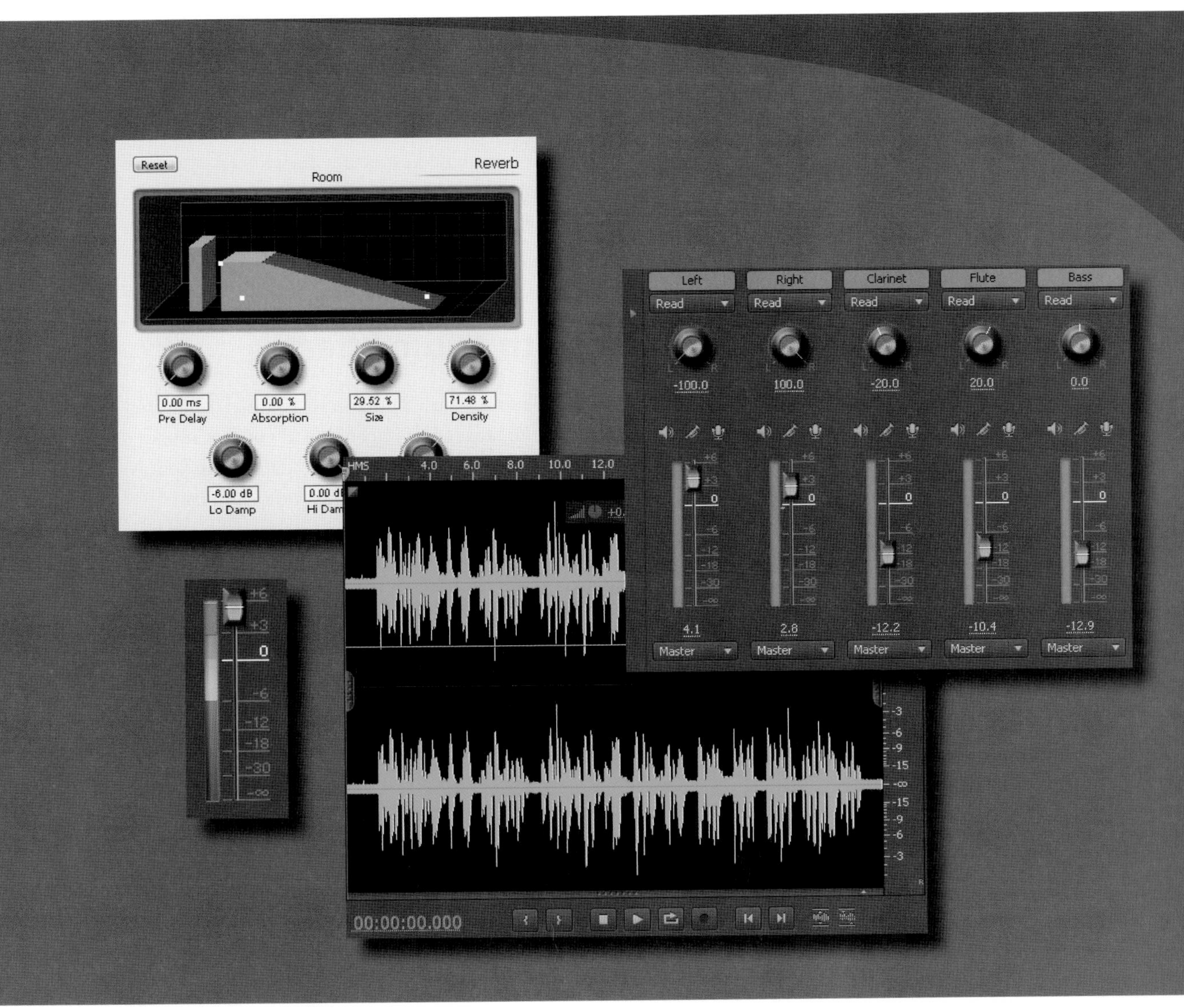

Audio effects in Adobe Premiere Pro CS4 can dramatically change the feel of your project. To take your sound to a higher level, leverage the integration and power of Adobe Soundbooth CS4.

Getting started

Adobe Premiere Pro contains more than 20 audio effects that can change pitch, create echoes, add reverb, and remove tape hiss. As you've done with video effects, you can set keyframeable audio effect parameters to adjust effects over time.

The Audio Mixer lets you blend and adjust the sounds from all the audio tracks in your project. Using the Audio Mixer, you can combine tracks into single submixes and apply effects, panning, or volume changes to those groups as well as to individual tracks.

Soundbooth is an audio application that is designed especially for video and Adobe Flash CS4 Professional editors. Soundbooth provides the tools video editors need to sweeten and repair typical audio challenges. Don't let the easy interface mislead you—Soundbooth is a powerful tool.

Sweetening sound with audio effects

For most projects, you will probably be happy to use audio in its original, unaltered state, but at some point you might want to start applying effects. If you use music from old cassette tapes, you can use the DeNoiser audio effect to detect and remove tape hiss automatically. If you record musicians or singers in a studio, you can make it sound like they were in an auditorium or a cathedral by adding the Reverb effect. You can also use Delay to add an echo, DeEsser to remove sibilance, and Bass to deepen an announcer's voice.

You'll try a few audio effects in this lesson, but you can expand your knowledge by going beyond that. Experiment. Listen to the possibilities. Test some effects not covered here. Each effect is nondestructive—that is, it does not change the original audio clip. You can add any number of effects to a single clip, change parameters, and then delete those effects and start over.

1 Start Adobe Premiere Pro and open Lesson 14-1.prproj.

2 Drag Ad Cliches Mono.wav from the Project panel to the Audio 1 track (it's a mono track) of the Practice sequence.

   Play the clip.

3 Open the Audio Effects > Mono folder in the Effects panel.

Note: All the mono effects have the mono single-speaker icon (). If you open the Stereo folder, you'll see a double speaker icon (), and you'll also recognize the 5.1 icon ().

4 Drag Bass to the Ad Cliches clip, open the Effect Controls panel, and then click its two disclosure triangles to expand the parameters.

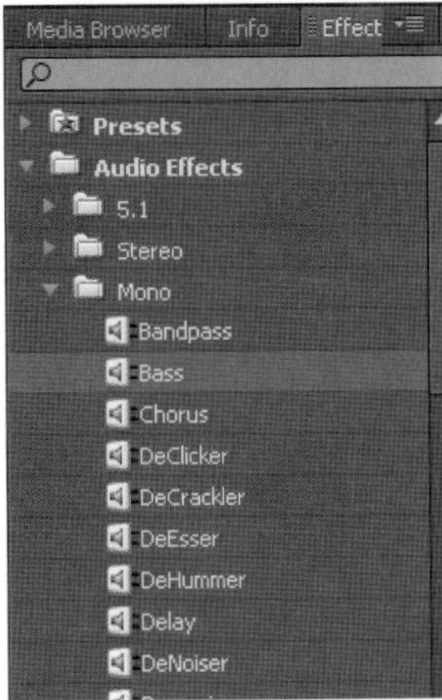

5 Play the clip, and then move the Bass Boost slider left and right. This increases or decreases bass.

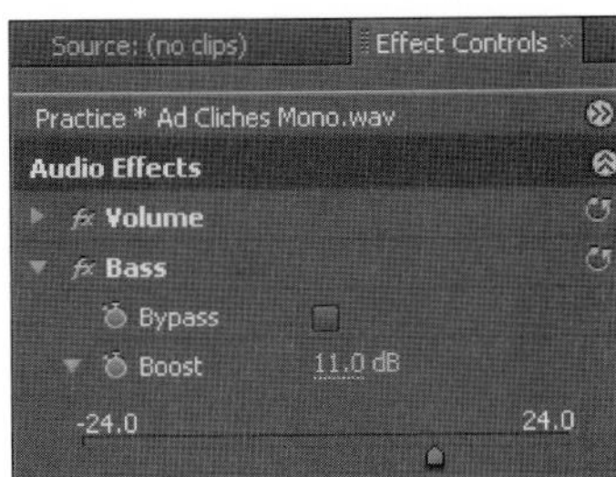

6 Delete Bass from the Effect Controls panel and add Delay.

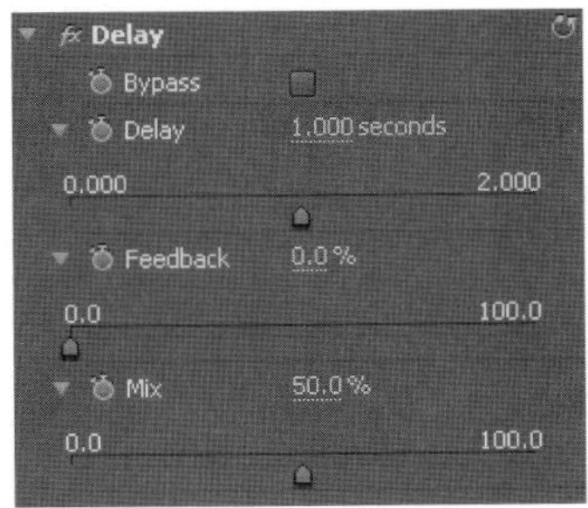

Try its three parameters:

- **Delay**: This refers to the time before the echo plays (0 to 2 seconds).
- **Feedback**: This is the percentage of echo added back to audio to create echoes of echoes.
- **Mix**: This is the relative loudness of echo.

Note: Listing all the attributes of all the audio effects is beyond the scope of this book. To learn more about audio effect parameters, search Adobe Premiere Pro Help.

7 Play the clip and move the sliders to experiment with the effect.

Lower values are more palatable, even with this over-the-top audio clip.

8 Delete Delay and add PitchShifter to the Effect Controls panel.

This panel includes three nifty items: knobs, presets, and a Reset button. You can tell an audio effect has presets by the tiny triangle next to what would normally be the Reset button and the addition of a rectangular Reset button (as shown here).

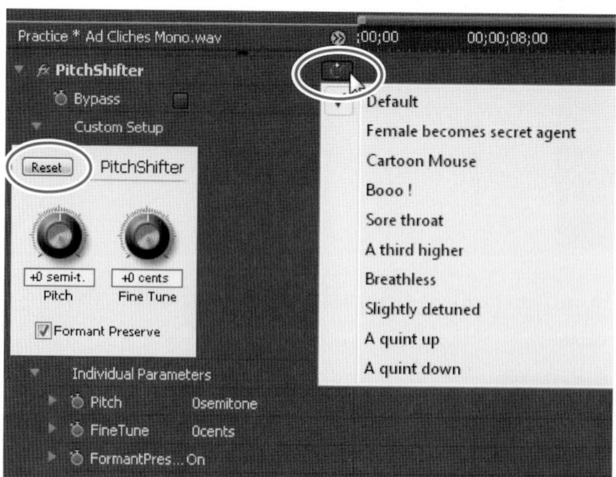

9 Try some of the presets, and note their values below the knobs in the Effect Controls panel.

10 Use the Individual Parameters sliders, and add keyframes at the beginning and end of a few phrases.

Use wildly different Pitch settings from -12 to + 12 semitone steps (two steps equals a second in musical parlance—from C to D, for example), and switch Formant Preserve on and off.

Note: *Formant Preserve* is not a misprint. *Formant* is the character, resonance, and phonetic quality of a particular voice, so Formant Preserve attempts to retain those elements even with severe pitch changes.

11 Delete Ad Cliches from the sequence and replace it with Music Mono.wav (you can do that by dragging Music Mono.wav to the beginning of the sequence, on top of Ad Cliches, to do an overlay edit).

12 Drag Treble to that clip and increase its parameter.

This guitar clip lends itself to a treble boost.

Note: Treble is not simply Bass in reverse. Treble increases or decreases higher frequencies (4,000 Hz and greater) while Bass changes low frequencies (200 Hz and less). The human audible frequency range is roughly 20 Hz to 20,000 Hz. Apply both Bass and Treble to a clip, and switch between them by clicking their Toggle effect on or off buttons.

13 Delete Treble, drag Reverb to the Effect Controls panel, and open Reverb's Custom Setup.

14 Play the clip, and drag the three white handles in the display to change the character of the reverb.

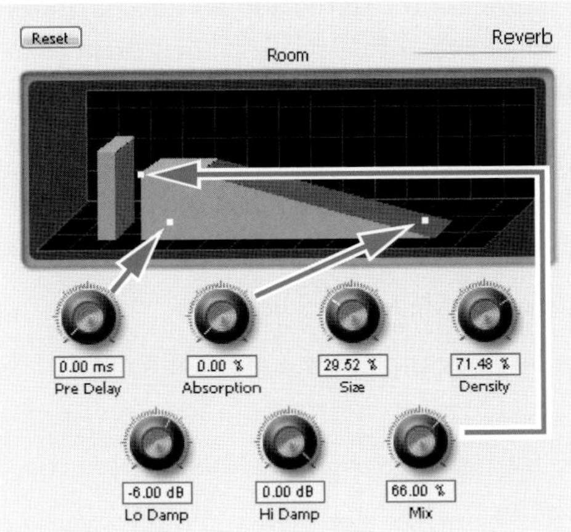

This is a fun effect that can give some real life to audio recorded in a "dead" room—a room like a recording studio with minimal reflective surfaces. As shown here, each of the three handles in the graphic control corresponds to a knob below it:

- **Pre Delay**: This is the apparent distance the sound travels to the reflecting walls and back.
- **Absorption**: This assesses how much of the sound is absorbed (not reflected).
- **Mix:** This is the amount of reverb.

These are the additional controls:

- **Size**: This refers to the apparent relative size of the room.
- **Density**: This is the density of the reverb "tail." The higher the Size value, the greater the Density range (from 0 to 100%).
- **Lo Damp**: Adjust this to dampen low frequencies to prevent the reverb from rumbling or sounding muddy.
- **Hi Damp**: This dampens high frequencies. A low Hi Damp setting makes the reverb sound softer.

A treasure trove of VST plug-ins

Reverb's rack of control knobs signals that this is a Virtual Studio Technology (VST) plug-in. These are custom-designed audio effects that adhere to a standard set by Steinberg audio. Invariably, those who create VST audio effect plug-ins want them to have a unique look and offer some very specialized audio effects. Many VST plug-ins are available on the Internet.

Trying stereo and 5.1 surround sound effects

The mono audio effects collection is a subset of the stereo and 5.1 effects. Those multichannel effect groups have additional effects that relate to their extra channels. You'll see here how they work in this exercise:

1 Open Lesson 14-2.prproj.

2 Drag Music Stereo.wav from the Project panel to the Audio 1 track in the sequence. In this project, the Audio 1 track is set up as a stereo track.

3 Attempt to drag any mono audio effect to the Music Stereo clip.

   You'll get a universal "No" symbol—you can't apply a mono effect to a stereo clip.

4 Drag Balance from Effects > Audio Effects > Stereo to the Music Stereo clip.

5 Drag the Balance slider in the Effect Controls panel left and right while you play this clip.

   This clip was mixed with the guitar panned all the way left and the honky-tonk piano panned hard right. If you move the slider all the way to either end, you will hear only one instrument.

6 Add two keyframes, and have the audio pan from left to right. (Using keyframes for audio effects is similar to using them for video effects, as you learned in Lesson 10.)

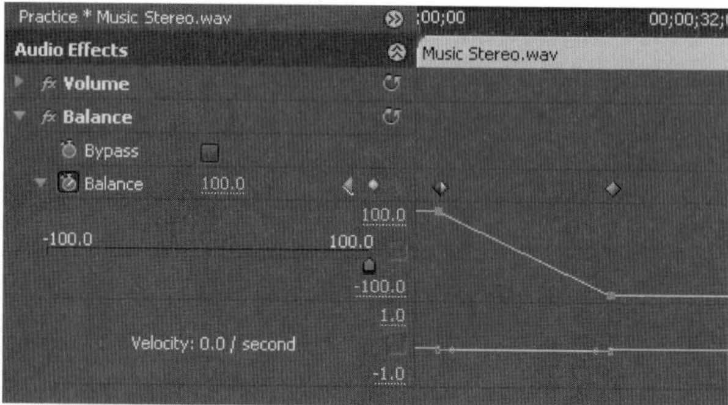

7 Play the clip.

The sound moves from left to right and, in this case, makes the guitar fade into the piano.

8 Delete Balance and apply Fill Right.

The Fill effects duplicate the selected channel, place it in the other channel, and discard that other channel's original audio. So, in this example, Fill Right plays the honky-tonk piano in both left and right channels and discards the guitar (the track in the left channel).

Use the same effect more than once

You've probably seen an equalizer. Many car and home stereos have them. They enable you to punch up or cut a number of preset frequency ranges. The EQ effect in Adobe Premiere Pro fits that bill, but it offers only five frequency ranges. If you want more possibilities, you can use Parametric EQ, which lets you select only one frequency range, but you can use it multiple times and select multiple frequencies. In effect, you can build a full graphic equalizer within the Effect Controls panel.

9 Drag Music 5.1.wav to the sequence, and Adobe Premiere Pro adds a 5.1 audio track to accommodate this new audio clip type.

10 Mute the Audio track containing the Music Stereo clip by clicking the speaker button on the left side of the track label.

11 Drag Channel Volume from the Audio Effects > 5.1 folder to the Music 5.1 clip.

Channel Volume lets you control the volume level for each of the six channels in a 5.1 surround sound clip and both channels of a stereo clip. The default setting for each channel is 0 dB, meaning no change from the original volume.

12 Play the clip and drag the sliders for each channel to experiment with this effect.

Note: If you don't hear all six channels, it's because you need to change the 5.1 Mixdown setting. Choose Edit > Preferences > Audio (Windows) or Premiere Pro > Preferences > Audio (Mac OS), and change 5.1 Mixdown Type to Front + Rear + LFE.

Looking at one more VST plug-in

Let's check out one more audio effect. This one is guaranteed to make your head spin. Drag MultibandCompressor to the Music 5.1 clip. You'll need to dramatically expand the Effect Controls panel to see its parameters (it might help to put the Effect Controls panel in a floating window).

The MultibandCompressor's purpose is to narrow the dynamic range for up to three sets of frequency ranges. Explaining its parameters could take a full lesson (refer to Adobe Premiere Pro Help for parameter details). Instead, note that it offers a collection of presets accessed by clicking the button shown here.

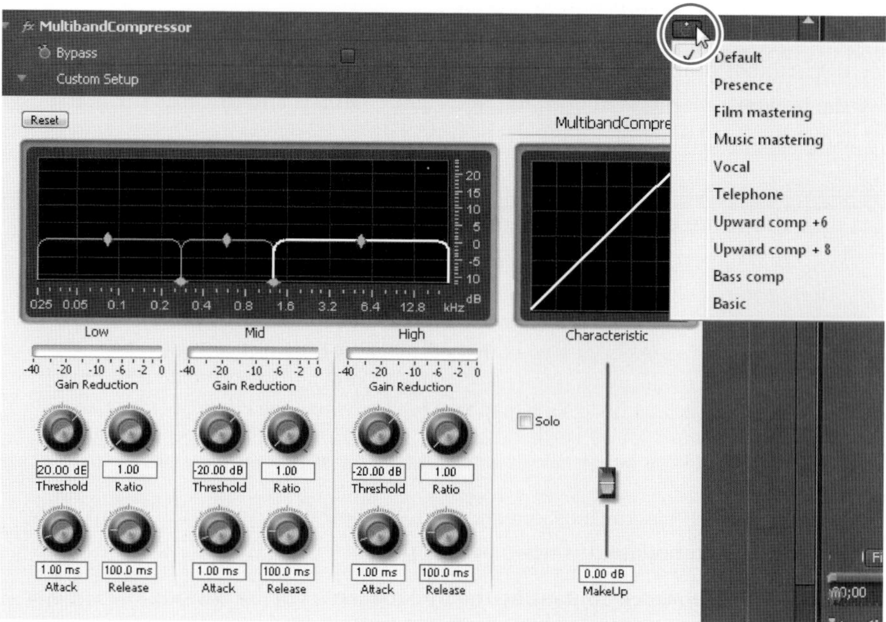

Editing keyframes by using the clip effect menu

You might have noticed that tucked away along the top edge of all clips—audio and video—is a pop-up menu of all the effects applied to a selected clip. You can find it just to the right of the clip name.

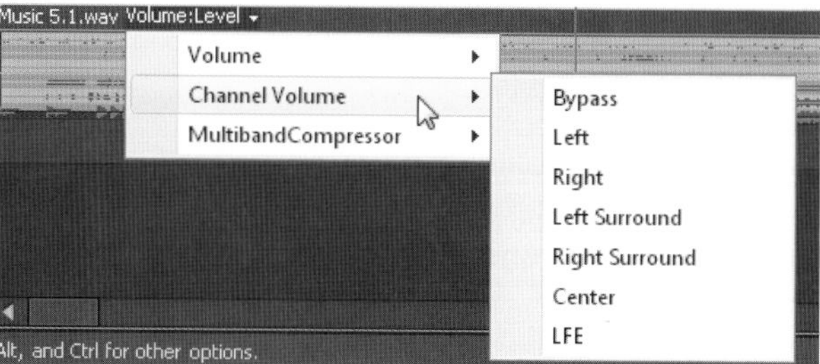

You might not be able to see the clip effect menu in all instances. The audio or video track needs to be in its expanded view. To do that, click the disclosure triangle to the left of the track name. If that does not reveal it, the clip is not wide enough. Zoom in on the Timeline to expand the width of the clip and reveal the clip effect menu.

For audio clips, the header is always Volume: Level. For Video clips, it's Opacity: Opacity (despite Motion residing on the top of that pop-up menu). Every time you add an effect—video or audio—Adobe Premiere Pro adds that effect (along with a list of its parameters) to the bottom of that clip's effect menu.

1 Delete the MultibandCompressor effect.
2 Open the clip effect menu by clicking Channel Volume.
3 Select Left.
4 Drag the yellow line, which now represents the left channel volume, up or down to change the left channel's volume.
5 Click the Show keyframes button on the left side of the audio track, and then set it to Show clip Volume. This causes the track to display the clip's volume, rather than the track's volume.
6 Ctrl-click (Windows) or Command-click (Mac OS) the yellow line to add a couple of keyframes, and adjust them by dragging them left or right along the graph line or dragging them up or down.

The advantages of clip-based effect and keyframe editing are that you can get a better overall view of the entire clip, and if you want to change only one or two parameters, you can easily access them. Some disadvantages are that you can't change the parameters while the clip is playing, setting an exact parameter value is challenging, and changing more than a couple of parameters in the Timeline panel gets tedious.

Working with the Audio Mixer

There is a big difference in how Adobe Premiere Pro handles layered audio tracks and layered video tracks.

Clips in higher-numbered video tracks cover what's below them on the Timeline. You need to do something to those higher video track clips—adjust opacity, create PIPs, or use specialized keying effects—to let clips below them show through.

Clips in audio tracks all play together. If you have 10 layered audio tracks loaded up with a variety of audio clips and do nothing to them in terms of adjusting volume levels and stereo panning, they'll all play as one grand symphony (or cacophonous mess).

Although you can adjust volume levels by using each clip's volume graph in the Timeline or Volume effect in the Effect Controls panel, it's much easier to use the Audio Mixer to adjust volume levels and other characteristics for multiple audio tracks.

Using a panel that looks a lot like production studio mixing hardware, you move track sliders to change volume, turn knobs to set left/right panning, add effects to entire tracks, and create submixes. Submixes let you direct multiple audio tracks to a single track so you can apply the same effects, volume, and panning to a group of tracks without having to change each of the tracks individually.

In this exercise, you will mix a song recorded by a choir in a studio:

1 Double-click Music - Sonoma Stereo Mix.wav, and play it in the Source Monitor. This is how your final mix should sound.

2 Open Lesson 14-3.prproj.

3 Play the Practice sequence, and note that the instruments are way too loud compared to the choir.

4 Choose Window > Workspace > Audio, and adjust the Audio Mixer panel so you can see all five tracks plus the master track.

5 Change the track names along the top row of the Audio Mixer by selecting each one in turn and typing a new name: **Left**, **Right**, **Clarinet**, **Flute**, and **Bass** (as shown here).

Those name changes also appear in the audio track headers in the Timeline.

6 Play the sequence, and adjust the sliders in the Audio Mixer to create a mix that you think works well. (A good place to start is setting Left to 4, setting Right to 2, and dropping the Clarinet, Flute, and Bass to -12, -10, and -12, respectively.)

7 Watch the master track VU (volume unit) meter as you make your adjustments.

Little hash marks (shown here) indicate the loudest passages. They remain for a couple of seconds and then move as the music volume changes. These hash marks provide a good way to see how balanced your left and right channels are. You want them to approximately line up most of the time.

Note: You want to avoid setting the volume too high (the VU meter line will turn red). That leads to distortion.

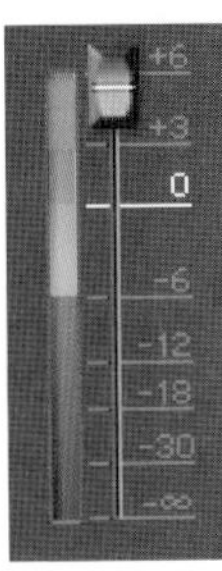

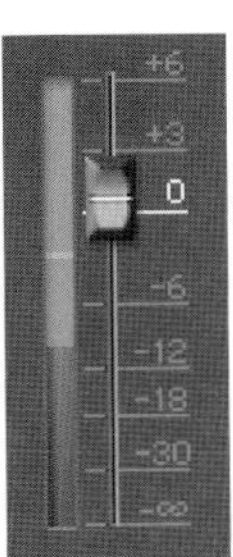

8 Adjust each channel's Left/Right Pan by using the knobs at the top of each track (when completed, your parameters should match those shown here):

- **Left**: All the way left (-100)
- **Right**: All the way right (+100)
- **Clarinet**: Left-center (-20)
- **Flute**: Right-center (+20)
- **Bass**: Centered (0)

9 Click the Show/Hide Effects and Sends button.

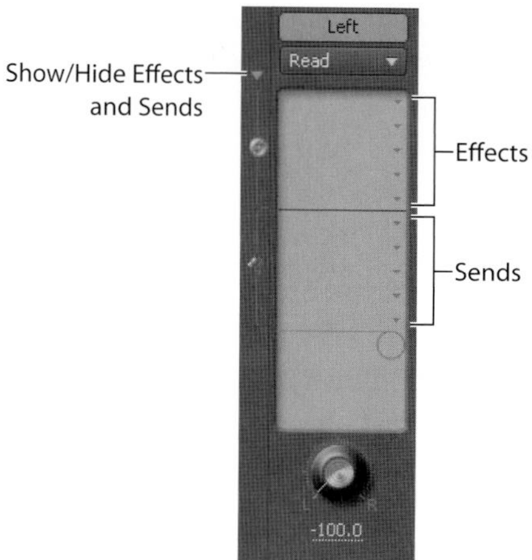

This opens a set of empty panels where you can add effects to entire tracks and assign tracks to submixes.

10 Click the Effect Selection button for the Left track and choose Reverb from the pop-up menu.

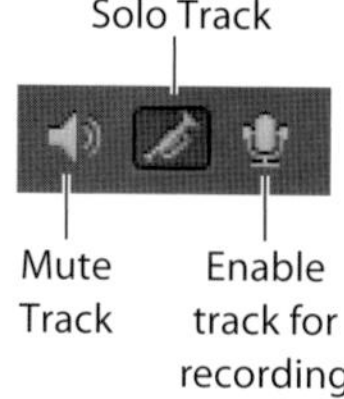

11 Isolate that track by clicking its Solo button (that mutes the rest of the channels).

You can click Solo buttons on more than one track to listen to a group of tracks. You can also click the Mute button to switch off audio playback for one or more tracks. You'll use the Enable Track For Recording button in the next lesson.

12 Click the Reverb effect pop-up menu, and make changes to each parameter.

Note: It's easier to apply effect parameters in the Effect Controls panel, but you can edit only clips there—not audio or video tracks. In this case, you could apply this effect to the clip instead of the track because there is only one clip on the track, but it's good to see how track-based effects work.

Play the clip to listen to your changes as you make them.

13 Undo your settings by removing the Reverb effect. To do that, click the Effect Selection button and select None.

Keep tabs on Mute and Solo settings

After working in the Audio Mixer for a while and then returning to the Timeline, you might not hear anything. Audio Mixer Mute and Solo settings do not show up in the Timeline but are still in effect when you play a clip in the Timeline, even if the Audio Mixer is closed. So, check those Mute and Solo settings before shutting down the Audio Mixer.

Automating changes in audio tracks

In the previous section, you set volume and panning values for entire tracks while listening to the audio. Adobe Premiere Pro also lets you apply volume and panning values that change over time, and you can apply them as you play your sequence.

To do so, use automation modes, accessed via pop-up menus at the top of each track in the Audio Mixer. Using one of the automation modes creates a series of track (as opposed to clip) keyframes for volume and panning, saving you from adding them one at a time.

Briefly, here's what each setting means (you can read more about this in Adobe Premiere Pro Help):

- **Off**: This setting ignores any changes you apply and thus lets you test some adjustments without recording them.
- **Read**: Adjusting a track option (such as volume) affects the entire track uniformly. This is the default setting you used when setting the mix volume in step 6 of the previous exercise.
- **Latch**: This works like Write but won't apply changes until you move the volume slider or panning knob. The initial property settings are from the previous adjustment.
- **Touch**: This works like Latch except that when you stop adjusting a property, its option settings return to their previous states before the current automated changes were recorded.
- **Write**: This setting records adjustments you make as you listen to a sequence.

Outputting tracks to submixes

You place your audio clips into audio tracks on the Timeline. You can apply effects and set volume and panning on a clip-by-clip basis. Or you can use the Audio Mixer to apply volume, panning, and effects to entire tracks. In either case, by default Adobe Premiere Pro sends audio from those clips and tracks to the master track.

But sometimes you might want to route tracks to submix tracks before sending them on to the master track.

The purpose of submix tracks is to save you steps and ensure some consistency in how you apply effects, volume, and panning. In the case of the Sonoma recording, you can apply Reverb with one set of parameters to the two choir tracks, and you can apply Reverb with different parameters to the three instruments. The submix can then send the processed signal to the master track, or it can route the signal to another submix.

1 Open Lesson 14-4.prproj. This project picks up where you left off with the Sonoma Choir.

2 Right-click (Windows) or Control-click (Mac OS) an audio track header in the Timeline and, using the figure shown here as a guide, choose Add Tracks. Set the Add values for Video Tracks and Audio Tracks to 0, set the Add value for Audio Submix Tracks to 2, and set Track Type for Audio Submix Tracks to Stereo; then click OK.

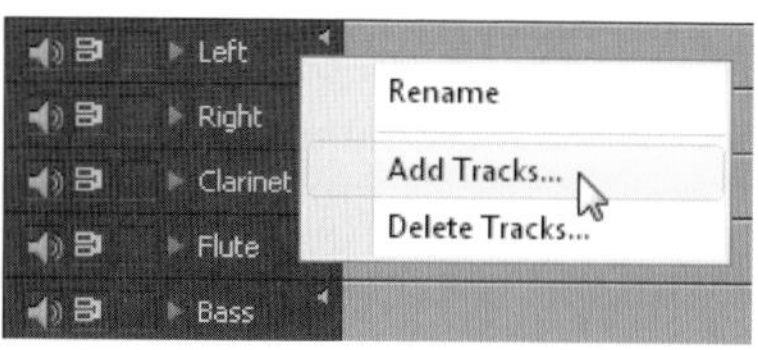

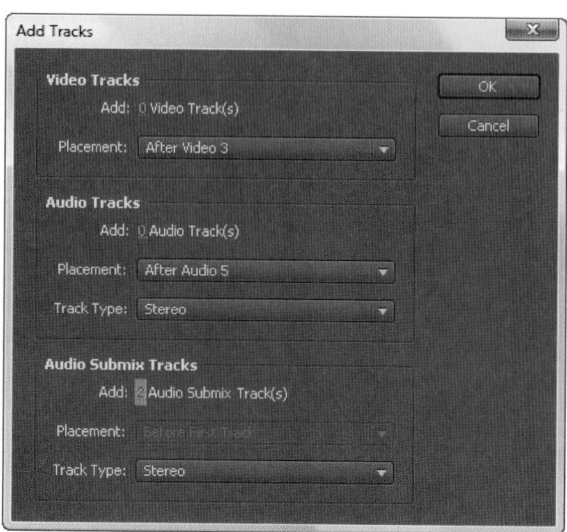

That adds two submix tracks to the Timeline and two tracks to the Audio Mixer (they have a darker hue), and it adds those submix track names (Submix 1 and Submix 2) to the pop-up menus at the bottom of the Audio Mixer.

3 Click the Left track's Track Output Assignment pop-up menu (at the bottom of the Audio Mixer), and select Submix 1.

4 Do the same for the Right track.

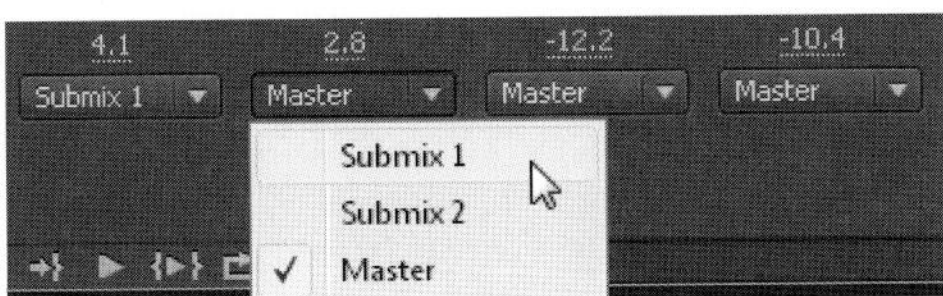

Now both the Left and Right tracks have been sent to Submix 1. Their individual characteristics—panning and volume—will not change.

5 Send the three instrument tracks to Submix 2.

6 Apply Reverb to the Submix 1 track by clicking the Show/Hide Effects triangle and adding Reverb as an effect. Click its Solo button, play the audio, and adjust the Reverb parameters to make it sound like the choir is singing in a large auditorium (setting Size to about 60 is a good place to start).

7 Apply Reverb to the Submix 2 track, click its Solo Track button, switch off the Submix 1 Solo button (remember you can solo more than one track, but in this case you want to solo only Submix 2), play its audio, and set its parameters to create a sound a bit less dramatic than the voices.

8 Click the Solo button on Submix 1, and listen to these two submixes as a single mix to see how they sound.

Feel free to tweak the Volume and Reverb settings.

Recording voice-overs

The Adobe Premiere Pro Audio Mixer is also a basic recording studio. It can record anything you can connect to your sound card. In this case, you'll use your computer's microphone to do a voice recording:

1 Remove any audio files from the Timeline, and set your current-time indicator at the beginning.

2 Make sure your computer's microphone is plugged in to the Mic input on your sound card, and make sure your audio setup is set to recognize and record from the microphone and that it is not muted. Check your computer's documentation if you are not sure how to set up a microphone to record.

3 Choose Edit > Preferences > Audio Hardware (Windows) or Premiere Pro > Preferences > Audio Hardware (Mac OS), and ensure that your default device is the hardware to which you have connected your microphone.

Note: Selecting Default will work in most circumstances. However, if you have a higher-end audio card, you should select it, refer to its product manual, and make any needed changes to its ASIO settings.

4 In the Audio Mixer, click the Enable Track For Recording button (the microphone) at the top of the audio track to which you want to record.

You can enable as many tracks as you like, but you can't record to the master track or a submix track. If you have more than one microphone enabled on your system, choose the microphone you want to use in the pop-up menu that appears above the microphone button.

5 Click the red Record button at the bottom of the Audio Mixer. The button starts blinking.

6 Move the current-time indicator to where you want this narration to begin (it'll cover up any audio on the selected track at that location).

Note: If you chose to locate the current-time indicator in the music, you'll hear the music as you record your voice. Being able to hear your sequence's audio as you narrate can be a big help. Laying down video clips and then recording a narration is a workflow some editors follow.

7 Click the Play button in the Audio Mixer, and start your narration.

8 When you finish recording, click the Stop button.

An audio clip appears on the selected audio track and in the Project panel. Adobe Premiere Pro automatically names that clip based on the audio track number or name and adds that audio file to the project file folder on your hard drive.

What about feedback?

If you record audio and you have not taken steps to mute the output, you might get feedback—that lovely screeching noise that happens when a microphone gets too close to a loudspeaker. You can deal with that in several ways: You can click the Mute button for the track, turn down your speakers (use headphones to listen to yourself), or choose Edit > Preferences > Audio (Windows) or Premiere Pro > Preferences > Audio (Mac OS) and then select Mute input during timeline recording.

Creating a 5.1 surround sound mix

Adobe Premiere Pro lets you create a full, digital, 5.1 surround sound mix. You can use 5.1 surround sound in two places: audio on a DVD or Blu-ray Disc or an audio file for playback on a computer with 5.1 surround sound speakers.

5.1 digital audio has six discrete channels: left front, front center, right front, right rear or surround, left rear or surround, and the low-frequency effects (LFE) channel designated for a subwoofer.

If you have a 5.1 surround sound setup on your computer, this section will be a lot of fun and lead to much experimentation. If you don't have a six-speaker setup, this at least will give you a feel for how to add 5.1 surround to a DVD.

Here are the basic steps to follow:

1 Open Lesson 14-5.prproj. This project has seven mono tracks and a 5.1 audio master track.

2 Drag the music clips to the Timeline as shown here. Note that Sonoma-Left and Sonoma-Right appear on the Timeline twice.

3 In the Audio Mixer, drag each track's 5.1 Panner puck to the proper location (shown here).

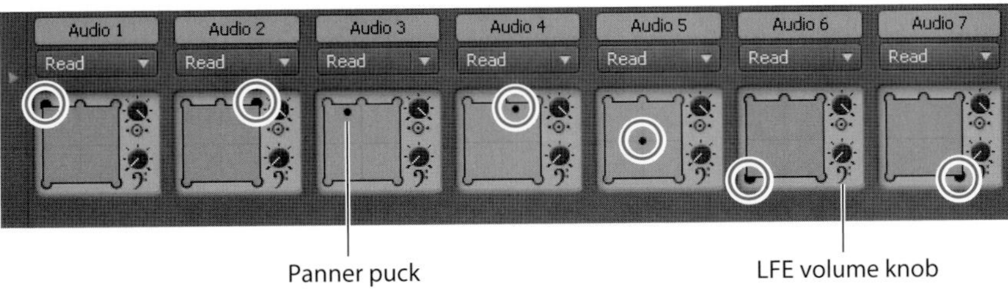

4 Set volume levels for tracks 1–5 that are similar to those you set for the stereo mix. For Audio 5 (the bass), adjust the volume using the LFE volume knob, and place its puck in the center. Set volume levels for tracks 6 and 7 (left-rear and right-rear) to 0 and -2, respectively.

Now you have some options:

- You can move the clips on Audio 6 and Audio 7 about a tenth of a second (three frames) into the Timeline (causing them to play a little after the rest of the clips) to make it sound like they're coming from the back of the room. To do that, select each clip in turn, press the plus sign (+) on the numeric keypad, type **3** on the numeric keypad, and press Enter on the numeric keypad.
- You can add a Reverb with a Size parameter a bit higher than what you set for the front channels. You might find that you don't need to have as much reverb for the front channels when you work in 5.1 surround sound.

Fixing, sweetening, and creating soundtracks in Soundbooth

Soundbooth is audio software designed especially for video and Flash editors. Soundbooth can be run as a stand-alone audio tool, or it can be launched from Adobe Premiere Pro. Although many audio tools are built into Adobe Premiere Pro, Soundbooth is designed to deal with specific audio challenges that video editors face every day. You will find Soundbooth easy to use yet very powerful.

Note: Soundbooth is not included with Adobe Premiere Pro. You must purchase Soundbooth separately or as part of Adobe Creative Suite CS4. The basics of Soundbooth are included in this book to demonstrate its integration and easy workflow with Adobe Premiere Pro.

Rather than give you a series of full-blown lessons on Soundbooth, we will review the most common uses you will run into: adding effects and cleaning up noisy audio.

Cleaning up noisy audio

Of course, it's always best to record perfect audio at the source. However, sometimes you cannot control the origin of the audio and it's impossible to re-record it, so you are stuck needing to repair a bad audio clip. To that end, the sample you will work on is a real-world nightmare—a voice-over narration with a horrible 60 Hz hum and a cell phone ringing in the background—but don't pull your hair out, because Soundbooth is up to the task.

Note: A 60 Hz or 50 Hz hum can be caused by many electrical problems, cable problems, or equipment noise.

1 Open Lesson 14-6.prproj.

2 Double-click audio problem.wav to open it in the Source Monitor. Play the clip, and notice the 60 Hz hum throughout and the cell phone ringing near the end.

3 Open audio problems fixed.wav in the Source Monitor, and listen to it. Soundbooth was used to remove the hum and the cell phone without noticeably affecting the voice.

4 Drag audio problems.wav to the Audio 1 track on the Timeline.

Note: You can also choose to edit the source file if you don't need to keep the original file. The Render And Replace command does not affect the original file. Rather, it renders a new copy of the file and replaces it automatically on the Timeline, so the original file is not changed.

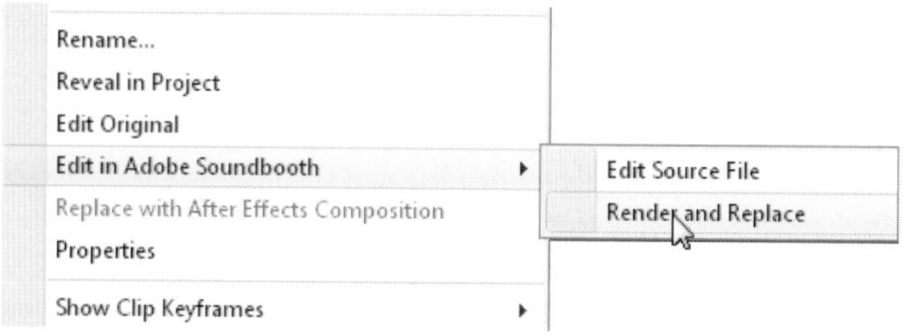

5 Right-click (Windows) or Control-click (Mac OS) the audio problems clip on the Timeline and choose Edit in Adobe Soundbooth > Render And Replace from the context menu. Soundbooth starts and displays the clip.

Rename...
Reveal in Project
Edit Original
Edit in Adobe Soundbooth
Edit Source File
Render and Replace
Replace with After Effects Composition
Properties
Show Clip Keyframes

6 Soundbooth displays two views of your audio file: the common waveform view showing audio amplitudes near the top of the screen and a colorful spectral display view showing audio frequencies near the bottom of the screen. If you can't see both views, drag the horizontal divider between the panels up or down so they are both visible. Give the frequency display more room.

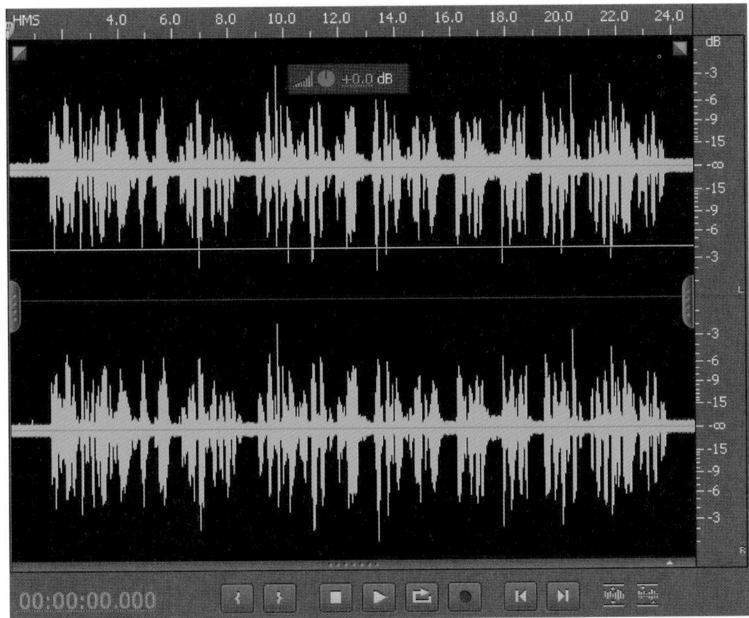

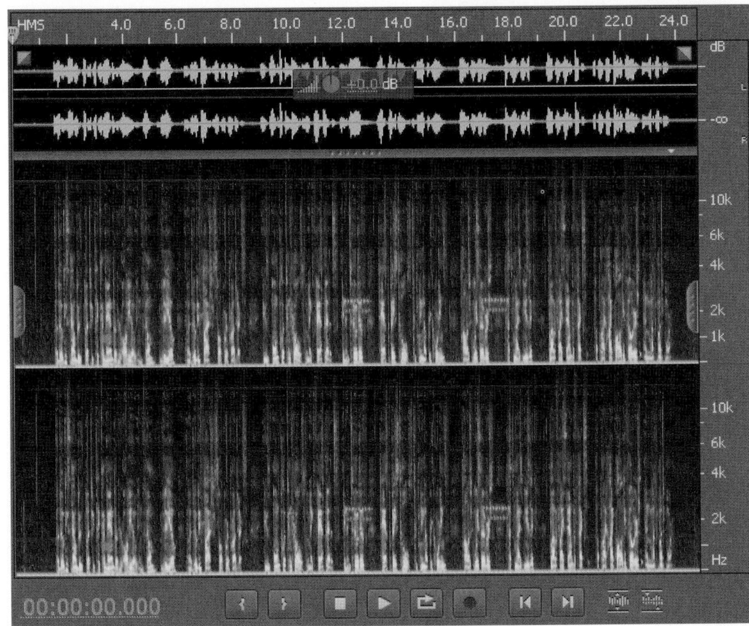

Note: The spectral display shows frequencies over time rather than amplitudes over time. In this display, colors represent amplitude—dark blue for low amplitude and bright yellow for high amplitude.

7 Play the file again to hear the problems, the hum and the cell phone ringing. You can drag the current-time indicator, much as you would in Adobe Premiere Pro, and use the playback controls at the bottom of the screen.

8 To remove the 60 Hz hum, click the Effects tab in the left-center panel. Click the Stereo Rack Preset pop-up menu, and choose Fix:Remove 60 Cycle Hum.

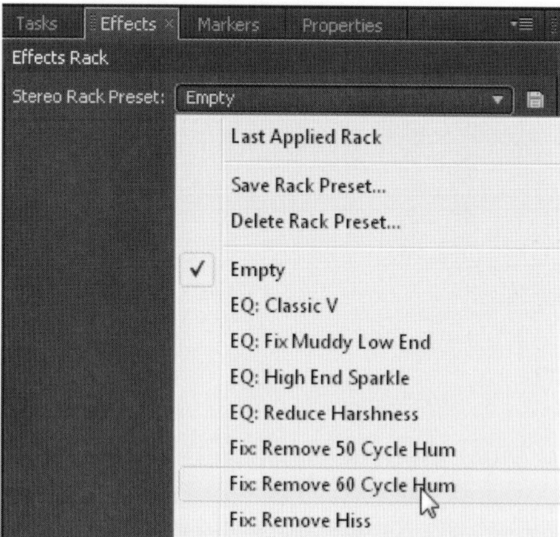

9 Play the file again, and hear the amazing difference.

10 The effect is not permanently applied to the file yet. To permanently apply this change, click the Apply to File button at the bottom of the Effects Rack.

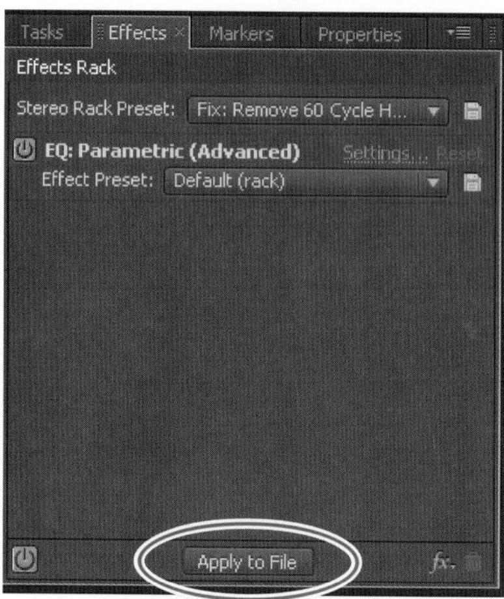

11 To remove the cell phone sound, you need to use the spectral display. The ringing cell phone is not visible as a change in amplitude, so you can't use the waveform display to locate this problem. However, if you zoom out so the whole file is visible, the cell phone rings are quite obvious in the spectral display as short horizontal dashes between 2 kHz and 3 kHz.

12 Position the current-time indicator over the first cell phone ring, and zoom in by pressing the equal sign key (=) on the keyboard or the plus sign (+) on the numeric keypad.

13 Select the Rectangular Marquee tool, and then select the cell phone ring. Make the marquee selection just slightly bigger than the visible ring. Be as precise as possible. When you are finished, the selection appears as an opaque box around the cell phone ring with a dB adjustment tool floating above it.

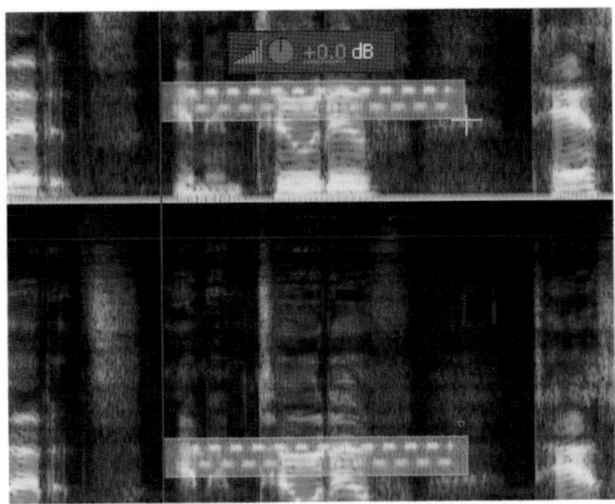

14 Adjust the selection to -34 dB. This reduces the frequencies you selected with the Marquee tool by negative 34 dB.

15 Zoom out, and play the clip. Even though it appears that some of the ring tone is still there, notice it is dark blue, which means very low volume.

16 Save the changes to the clip by choosing File > Save. Switch back to Adobe Premiere Pro, and notice that the audio file on the Timeline has been updated with the changes.

Note: A common mistake is to reduce noise selections to the maximum (-96 dB) to remove them completely. However, this creates a complete void in that frequency spectrum for your selection, which is often noticeable. Most noises are soft enough that -34 db is enough to eliminate them without removing the frequency space completely. Experiment by removing the least amount possible to keep your audio sounding natural.

Adding audio effects in Adobe Soundbooth

You will use the same audio file to add a few effects in Soundbooth. Continue where you left off in Soundbooth with the audio problem.wav file:

1 Another way to add an effect to the Effects panel is to click the Add an effect to the rack icon () in the lower-right corner of the panel. Choose Vocal Enhancer from the Effects menu. In the Effects panel, choose Male as the effect preset for the Vocal Enhancer effect.

2 Play the file to hear the effect.

3 Choose Analog Delay from the Add an effect to the rack icon, and experiment with the many presets available.

   You can add multiple effects to the Effects Rack at the same time. When you get a combination of effects you like, you can save them as a Rack preset. There are many preloaded Rack presets you can choose from and experiment with.

4 Try one of the Rack presets—Choose Voice: Old Time Radio—and play the effect.

5 If you want to get more advanced and tweak some of the settings yourself, click the Settings link to the right of each effect name. This gives you access to the detailed settings of each effect.

Using multiple tracks and Dynamic Link with Soundbooth

Soundbooth has the ability to work with more than one audio file at once. This is called *multitrack editing*. In this mode, an Adobe Premiere Pro project can be imported and used as a reference for creating a complex soundtrack in Soundbooth.

1 Open Soundbooth, and choose File > New > Multitrack File.

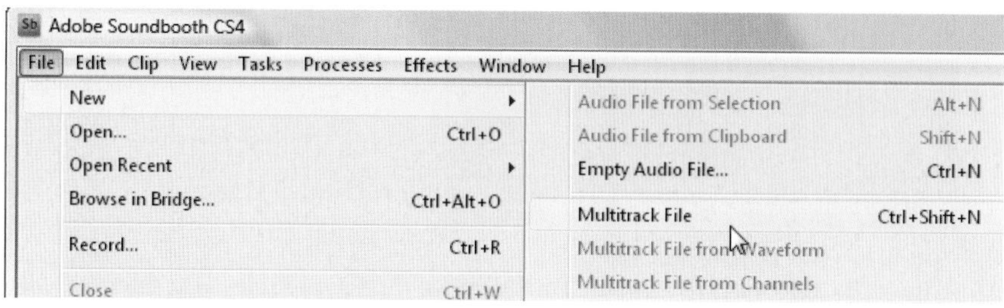

● **Note:** Adobe Creative Suite needs to be installed to enable the Dynamic Link functionality.

You'll import one of the Adobe Premiere Pro projects you worked with earlier in this book to use as a reference in Soundbooth to create a musical soundtrack. Soundbooth uses Dynamic Link to perform this function. Adobe Premiere Pro does not even need to be open.

2 Choose File > Adobe Dynamic Link > Import Premiere Pro Sequence.

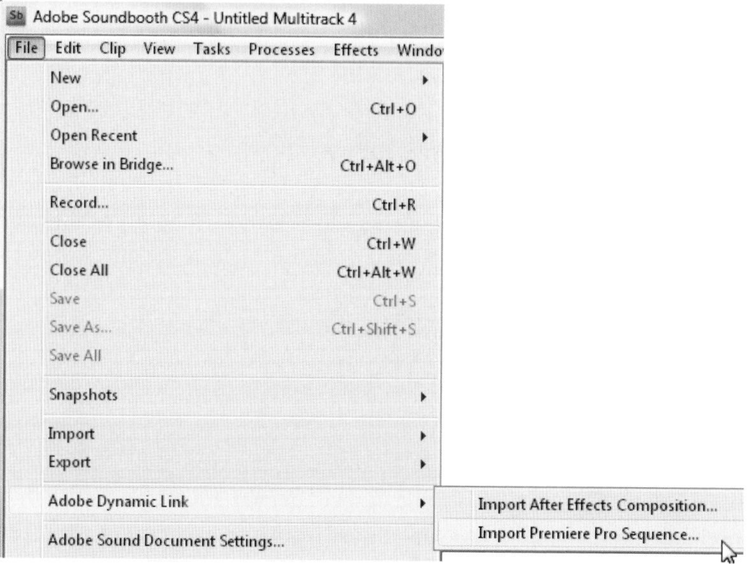

3 Navigate to the Lesson 06 folder, click Lesson 06-5.prproj, and the sequences within that project will be displayed in the right Sequence pane. Choose the Complete sequence, and click OK.

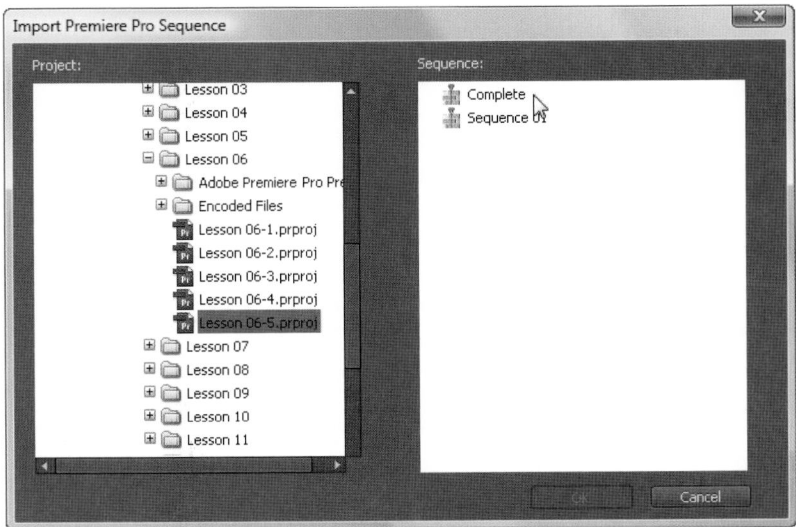

This imports the sequence from the selected Adobe Premiere Pro project and displays it in Soundbooth. You can play the sequence to hear the existing soundtrack and see the video. You are now going to have Soundbooth generate a score to use with this sequence.

4 Click the Scores tab in the upper-left panel. Two scores come with Soundbooth, but many more can be downloaded. Check Soundbooth Help for instructions on downloading additional scores.

5 Drag the AqoVisit score to the Audio 1 track.

6 The score is longer than the sequence you added. Press the backslash key to zoom the Timeline so you can see the entire score.

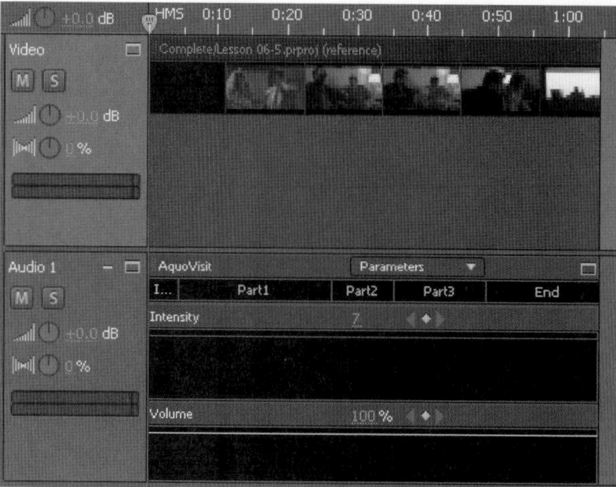

7 Drag the right edge of the score to the left until it is the same length as the video sequence. Soundbooth composes the score on the fly as you change its length.

8 Play the sequence with the new score added. Notice the score is too loud and is covering the narration. Lower the volume of the score by lowering the dB to -12.

You can save or export this soundtrack to be used in other applications or imported into Adobe Premiere Pro.

Review questions

1 There are at least four ways to make audio move from the right channel to the left and back. What are they?

2 You are playing a 5.1 surround sound clip but can't hear all the channels. What's a possible cause?

3 What's the difference between the Delay and Reverb effects?

4 Can you record a voice-over while other audio is playing on the Timeline?

5 How do you apply the same audio effect with the same parameters to three audio tracks?

6 Describe the difference between the Edit Source File and Render And Replace commands when editing a file from Adobe Premiere Pro in Soundbooth.

7 How is using Dynamic Link to import an Adobe Premiere Pro project into Soundbooth useful?

Review answers

1 Balance adjusts the overall balance, left or right. Channel Volume enables you to adjust the volume of each channel individually. You can also use the Audio Mixer's Left/Right Pan knob or use clip or track keyframes on the Timeline.

2 Check the audio preferences, and make sure the 5.1 Mixdown setting includes all channels.

3 Delay creates a distinct, single echo that can repeat and gradually fade. Reverb creates a mix of echoes to simulate a room. It has multiple parameters that take the hard edge off the echo you hear in the Delay effect.

4 Yes. When you start recording the voice-over, any other audio tracks on the Timeline will be heard as you record.

5 The easiest way is to create a submix track is to assign those three tracks to that submix track and apply the effect to the submix.

6 Edit Source File changes the original source audio file. Render And Replace creates a new copy of the audio file and changes the copy rather than the original.

7 Adobe Dynamic Link allows you to import a sequence into Soundbooth without having to render it first.

15 AUDIO TRANSCRIPTION

Topics covered in this lesson

- Transcribing audio to text
- Searching a transcription for keywords
- Modifying an audio file's metadata

This lesson will take approximately 15 minutes.

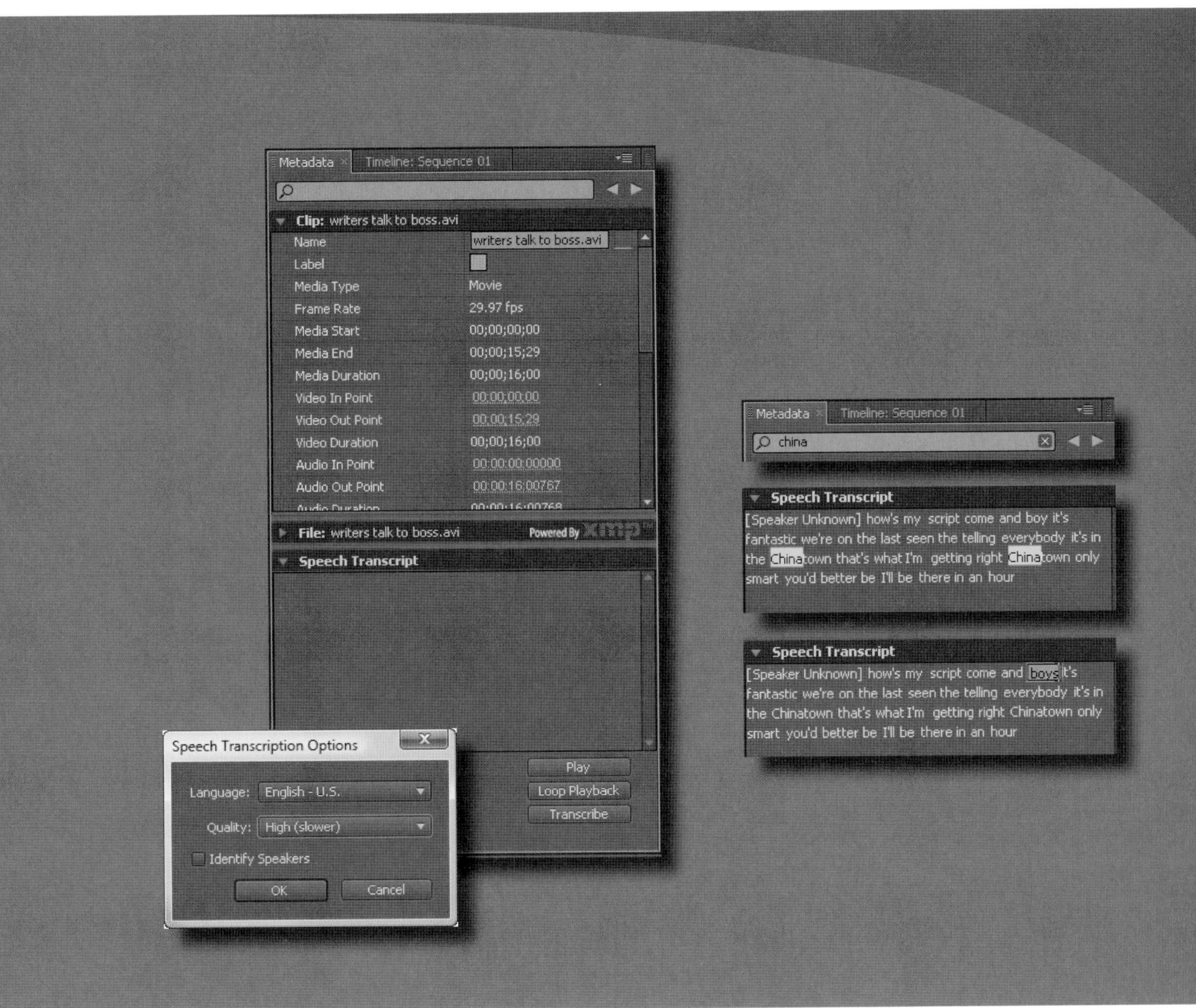

Adobe Premiere Pro CS4 can convert an audio file containing speech to a text transcription file. This allows you to search an audio file for keywords, or even to locate a specific video frame using a text search tool.

Getting started

While it may not be obvious from the small sample files used in this lesson, speech transcription can be a huge timesaver, allowing you to do text searches to find a video frame where a specific word is spoken. You can easily add markers or edit points after using this feature to locate keywords. Without this feature, you would need to scrub or play the audio of the file to listen for keywords.

You will notice that it does take some time for Adobe Premiere Pro CS4 to transcribe an audio file to text. But this process can run in batch mode in the background while you do other work. It's also worth noting that once the transcription occurs, the transcribed text becomes part of the audio file's metadata. Even if you export the file, the transcription will remain with the file.

Transcribing audio to text

The first step in transcribing audio to text is to get your workspace into its Metalogging workspace and make the metadata associated with your files visible in the Premiere Pro interface.

1 Open Lesson 15-1.prproj.

2 Click Window > Workspace > Metalogging to change the workspace layout to Metadata.

This workspace layout is designed to make it easy for you to see the metadata associated your audio and video files.

Note: XMP metadata is text information about a source file that is stored with the source file. The text transcription we are about to do will store the words transcribed from the audio file and store them as metadata. Transcriptions are special in that the metadata is associated with time as well, so that the transcribed text is in sync with the audio file.

3 Double-click the "writers talk to boss.avi" clip in the Project panel to load it into the Source Monitor.

4 Click the Play button in the Source Monitor to play the clip.

The words spoken by the actors are what we want to convert to a text transcript.

5 On the right side of the workspace is the Metadata panel. Near the bottom is the Speech Transcript field. Click the Transcribe button (highlighted here) to start the transcription process.

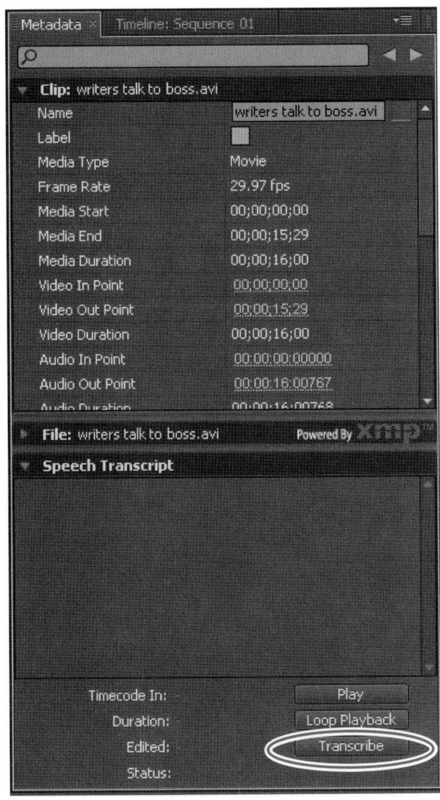

The Speech Transcription Options dialog box appears.

6 In the Speech Transcription Options dialog box, choose the options shown in this figure and click OK.

Note: Choose the Identify Speakers option if you want the transcription process to attempt to tag the text with different speaker tags. This function works best if each speaker has a unique voice.

This will launch the Adobe Media Encoder. This is our first encounter with the Adobe Media Encoder but it will not be our last. Adobe Media Encoder is a standalone application that handles some batch processing tasks for Adobe Premiere Pro, including exporting media (which we will cover in detail in

Lesson 20) and speech transcription. Since it is a standalone application, it can process these tasks while you continue to work on other things in Adobe Premiere Pro CS4 or other applications.

7 You will see the file we want to transcribe loaded into Adobe Media Encoder. Click Start Queue.

Adobe Media Encoder processes and transcribes the file.

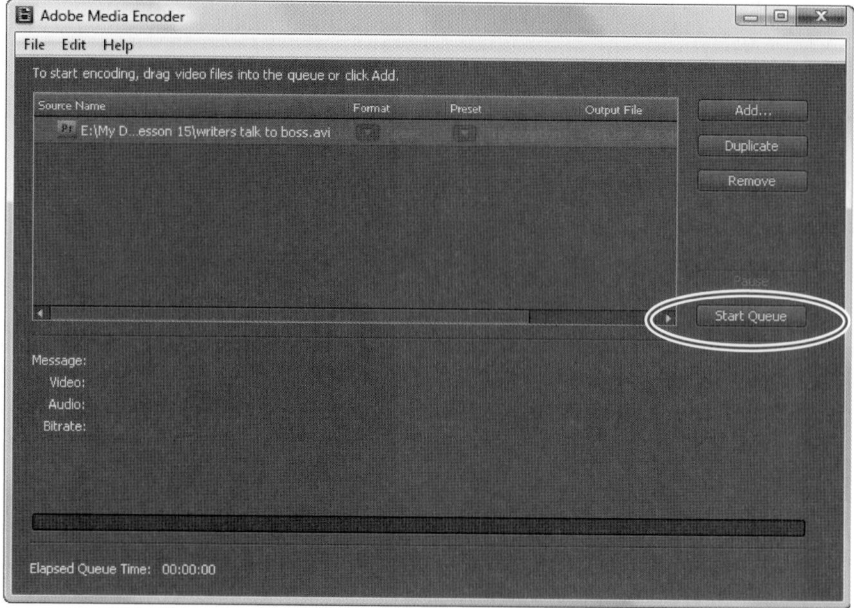

8 Switch back to Adobe Premiere Pro and note that there is a progress indicator at the bottom of the Metadata panel.

When the encoding and transcription process is complete, the text transcription will appear in the window.

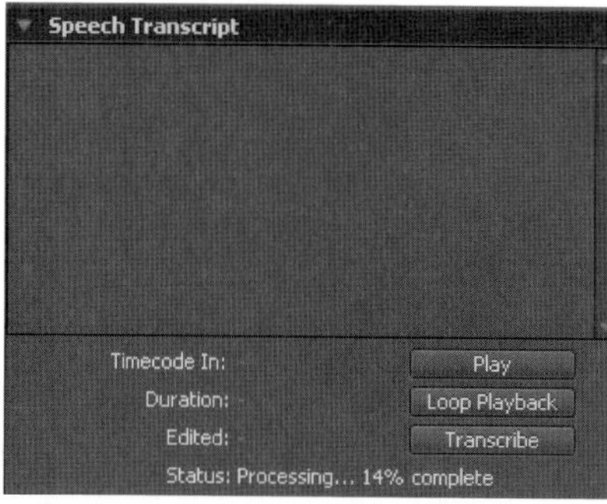

Your transcription should look very similar to what is shown here. The time it takes to complete the transcription depends on the length of the source file and the speed of your system.

9 Click the Play button to play the clip. Notice that the words in the transcription are highlighted as they are spoken.

Searching transcription for keywords

Now that we have the transcription, what can we do with it? One of the most useful applications for transcribed text is to search for a keyword in order to find a specific frame of video.

1 Continue working with the transcribed file you just created. At the top of the Metadata panel there is a search bar. Type **China** in the search bar and note that both instances of "china" are highlighted in the transcribed text.

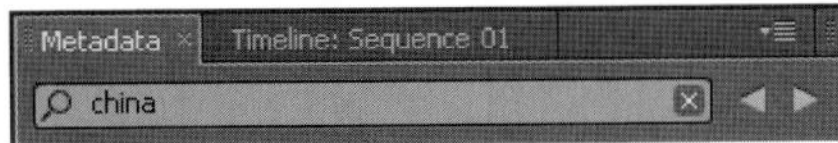

2 Click the word "china."

The playhead in the Source Monitor moves to the corresponding frame of video. The timecode is also displayed at the bottom of the Metadata panel.

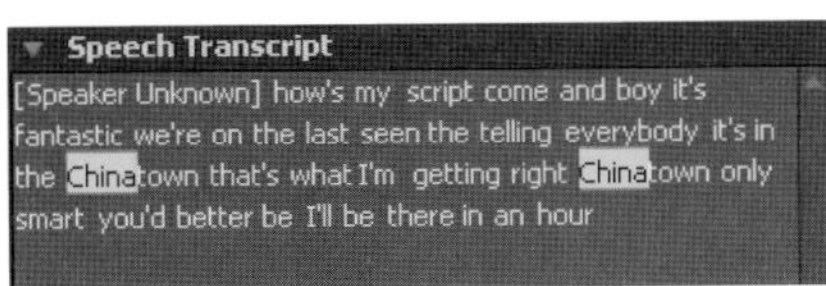

Note: The transcribed text can be copied into your clipboard and pasted into another application by right-clicking the transcribed text and choosing Copy All.

3 Click different words in the transcription and notice the playhead moving to match that location in the Source Monitor.

Modifying the metadata

You will notice that there are a couple of words in the transcription that are not perfect. You may edit the transcribed text by adding, modifying, or deleting words, and the transcribed audio will not go out of sync with the corresponding clip.

1 Clear the Metadata search bar so that no words are highlighted in the transcribed text.

2 Double-click the word "boy" in the transcribed text. This will allow you to edit that word. Change it to **boys**, as this is what the actor actually said.

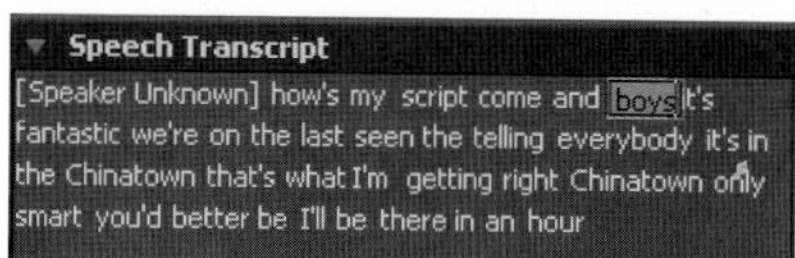

3 Double-click the word "smart" and change it to *smarter*, as this is what the actor actually said.

● **Note:** You may copy the transcribed text into your clipboard and paste into other applications.

This metadata is saved with the source file, so if you use this file in another project, the transcription will already be there.

This feature can be a huge timesaver for applications like long interviews where you could spend a long time trying to find a specific frame by listening for the keywords. The accuracy of the transcription is dependent on the quality and clarity of the source file. For example, background noise behind speech will make transcription difficult.

Review questions

1 What is the main benefit of Adobe Premiere Pro CS4's Speech Transcription feature?

2 Transcription can take a long time with a long file. Can you continue to work while the transcription is running?

3 Can you close Adobe Premiere Pro CS4 while the transcription process is running or open a different project?

4 If you edit or add words manually to the transcription, will it mess up the timing of the existing words?

5 If you use the same source file that is already transcribed in a new project, will you have to run the transcription process again?

Review answers

1 The main benefit is to be able to use text searches to locate a specific keyword or frame of video.

2 You may continue to work in Premiere Pro CS4 or any other application while Adobe Media Encoder processes the file.

3 You may close Premiere Pro or open a new project file while Adobe Media Encoder is processing the file.

4 The timing will remain in sync even if you add or delete words.

5 The transcribed text is added as metadata to the source file, so it is not necessary to transcribe the file again.

16 COMPOSITING TECHNIQUES

Topics covered in this lesson

- Making compositing part of your projects
- Working with the Opacity effect
- Using blending modes
- Working with alpha-channel transparencies
- Color keying a greenscreen shot
- Blurring a moving object with a track matte

This lesson will take approximately 50 minutes.

An important feature of Adobe Premiere Pro CS4 is its ability to composite (or layer) any number of video clips, graphics, and still images. Compositing will become a significant part of your video productions.

Getting started

Adobe Premiere Pro and other Timeline-based, multitrack nonlinear editors have a general operating practice: Clips in video tracks above Video 1 trump clips in tracks below them. In other words, whatever appears on a track covers up whatever is below it.

However, the object isn't to use clips in tracks above Video 1 to obliterate what's beneath them. It's to use compositing to enhance what's down there. Adobe Premiere Pro gives you many ways to layer videos, graphics, and images for best effect.

You use compositing techniques on clips so the clips below them on the Timeline can show through. The five basic compositing methods are as follows:

- Reducing the opacity of an entire clip
- Combining layers based on a blending mode
- Using alpha-channel transparencies in clips and effects
- Color keying a greenscreen shot
- Using matte keying effects

In this lesson, you will try all of these compositing methods and use different techniques with a few you've already tried. Once you see all the possibilities, you'll start to plan and shoot your projects with layered videos, graphics, and images in mind.

Making compositing part of your projects

You see compositing when you watch a TV meteorologist standing in front of a map or some other graphic background. As shown in the photos here, most times they're standing in front of a green or blue wall. The technical director uses a *keying* effect to make that wall transparent and then inserts a weather graphic. You can do the same thing in your video projects by using an Adobe Premiere Pro video keying effect.

Matt Zaffino, chief meteorologist—KGW-TV, Portland, Oregon

Many movies, as well as most computer games with live actors, use compositing. *Greenscreen* studios enable game developers and film directors to place actors in science fiction and other artificial settings created with 3D computer graphics. Such sets make it possible for actors to work in relative safety while the finished product shows them dangling from a skyscraper, hundreds of feet in the air.

Shooting videos with compositing in mind

Making keying effects work well takes some extra effort. Proper backdrop colors, lighting, and keying techniques all come into play. You need to consider which keying effect will work best for your project.

Some keys use textures or graphics, so you don't need to do a whole lot of planning, but most keying effects take some extra thought and work:

- High-contrast scenes lend themselves to making either the dark or the light portions transparent. The same holds true for shooting light objects against a dark background, or vice versa.
- Solid-color backgrounds are fairly easy to make transparent. Take care that the subjects you *don't* want to key out aren't wearing clothing with colors that match the background.
- For most keying shots, you need to use a tripod and lock down your camera. Bouncing keyed objects creates viewer disconnects. There are exceptions to this rule; typically, if you're keying in wild, animated backgrounds, then camera movement will not be a problem.
- Most times you want your background (or the other images you'll insert in the transparent areas you create with keying effects) to match those keyed shots. If you're working with outdoor scenes, try to shoot the keyed shots outside or use lights balanced for daylight.

Working with the Opacity effect

One easy way to see compositing at work is to place a video or graphic on a superimposing track and then make it partially transparent—turn down its opacity—to let videos on lower tracks show through. You can accomplish this using the Opacity effect. Though it can be very useful, you'll discover in this exercise that the Opacity effect's blanket approach to compositing is not always effective. In certain circumstances, you might want to use some other similar Adobe Premiere Pro tools.

In this exercise, you'll reduce the opacity of several items. Later you'll learn ways to achieve more effective results using some of the same clips.

1 Open Lesson 16-1.prproj.

2 Play the clip in the Video 1 track.

3 Drag brown matte to the Video 2 track directly above the video clip in the Video 1 track. Stretch brown matte to be the same length as the video clip in the Video 1 track.

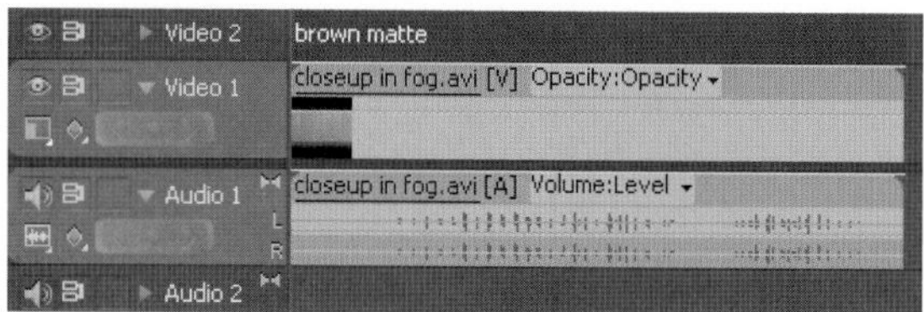

The matte completely covers the video. You cannot see any of the video because the brown matte clip in the Video 2 track is covering it.

4 Select the brown matte clip and expand Opacity in the Effect Controls panel.

5 Use keyframes to set an Opacity effect of 100% (opaque) at the beginning of the clip and an Opacity effect of 0% (completely transparent) at the end.

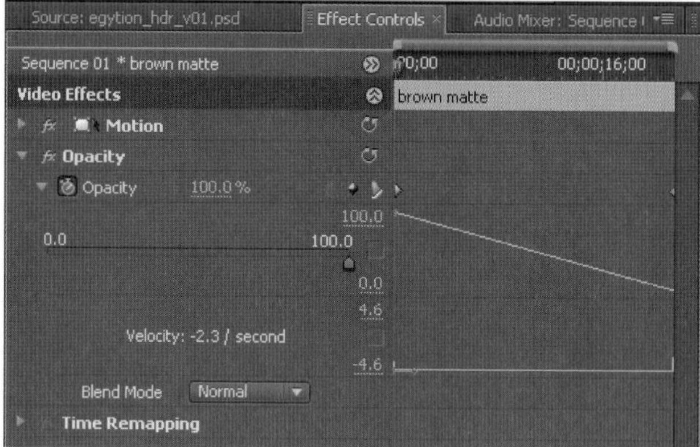

6 Play the clip.

The brown gradually becomes less opaque and more like a tint. Finally, it disappears altogether.

7 Right-click (Windows) or Control-click (Mac OS) the brown matte clip and then choose Copy.

You'll paste the Opacity parameters on another clip to save a few steps.

8 Drag the gradient circle on top of the brown matte clip in Video 2 to do an overlay edit. You will need to delete part of the brown matte clip not covered by the new clip and stretch the gradient circle clip to the same length as the video clip in Video 1.

9 Right-click (Windows) or Control-click (Mac OS) the gradient circle clip and choose Paste Attributes.

This applies the Opacity parameters with the keyframes you set for the brown matte clip to the Gradient clip.

Copy a clip and paste its attributes

Adobe Premiere Pro allows you to copy a clip and paste it somewhere else in any sequence. Or you can merely paste its attributes—any effects applied to it along with their parameters and keyframes—onto another clip. That latter feature is a great way to achieve consistent results. If you do PIPs, you can set a clip size and then apply that to all the clips in the PIP, changing only their screen locations.

10 Play the composited clips.

This gradient was set up using the Titler. It's simply a rectangle with a radial gradient fill applied. You can double-click the gradient circle clip in the Project panel to open the Titler and change the characteristics of the gradient.

It is fairly effective to use the Opacity effect to composite a scene with another clip that has a bright object with a dark background. But sometimes shots composited using the Opacity effect have a washed-out look; later you'll see ways to avoid that undesirable effect.

Combine layers based on a blending mode

If you have used Adobe Photoshop CS4, you may already be familiar with blending modes. Adobe Premiere Pro CS4 uses blending modes in a similar way.

1 Open Lesson 16-2.prproj. Notice the same gradient circle is in Video 2.

2 Select the gradient circle clip in the Video 2 track.

3 Expand the Opacity effect in the Effect Controls panel and make sure it is set to 100%.

4 Change the blending mode to Multiply and then play the sequence to see the effect.

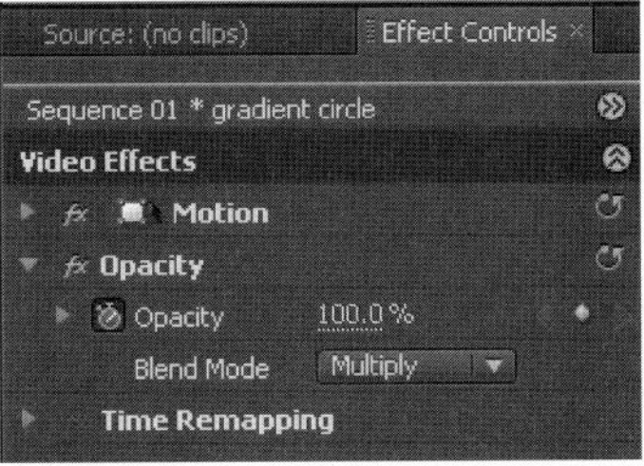

Rather than making portions of the clip transparent by changing the opacity, the blending modes actually blend the clip with the clip below it based on the blending mode selected.

5 Try a few other blending modes and observe their effect.

6 Delete the gradient circle clip from Video 2 track and drag the blend title where it was. Stretch the title to the same length as the video clip in the Video 1 track.

7 Change the blending mode on the Blend title menu to Color Dodge and then play the clip. Notice how the color of the video clip now interacts with the colors in the title.

Working with alpha-channel transparencies

Many graphics, some of the Adobe Premiere Pro transitions, and some video clips have what are called *alpha channels*—portions of the clips or gaps in the transitions that can be made transparent, revealing what's below those clips and transitions on a sequence. You'll work with both in this exercise:

1 Drag logo.psd to Video 2, overlaying the blend title.

2 Adjust the position parameters to 600 and 340, as shown here on the left. This moves the logo to the lower-right corner where logos (or bugs) are commonly displayed.

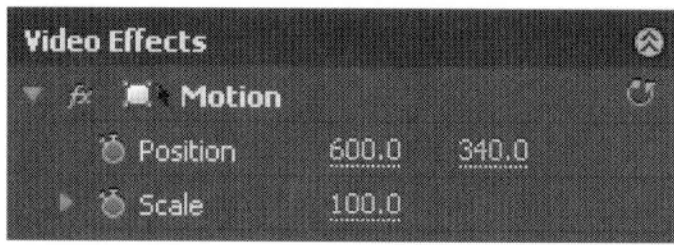

This is a Photoshop graphic with an alpha channel. By default, Adobe Premiere Pro makes the graphic opaque and its alpha channel transparent, allowing whatever is below the alpha channel on the sequence to show through. You can use the Alpha Adjust effect to see the alpha channel.

3 Choose Video Effects > Keying > Alpha Adjust to apply Alpha Adjust to Logo.psd.

Alpha Adjust is the clip-based version of the Opacity fixed effect. As with the Transform effect's connection to Motion, you can use Alpha Adjust to apply Opacity at some other point in the effect chain, instead of second-to-last, where it would occur if you were to use the Opacity fixed effect. Alpha Adjust has a few extra parameters in addition to Opacity:

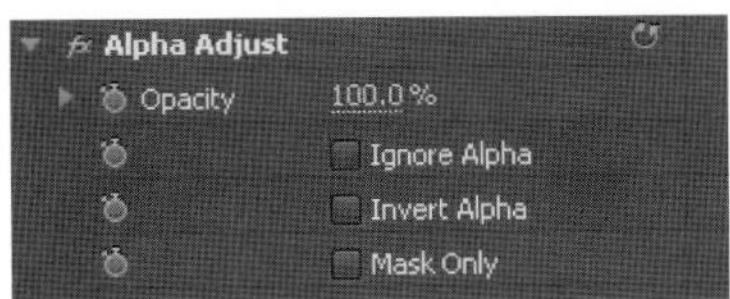

- **Ignore Alpha**: This makes the alpha channel opaque, covering up the clip below it.
- **Invert Alpha**: This makes the graphic transparent and the alpha channel opaque.
- **Mask Only**: This converts the graphic to a white silhouette.

4 Select Ignore Alpha to see the alpha channel as opaque rather than transparent.

5 Select Alpha Adjust in the Effect Controls panel and press Delete.

Using video effects that work with graphic-file alpha channels

Four video effects work well with graphic-file alpha channels: Alpha Glow, Bevel Alpha, Channel Blur, and Drop Shadow. You've already seen Drop Shadow, so here you'll use the other three:

1 Choose Video Effects > Stylize > Alpha Glow to apply an Alpha Glow effect to the graphic in Video 2, open its Settings dialog box, and experiment with its settings.

The Start Color and End Color parameters set the colors of the glow.

2 Delete Alpha Glow from the Effect Controls panel, choose Video Effects > Perspective > Bevel Alpha, and then drag the Bevel Alpha effect into its place.

Give this graphic a 3D beveled feel by adjusting the effect's parameters.

3 Choose Video Effects > Perspective and add a Drop Shadow effect below the Bevel Alpha effect in the Effect Controls panel. Set Shadow Opacity to 70%, Distance to 10, and Softness to 40, as shown here on the left.

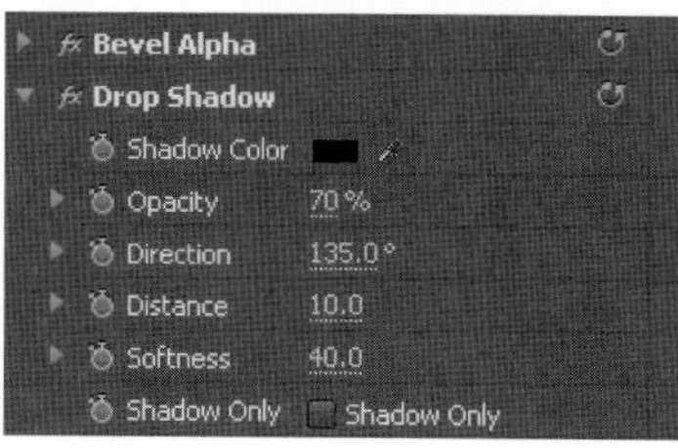

Some video formats may also contain alpha channels. DV cannot, but the QuickTime .mov and uncompressed .avi formats are examples of formats that can contain alpha channels.

4 Drag the scratches.mov clip over the logo clip in Video 2 to overlay it. This .mov clip contains moving scratches and flicker to simulate an old movie. It contains an alpha channel that makes the areas where there are no scratches transparent, so the movie under it can be seen. Play the sequence to observe the effect.

5 To enhance the old movie look, drag the brown matte clip to Video 3 and set its Opacity parameter to 20%. Press Enter (Windows) or Return (Mac OS) to render and play the sequence.

Color keying a greenscreen shot

Using the Opacity effect to combine two or more clips works well for some images, but it's an inexact science. You can get more precise compositing results by using keying effects.

Keying effects use various methods to make portions of a clip transparent. To get a quick overview, choose Video Effects > Keying in the Effects panel. You'll see many effects. With the exception of Alpha Adjust (the clip-based Opacity video effect), they fall into three basic categories:

- **Color/chroma**: Blue Screen (Windows only), Chroma (Windows only), Color, Non-Red, and RGB Difference (Windows only)
- **Luminance**: Luma, Multiply (Windows only), and Screen (Windows only)
- **Matte**: Difference, Garbage, Image, Remove, and Track

Color keys and chroma keys all work in basically the same way: You select a color for them to make transparent and then apply a few other parameters (basically adjusting the width of that color selection).

Luminance keys look for dark or light areas in a clip and make them transparent or opaque. In this lesson, you'll use the color keying effect.

Mattes typically do the equivalent of cutting a hole in a clip using a graphic or some other user-defined region.

Using the color key effect

In this exercise, you'll learn how to get a good color key:

1. Load Lesson 16-3.prproj.
2. Scrub the Timeline to see the background you are using for the greenscreen clip.
3. Drag green screen shot.avi to Video 2. Play the Timeline now to see the woman walking in front of a greenscreen. Leave the current-time indicator in the middle of the clip where the woman is in full view.

   You need to apply a color key filter to make the greenscreen behind the woman become transparent.
4. Choose Video Effects > Keying and apply a color key to the clip in Video 2.
5. Drag the eyedropper from the Key Color parameter into the clip in the Program Monitor and click the green area on the left side of the woman.

Get an average color value to improve keying

The eyedropper selects a color from a single pixel. Frequently that single pixel does not represent the average color of the region you want to key out, leading to keying results that are less than satisfactory. When using the eyedropper to get a color sample for a key, Ctrl-click (Windows) or Command-click (Mac OS) to get a subsample—a 5x5-pixel area.

6. Adjust the Color Tolerance slider until as much of the green disappears without any of the woman's skin or clothing becoming transparent—to about 26%. Adjust Edge Feather to 2.

If you have not seen a color key at work before, that little parameter change is sure to get your attention, but the key is not nearly perfect. Some of the green on the right is likely still visible. You will fix that next. At this point, your key should look similar to the one shown here.

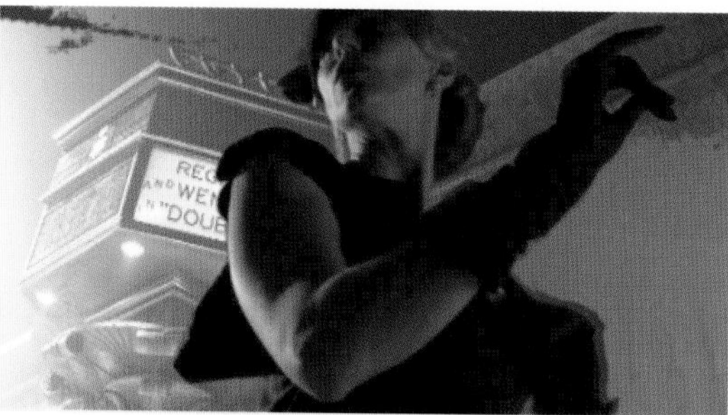

7 Drag a second color key filter to the green screen shot.avi clip.

8 Drag the eyedropper from the Color parameter into the clip in the Program Monitor and click the green that is on the right side of the woman.

9 Adjust the Color Tolerance slider to about 33%, until as much of the green disappears as possible without any of the woman's skin or clothing becoming transparent. Adjust Edge Feather to 2.

10 You may have a portion of greenscreen still showing in the upper left of the frame. If so, drag a third color key filter to the clip and repeat the procedure, sampling the green that is left.

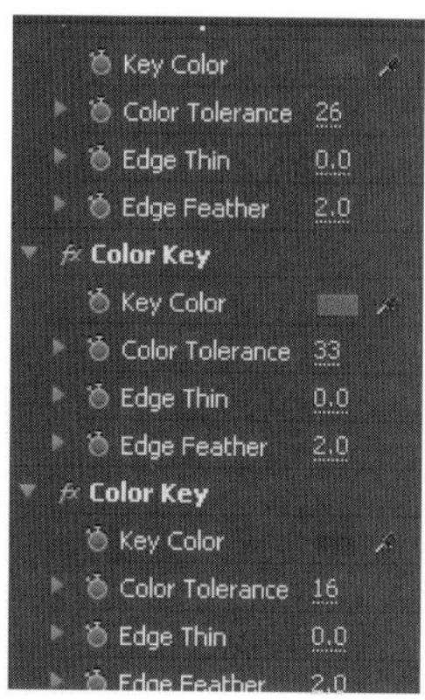

11 Press Enter to render and play the sequence.

The reason three color key filters were necessary is that the greenscreen in the clip was not lit evenly. It had darker and lighter areas that made it essentially several colors of green.

Tips for effective color or chroma key shots

Chroma key video shoots don't always go smoothly. For the key effects to work effectively, you should follow these tips:

- Use flat lighting (two lights at 45° angles to the screen) to avoid creating hot spots. Don't overdo the lighting. Simply make it even.
- The actor's lighting does not have to be flat. Controlled spotlights or lights with "barn doors" work well.
- If you're going to key in an outdoor background, use daylight-balanced blue gels over your lights to re-create outdoor lighting, or shoot your chroma key shots outdoors. If you're working with live actors, use a fan to blow their hair around to enhance the illusion.
- Avoid chroma key spill—keep actors at least 4 feet away from the backdrop to avoid picking up its reflected color. A backlight on the actors minimizes spill.
- The tighter the shot, the more realistic the finished look will be.
- Fast-paced action is harder to key right to the edges of your subjects.
- Use a wide-open iris on your camcorder to limit the depth of field and to throw the bluescreen or greenscreen a bit out of focus, making it easier to key out.
- Chroma key fabric and paper cost about $8 a square yard, and paint costs about $60 a gallon. You can find many dealers online.
- Which color should you use? With chroma key green, you have a reasonable assurance that no one will have clothing that matches it and therefore will key out. Chroma key blue works well because it's complementary to most skin tones.
- Consumer and prosumer camcorders do not key as well as professional camcorders because they record less color information. However, because they give more weight to green colors to correspond to the color sensitivity of human eyes, greenscreens key more cleanly than blue.

Using matte keys

Matte keys cut "holes" in one clip to allow portions of another to show through or to create something like cutout figures you can place on top of other clips.

The nomenclature can be confusing. Matte keys are not the same as color mattes, such as the orange matte you used earlier in this lesson. However, matte keys generally use matte graphics that you create to define the areas you want to make transparent or opaque.

Two basic types of matte keys exist:

- **Garbage**: Garbage mattes are four-, eight-, or sixteen-sided polygons. They're named *garbage* because you typically use them to remove something you don't want in the video. You move their vertices to define the outline of an area you want to display.
- **Graphic**: Graphic mattes are shapes that you create for keying out or keying in another graphic or a clip. Types of graphic mattes include Difference Matte Key, Image Matte Key, Remove Matte Key, and Track Matte Key.

In this exercise, you'll work with the Four-Point Garbage Matte Key effect and the Track Matte Key effect:

1 Load Lesson 16-4.prproj.

2 Drag the theater.psd clip to Video 2 and stretch it to be the same length as the video clip.

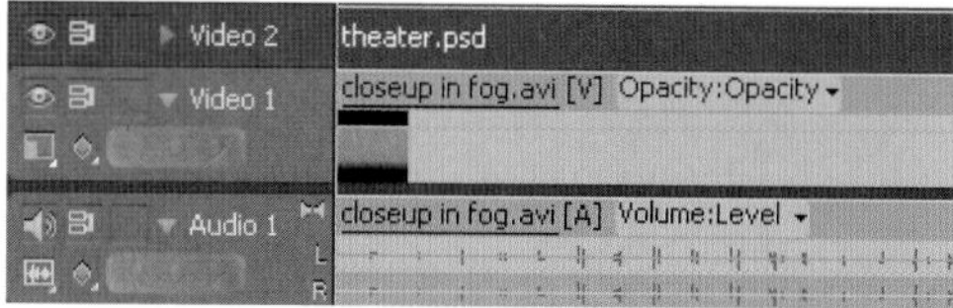

Your goal is to cut out the theater's lighted sign and make it a "bug" in the bottom right of the video.

3 Drag the Four-Point Garbage Matte Key effect from the Keying folder to the theater.psd clip.

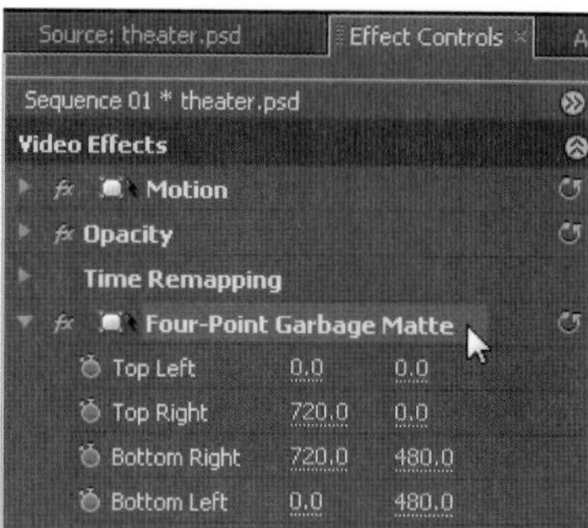

4 Use your mouse to drag the four control points in the Program Monitor to the four corners of the sign. Zoom the Program Monitor to make finer adjustments.

5 Set the zoom of the Program Monitor back to Fit when you are done adjusting the Four-Point Garbage Matte control points.

6 Expand the Motion field, and adjust the Position and Rotation fields so that the sign appears in the lower-right corner, as shown here on the right.

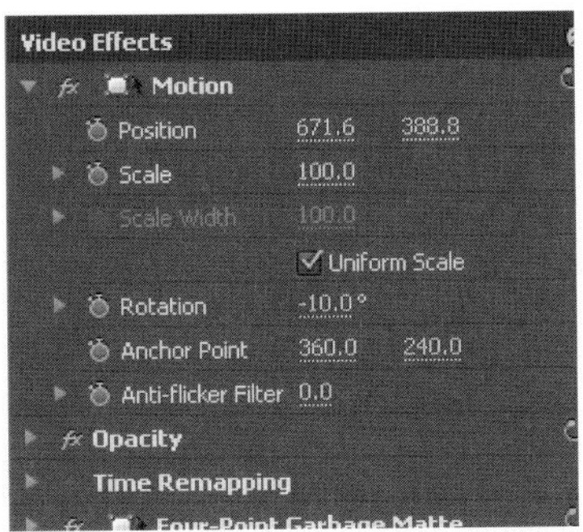

Creating a split-screen effect

You can use garbage mattes to create split-screen effects. The most frequent application is simply to layer two clips, apply the Four-Point Garbage Matte effect to each, and move the vertices to create two side-by-side rectangles. You can also layer more clips and use the Eight- and Sixteen-Point Garbage Matte effects to create all sorts of shapes.

The one little gotcha is that the garbage matte effects reveal part of a clip—they don't shrink the clip to fit it in the borders of the garbage matte, as happens when you use Motion to make PIPs. So plan your shots accordingly. If you want to put more of the scene within the garbage matte's borders, use Motion or some other effect to accomplish that.

You can achieve a cool effect by locking down your camcorder on a tripod; ensuring the lighting, focus, and exposure settings don't change for the duration of the shoot; and having an actor do a scene on one side of a set and then play another role on the other side of the set. You can use a garbage matte on one of the scenes to have the actor appear on both sides of the set at once.

This takes some planning. The actor shouldn't cross the line that divides the set in two (though you can keyframe the garbage matte box edges to accommodate some overlap), and there can't be any movement in the vicinity of the scene's dividing line.

Using mattes that use graphics or other clips

Four keying effects fall into the matte category. You'll work with the Track Matte Key effect, because it's the most useful and works the best. Here's a quick rundown on the others:

- **Difference Matte Key**: Making this effect work smoothly is very difficult. In theory, you use it to place in a single set multiple actors, animals, or objects that could not all be in a scene at the same time in the same set. You have to create the various shots with the same lighting and camera angle, and you need to work with high-end video to have a chance of making it work. It's best to stick with greenscreens/bluescreens.
- **Image Matte Key**: This matte works like the image mask used in the Gradient Wide transition. You apply it and open a graphic or still image, and the effect makes dark areas transparent and makes light areas opaque. This is a static effect with limited usability.
- **Remove Matte Key**: The Remove Matte effect is designed specifically for graphics that, when used in keyed shots, have something akin to a thin halo around their edges. Apply the effect to remove it.

Using Track Matte Key

Track Matte Key works like Image Matte Key, but it has several advantages and one obvious difference. What makes it different is that you place the matte—a still image, graphic, or something you created in the Titler—in a video track (thus its name) rather than applying it directly to the clip.

Track Matte Key uses the clip in a separate track to define areas of transparency in the selected clip and reveal whatever is below it on a sequence. Its huge advantage is that you can animate the matte. For example, you can use Motion's Scale parameter to gradually reveal the matte or move it in the clip to follow some action. The latter application of Track Matte Key is called a *traveling matte.*

Making a traveling matte

You will use this effect time and time again. It's a great way to follow action or hide an object. In this case, you will use Track Matte Key to blur the moving face of a woman walking through the fog. If necessary, refer to the example of this effect in the Lesson 16 Finished sequence.

1 Open Lesson 16-5.prproj. Notice that the same video clip is on Video 1 and Video 2.

2 Drag the face matte to Video 3. Stretch the face matte clip to the same length as the other clips. If you play this sequence, you will notice the face matte just stays in the middle of the frame. You need to animate the face matte so it follows the woman's face.

3 Select the face matte clip and then expand the Motion effect in the Effect Controls panel.

4 Set a Position keyframe at the beginning of the clip by clicking the Toggle Animation button to the left of Position. Position the white circle where the woman's face is, even if it is off-screen.

● **Note:** Keyframing motion can be a tedious task, but you don't have to set a keyframe at every frame. A good technique is to set a keyframe at the beginning, then the end, and then in the middle. The in-between times will be smoothly calculated. If the motion is constant and there is no camera movement, you will not need to set many in-between keyframes. If you need to add more keyframes, keep dividing the space between keyframes in half until the animation is correct.

5 Scrub the Timeline to about the halfway point of the clip and adjust the matte to be over the woman's face. Move halfway across the remainder of the clip and do the same thing again. Continue setting keyframes until you can scrub the clip and have the matte over the face at all times.

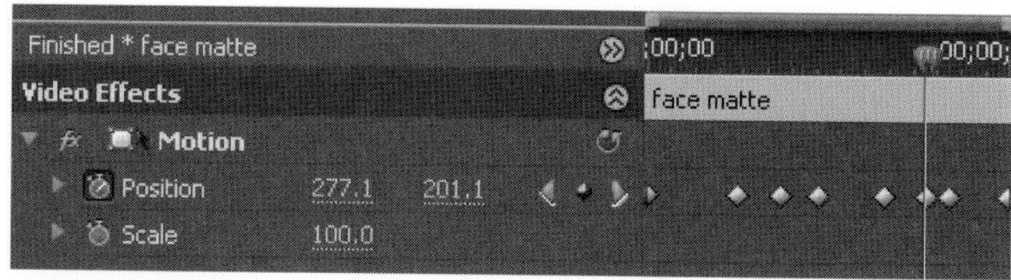

6 Select the Video 2 clip, select Video Effects > Stylize, and apply the Mosaic effect to it. Set the horizontal and vertical blocks' values to 30. This makes the clip in Video 2 a mosaic. Now you need to use the Track Matte Key effect to make the mosaic appear over only the face as it moves.

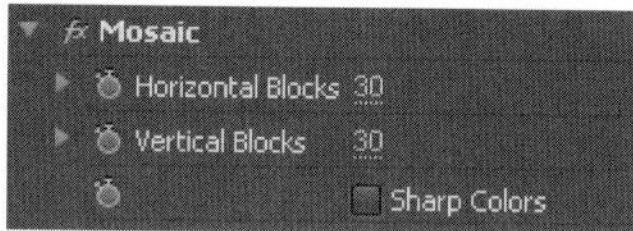

7 Locate the Track Matte Key effect in Video Effects > Keying and apply it to the clip in Video 2. This is the same clip to which you applied the Mosaic effect.

8 Set Matte to Video 3 and Composite Using to Matte Alpha.

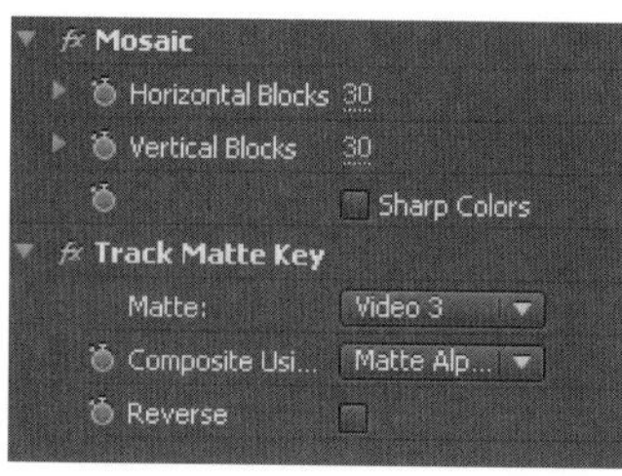

● **Note:** You can also use this technique to highlight, rather than obscure, a person or object in motion. To highlight with a track matte, simply change the effect on the matted clip from Mosaic to a tinted color, a brighter color, or even black and white.

9 Play the sequence.

The Mosaic effect is now on the woman's face only.

Review questions

1 Explain how to copy all the effects from one clip to another.

2 How do you create a logo with beveled edges and a glow that grows and then shrinks?

3 Why is it helpful to light a greenscreen evenly when shooting a scene?

4 How is using the blending modes different from just adjusting the Opacity setting's percentage?

5 Describe what a track matte is.

Review answers

1 Select the clip from which you want to copy the attributes, and choose Edit > Copy. Then select the clip or clips to which you want to copy the attributes, and choose Edit > Paste Attributes.

2 Apply Bevel Alpha and Alpha Glow. Use keyframes in Alpha Glow to animate the size of the glow.

3 If a greenscreen is not lit evenly, it will be more difficult to key out. Multiple key filters may be necessary to select the various shades of green in a poorly lit greenscreen.

4 The Opacity setting adjusts the amount of transparency of all the pixels in the frame evenly. Blending modes allow you to blend the clip with the clip below it based on the blending mode selected.

5 A matte allows you to make a portion of the video frame transparent. A track matte can be static, or it may be animated to follow motion in the video.

17 COLOR, NESTED SEQUENCES, AND SHORTCUTS

Topics covered in this lesson

- Exploring color-oriented effects
- Adjusting and enhancing color
- Using nested sequences
- Applying recommended keyboard shortcuts

This lesson will take approximately 60 minutes.

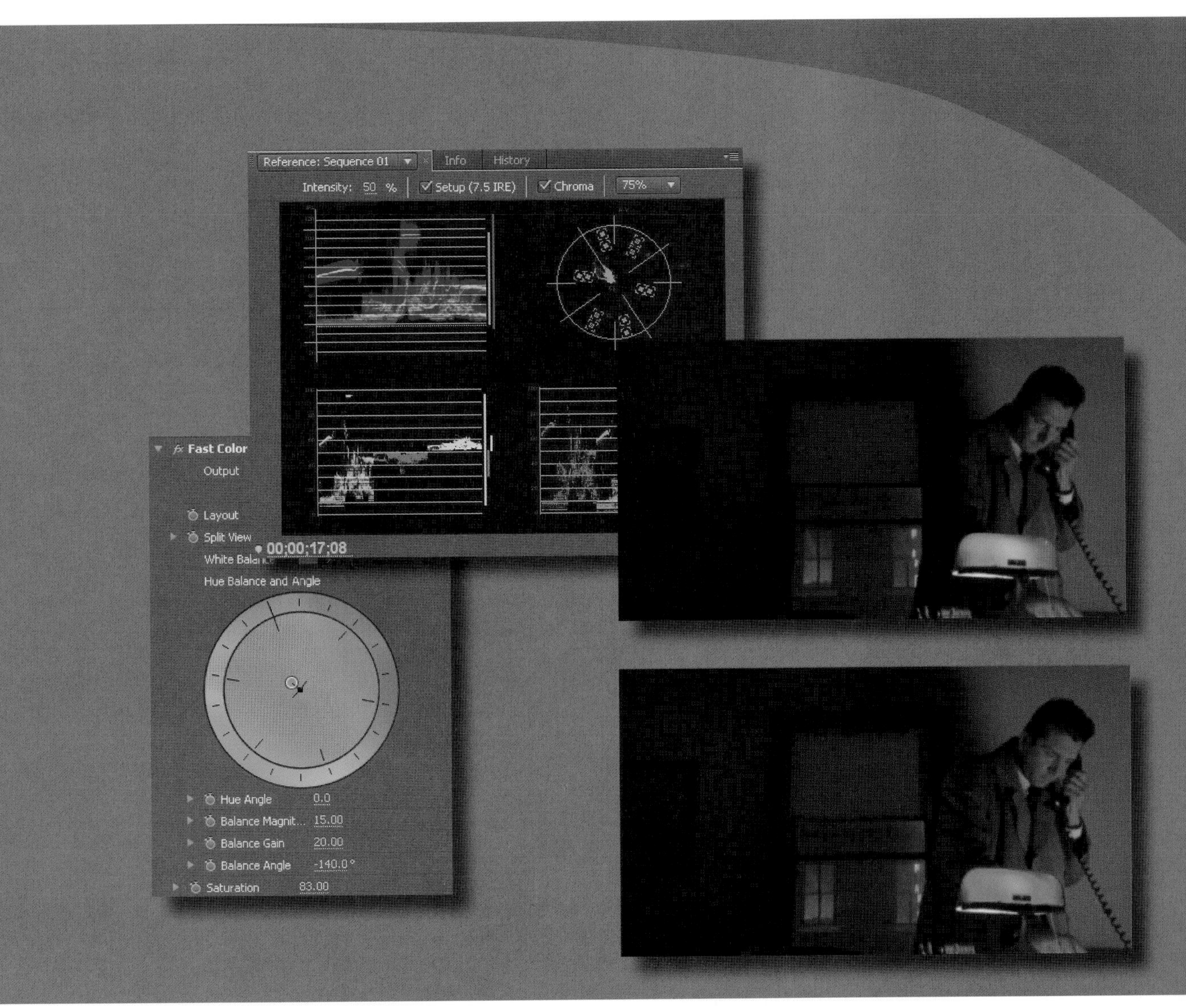

Adobe Premiere Pro CS4 offers a dozen video effects for enhancing or adjusting colors. In this lesson, you'll explore some specialized editing techniques, including nesting clips and sequences, and you'll learn some keyboard shortcuts to speed up your editing.

Getting started

Most feature films are color-corrected. The purpose of *color correction* is less to fix a shot gone bad than it is to give the film a look that matches its mood or genre: from warm reds for landscapes and sepia tones for historic shots to cold blues for hard-edged films or a gritty look for urban dramas. Color correction (also known as *color enhancing*) is big business, and Adobe Premiere Pro has a full suite of professional color-enhancing effects.

These color-oriented effects offer more than just color correction. You can select a color and change it, convert a clip to grayscale (with the exception of a single color), or remove all colors outside a specific color range. You'll see samples of some of these in this lesson.

You'll also learn about the power of nested sequences as you change the look of a complex effect by changing one nested clip.

The default keyboard shortcuts in Adobe Premiere Pro are too numerous to use all of them, much less memorize them, but you will come to rely on several. In this lesson, you'll also learn how to customize keyboard commands to suit your editing style.

An overview of color-oriented effects

Adobe Premiere Pro has many video effects that adjust or enhance color. Some have narrow functionality, while others are professional-level tools that take a lot of trial and error to gain some level of expertise. Entire books are devoted to color correction, and a good number of video editors specialize in that field.

Adobe Premiere Pro offers a wide range of "colorful" possibilities—more than enough to spark some ideas for your upcoming video projects.

To see what Adobe Premiere Pro has to offer in the color effects department, click the Effects tab and type **color** in the Contains text box. However, that's just a start; Adobe Premiere Pro has several more effects that have to do with color.

Here, the color-oriented effects have been grouped into four categories and are listed within those groups more or less from simplest to most complex. (This taxonomy is one example of why you might want to create and organize some custom effects bins.) The following sections offer a brief overview of the color effects.

Coloring effects

These are the coloring effects:

- **Tint**: This is a simple way to apply an overall color cast to a clip.
- **Change Color**: Like Tint, Change Color applies a color cast but adds more control, and it allows you to change a wider range of colors.
- **Ramp**: This creates a linear or radial color gradient that blends with the original image colors.
- **4-Color Gradient**: This gradient is like the Titler's eponymous feature, but it has more options, and it allows you to keyframe the parameters for some wild results.
- **Paint Bucket**: This effect paints areas of a scene with a solid color.
- **Brush Strokes**: This effect applies a painted look to a clip.
- **Channel Blur**: This creates a glow by blurring red, green, or blue channels separately and in user-specified directions.

Color removal or replacement

These are the color removal or replacement effects:

- **Color Pass**: This Windows-only effect converts an entire clip to grayscale, with the exception of one user-specified color.
- **Color Replace**: This Windows-only effect changes a user-selected color in a scene to a different user-specified color.
- **Leave Color**: Though similar to Color Pass, Leave Color offers much more control.
- **Change to Color**: This effect is like Color Replace, but it has more options and control.

Color correction

These are the color-correction effects:

- **Color Balance, Color Balance (HLS), and Color Balance (RGB)**: Color Balance offers the most control over the red, green, and blue values in midtones, shadows, and highlights. Color Balance (HLS) controls only the overall hue, lightness, and saturation; Color Balance (RGB) controls only the red, green, and blue color values.
- **Auto Color**: This effect is a simple generic color balance.
- **RGB Color Corrector and RGB Curves**: Offering even more control than Color Balance, these effects include controls over the tonal range of shadows and highlights, as well as controls for midtones values (*gamma*), brightness (*pedestal*), and contrast (*gain*).

- **Luma Color and Luma Curve**: These filters adjust brightness and contrast in the highlights, midtones, and shadows of a clip. They also correct the hue, saturation, and luma in a selected color range.
- **Color Match**: A useful but difficult-to-master tool that lets you match up the overall color schemes in scenes with different color lighting, the Windows-only Color Match makes it possible to color-match scenes shot under fluorescent lights (blue-green) with scenes shot under tungsten lights (orange).
- **Fast Color Corrector**: This effect lets you make instant color changes that you can preview in a split-screen view within the Program Monitor. This is a tool you are likely to use frequently.
- **Three-Way Color Corrector**: This tool eanables you to make more subtle corrections by letting you adjust the hue, saturation, and luminance for highlights, midtones, and shadows.

Technical color effects

These are the technical color effects:

- **Broadcast Colors**: The Broadcast Colors effect conforms video to display properly on TV sets. It corrects problems created by overly bright colors and geometric patterns due to some effects or added graphics.
- **Video Limiter**: Like Broadcast Colors but with much more precise control, Video Limiter enables you to preserve the original video quality of your clip while conforming to broadcast TV standards.

Adjusting and enhancing color

In this exercise, you will work with five color-oriented effects: Leave Color, Change to Color, Color Balance (RGB), Auto Color, and Fast Color Corrector.

The Leave Color effect

You'll begin with the Leave Color effect:

1. Open Lesson 17-1.prproj.
2. Drag the enters office.avi clip to Video 1 and position the current-time indicator at about halfway so you have a good view of the blue desk lamp.
3. Choose Video Effects > Color Correction and apply the Leave Color effect to the clip.
4. Expand Leave Color in the Effect Controls panel. Using the eyedropper next to Color To Leave, click the blue lamp to select the color to retain.

5 Set Amount to Decolor to 100%. This turns everything but the selected color to grayscale.

6 Set Tolerance to about 36%. You might need to adjust this figure a little to get the effect you want.

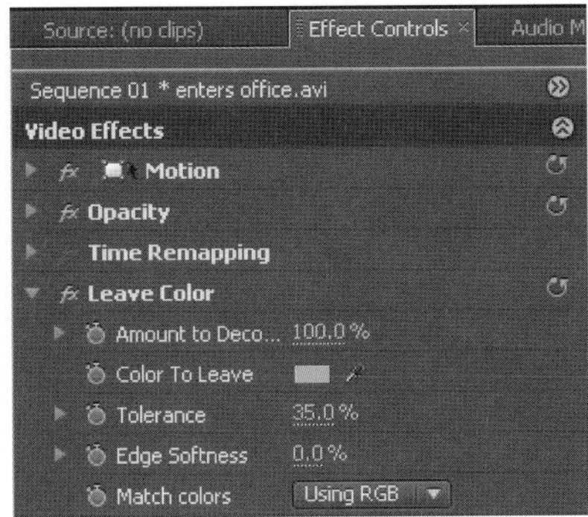

7 Play the clip. Only the blue lamp is in color.

The Change to Color effect

Next let's work with the Change to Color effect:

1 Remove the Leave Color effect, choose Video Effects > Color Correction, and apply the Change to Color effect to that clip.

2 Expand the Change to Color effect in the Effect Controls panel.

3 Move the current-time indicator over the clip so you can see the blue lamp clearly in the Program Monitor.

4 Use the eyedropper next to From to sample the blue color from the lamp.

5 Click the To color swatch and select a red.

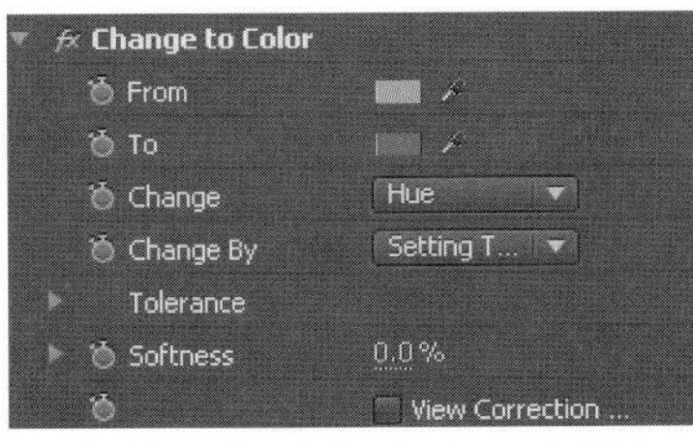

The lamp should change from a blue hue to a red hue. The color you select will retain the shadows, midtones, and highlights of the scene it's replacing. If the scene is generally dark, the color in the scene will look darker than the color you select.

Color correction

Depending on how you define *color correction*, Adobe Premiere Pro offers several color-correction effects. They run the gamut from basic color balance (like an auto white balance on a camcorder) to the richly detailed and complex Three-Way Color Corrector effect. In this lesson we'll devote the most attention to the middle ground: Fast Color Corrector.

Note: The Three-Way Color Corrector effect lets you make separate adjustments, using individual wheels, to adjust tonal ranges for shadows, midtones, and highlights.

The Fast Color Corrector and Three-Way Color Corrector effects offer what are called Hue Balance and Angle color wheels. You use them to balance the red, green, and blue colors to produce the desired white and neutral grays in the image.

Depending on the desired effect, you might not want the color balance in a clip to be completely neutral. That's where color enhancement comes in. For example, you can give your videos a warm orange color or a cool blue color.

Before tackling the Fast Color Corrector effect, you'll learn briefly about two other color-correction effects.

The Color Balance (RGB) effect

Let's begin with Color Balance (RGB), which is probably the most intuitive color-correction effect:

1 Load Lesson 17-2.prproj.

2 Drag the Color Balance (RGB) effect from the Image Control folder to the clip on the Timeline.

   Color Balance (RGB) has a Settings window where you can manually adjust the red, green, and blue levels. The starting point for all clips is 100 no matter what the actual color levels in the clip are.

3 Change the Red, Green, and Blue settings to give this scene a cooler appearance (more blue). Try 98% for Red, 104% for Green, and 116% for Blue, as shown in the figure on the left.

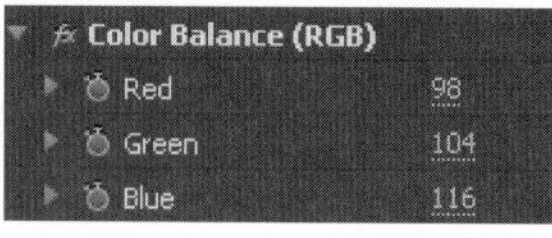

The Auto Color effect

The next color-correction effect you'll learn is Auto Color, which analyzed frames based on your parameter settings:

1 Delete Color Balance (RGB) from the start clip, choose Video Effects > Adjust, and replace Color Balance (RGB) with the Auto Color effect.

2 Try some parameters.

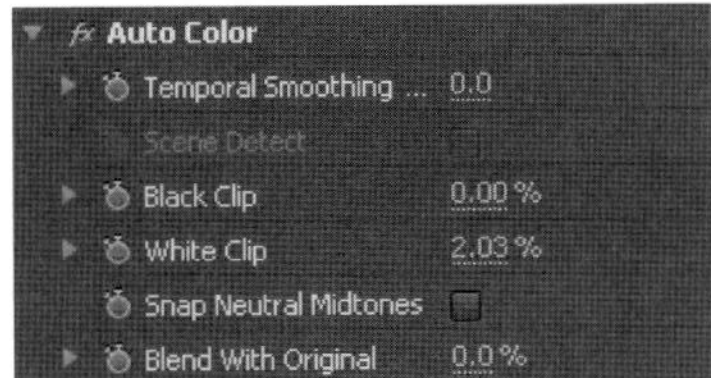

Temporal Smoothing looks at several frames at once and averages their values to smooth any color-balance differences. Higher Black Clip and White Clip values increase contrast.

The Fast Color Corrector effect

Fast Color Corrector is the workhorse of color-correction filters in Adobe Premiere Pro. It is extremely useful when correcting the color or lighting of a clip.

1 Drag writers 3.avi to the sequence to the right of the previous clip.

2 Choose Video Effects > Color Correction and apply the Fast Color Corrector effect to the writers 3.avi clip.

   Notice that writers 3.avi is more saturated with color than writers 2.avi. By using the Fast Color Corrector effect, you can make the writers 3 clip more closely match the look of writers 2, even though they were filmed with different exposures. This very detailed effect signals a tidal shift in editing possibilities. It's loaded with options, including two color wheels—an intuitive means of adjusting hue and saturation.

3 Click the Balance Magnitude control point in the middle of the color wheel and drag it a little toward yellow (shown in the next figure).

   Note that the Balance Magnitude value and Balance Angle values change when you drag this control point.

4 Notice how the blue cast to the clip is now gone. Select the Show Split View option (under the Output parameter) to see the difference.

5 Adjust the amount of color correction by increasing Balance Magnitude to about 15 and the Balance Angle to -140. This shifts the tone a little toward yellow to better match the writers 2 clip. Notice that the circle near the center of the color wheel moves farther from the center as you adjust the Balance Magnitude parameter.

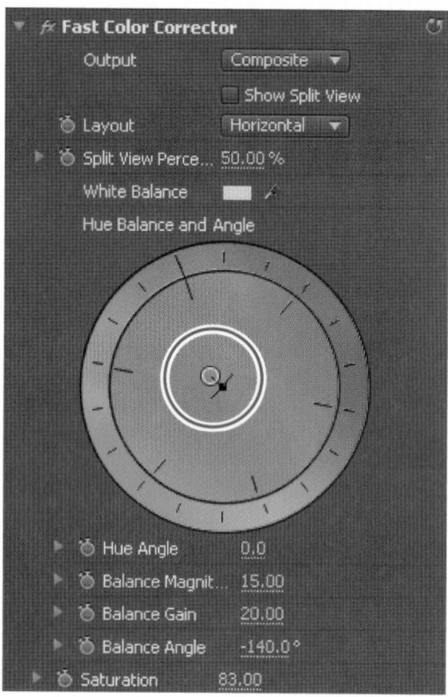

Take a look at the color wheel. Here are its parameters:

- **Hue Angle**: Move the outer ring clockwise to shift the overall color toward red; move it counterclockwise to shift it toward green.
- **Balance Magnitude**: Move the circle out from the center to increase the magnitude (intensity) of the color introduced into the video.
- **Balance Gain**: Set the relative coarseness or fineness of the Balance Magnitude and Balance Angle adjustments. Moving the handle toward the outer ring makes the adjustment very obvious. Keeping the perpendicular handle of this control close to the center of the wheel makes the adjustment very subtle.
- **Balance Angle**: Shift the video color toward a target color.

6 Change the Saturation parameter (below the color wheel) to about 83 to make the colors a bit less intense.

7 Slide the midtone input level to about 1.6 to lighten the midtones.

8 Deselect the Show Split View option, and play both the writers 2 and writers 3 clips.

They now match much better than before.

9 Choose Window > Workspace > Color Correction.

Note that you have a new video panel: a Reference Monitor.

10 Click the Reference Monitor panel menu and choose All Scopes.

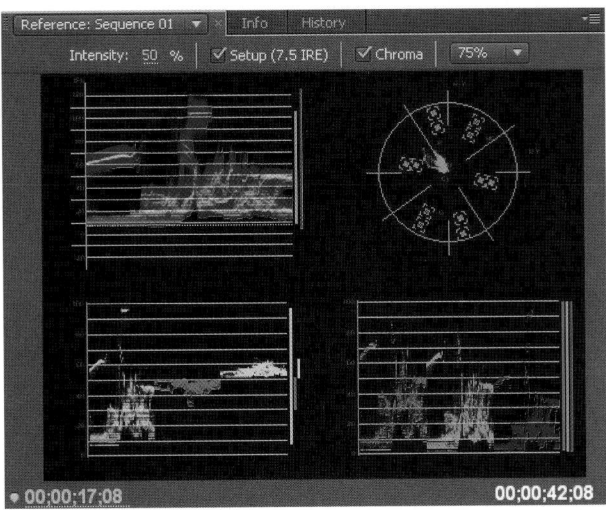

These are three Waveform Monitors and a Vectorscope (in the upper-right corner). For decades, broadcast TV engineers have used these to ensure that TV signals meet standards (that is, they don't get too bright or have too much contrast).

As you ramp up your color-enhancing skills, you might want to use them for that reason as well as to adjust color. To learn more about them, choose Help > Adobe Premiere Pro Help, and then open Applying Effects > Vectorscope and Waveform Monitors.

Using nested sequences

A *nested* sequence is a sequence in a sequence. You can break your project up into more manageable chunks by creating a project segment in one sequence and dragging that sequence—with all its clips, graphics, layers, multiple audio/video tracks, and effects—into another sequence. There it will look and behave like a single audio/video clip.

One great way to take advantage of a nested sequence is to apply color correction to a long sequence with multiple edits. Instead of applying that effect to each clip in turn, you simply place—nest—that sequence in another sequence and apply a single instance of that effect to it. If you want to change the effect parameters, you can then do it on one nested sequence clip, rather than changing each clip in that original sequence.

Multiple uses for nested sequences

Nested sequences have many other uses:

- They allow you to apply an effect or effects to a group of layered clips. That saves having to apply effects to each layer, one at a time.
- They simplify editing by creating complex sequences separately. This helps you avoid running into conflicts and inadvertently shifting clips on a track that is far from your current work area.
- They let you reuse sequences, as well as use the same sequence but give it a different look each time.
- They organize your work in the same way you might create subfolders in the Project panel or in Windows Explorer. This avoids confusion and shortens editing time.
- They allow you to apply more than one transition between clips.
- They make it possible to build multiple picture-in-picture effects.

Nesting a video in a newspaper

In this exercise, you will learn to create the classic newspaper spinning onto the screen—except you will use a nested sequence to add a motion video as a "picture" on this spinning newspaper. Using nested sequences will make it very easy.

1. Open Lesson 17-3.prproj.
2. Select the completed sequence and play it to see the effect you will create.

   The spinning newspaper is the last set of clips in the sequence.
3. Open the nested practice sequence. Initially, it is empty.
4. Drag the enters office.avi clip to the Video 1 track of the nested practice sequence. Press backslash (\) to zoom in the Timeline.
5. Drag newspaper.psd to the Video 2 track, directly above the Enters office.avi clip. Adjust the length of the newspaper clip to match the movie clip.

   The newspaper clip has a square transparent area where the movie clip underneath shows through.

6 Select the enters office clip in Video 1, and using the Scale and Position parameters of the Motion effect, adjust the video to fit in the window of the newspaper. Set Scale to 56 and Position to 261, 292, which should work well.

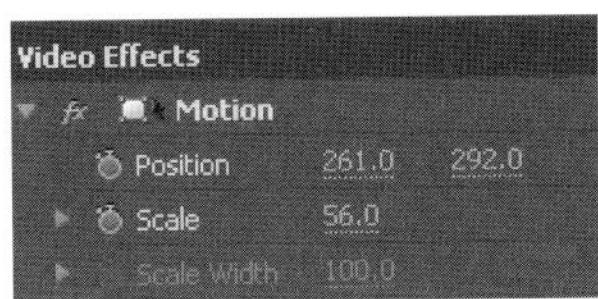

7 Delete the audio of the Enters office.avi clip by Alt-clicking (Windows) or Option-clicking (Mac OS) the audio track and pressing Delete.

That's all you need to do with the nested sequence. You will animate the newspaper and video together by animating the sequence, not the individual clips.

8 Click the practice sequence to make it active.

9 Drag writers 2.avi to the Video 1 track of the nested practice sequence.

10 Drag the nested practice sequence to the Video 2 track, directly above the interview clip. Make the clip in Video 1 the same length as the nested practice sequence in Video 2.

11 With the nested practice sequence clip selected, add a Scale keyframe in the Motion effect at about 3 seconds from the beginning of clip. Set its value to 80. Set another Scale keyframe at the beginning of the clip and set its value to 0.

12 Set a keyframe for the Rotation parameter in the Motion effect at the beginning of the clip. Set its value to -4x0.0. Set another Rotation keyframe at the same point in the Effect Controls Timeline as the second Scale keyframe. The keyframes snap to each other to make this easy. Set the value of this Rotation keyframe to 0.0.

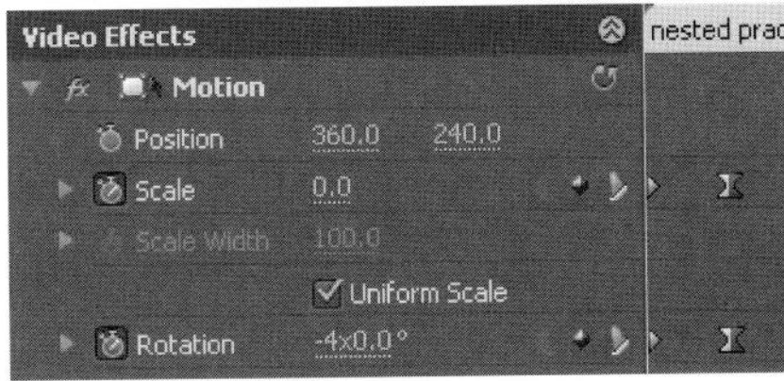

13 As a nice touch, you can right-click (Windows) or Control-click (Mac OS) the last Rotation keyframe you set and set it to Ease In.

This will make it gradually stop rotating, rather than stop suddenly.

14 Play the clip.

The power of nesting allows you to apply effects to multiple clips at once by nesting clips in a sequence. You can also nest sequences in sequences.

Nesting clips

In the previous exercise, you nested an entire sequence in another sequence. It is also possible to select a group of clips and nest them in a sequence. It does not have to be all the clips in a sequence. This can be useful for collapsing a complex set of clips into a single nested sequence.

1 Open Lesson 17-4.prproj. Play the Timeline.

You want create a Page Turn transition at the edit point of the writers 2 and writers 3 clips. Since there are two other clips composited over the writers 2 clip, a Page Turn transition is difficult—but not if you collapse the first segment to a single nested clip.

2 Shift-click the three clips that make up the first segment—Title 01, nested complete, and writers 2.avi—to select them.

3 Right-click the selected clips and choose Nest.

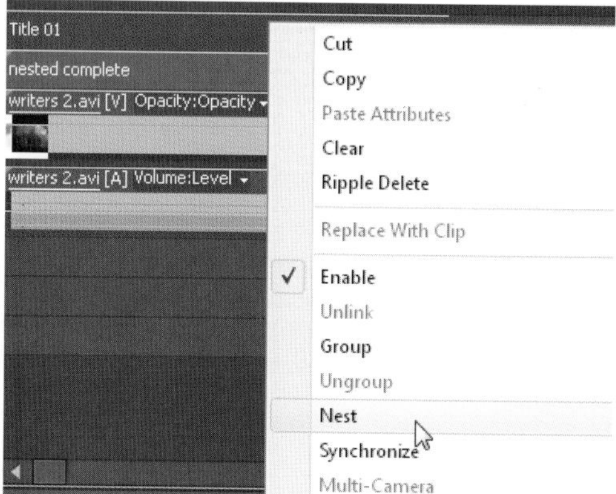

The three clips are collapsed to a single nested clip. Play the clip to see that the nest contains the three clips.

4 Drag the Page Turn transition from Effects > Video Transitions > Page Peel to the edit point between the two clips.

Note: To edit a nested set of clips, double-click the nested sequence in the Timeline. The nested sequence becomes the active sequence, which you can edit.

Getting to know the recommended keyboard shortcuts

Adobe Premiere Pro has more than 100 keyboard shortcuts. You won't use all of them, but about 25 should become part of your repertoire. You can customize them and create additional ones to suit your needs.

To get an idea of just how vast the shortcut opportunities are, choose Edit > Keyboard Customization. Not surprisingly, that opens the Keyboard Customization dialog, shown here.

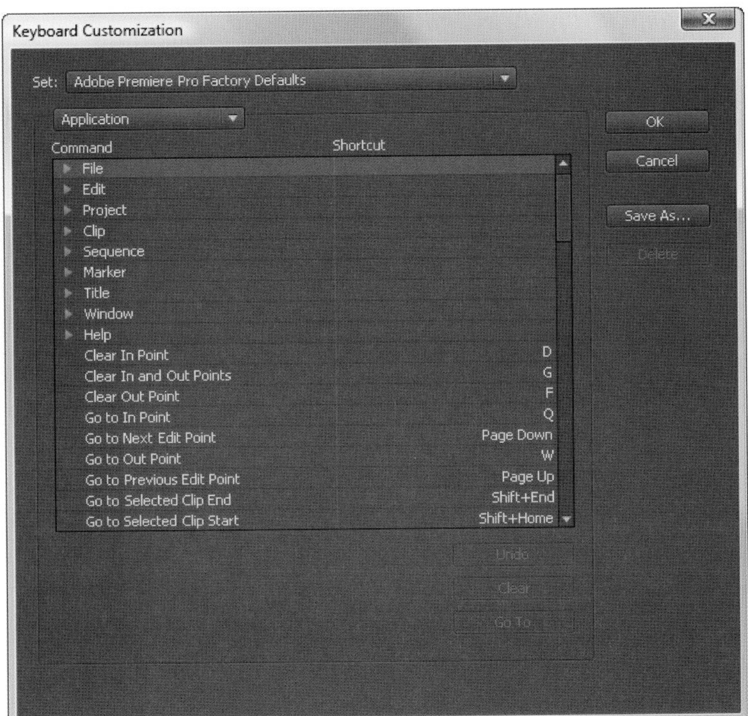

Note that the Adobe Premiere Pro Factory Defaults list includes the main menu headings: File, Edit, Project, and so on. You can open each of those lists and find commands that match virtually everything available in the menus.

Many mimic standard system-level shortcuts:

FUNCTION	WINDOWS	MAC OS
Save	Ctrl+S	Command+S
Copy	Ctrl+C	Command+C
Undo	Ctrl+Z	Command+Z

Adobe Premiere Pro has three sets of keyboard shortcuts: the factory defaults and sets for two competing products, Avid Xpress DV 3.5 and Final Cut Pro 4.0. The latter two facilitate migration from those products to Adobe Premiere Pro.

Changing a shortcut

You can create a fourth, custom set of shortcuts. The more you work with Adobe Premiere Pro, the more you'll want to do that. Here's how:

1 Choose Edit > Keyboard Customization.

2 Open the Edit list and click Redo.

You'll see that the keyboard shortcut to redo something you've undone is Ctrl+Shift+Z (Windows) or Command+Shift+Z (Mac OS). That shortcut is valid in various Adobe products. Your experience with other products might be to use Ctrl+Y (Windows) or Command+Y (Mac OS).

3 Click the Redo shortcut in the Shortcut column (not the word *Redo*) and then press Ctrl+Y (Windows) or Command+Y (Mac OS).

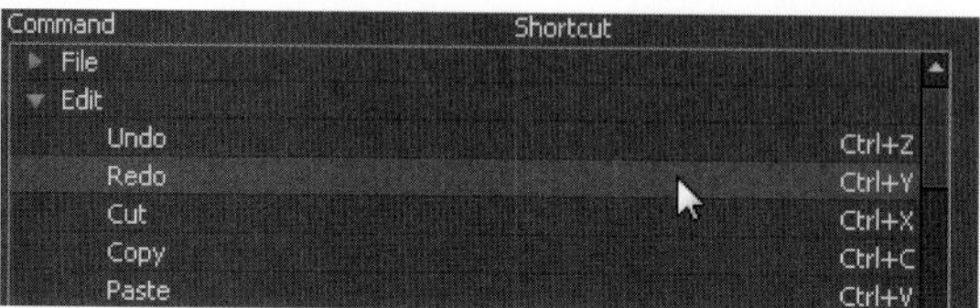

[Custom] appears in the Set menu. You'll name and save this as a custom set in a moment, but first check out what happens when you try to change a keyboard shortcut to one that's already in use.

4 Click Copy to highlight it in the list, and then click its shortcut—Ctrl+C (Windows) or Command+C (Mac OS)—to clear that entry.

5 Press Ctrl+Y (Windows) or Command+Y (Mac OS).

A small warning (shown here) opens, noting that you are about to redefine an existing shortcut. Click anywhere in the dialog box to make that change.

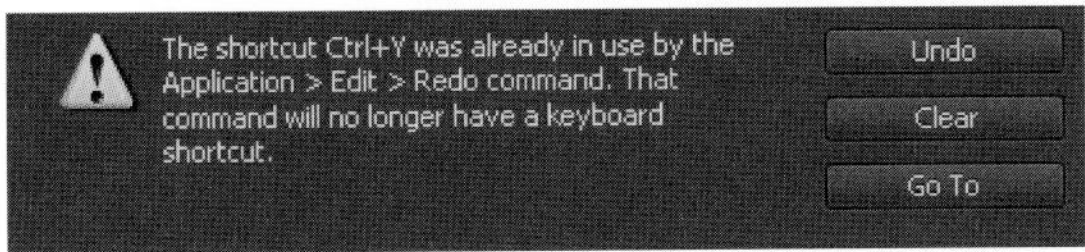

6 Click Undo to undo that change.

If you were to click OK, you would close the dialog box, and the [Custom] set would have the new shortcut for Redo and would be the currently selected set of keyboard shortcuts. If you click Save As instead, you can give that [Custom] collection a more descriptive name.

7 Click Save As, give your customized keyboard shortcut collection a name, and then click Save.

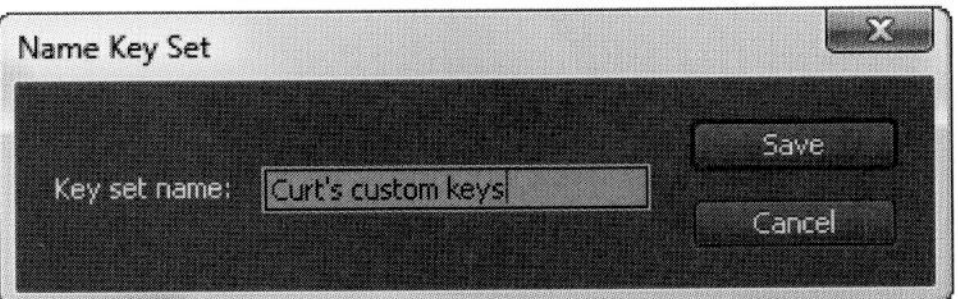

Most frequently used shortcuts

About 25 shortcuts seem to be the most frequently used (including system-level "imitations" such as Ctrl+C/Command+C). In no time at all, the following shortcuts will become second nature to you:

- **Tools**: Each tool has a single-letter keyboard shortcut. To remind yourself of those shortcuts, open Keyboard Customization and choose the Tools menu.

You'll use these frequently. At the very least, Selection (V), Ripple Edit (B), Rolling Edit (N), and Razor (C) should be ingrained in your brain. In case you need reinforcement, roll your pointer over each icon in the Tools panel to see a tool tip with the tool's keyboard shortcut.

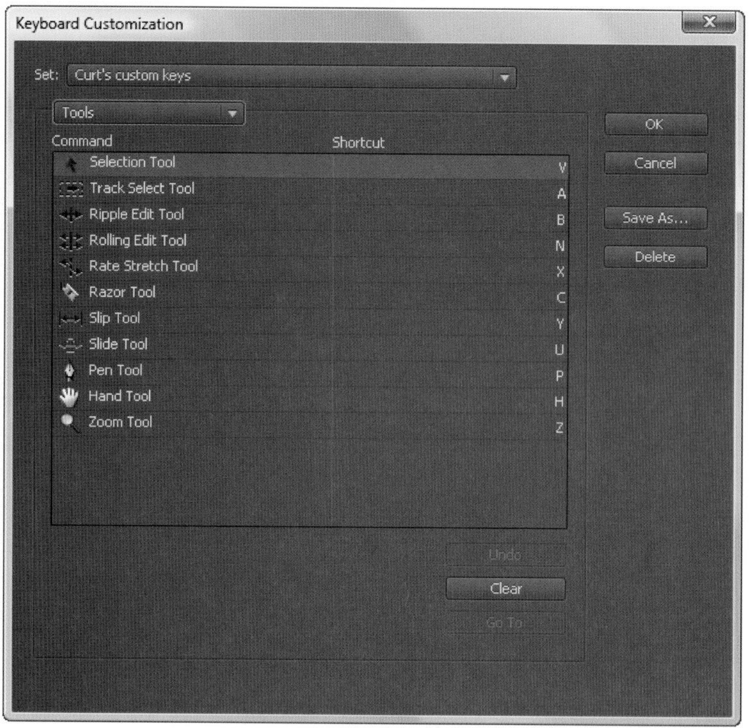

Note: Pressing the backslash twice will return you to the previous zoom level. This is a great time-saver.

- **Backslash (\)**: This resizes the Timeline to display your entire project. It's a great way to get a handle on where you are in the workflow.
- **J and L**: These are playback controls. J is reverse; L is forward. Press one of these keys two or three times to increase speed incrementally.
- **K**: This is a multifunction playback modifier key. Press K to stop playback. Hold down K while either pressing or holding down the J or L key to change playback speeds.
  - **Hold down K while pressing J**: Do this to play in reverse one frame at a time.
  - **Hold down K while pressing L**: Do this to play forward one frame at a time.
- **Press and hold down K+J**: Do this to play in reverse slowly (8 fps).
- **Press and hold down K+L**: Do this to play forward slowly (8 fps).

- **Plus sign (+) or minus sign (-) and a number**: Use this keystroke combination to move a clip by a specified number of frames. Select the clip, and then press + or - on the numeric keypad (not Shift+= or the hyphen key) followed by the number of frames (you also need to use the numeric keypad). Press Enter (Windows) or Return (Mac OS) to move the clip.
- **Home and End**: Use these to move to the beginning or end of a sequence if the Timeline is active or to the first or last clip in the Project panel if it's active.
- **Page Up and Page Down**: Use these to move to the beginning or end of the selected clip or next edit point in the Timeline, or to the top or bottom clip currently displayed in the Project panel.
- **Asterisk (*)**: This adds a marker. The asterisk key on the numeric keypad (not Shift+8) adds a marker to the Timeline. (Markers will be covered in more detail in Lesson 21.)
- **S**: Pressing S turns on or turns off the Snap feature (the little two-pronged icon in the upper-left corner of the Timeline). You can toggle Snap on or off even while dragging or trimming a clip.
- **Alt/Option**: This shortcut temporarily unlinks audio and video. Press the Alt (Windows) or Option (Mac OS) key as you click the video or audio portion of a linked audio/video clip to unlink that portion, enabling you to trim or move that portion of the clip without affecting the other portion.
- **Alt+[/Option+[and Alt+]/Option+]**: This shortcut sets work area bar end points (shown here). If you want to render or export a part of your project, you need to set the beginning and end of that section. Pressing Alt+[(Windows) or Option+[(Mac OS) sets the beginning to wherever the current-time indicator edit line is. Alt+] (Windows) or Option+] (Mac OS) sets the end. You can simply drag the ends of the bar to those points as well. The work area bar end points will snap to clip edit points.

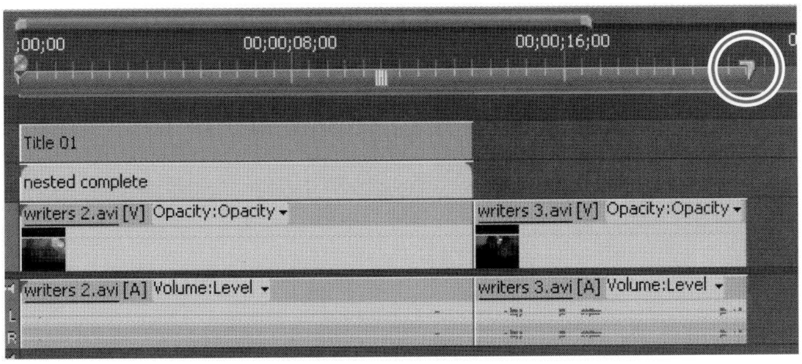

Note: When viewing the Timeline panel in audio units, the clip will move by the specified number of audio samples.

Note: The current-time indicator does not snap to items—items snap to it. If the current-time indicator did snap to edit points, moving the current-time indicator through the sequence would become a jumpy mess.

Note: Double-clicking the center of the work area bar sets the bar ends to the visible area of the sequence, or to the full length of the sequence if it's visible in its entirety in the Timeline.

- **F1**: This opens Adobe Premiere Pro Help.
- **Ctrl+T/Command+T**: Pressing Ctrl+T (Windows) or Command+T (Mac OS) opens the Titler.
- **Marquee-select**: Drag a marquee to select a group of clips in the Timeline or Project panel. This should be a routine part of your workflow. Marquee-selecting clips in the Timeline lets you move a whole group of clips, and marquee-selecting clips in the Project panel lets you add all those clips at once to a sequence.
- **Import folders**: Instead of importing a file or collection of files, you can import an entire folder. Select Import and click the Import Folder button in the lower-right corner of the Import dialog box. That creates a bin in the Project panel with the exact folder name and imports the associated files.

Review questions

1 What's the difference between the Leave Color effect and the Change to Color effect?

2 What is a way to use the eyedropper to sample a wider range of pixels?

3 What is the purpose of the split-screen option in the Fast Color Corrector effect?

4 What are the basic settings you apply with the color wheel in the Fast Color Corrector effect?

5 How can you edit a nested sequence once you nest selected clips on a Timeline?

6 What keyboard shortcuts enable you to rewind, stop, and play your project?

Review answers

1 Leave Color turns everything in a scene gray with the exception of objects that have a user-selected color. Change to Color replaces a user-specified color with another color.

2 Holding down the Control (Windows) or Command (Mac OS) key while sampling a color with the eyedropper causes it to sample more pixels.

3 The split-screen function allows you to instantly preview the effect of your color corrections and compare it to the original.

4 The settings are Balance Angle (the color added to the clip) and Balance Gain (the intensity of that color). You can also adjust the overall Hue Angle parameter to move all colors in a clip toward a selected color.

5 Double-click the nested sequence, and the original sequence will become active.

6 The shortcuts are J, K, and L. Pressing J or L more than once speeds up the reverse and forward speeds. K stops playback.

18 MANAGING YOUR PROJECTS

Topics covered in this lesson

- Working in the Project menu
- Using the Project Manager
- Conducting a Clip Notes review
- Importing projects or sequences

This lesson will take approximately 30 minutes.

Managing assets and tracking client comments are critically important to professional video producers. The Project Manager lets you easily consolidate a project, and Clip Notes lets you embed a project into a Portable Document Format (PDF) file for client review.

Getting started

If you are a one-person band, tracking projects is probably a snap for you. However, once you start bringing others into the production mix, you need to find ways to manage your assets. Adobe Premiere Pro CS4 has a slick project-management tool, called the Project Manager, that reduces a project's storage size and consolidates the files associated with a project.

The Clip Notes feature in Adobe Premiere Pro streamlines a collaborative workflow by facilitating feedback from clients and colleagues. You can either embed a rendered sequence as a video file within a PDF file or store it on a server and put a link to that file in the PDF file. In either case, a reviewer can open the PDF file, play the movie, and enter comments directly in the PDF file. Later you can read those comments from within the Timeline.

The Project Manager allows you to save or consolidate your project for easy archiving, and its import features allow you to share complete projects or portions of projects.

Project menu overview

Project management starts in the Project menu. It presents several options that let you track projects and reuse assets. In particular, it offers two ways to export your project:

- **Batch list**: A Batch list is a text file of audio/video asset names and timecodes. It contains no information about your project such as edits, transitions, or graphics.
- **Project Manager**: The Project Manager creates a trimmed version of your project by saving only the portions of the assets you used in your sequences or consolidates the project by storing all its assets in a single file folder. If you choose to create a trimmed project, you can use only offline filenames that you later recapture. Whether you trim or consolidate your project, the Project Manager also stores a copy of your original Adobe Premiere Pro project file with all its information about edits, transitions, effects, and Titler-created text and graphics.

In the following exercise, you will briefly run through the Project menu commands and then focus on the menu's most important feature—project management:

1 Load Lesson 18-1.prproj.

2 Click in the Project panel to select it, but don't select any of the clips (otherwise several options in the Project menu will be unavailable).

Note: If you select a clip, that will be the sole entry in the Batch list you will make in step 4.

3 Open the Project menu in the menu bar.

You'll see the following options:

- **Project Settings**: You worked with project settings in Lesson 4.
- **Link Media**: Use this to link offline filenames to their actual files or videotapes.
- **Make Offline**: This allows you to convert an online file to offline.
- **Automate to Sequence**: Use this to move selected files to a sequence, as you did in Lesson 6.
- **Import/Export Batch List**: Use this to create or import a list of filenames.
- **Project Manager**: You'll work with the Project Manager in this lesson.
- **Remove Unused**: This is a quick and easy way to clean up your project. Choose it to remove any assets from the Project panel that you are not using in your project.

Note: Some of these options will be dimmed depending on what files or panel you have selected.

4 Choose Export Batch List, accept the default name and location (the current project folder), and click Save.

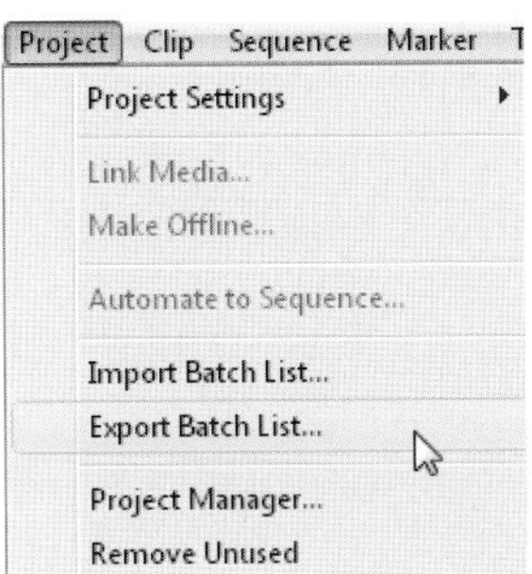

That creates a comma-delimited or comma-separated value (CSV) file that you can read with most text editors. The contents are simply the filenames, timecodes, and original source tape names (if any). The Batch list stores only audio and video filenames, not graphics or images.

5 Choose Import Batch List from the Project menu and double-click Adobe Premiere Pro Batch List.csv (the file you just created in step 4).

A Batch List Settings dialog box opens.

6 Accept the defaults, which should be the same as your sequence settings, as shown here. Click OK.

This adds a new bin to the Project panel.

7 Open the Adobe Premiere Pro Batch List bin.

The status of each clip is Offline, which is evident because of the icons next to each clip.

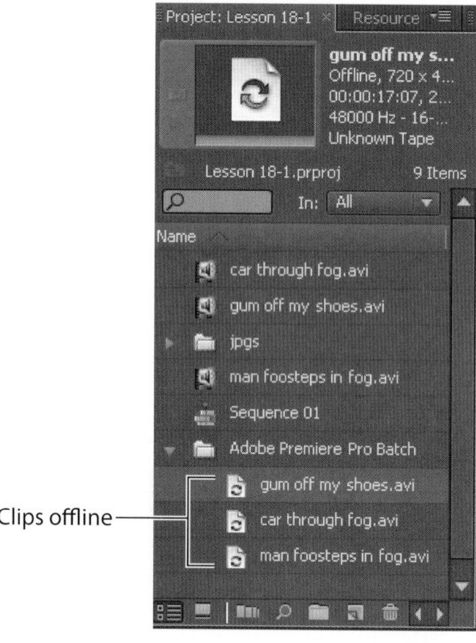

8 Click gum off my shoes.avi in the Adobe Premiere Pro Batch bin.

9 Choose Project > Link Media.

10 In the Link Media dialog box, navigate to the Lesson 18 folder and then double-click gum off my shoes.avi.

Note: If you select more than one offline file, the Link Media dialog box appears in turn for each file you select. Pay attention to the offline filename in the title bar of the dialog box so that you relink the correct source file to each offline file.

Note: The Import Batch List feature has a limitation in functionality. It can link to A/V files only. If you attempt to link to audio-only or video-only files, you will get an error message.

Making a clip offline

It's possible to purposely make clips offline and still work with them in the Timeline. This can be useful for saving disk space while working in the early stages of a project or for relinking to a clip that is being reshot.

1 Delete the Adobe Premiere Pro Batch bin you just imported.

2 Click the car through fog.avi clip in the Project panel to select it.

3 Choose Project > Make Offline.

4 In the Make Offline dialog box, select Media Files Remain on Disk and click OK.

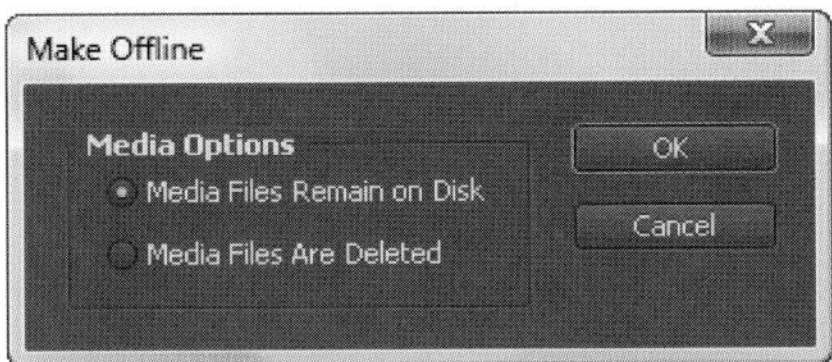

The file becomes offline in the project but remains on the hard drive. Selecting Media Files Are Deleted takes the file offline and removes it from the hard drive. If you select that option and you want to use that file in a project, you'll need to recapture it (or, in this case, copy it from the DVD).

5 Move the current-time indicator over the first clip in the Timeline.

Note these two things:

- The clip remains in the project with all its effects applied. (The first clip has scaled motion and a transition at the end.)
- The Program Monitor displays a Media Offline placeholder graphic for that clip.

This is useful if you work with massive files and want to speed up editing. The drawback is that you can't see the video if you want to make frame-specific edits.

Note: If you're using the clip in another project, it will still be online there.

Using the Project Manager

Typically the Project Manager comes into play after you complete a project.

You can use it to create a separate file folder that consolidates into one spot all the assets used in your sequences. This is a great way to archive a project and make it easier to access later. Once consolidated, you can remove all the original assets if you choose.

You can conserve hard-drive space by saving only those assets you used in the project, trimming them to the portions you used in your sequences, and then saving them (or offline references to them) in a single file folder.

To see your options, choose Project > Project Manager.

You can choose to save all sequences (the default) or only specific sequences.

You have two basic choices that determine how the project will be saved, each with its own set of options (shown here):

- Create New Trimmed Project
- Collect Files and Copy to New Location

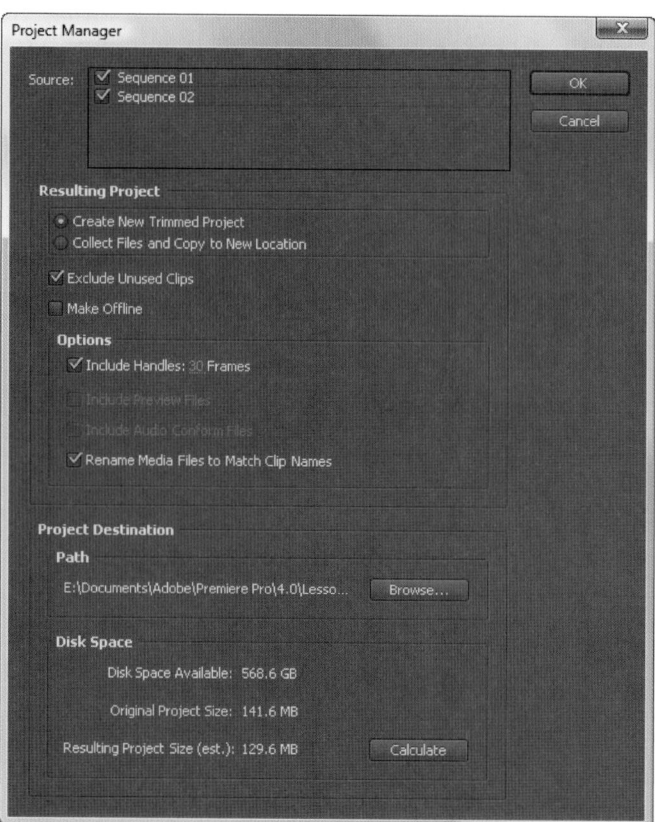

Working with a trimmed project

In the trimmed project, the resulting files (or offline file references) refer only to the portions of the clips you used in the project sequences. You have some options, as shown in the previous figure:

- **Exclude Unused Clips**: This almost goes without saying when you are making a trimmed version of your project.
- **Make Offline**: Instead of storing the clips as files, create a list of file data so that you can capture the clips from videotape.
- **Include Handles**: This works the same as video capture in that you retain some extra head and tail frames to allow for smooth transitions or slight editing changes later.
- **Rename Media Files to Match Clip Names**: If you changed the clip names to make them more descriptive, you can use the new names in the trimmed project.

Note: If you select Make Offline, the Project Manager checks all the video files to see whether they have source tape names associated with them. If not, because they can't be recaptured, the Project Manager will copy those files into the newly created project rather than just list them as offline.

Collecting files and copying them to a new location

The Collect Files and Copy to New Location option in the Project Manager menu will store all the media assets from the current project to a single location. You might use it to prepare a project for sharing or archiving. This feature is useful if you have media assets stored in many different folders or many different drives. It will organize all your files into one location.

This selection shares two options with the trimmed project selection: Exclude Unused Clips and Rename Media Files to Match Clip Names. In addition, it has two other choices:

- **Include Preview Files**: These are files created when you render effects. Using this approach saves you time later but takes up more disk space.
- **Include Audio Conform Files**: This is only a minor time-saver. Audio conforming runs in the background when you import files with audio into a project. There is generally no need to include audio conform files.

Note: Because the video files in all the lessons in this book do not have source tape names associated with them, clicking Calculate with Make Offline selected or unselected will yield the same results. By default, even if you select Make Offline, the Project Manager copies all video files that don't have source tape names associated with them to the new project to ensure you don't delete them accidentally.

Final project management steps

Click Calculate (at the bottom of the Project Manager), and Adobe Premiere Pro will determine the size of the files in the current project and the resulting trimmed project's estimated size. You can use this to check what difference it will make to select Make Offline or to include preview files, audio conform files, or handles.

Finally, select (or create) a file folder for the trimmed or consolidated project and click OK.

Conducting a Clip Notes review

Anyone who has sought feedback on a project from a client will embrace Clip Notes. This feature resolves the headaches and miscommunications common to collaboration.

You use the Clip Notes feature in Adobe Premiere Pro to create an Adobe PDF file. PDF files have become the de facto standard in multiplatform document exchange. A Clip Notes PDF contains either a video of your selected sequence or a link to a video on a server.

A reviewer opens the PDF, plays the video, and enters comments into the PDF, which automatically tags the comments directly to the timecode. You import those comments into Adobe Premiere Pro, and they appear as markers in the Timeline.

You don't need Adobe Acrobat to create a Clip Notes PDF, because the engine is built into Adobe Premiere Pro. To make comments, you do need Adobe Acrobat 8 Standard, Adobe Acrobat 8 Professional, or Adobe Reader (Adobe Reader is available as a free download at www.adobe.com/reader).

1 Open Lesson 18-2.prproj and select Sequence 01.

2 Choose File > Export > Adobe Clip Notes.

   You have two main options for Export Settings:

   - **Format**: Windows Media or QuickTime (Windows) or QuickTime only (Mac OS)
   - **Preset**: Presets for high- and low-quality bit rates for NTSC, PAL, and widescreen formats

   Below the main settings are five tabs for various detailed settings:

   - **Filters**: You can enable the Gaussian Blur filter to reduce noise introduced in the encoding process. Setting this value too high will make the video blurry. As a rule of thumb, use the least amount of noise reduction you can for a clean picture. Test your export with this option turned off, and then increase it by small amounts, if needed.
   - **Clip Notes**: Your choices here are Embed Video or Stream Video. Embedding the video means a larger PDF file size but ensures that all reviewers will be able to play the movie regardless of their network connection. Streaming the video means a smaller PDF file size, but reviewers must have access to the server you're using to post the video file. If you choose to stream the video, enter the URL where the file is located. You can also set a password if you want the PDF document secured from anyone except those with a password. You can also add an e-mail address to which comments will be returned when the review is complete.

- **Video**: The recommended settings for video frame size and bit rate are determined by the preset you choose, but you can customize these settings and save them as your own customized preset.
- **Audio:** As with the Video tab, the Audio setting is determined by the preset you choose but is customizable to many other audio encoding options.
- **Others**: If you choose the Stream Video option on the Clip Notes tab, you can have the video automatically uploaded to your FTP server. Add the FTP server information in the boxes on this tab, as specified by your FTP server host.

3 Set Preset to NTSC Widescreen Source to 1024kbps, leave the format set to Clip Notes QuickTime, set Output Name to Clip Notes Test.pdf in the Lesson 18 folder, and click OK.

4 Adobe Media Encoder starts. Click Start Queue to encode and create the Clip Notes PDF document.

Adobe Media Encoder processes the file and creates the PDF. Close Adobe Media Encoder when it has finished processing the file.

Reviewing your Clip Notes PDF file

You can e-mail the PDF file to a client or circulate it within your organization. In either case, anyone with access to the file can view its associated rendered sequence and make comments.

1 Minimize Adobe Premiere Pro.

2 Navigate to the newly created PDF file and open it by double-clicking.

3 Make a selection that suits you in the Manage Trust for Multimedia Content dialog box.

4 Read the instructions (you can access them at any time by clicking the View Instructions button in the reviewing area) and click OK.

5 Type your name in the Reviewer Name text box.

6 Click the Play button in the movie viewer.

● **Note:** You will find a sample PDF file (Lesson 18 clip notes.pdf) for your use and reference, if needed, in the Lesson 18 folder.

7 Click Pause when you want to enter a comment (clicking Stop will return the current-time indicator to the beginning of the video).

Adobe Premiere Pro automatically enters a timestamp in the comment box.

8 Type your comment.

9 Click Play to continue reviewing the movie and adding more comments.

10 Click the Go To pop-up menu to jump to any of your comments.

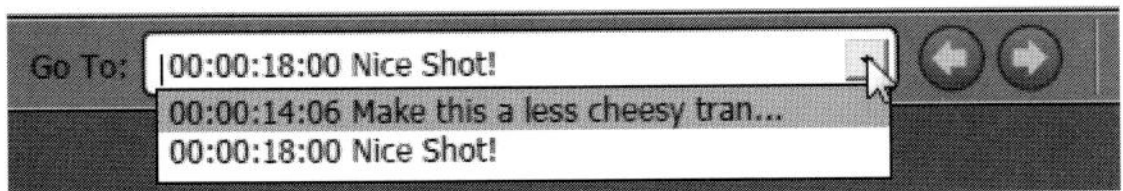

11 When you finish entering comments, click the Export button (in the lower-right corner below the screen), give your comments a name (the default is [*original PDF filename*]_data), put the file in the Lesson 18 folder, and click Save.

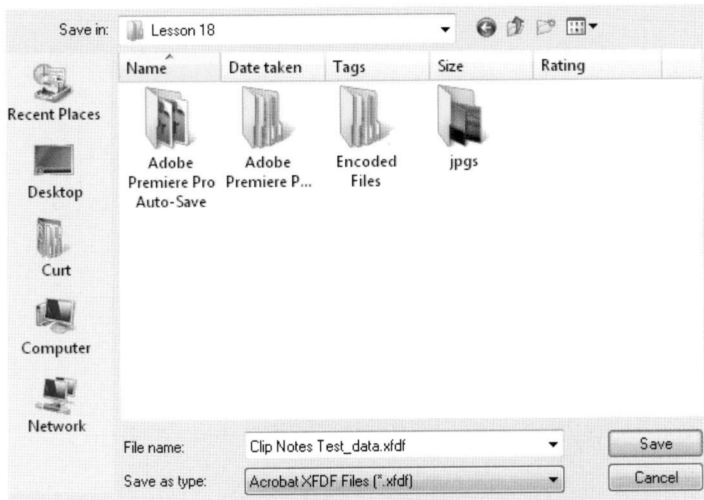

That creates an Extensible Markup Language forms data format (XFDF) file.

Viewing Clip Notes comments in Adobe Premiere Pro

To view Clip Notes comments in Adobe Premiere Pro, follow these steps:

1 Quit Adobe Acrobat and return to Adobe Premiere Pro.

2 Make sure the sequence you sent out for review is open in the Timeline panel.

3 Choose File > Import Clip Notes Comments, navigate to that file, and click Open.

Comments appear as markers in your sequence.

Note: You will find a sample Clip Notes comments file (Lesson 18 Clip Notes Test_data.xfdf) for your use, if needed, in the Lesson 18 folder.

4 Double-click a marker to view the comments.

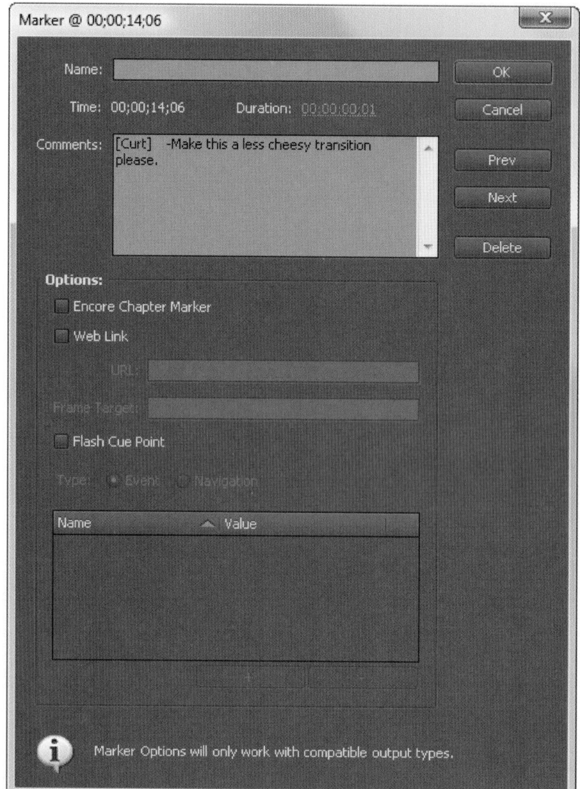

Alternatively, choose Marker > Go To Sequence Marker to move from one marker to another.

Notice that the comments the reviewer makes are accurate in time on the Timeline. This is an extremely helpful tool for reviewing draft videos with customers or clients.

Importing projects or sequences

It is helpful to be able to use one Adobe Premiere Pro CS4 project in another. You can save hours of time by importing a project, or a portion of a project, into a new project.

1 Load Lesson 18-3.prproj.

   You want to import the twirling newspaper sequence you created in Lesson 17 and add it to this project.

2 Choose File > Import and navigate to the Lesson 17 folder to select Lesson 17-3.prproj. Click Open.

   An Import Project dialog box pops up.

3 Selecting the Import Entire Project option will do as it suggests. In this case, you just want the twirling newspaper sequence, not the entire project. So select Import Selected Sequences and click OK.

   The Import Premiere Pro Sequence dialog box pops up, displaying all the sequences available in the imported project.

4 Choose the completed sequence and click OK.

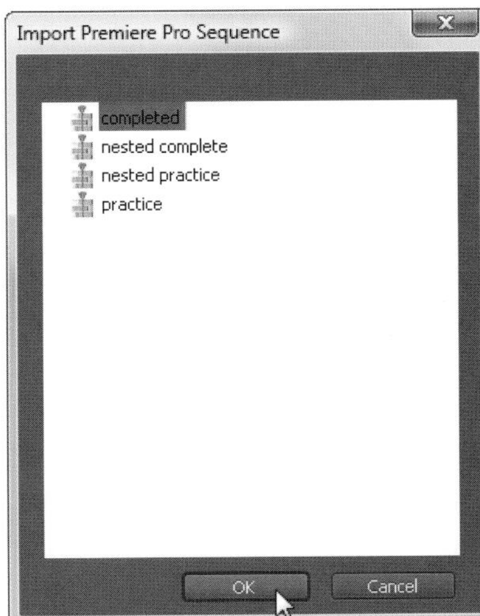

A new bin appears in the Project panel with the name of the imported project. Expand this bin, and you will notice it has the completed sequence and associated clips you requested, but it also imported the nested complete sequence, which you did not request. Adobe Premiere Pro analyzed the request and determined that the nested complete sequence was also required because it was nested inside the complete sequence.

5 Drag the completed sequence to the Timeline and play it to see that the imported sequence plays as expected.

Review questions

1 What are the basic differences between Batch lists and Project Manager-trimmed projects?

2 Explain the two principal uses of the Project Manager.

3 Why does selecting Make Offline in the Project Manager have no effect on clips with no source tape name associated with them?

4 How do you access Clip Notes comments from within Adobe Premiere Pro?

5 When you import a project into a project, must you import the entire project?

Review answers

1 Batch lists are simply text files consisting of audio/video filenames, timecodes, and their source tape names. Project Manager trimmed projects have full project information, plus trimmed original clips or offline filename references.

2 You use the Project Manager either to create a trimmed version of your project or to consolidate the original, untrimmed project files in one folder. In either case, you can store all your assets in one easily accessible spot to simplify collaboration and archiving.

3 Adobe Premiere Pro has a built-in fail-safe mechanism. If it sees that a video clip has no source tape associated with it, it won't allow the Project Manager to make that an offline clip, since you might not be able to recapture it.

4 Open your project to the sequence you created the Clip Notes for, choose File > Import Clip Notes Comments, and double-click any of the markers that appear along the sequence time ruler.

5 No. Adobe Premiere Pro allows you to import an entire project or one or more sequences.

19 USING PHOTOSHOP AND AFTER EFFECTS TO ENHANCE YOUR VIDEO PROJECTS

Topics covered in this lesson

- Working with Adobe Creative Suite 4 Production Premium
- Importing Photoshop files as sequences
- Using Adobe Dynamic Link with After Effects
- Replacing a clip with an After Effects composition

This lesson will take approximately 50 minutes.

Adobe Photoshop CS4 and Adobe After Effects CS4 can play valuable roles in your video production workflow. You can animate Photoshop layered graphics in Adobe Premiere Pro CS4, and you can use After Effects to dynamically link text and graphic animations with Adobe Premiere Pro.

Getting started

Adobe Premiere Pro is a powerful tool on its own, but it is also part of Adobe Creative Suite 4 Production Premium. You can purchase Adobe Premiere Pro by itself and use all its built-in features, or you can purchase it as part of the Production Premium, where it becomes one piece of a powerful combination of integrated components.

Anyone who works with print graphics or does photo retouching has probably used Adobe Photoshop. It is the workhorse of the graphic design industry. Photoshop is a powerful tool with great depth and versatility, and it is becoming an increasingly important part of the video production world. In this lesson, you will explore how to use the integration features between Photoshop and Adobe Premiere Pro.

Adobe After Effects is the *de facto* standard in the video production industry as a text animation and motion graphics tool. In this lesson, you will explore the unique integration between Adobe Premiere Pro and After Effects for powerful and time-saving techniques.

Exploring Creative Suite Production Premium

Creative Suite 4 Production Premium is not just a collection of software bundled together in a box. This suite of components is designed to work together through common interface elements and tight integration to provide you with the tools you need to move from vision to output on virtually any platform.

Adobe Premiere Pro by itself is a powerful tool for acquiring, editing, and outputting video projects. As part of Creative Suite Production Premium, however, it becomes even stronger. If you purchased Adobe Premiere Pro by itself, you may not be able to follow along with all the examples in this lesson, but please read through them to understand how Adobe Premiere Pro fits into the larger picture of this suite of products. If you purchased Adobe Premiere Pro as part of Creative Suite Production Premium, read on to experience the impressive integration and timesaving techniques engineered into the product.

Creative Suite Production Premium combines Adobe Bridge CS4, Dynamic Link, and Adobe Device Central CS4, and includes the following components:

- Adobe Premiere Pro CS4
- Adobe After Effects CS4
- Adobe Photoshop CS4 Extended
- Adobe Flash CS4 Professional

- Adobe Illustrator CS4
- Adobe Soundbooth CS4
- Adobe Encore CS4
- Adobe OnLocation CS4

You have already had a look at capturing with Adobe OnLocation, importing Photoshop and Illustrator files, and sweetening and mixing audio with Soundbooth.

Adobe Encore CS4 is now included with the purchase of Adobe Premiere Pro as a full-featured DVD-authoring tool. You will learn how to export to Encore to produce DVDs, Blu-ray Discs, and Flash Video in Lesson 21.

In this lesson, you'll focus on the integration among Adobe Premiere Pro, After Effects, and Photoshop.

Note: For more information on any of these products, please visit www.adobe.com/products.

Importing Photoshop files as sequences

Making the move to Photoshop means joining forces with just about every image-editing professional on the planet. It's that ubiquitous. Photoshop is the professional image-editing standard.

Note: In this exercise, you will animate a Photoshop PSD file in Adobe Premiere Pro. The PSD file is provided on the DVD, so it is not necessary to have Photoshop to complete this lesson.

Photoshop has some strong ties to Adobe Premiere Pro and the entire DV production process:

- **Editing in Photoshop**: Right-click (Windows) or Control-click (Mac OS) any Photoshop graphic in Adobe Premiere Pro—in either the Timeline or the Project panel—and choose Edit In Adobe Photoshop (or Edit Original). This launches Photoshop and lets you immediately edit the graphic. Once saved within Photoshop, the new version of the graphic appears in Adobe Premiere Pro.
- **Exporting a filmstrip**: This feature is specifically designed to export a sequential collection of video frames for editing in Photoshop. You open the filmstrip in Photoshop and paint directly on the clips—a process called *rotoscoping*.
- **Creating mattes**: Export a video frame to Photoshop to create a matte that will mask or highlight certain areas of that clip or other clips.
- **Cutting objects out of a scene**: Photoshop has several tools that work like a cookie cutter. You can remove an object and use it as an icon, make it into a button in a DVD menu, or animate it over a clip.
- **Importing PSD files**: You can natively import Photoshop PSD files with video, blending modes, and layers.

You looked briefly at importing Photoshop CS4 files as footage in Lesson 4. In this exercise, you will take a closer look at importing a layered Photoshop file into Adobe Premiere Pro as a sequence:

1 Open Lesson 19-1.prproj. Notice there is a bin in the Project panel named Finished. Expand the Finished bin, and open the Finished sequence if it's not already open.

2 Play the Finished sequence, and notice that the title at the bottom of the screen is animated in layers. Titles appearing at the bottom of the frame like this are often referred to as *lower thirds*. The lower-third graphic is a nested sequence called finished lower third. In the following steps, you are going to open that sequence to see how it was made and then re-create it.

3 Inside the Finished bin is another bin named Finished lower third. From that bin, open the sequence named Finished lower third.

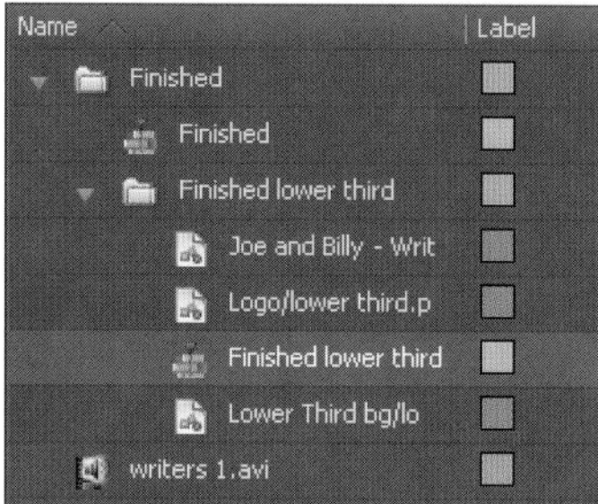

This sequence is built from a Photoshop image that has three layers.

4 Move the current-time indicator to about 2 seconds into the sequence. Toggle the track output off for each video track (click the eye icon), and then toggle them back on to see the contents of each track. Examine the Motion settings of each clip, and notice that the Motion effect was used to animate each clip to achieve an interesting appearance. You will now re-create this lower third by importing the Photoshop graphic into a new sequence.

5 Collapse the Finished bin in the Project panel so you are back at the root level of the bins.

6 Import lower third.psd from the Lesson 19 folder. When prompted, choose to import as a sequence rather than as layers, and click OK.

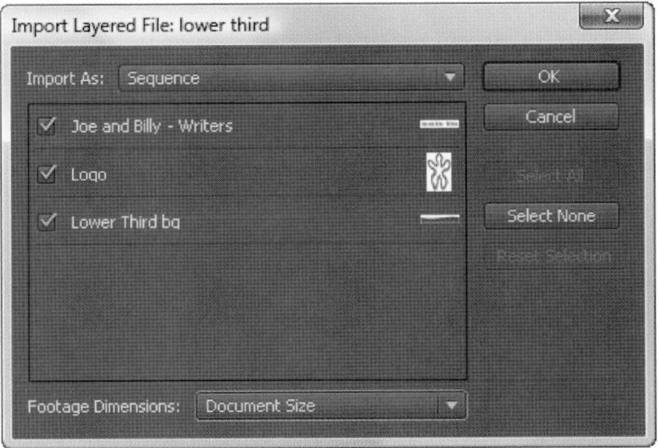

7 Expand the new bin called lower third that has been added to the Project panel. This bin contains three clips that constitute the three-layered Photoshop file. It also contains a sequence called lower third that has the three layers assembled in the same layered order as they were in Photoshop.

8 Open the lower third sequence by double-clicking it in the Project panel, and press the backslash (\) key to expand the view in the Timeline.

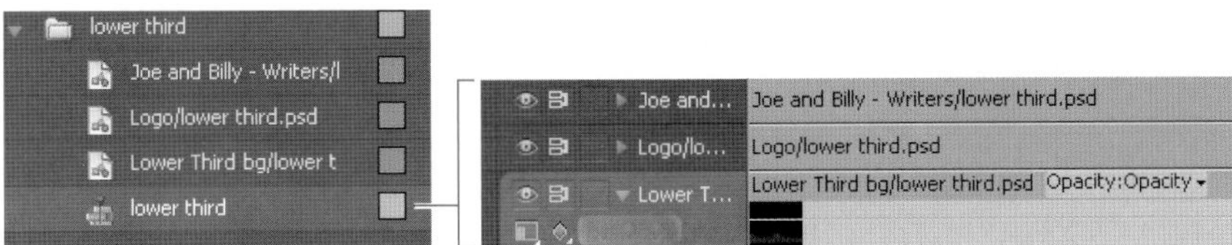

Re-creating the lower third animation

The next step is to re-create the lower third animation. Here's how:

1 Select the Lower Third bg/lower third clip and open the Effect Controls panel.

2 Expand the Motion fixed effect, and then position the current-time indicator at about 1 second into the clip.

3 Enable keyframes for the Position parameter by clicking the stopwatch. This places a keyframe at the position of the current-time indicator. Move the current-time indicator to the beginning of the clip and adjust the Position value to 360, 400. This adds a keyframe at this position and moves the lower third background below the bottom of the frame.

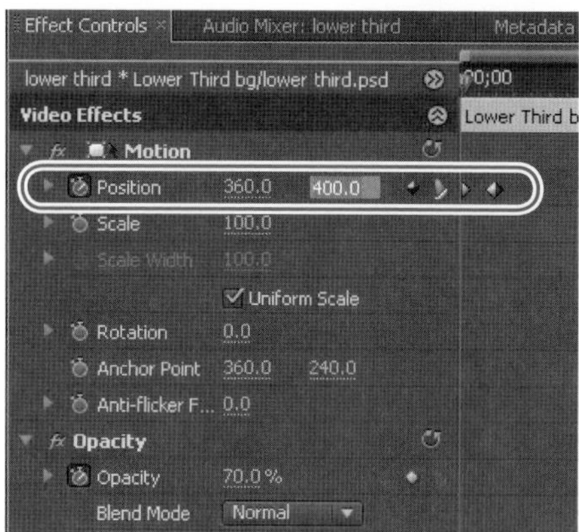

4 Play the sequence to verify that the lower third background rises from the bottom of the screen over the first second of the clip. Right-click (Windows) or Control-click (Mac OS) the second keyframe and set Temporal Interpolation to Ease In. Play the sequence again and notice what a nice touch the Ease In setting has on the animation.

Note: In this case, the blending modes in the imported Photoshop layers are set to Normal. But if you import Photoshop layers with other blending modes, Adobe Premiere Pro will import and use the blending modes as they were set in Photoshop.

5 Expand the Opacity effect, and notice that Opacity is set to 70%. This Opacity value was set in Photoshop and is imported correctly in Adobe Premiere Pro.

6 Select the Logo/lower third clip, and expand the Motion fixed effect in the Effect Controls panel. Set a Position keyframe just after 1 second, at about 00;00;01;15. Set another keyframe at the 1-second point. Set the value of this position keyframe to -300, 240. This positions the logo off the left side of the frame at the beginning of the clip.

7 Play the sequence. You can adjust the speed the logo travels by moving the second keyframe farther from or closer to the first keyframe. Experiment with this until you have the speed you desire. Also set the Ease In option on the second keyframe as you did on the background clip motion.

8 The text of the lower third should follow the logo so you can copy the logo's animation and paste it in the text clip. Select the Logo/lower third clip, click Motion, and choose Edit > Copy.

9 Select the Joe and Billy – Writers/lower third clip, click a blank area inside the Video Effects panel, and choose Edit > Paste.

The animation of the sequence is complete. The only step left is to superimpose this lower third over the interview clip.

10 Create a new DV – NTSC Widecreen 48 kHz sequence by choosing File > New Sequence. Name it Practice.

11 Drag the writers 1.avi clip to the Video 1 track of the Timeline and press the backslash (\) key to expand the view in the Timeline.

12 Drag the lower third sequence you just animated to the Video 2 track above the writers 1 clip. Adjust the position of the lower third so it starts about 1 second after the interview clip starts.

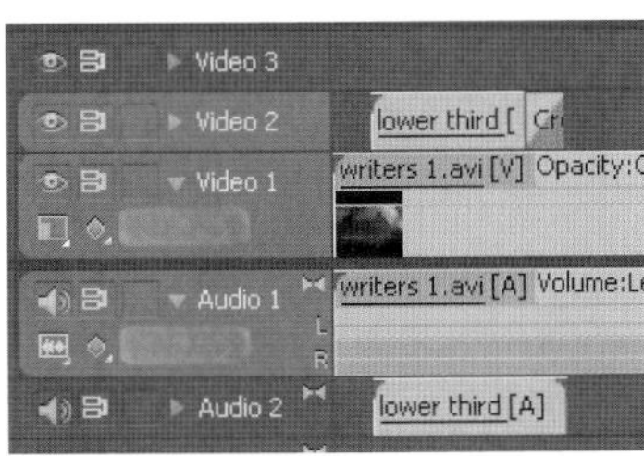

13 To polish it all off, drop a Cross Dissolve transition on the end of the lower third sequence clip.

The lower third animation sequence references the original Photoshop file. So, if you change the original Photoshop file, the changes will ripple through any instances where it was used in Adobe Premiere Pro. For example, you might open the lower third.psd file in Photoshop and change the background or text color. When you save the Photoshop file, the changes will immediately be reflected wherever that file was used in Adobe Premiere Pro.

Using Dynamic Link with After Effects

After Effects is the tool of choice for editors who want to produce exciting and innovative motion graphics, visual effects, and animated text for film, video, DVD, and the Web.

After Effects users tend to fall into two distinct camps: motion graphics artists and animated text artists. Some production houses specialize in one or the other. After Effects can do so much that it's hard to wrap your brain around all of it. You are likely to use only a subset of its creative prospects.

Note: Dynamic Link requires Creative Suite Production Premium. Purchasing Adobe Premiere Pro and After Effects separately will not allow Dynamic Link to work. Dynamic Link is a suite-based feature.

Surveying After Effects features

After Effects has numerous options:

- **Text creation and animation tools**. Create animated text with unprecedented ease. After Effects offers dozens of groundbreaking text animation presets. Simply drag them to your text to see them in action.
- **Leading-edge visual effects**. More than 150 effects and compositing features enhance your images well beyond the capabilities of Adobe Premiere Pro.
- **Vector paint tools**. Use built-in vector paint tools based on Photoshop technology to perform touch-up and rotoscoping tasks.
- **Comprehensive masking tools**. Easily design, edit, and work with masks using flexible autotracing options.
- **Tight Adobe integration**. Copy and paste assets, compositions, or sequences between Adobe Premiere Pro and After Effects. Preserve layers and other attributes when you import Photoshop and Illustrator files. The Dynamic Link feature (remember, available only in Creative Suite Production Premium) means you will not need to render an After Effects composition before moving it between After Effects and Adobe Premiere Pro or Encore.
- **Motion Tracker**: This option accurately, quickly, and automatically maps the motion of an element and lets you add an effect to follow that action.

Looking at the After Effects workspace

In this exercise, you will animate the same lower third graphic that you did at the beginning of this lesson. You will import the same Photoshop file into After Effects, use After Effects tools to animate the three layers of the graphic, and then use Dynamic Link to link the After Effects animation into the Adobe Premiere Pro Timeline.

1. In Adobe Premiere Pro, open Lesson 19-2.prproj.
2. Launch Adobe After Effects.
3. In After Effects, open the ae finished.aep file by choosing File > Open Project and selecting ae finished.aep from the Lesson 19 folder.

Notice many similarities to the Adobe Premiere Pro user interface.

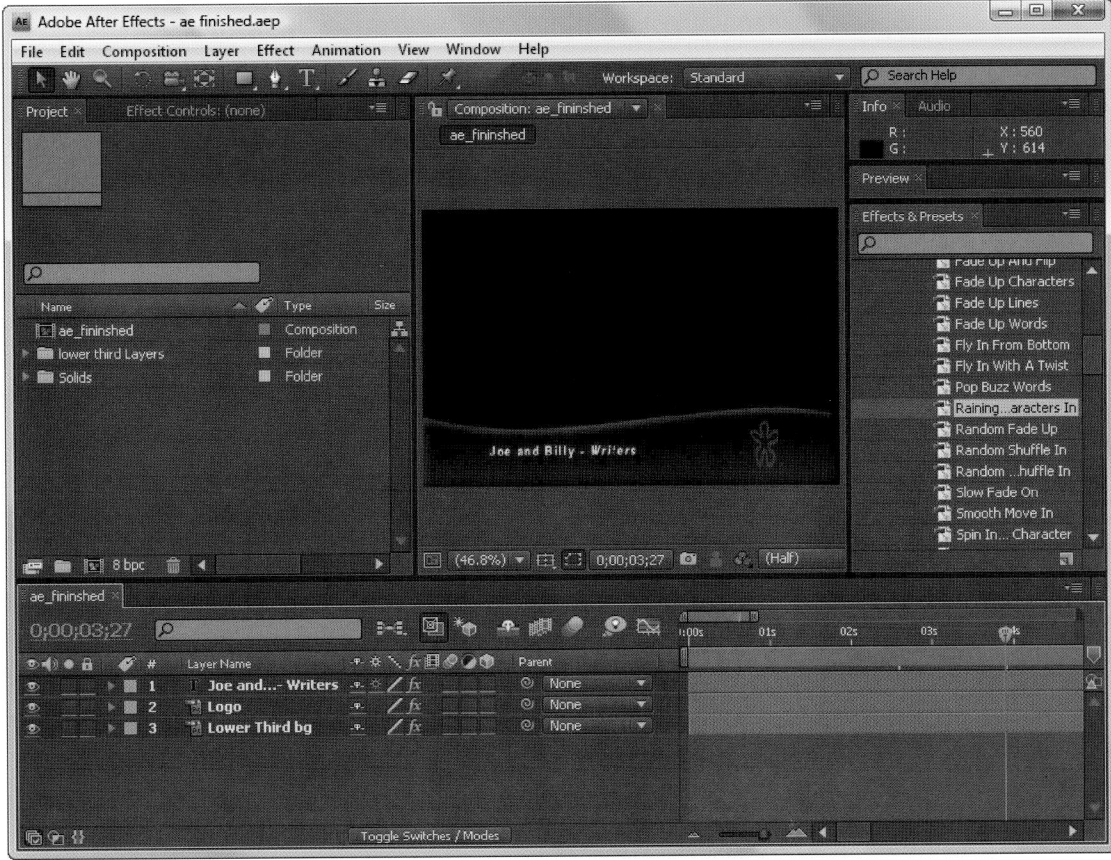

As with Adobe Premiere Pro, After Effects has a Project panel, but the icons and terminology are a bit different. For instance, Adobe Premiere Pro sequences become *compositions* in After Effects.

Double-clicking a composition (as shown here) opens it in the Timeline panel. Instead of tracks, you work with *layers* in After Effects.

4 Scrub the After Effects Timeline to see the final animation you will create.

5 After Effects may not be able to play back the animation in real time, depending on your computer speed. However, After Effects can do a RAM preview when you press the 0 (zero) key on the numeric keypad. This renders the Timeline to RAM and then plays it back smoothly in real time.

6 Close ae finished.aep by choosing File > Close Project.

Animating the lower third

In this exercise, you will start a new project in After Effects and create the animation you just saw in the finished example:

1 With After Effects still open, import the lower third.psd file by choosing File > Import > File and selecting lower third.psd from the Lesson 19 folder. Change the Import As parameter from Footage to Composition and click Open.

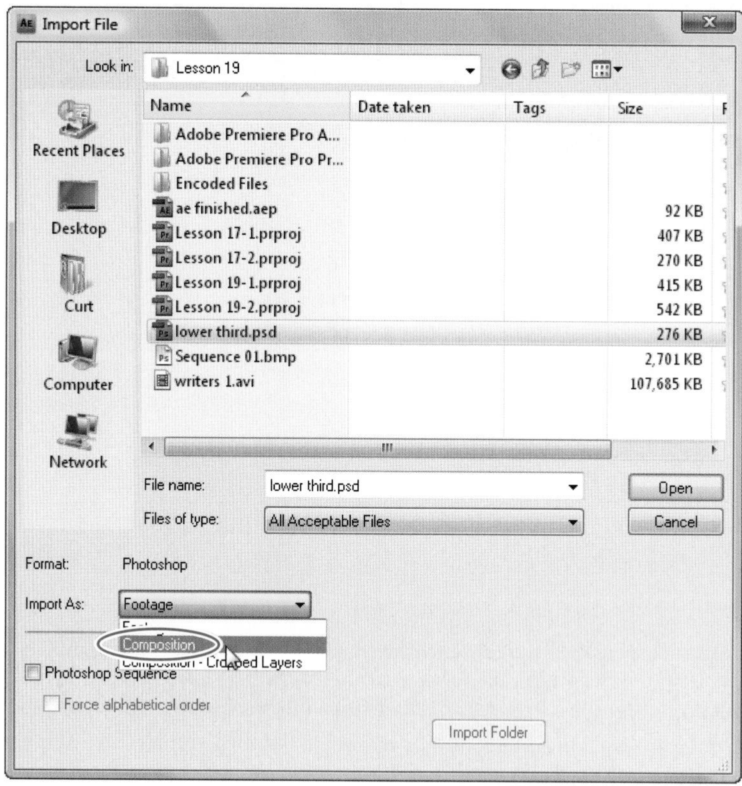

2 A dialog box will open where you can specify the kind of composition import. Accept the default, as shown here, and click OK.

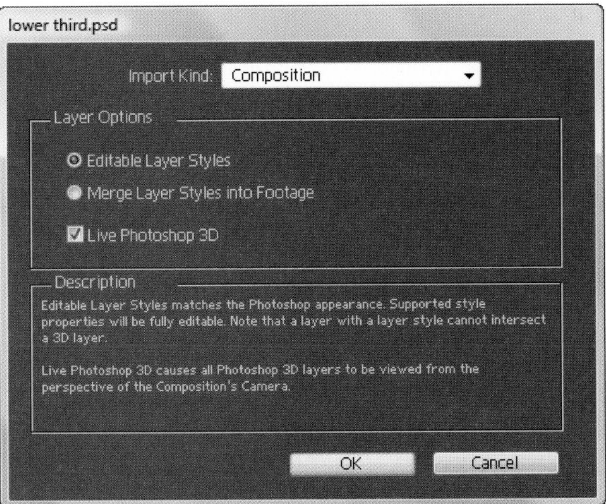

3 Double-click the lower third composition icon in the Project panel to open the composition in the Timeline.

4 Notice the Photoshop CS4 layers are intact and in the correct order in the Timeline. Scrub the Timeline, and you will see this is a static graphic. No animation has been applied yet. Return the current-time indicator to the beginning of the clip.

5 Locate the Effects & Presets panel, and expand the * Animation Presets folder. Within that folder, expand the Transitions – Movement folder. Drag the Zoom – 3D tumble preset to the Lower Third bg layer of the Timeline.

Note: The preset will be applied at the current-time indicator location on the layer where you dropped the preset, so make sure the current-time indicator is at frame 0 for step 5.

6 Do a RAM preview of this effect by pressing the 0 (zero) key on the numeric keypad.

Next you will animate the logo.

7 Position the current-time indicator at the 1-second mark, just as the lower third background animation is finishing.

8 Drag the Slide – Swoop preset (located in the Transitions – Movement folder) to the Logo layer. RAM preview the Timeline.

After Effects has some dazzling animation presets designed especially for text. These animations are aware of individual characters, words, or lines of text. You'll use one of these text effects on the text layer. However, because you didn't create the text in After Effects, After Effects doesn't know the layer is text. You need to tell After Effects that the top layer (Joe and Billy – Writers) is text.

9 Select layer 1 (the Joe and Billy – Writers text layer), and choose Layer > Convert to Editable Text. Now After Effects will treat this layer as text; the text can now be edited and animated with special text effects or presets. After Effects indicates this is a text layer by showing a T icon to the left of the layer name.

10 Position the current-time indicator at the 1-second mark on the Timeline.

11 In the Effects & Presets panel, expand the Text folder within the *Animation Presets folder. Within the Text folder, expand the Animate In folder and drag the Raining Characters In preset to the Joe and Billy – Writers text layer in layer 1.

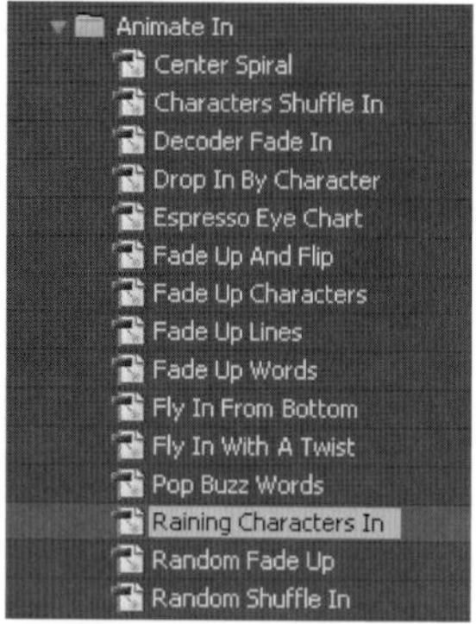

12 Do a RAM preview.

13 Save the project by choosing File > Save. Save the project in the Lesson 19 folder and name it ae practice.aep.

Importing a project from After Effects to Adobe Premiere Pro using Dynamic Link

With the animation complete, it's time to use it in your Adobe Premiere Pro project, superimposed over the interview clip. In the past, this would involve rendering the animation out to a movie, importing the movie into Adobe Premiere Pro, and then placing it in the Timeline. If you ever wanted to change the animation, you would have to edit the movie in After Effects, rerender it, and re-export it, which would be very time-consuming. With Dynamic Link, the process is much simpler:

1 Leave After Effects open, and open or switch back to Adobe Premiere Pro. It is not necessary to leave After Effects open for Dynamic Link to work, but you will be editing the animation again, so to save time here, leave it open.

2 In Adobe Premiere Pro, open Lesson 19-2.prproj, and then open the Practice sequence.

3 Drag writers 1.avi from the bin to the Video 1 track.

4 Import the After Effects composition you just made via Dynamic Link by choosing File > Adobe Dynamic Link > Import After Effects Composition.

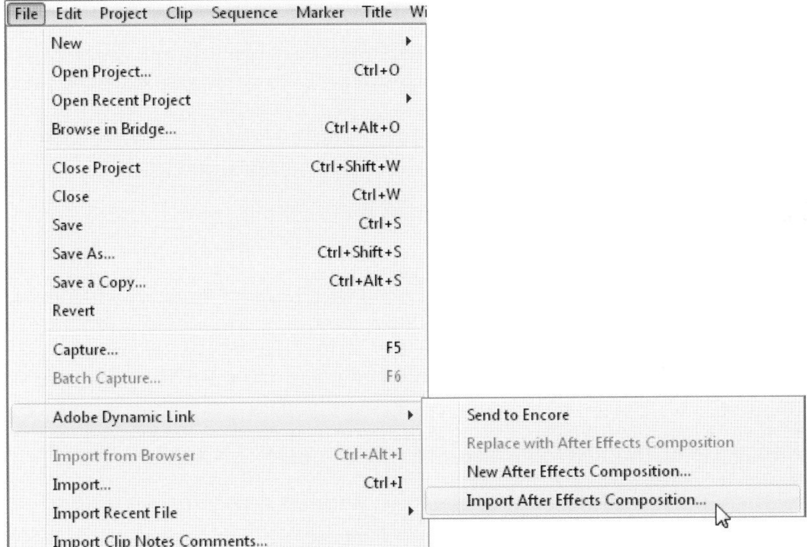

5 On the left side of the Import Composition dialog box, navigate to the Lesson 19 folder, select ae practice.aep, select the lower third/ae_practice composition in the right window, and click OK.

6 This adds the lower third/ae practice composition to the Adobe Premiere Pro Project panel. Drag it to the Video track above the writers 1 clip. Position it about 1 second after the start of the interview. Trim the end of the ae_practice composition so it is about 7 seconds long.

7 As a nice finish, add a Cross Dissolve transition to the end of the lower third Dynamic Link clip so it dissolves away.

8 Render and play the sequence in Adobe Premiere Pro.

You now have an After Effects animation playing in Adobe Premiere Pro—and you didn't need to render or export the animation in After Effects. This is a real timesaving feature. The power of this feature becomes more obvious when you need to edit or tweak your animation.

Editing an existing dynamically linked animation

In this exercise, you will make an adjustment to the animation in After Effects to show the dynamic nature of this feature:

1 Leave the project open in Adobe Premiere Pro, and switch over to After Effects, which should still be open, with the lower third composition open.

2 Set the current-time indicator position to the beginning of the After Effects Timeline.

3 In the Effects & Presets panel, expand the Backgrounds folder, which is inside the * Animation Presets folder.

4 Drag the Silk preset to the Lower Third bg layer. Do a RAM preview to see this effect.

5 Without saving the After Effects project, switch back to Adobe Premiere Pro.

6 Play the sequence in Adobe Premiere Pro. Without saving the After Effects project, the changes you made in After Effects are already updated in Adobe Premiere Pro. That's why they call it Dynamic Link!

Replacing a clip with an After Effects Composition

There are times when you are editing an Adobe Premiere Pro project and you want to apply some special effects that are available in After Effects. You could create a new After Effects composition and import it into Adobe Premiere Pro with Dynamic link, but there is an even faster way to do it. You can convert a clip or clips on an Adobe Premiere Pro sequence to an After Effects composition right from the Timeline. Let's give it a try:

1 Open Lesson 19-3.prproj. This project already has the After Effects title sequence linked via Dynamic Link in the Video 2 track.

  You want to apply a special affect to the writers 1.avi clip to make it look like bad TV reception. After Effects has this effect as a preset.

2 Right-click the writers 1.avi clip in the practice sequence, and choose Replace with After Effects Composition.

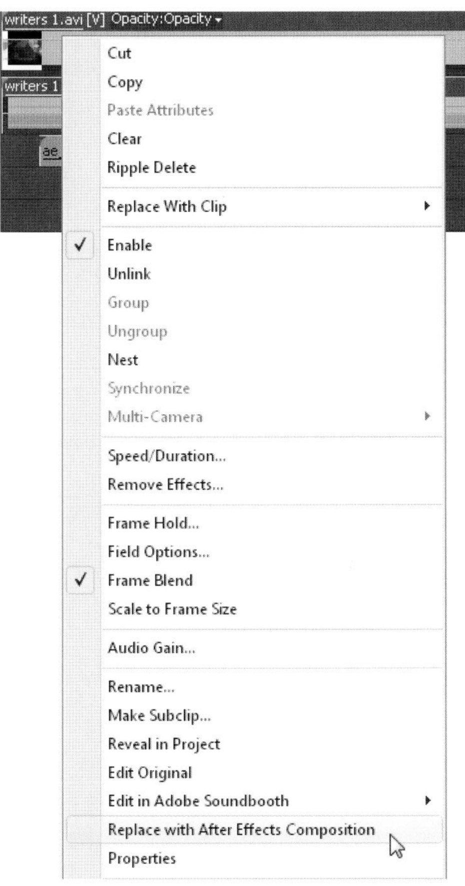

3 You will be prompted to name the new After Effects project. Name it writers bad tv.aep in the Lesson 19 folder, and click Save.

This launches After Effects, if it is not already open, with the writers clip in a new composition.

4 Locate the Bad TV 2 – old effect in *Animation Presets > Image – Special Effects, and drag it to the writers 1.avi clip.

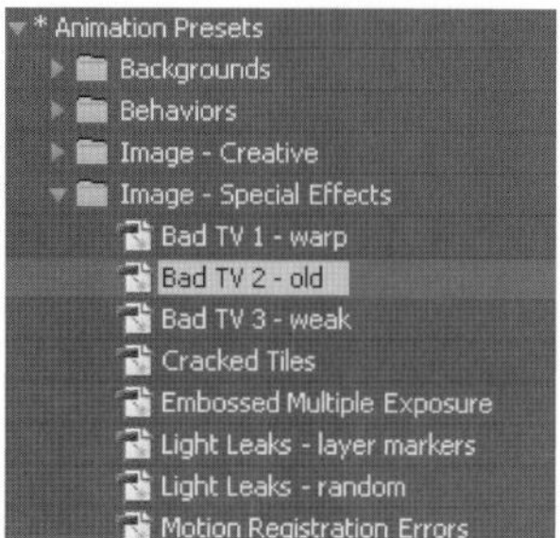

Without saving the After Effects composition, switch back to Adobe Premiere Pro, and notice the Bad TV 2 effect is applied to the writers clip. You may need to render the sequence in Adobe Premiere Pro to see it play back smoothly. This is a fast way to apply special After Effects effects to a clip in Adobe Premiere Pro.

Review questions

1 What is the difference between importing a Photoshop file into Adobe Premiere Pro as footage and importing it as a sequence?

2 If you set the Opacity value of a layer to something less than 100% in Photoshop, what will be the Opacity setting for the clip when imported into Adobe Premiere Pro?

3 Can Adobe Premiere Pro import blending modes set in Photoshop layers?

4 In some ways, Adobe Premiere Pro and After Effects have similar functionality. Only the terms are different. Give a couple of examples.

5 Once a dynamic link is established between an After Effects composition and an Adobe Premiere Pro project, must the After Effects composition be rendered after making changes?

Review answers

1 Importing Photoshop files as layers brings them in as a single clip, with either all the layers collapsed or a single layer selected. Importing as a sequence brings all the Photoshop layers into Adobe Premiere Pro in the same stacking order as in the Photoshop file. An Adobe Premiere Pro sequence is created to nest them all together.

2 Adobe Premiere Pro imports the opacity as set in Photoshop.

3 Yes. Adobe Premiere Pro respects the blending modes set in Photoshop.

4 Adobe Premiere Pro has sequences and tracks. After Effects has compositions and layers.

5 No. Once a dynamic link is established, changes made in After Effects are immediately available in Adobe Premiere Pro.

20 EXPORTING FRAMES, CLIPS, AND SEQUENCES

Topics covered in this lesson

- Choosing export options
- Recording to videotape
- Making single frames
- Creating movie, image sequence, and audio files
- Using Adobe Media Encoder
- Exporting to mobile devices
- Working with edit decision lists

This lesson will take approximately 45 minutes.

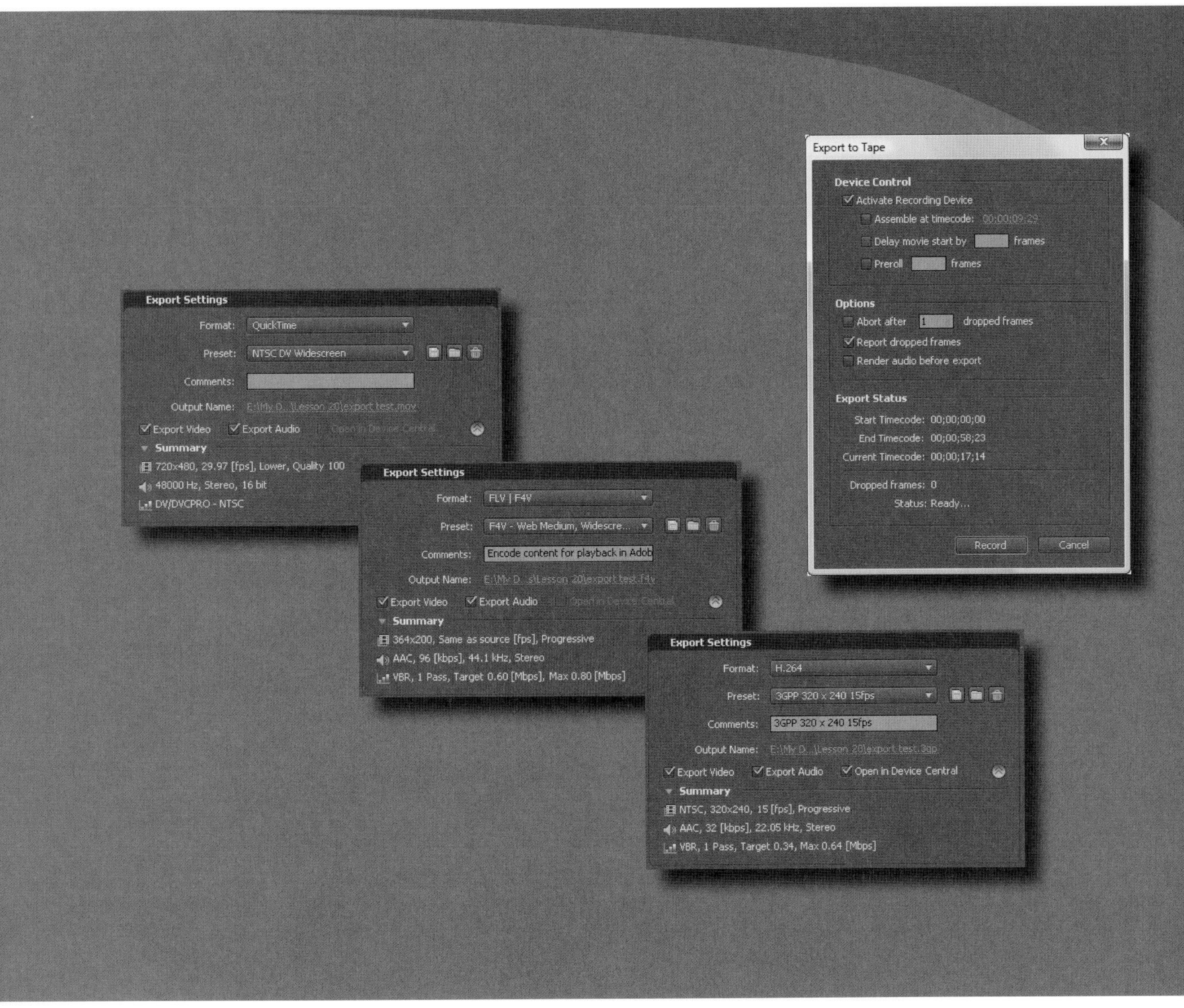

Exporting your project is the final step in the video production process. Adobe Media Encoder offers multiple high-level output formats: Windows Media, QuickTime, RealMedia, Adobe Flash, and MPEG. Within those formats you have dozens of options and can also export in batches.

Getting started

Adobe Premiere Pro CS4 offers a full array of export options—methods of recording your projects to videotape, converting them to files, or burning them to DVDs.

Recording to videotape is straightforward, while file creation has many more options. For example, you can record only the audio portion of your project; convert a video segment or entire project into one of several standard file formats; or create still frames, sequences of still frames, or animation files.

Of greater relevance are the higher-level video encoding formats available in Adobe Media Encoder. You'll use that powerful tool to create projects for posting on a website, for burning to multimedia CDs, or for exporting to mobile devices using the new Adobe Device Central CS4 software. If you need to create Flash Video for websites, use the new tools to export Flash Video with web markers. Adobe Media Encoder is a stand-alone application that handles exports in batches, meaning you can send several exports in various formats to Adobe Media Encoder and allow it to process them all in the background while you work on other applications.

Overview of export options

When you complete a project, you have a number of export choices:

- You can select a single frame, a series of frames, a clip, or an entire sequence.
- You can choose audio-only, video-only, or full audio/video output.
- You can export directly to videotape; create a file for viewing on a computer or the Internet; or put your project on a DVD with or without a complete set of menus, buttons, and other DVD features.

Beyond the actual export formats, you can set several other parameters as well:

- Any files you choose to create can be at the same visual quality and data rate as your original media, or they can be compressed.
- You need to specify the frame size, frame rate, data rate, and audio and video compression techniques.

You can use exported project files for further editing, in presentations, as streaming media for Internet and other networks, or as sequences of images to create animations.

Checking out export options

The first step in exploring export options, naturally, is importing some content to export:

1 Start Adobe Premiere Pro and open Lesson 20-1.prproj.

2 Click somewhere in the Timeline to select the project and its single sequence (otherwise Adobe Premiere Pro will not present Export as an option in the File menu).

3 Choose File > Export.

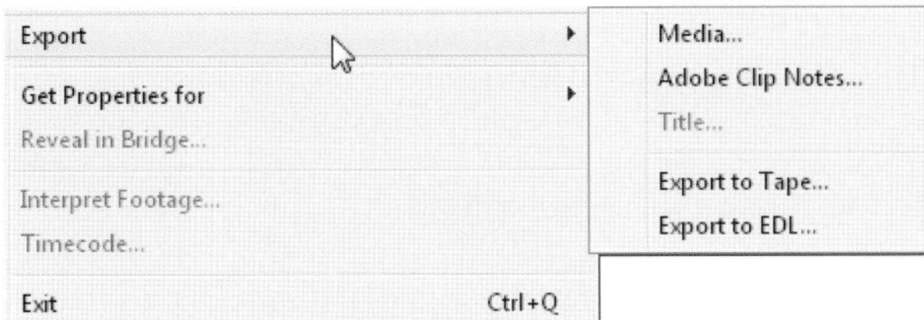

Adobe Premiere Pro offers nine export options (some options might be dimmed because of the particulars of the files in your sequence):

- **Media**: Selecting this option opens the Export Settings dialog box, which allows you to export to all popular media formats.

- **Adobe Clip Notes**: Select this option to send your project to a PDF file for review. We covered this in Lesson 18.
- **Title**: Since Adobe Premiere Pro stores Titler-created objects in the project file, the only way to use the same title in more than one project is to export it as a file. To use this option, you need to select a title in the Project panel.
- **Export to Tape**: This option transfers your project to videotape.
- **Export to EDL**: Use this to create an edit decision list (EDL) to take your project to a production studio for further editing.

Recording to videotape

Even with something as straightforward as dubbing your sequence to videotape, Adobe Premiere Pro gives you multiple options. All you need is a video recording device—most commonly, the same DV camcorder you used to import the original raw video.

You can use an analog videotape recorder without video control, but doing so takes some extra effort. That will be explained later in this lesson.

1 Connect your DV camcorder to your computer, just as you did when you captured the video.

2 Turn it on and set it to VCR or VTR (not to Camera, as you might expect).

3 Cue the tape to where you want to start recording.

Bars and tone or black video

If you're going to have a postproduction studio duplicate your tapes, add 30 seconds of bars and tone to the beginning so the studio can set up its gear. Otherwise, give your project a little breathing room on your DV tape by adding black video to its beginning. To do either one, click the New Item button at the bottom of the Project panel, and select Bars and Tone or Black Video. The default duration is 5 seconds. Right-click (Windows) or Control-click (Mac OS) the clip in the Project panel, choose Speed/Duration, and change the time to suit your needs. Then drag that clip from the Project panel to the start of your project by holding down Ctrl (Windows) or Command (Mac OS) to insert it and sliding all other clips to the right.

Note: When using the standard DV device control videotape export method, you can export only an entire sequence, as opposed to a selected segment. To export a segment, follow the analog videotape recording instructions later in this exercise.

4 Select the sequence you want to record.

5 Choose File > Export > Export to Tape.

That opens the Export to Tape dialog box shown here.

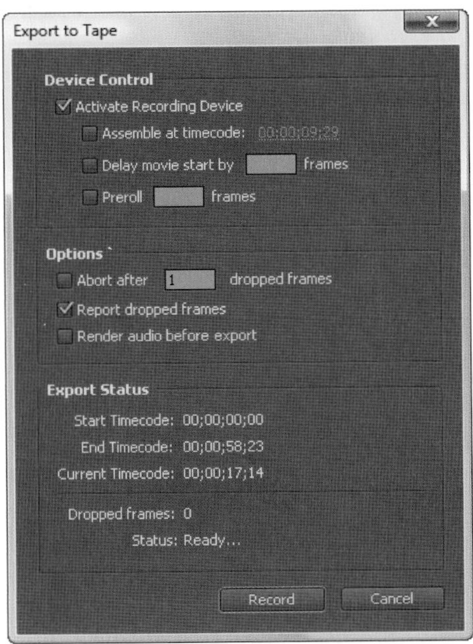

Here's a rundown of options:

- **Activate Recording Device**: When you select this option, Adobe Premiere Pro will control your DV device. Deselect it if you want to record to a device that you'll control manually.
- **Assemble at timecode**: Select this option to pick an In point on the tape where you want recording to begin. When this option is not selected, recording will begin at the current tape location.
- **Delay movie start by *x* frames**: This is for the few DV recording devices that need a brief period of time between receiving the video signal and recording it. Check your device's manual to see what the manufacturer recommends.
- **Preroll *x* frames**: Most decks need little or no time to get to the proper tape recording speed. To be on the safe side, select 150 frames (5 seconds), or add black video to the start of your project (see the previous "Bars and tone or black video" tip).

The remaining options are self-explanatory.

6 Click Record (or Cancel if you don't want to make a recording).

If you haven't rendered your project (by pressing Enter for playback instead of the spacebar), Adobe Premiere Pro does that now. When rendering is complete, Adobe Premiere Pro starts your camcorder and records your project to it.

Recording to an analog recorder without device control

To record to an analog machine without device control, set up your camcorder for recording:

1. Render the sequence or portion you want to record by pressing Enter.
2. Play the sequence to make sure you see it displayed on your external recording device.
3. Cue your tape to where you want recording to begin, position the Timeline current-time indicator to where you want playback from your sequence to begin, press the Record button on your device, and play the sequence.
4. When the sequence or segment finishes, click the Stop button in the Program Monitor and then stop the tape on the device.
5. Choose an output path and filename, and click OK.

   Adobe Media Encoder launches with this export added to its queue.

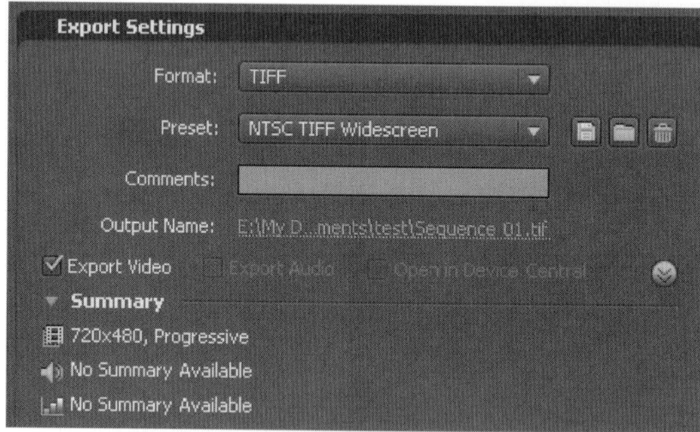

6. Click Start Queue to execute the export.

Using Adobe Media Encoder

Adobe Media Encoder is a stand-alone application that can be run by itself or when invoked from Adobe Premiere Pro. After choosing your export settings and clicking OK, Adobe Media Encoder adds your export to its queue. You can control the order of the queue and choose when to start and stop the queue. You will explore a few of the common export formats in the following sections.

Making single frames

1. Move the current-time indicator to the frame you want to export.
2. Choose File > Export > Media.

   The Export Settings dialog box appears.

3 Change Format to TIFF.

4 Change Preset to match your source sequence settings—in this case, NTSC TIFF Widescreen.

5 Set the Output Name to the desired path and filename.

6 On the Video tab make sure Export to Sequence is not checked, then click OK.

The export will be added to Adobe Media Encoder.

7 Click Start Queue to complete the export.

Note: Windows users can choose Windows Bitmap, TIFF, or Targa as a valid still image format. Mac users can choose TIFF or Targa.

Exporting editable movie and audio files

You can export a clip, an entire sequence, or a portion of a sequence as an audio/video, audio-only, or video-only file or as a sequence of still image files. The two most common file formats used for editing SD video are Microsoft DV AVI and QuickTime. In this exercise, you will export to QuickTime .mov format.

Let's begin by exporting a complete sequence:

1 Select the sequence in the Timeline or Program Monitor.

2 Choose File > Export > Media.

3 Choose QuickTime as the Format and NTSC DV Widescreen as the preset.

4 Choose Lesson 20 as the output folder and export test as the filename.

Tip: To export a portion of a sequence, place the ends of the work area bar at the beginning and end of the segment you want to export. To export a clip, select the clip in the Source Monitor or Project panel, and click in the appropriate panel to make it active. To specify a range of frames within the clip to export, set an In point and Out point in the Source Monitor.

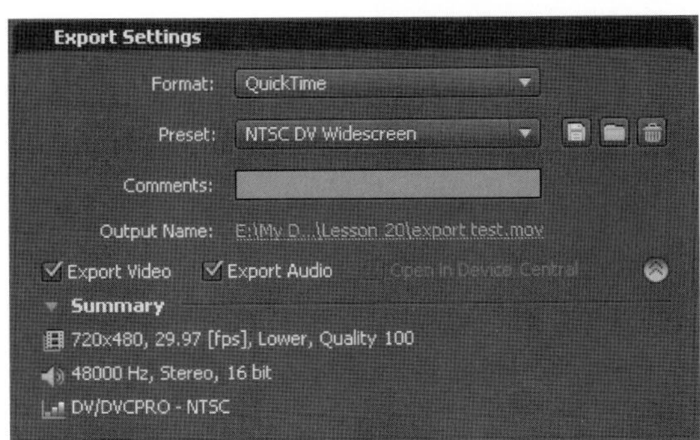

Choosing a preset that matches your source sequence will set all the detailed video and audio settings for you. Typically, you won't need to change any of the detailed settings under the advanced mode.

5 Click OK.

Adobe Media Encoder will load (if it's not already loaded), and this export will be added to its queue. Do not click Start Queue yet. We're going to add a few jobs to the queue and let it process them all at once.

Tip: To create editable movie files for HDV or HD source video, export to Uncompressed Microsoft AVI (Windows users) or H.264 Blu-ray (Windows or Mac OS users).

Exporting for the Web

Adobe Media Encoder offers a range of options for exporting and encoding video and audio for delivery on the Web. You'll start by exporting video to Adobe Flash Video.

Adobe Flash Video is based on Adobe Flash Player technology, so it's ready to play on any computer with a Flash-enabled browser. You don't have to worry about the platform or the format. With Adobe Flash Video, when the page loads, the video plays. Follow these steps to export your video:

1 Return to Premiere Pro. Select the same sequence you used in the previous exercise, then choose File > Export > Media.

2 Choose the FLV|F4V format and the F4V – Web Medium, Widescreen Source Flash 9r.115 and Higher as the preset.

3 Set Lesson 20 as the output folder and export test as the filename.

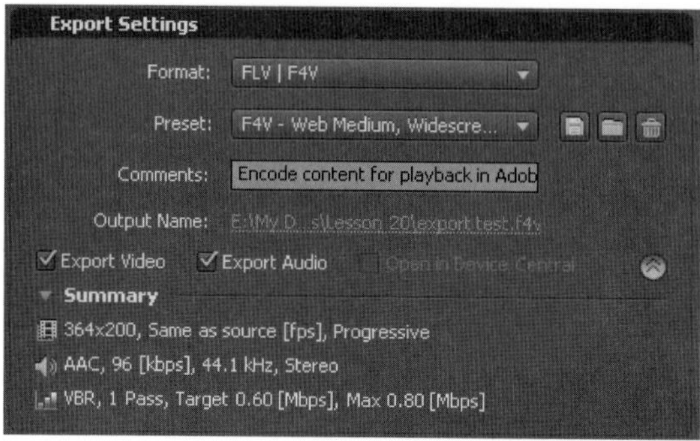

This is all you have to set to export your project to Flash Video. However, you can optionally fine-tune the export settings on the following five tabs:

- **Filters**: The filter available for encoded output is Gaussian Blur. Enabling this filter reduces the video noise introduced by slightly blurring the video. Export the project without this filter to see whether noise is a problem. If it is, increase noise reduction in small amounts. Increasing noise reduction too much will make the video blurry.
- **Format**: This determines the type of stream to which the video and audio are multiplexed.
- **Video**: The Video tab allows you to adjust the frame size, frame rate, field order, and profile. The default values are based on the preset you chose.
- **Audio**: The Audio tab allows you to adjust the bit rate of the audio and, for some formats, the codec. The default values are based on the preset you chose.
- **Others**: This tab primarily allows you to specify an FTP server for uploading the exported video when it is finished encoding. Fill in the appropriate FTP values supplied by your FTP host if you want to enable this feature.

4 Click OK.

Adobe Media Encoder loads (if it is not already loaded), and this export will be added to its queue. Do not click Start Queue yet.

Note: A unique feature of exporting to Flash is exporting flash cue markers to be used in a Flash application. Flash will read Adobe Premiere Pro flash cue markers as cue points that you can use to trigger events in the Flash composition.

Working with Windows Media (PC only)

Windows Media is the most versatile video format for use on Windows and for playback on the Internet. You can create single files with multiple-bandwidth bit rates (as a means to compensate for varying Internet user connection speeds), or you can create high-definition, wide-screen videos with 5.1 surround sound for playback in theaters or on HD TVs.

1 Export the same sequence as in the previous exercise, choosing Windows Media from the Format menu.

2 Choose NTSC Widescreen Source to High Quality Download as the preset.

3 Set Lesson 20 as the output folder and export test as the filename.

4 Click the Video tab. Notice the one- or two-pass encoding option for Windows Media encoding. Choose two-pass encoding for the best quality.

5 Click OK.

Adobe Media Encoder loads (if it is not already loaded), and this export will be added to its queue. Do not click Start Queue yet.

Note: Windows Media export is not available for Mac users.

Encoding MPEG files

Moving Picture Experts Group (MPEG) is a working committee of the International Organization for Standardization (ISO) and the International Electrotechnical Commission (IEC).

MPEG is in charge of the development of standards for digital audio and video compression. Established in 1988, the group has produced several compression standards, including the following:

- **MPEG-1**: This is the standard on which video CDs and MP3 audio are based. MPEG-1 video is VHS-quality video with CD-quality audio at up to a combined data rate of 1.5 megabits per second (Mbps). Its resolution is 352x240 (about 25 percent of full DV quality).
- **MPEG-2**: This codec is used for DVD and satellite digital video with a data rate for standard-definition video from 3 to 15 Mbps (7 to 9 Mbps is the generally accepted range for high-quality DVD video) and 15 to 30 Mbps for HD and Blu-ray. MPEG-2 also supports multichannel surround sound audio encoding.
- **MPEG-4**: This codec is used for multimedia for the fixed and mobile Web.

All MPEG standards use similar encoding techniques. They compress video by selecting keyframes or I-frames (intraframes) and then removing a few of the frames between I-frames and replacing them with B-frames (backward frames) and P-frames (predicted frames). The B- and P-frames store only the differences between I-frames. To encode your files, follow these steps:

1 To begin, open the Format menu, and note that there are five MPEG file formats:

- **MPEG4**: This file format has the file extension .3gp. This is a general MPEG4 preset. Adobe Media Encoder also has specific presets such as H.264 and QuickTime which may also use the MPEG4 standard.

Note: MPEG1 export and MPEG1-VCD export are not available for Mac users.

- **MPEG1**: This file format is specifically to view about an hour of less-than-VHS-quality video on a CD that will play on most consumer DVD video players and computer DVD and CD drives. You'll need to use stand-alone CD-writing software to create a VCD.
- **MPEG2**: The MPEG2 presets are geared to high-definition and progressive scan videos. If your goal is to create standard DVD content, select MPEG2-DVD. If you want to tweak the MPEG-2 parameters, select MPEG2.
- **MPEG2-DVD**: This option offers the most presets. Select a preset that gives you the best quality while not exceeding the 4.38 GB of space on a DVD. To help you find the right fit, Adobe Media Encoder has an Estimated File Size display that updates each time you change a preset or a customized setting. You'll take a look at that in a moment.
- **MPEG2 Blu-ray**: The MPEG2 Blu-ray presets are geared to high-definition video for distribution on Blu-ray Disc.

2 Select MPEG2.

3 Choose NTSC DV High Quality from the Preset menu.

4 Set Lesson 20 as the output folder and export test as the filename.

5 Click the Video tab, and change Pixel Aspect Ratio to Widescreen 16:9 (1.212).

6 Scroll through the many options available for fine-tuning the MPEG encoding settings. Many of these settings are beyond the scope of this book. Leave them at their default values unless you are confident in making changes and understand how the various settings interact. One of the most common settings you might want to adjust is the Bitrate Encoding setting, located on the Multiplexer tab:

- **CBR** (constant bit rate): This works well for Internet applications, because the bit rate does not fluctuate.
- **VBR** (variable bit rate): VBR generally gives you better picture quality than CBR at the same bit rate, because it increases the bit rate during action scenes. It offers a one- or two-pass option. Two passes take longer but create a higher-quality image. Use VBR when creating a video for a DVD.

7 Click the Audio tab and change Audio Format to Dolby Digital.

That gives you a wide range of options including surround sound in the Audio Coding Mode menu.

8 Click OK. Adobe Media Encoder adds the export to its queue. This time, go ahead and click Start Queue.

Adobe Media Encoder processes all the exports in its queue in the background. This may take a few minutes, but you can continue working on other projects while it is running. When it finishes, navigate to the Lesson 20 folder with your file explorer and observe the exported files.

Note: Adobe Media Encoder does not have to be used from Adobe Premiere Pro. You can start Adobe Media Encoder from your list of Adobe programs and add files to it that already exist on your file system.

Exporting to mobile devices

With the array of mobile devices that support video, it would be nice if there were a way to see what a video project would look like on various mobile devices. That is exactly what Adobe Device Central is designed to provide. In this exercise, you will export your project to Device Central and see how the video looks on various mobile devices.

Most mobile devices, such as iPods and 3GPP (third-generation) cell phones, support video encoded in the H.264 format. Two flavors of H.264 are available in the Adobe Media Encoder Format menu:

- **H.264**: This is an MPEG-4–based standard for encoding for a variety of devices, including high-definition displays, 3GPP cell phones, video iPods, and PlayStation Portable (PSP) devices.
- **H.264 Blu-ray**: This is an MPEG-4–based standard for encoding in high-definition for Blu-ray Disc media.

You'll be using H.264 for this exercise:

1 Make sure your Timeline sequence is selected in Lesson 20-1.prproj and then choose File > Export > Media.

2 Select H.264 as the encoding format.

3 Open the Preset menu.

Notice the variety of mobile devices set up for easy export. For example, it's easy to create video that will play on the Apple iPod by choosing the iPod preset. Many popular mobile device presets are already listed, and you can create or fine-tune your own presets. We'll work with a generic preset for now.

4 Choose the 3GPP 320 x 240 15fps preset, which you can test on multiple devices.

5 Make sure the Open in Device Central option (shown here) is selected and click OK.

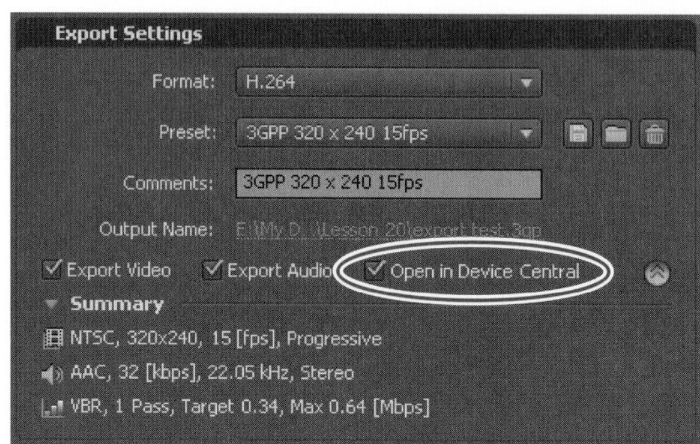

6 Name the file and click Save. This adds the export to the Adobe Media Encoder queue. Click Start Queue to process the file. If the files from the previous section are still encoding, the H.264 export will start when they are finished.

Adobe Device Central launches. The available devices are listed in the left panel of Adobe Device Central by category or manufacturer.

7 Open the Nokia category and choose Nokia 5300 cell phone by double-clicking it.

This loads your encoded video into an emulation of the Nokia 5300 phone.

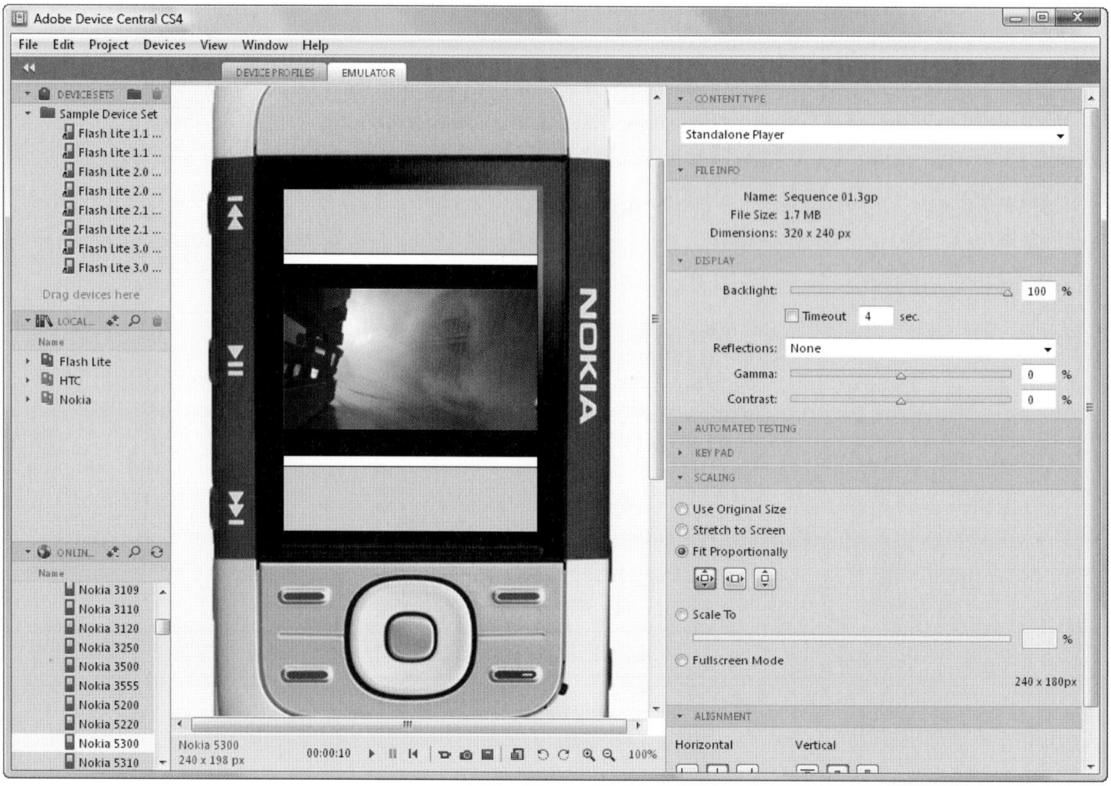

8 In the right panel under Scaling, select Fullscreen Mode, and then click the Play button under the phone emulation to see how the video will appear when it is played horizontally in the phone.

9 Choose different options from the Reflections menu under Display to see how the video might look under different lighting conditions.

10 Double-click Nokia 5200 to see how the video will look on this phone with a smaller screen.

11 Double-click Nokia 6151. Notice the video will not play on this phone. This phone does not support the video file format that was exported. You can click the Device Profiles tab to get more information about the mobile device you are viewing.

12 Quit Adobe Device Central. Remember your exported encoded file is in the file location you chose in the export options.

Working with edit decision lists

An EDL harks back to the days when small hard drives limited the size of your video files and slower processors meant you could not play full-resolution video. To remedy this, editors used low-resolution files in an NLE like Adobe Premiere Pro, edited their project, exported that to an EDL, and then took that text file and their original videotapes down to a production studio. They'd use expensive switching hardware to create the finished, full-resolution product.

These days, there isn't much call for that kind of offline work, but filmmakers still use EDLs because of the size of the files and other complexities associated with going from film to video and back to film.

CMX is gone but its EDL lives on

There is no standard EDL format. Adobe Premiere Pro uses a format compatible with the CMX 3600, a switcher created by CMX Systems, which was a pioneer of production studio and broadcast-TV computer-controlled video editors. Formed as a joint venture by CBS and Memorex in 1971, CMX owned 90 percent of the broadcast video editing market by the mid-1980s. It discontinued operations in 1998, but its EDL remains the de facto standard to communicate edit decisions.

If you plan to use an EDL, you need to keep your project within some narrow guidelines:

- EDLs work best with projects that contain no more than one video track, two stereo (or four mono) audio tracks, and no nested sequences.
- Most standard transitions, frame holds, and clip-speed changes work well in EDLs.

- Adobe Premiere Pro supports a key track for titles or other content. That track has to be immediately above the video track selected for export.
- You must capture and log all the source material with accurate timecodes.
- The capture card must have a device control that uses a timecode.
- Videotapes must each have a unique reel number and be formatted with the timecode before you shoot the video to ensure there are no breaks in the timecode.

To view the EDL options, choose File > Export > Export to EDL, which opens the EDL Export Settings dialog box.

Your options are as follows:

Note: The title can be different from the filename. After clicking OK in the EDL Export Settings dialog box, you will have the opportunity to enter a filename.

- **EDL Title**: This specifies a title to appear in the first line of the EDL file.
- **Start Timecode**: Here you set the starting timecode value for the first edit in the sequence.
- **Drop Frame**: Specify if the timecode should use the drop frame method of counting frames (usually with NTSC video) or non drop frame method (usually for Web).
- **Include Video Levels**: This includes video opacity–level comments in the EDL.
- **Include Audio Levels**: This includes audio-level comments in the EDL.
- **Audio Processing**: Here you specify when audio processing should occur. Options are Audio Follows Video, Audio Separately, and Audio at End.
- **Tracks To Export**: This specifies which tracks to export. The video track directly above the video track selected for export is designated as the key track.

Review questions

1 What are the main formats for exporting digital video if you want to be able to edit the files in the future?

2 When you click Record in the Export to Tape dialog box, your camcorder remains paused. What's going on?

3 What are three streaming media options in Adobe Media Encoder?

4 How are MPEG-1 and MPEG-2 different?

5 What is the encoding format used when exporting to most mobile devices?

6 Must you wait for Adobe Media Encoder to finish processing its queue before working on a new project?

Review answers

1 The primary options are Microsoft DV AVI and QuickTime MOV.

2 Before Adobe Premiere Pro can start recording a project to videotape, it has to render it. You can do that in advance by opening a sequence and pressing Enter. Otherwise, when you click the Record button, you'll have to wait a while for Adobe Premiere Pro to render the unrendered portions of your sequence.

3 Windows Media, QuickTime, and RealMedia are three streaming media options in Adobe Media Encoder. Windows Media offers the most options.

4 MPEG-1 is VHS quality and is intended for use on CDs or personal computers. MPEG-2 is much higher quality, has a wider spectrum of quality control possibilities, and is the standard video format for videos and movies on DVDs and satellite digital TV.

5 H.264 is the encoding format used when exporting to most mobile devices.

6 No. Adobe Media Encoder is a stand-alone application. You can work in other applications or even start a new Adobe Premiere Pro project while it's processing its render queue.

21 AUTHORING DVDS WITH ADOBE ENCORE CS4

Topics covered in this lesson

- Preparing projects for DVD authoring in Adobe Premiere Pro
- Adding Encore chapter markers to the Timeline
- Sending a sequence to Encore via Adobe Dynamic Link
- Creating an autoplay DVD
- Creating a menu DVD
- Creating a Blu-ray Disc
- Exporting DVD projects to Flash

This lesson will take approximately 30 minutes.

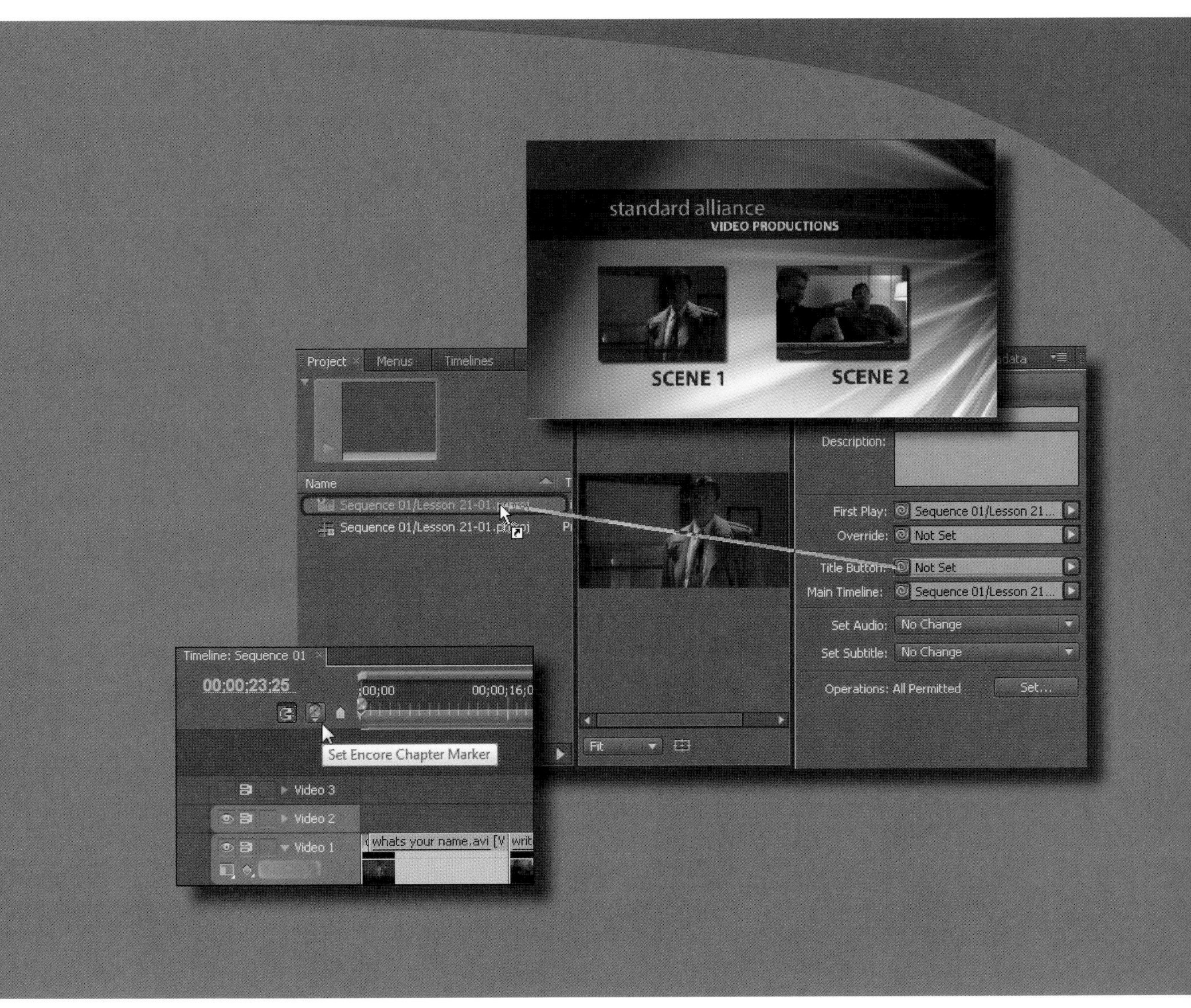

Send your Adobe Premiere Pro CS4 Timeline to Adobe Encore CS4 to create DVDs, Blu-ray Discs, or Adobe Flash CS4 Professional web projects.

Getting started

DVDs are a tremendous media delivery platform. Their images and videos are full-screen (including 16:9 wide-screen), the audio quality is good, and they are interactive. Simply click a menu button to jump immediately to a video, a scene, or behind-the-scenes stills.

Creating these interactive DVDs, with all their menus and buttons, used to take a Hollywood feature-film budget and expensive hardware. Now, with Adobe Premiere Pro and Encore, you can create professional-looking DVDs on your computer in minutes.

Encore is now included with Adobe Premiere Pro and has a collection of customizable DVD menu templates with backgrounds and buttons—static or animated. If you like, you can even use your own images or videos as backgrounds.

Encore CS4 takes DVD authoring much further than previous versions. You can use Encore to create standard-definition (SD) DVDs or high-definition (HD) Blu-ray Discs, and you can even output your DVD project to Flash.

Overview of DVD authoring in Adobe Premiere Pro

DVD authoring is the process used to create menus, buttons, and links to assets and menus. It also describes behaviors such as what the DVD player should do when it gets to the end of a video—does it return to the DVD's main menu, to some other menu, or to another video?

Each DVD-authoring product takes a different approach to creating interactive DVDs. Adobe Premiere Pro simplifies the authoring process by allowing you to send your Timeline to Encore, which is a full-featured professional authoring tool. When you author in Encore, you have two basic options for creating DVDs:

- **Autoplay DVDs**: These discs have no menus. They work best for short movies that you want your viewers to watch from start to finish. Before you create an autoplay DVD, you can add Encore chapter markers to the Timeline. Markers let viewers skip forward or backward through the movie by using the Next and Previous buttons on their DVD player's remote control.
- **Menu-based DVDs**: These DVDs have one or more menus with buttons that link to separate videos, slide shows, or scene-selection submenus. (Scene-selection submenus, as you probably know, let viewers navigate to scenes within the videos.)

Encore can output a project to any of three file formats:

- **SD DVD**: This is the traditional DVD format widely in use today for set-top DVD players.
- **Blu-ray Disc**: This is a delivery medium for HD video.
- **Flash**: With one step, Encore can export your DVD project to Flash content for the Web. Not only is the video converted to Flash Video, but the menu system and actions are converted to Flash content as well. Encore also produces a web-ready HTML page with links to the Flash content, ready to be uploaded to your website for client review or demonstration.

You have two options to get your Adobe Premiere Pro Timeline into Encore for authoring:

- **Send it via Dynamic Link to Encore**: The preferred method is to use Dynamic Link to "send" the Timeline to Encore. The advantage of this method is you don't need to create an intermediate file to load into Encore. This is a fast, efficient workflow. Another advantage of this method is that any changes you make later to your Timeline in Adobe Premiere Pro will be reflected immediately in Encore, without you having to render or even save the file. This is the method you will explore in this lesson.
- **Export it as media**: Adobe Premiere Pro allows you to export an intermediate temporary file to import into Encore. You can export an encoded file that Encore can import and use directly, or you can export an intermediate format that is editable, such as AVI or QuickTime format, and allow Encore to encode it for you. Using this method, you could author a DVD with any third-party tool; however, you lose the advantages associated with Dynamic Link. This method consumes more hard disk space for the temporary intermediate file and requires more render time.

Adding Encore chapter markers to the Timeline

Once you have finished editing a video in Adobe Premiere Pro, you can add Encore chapter markers to the Timeline to denote chapters for the final DVD. You can move, remove, and add markers at any time in the sequence.

1 Open Lesson 21-01.prproj and open Sequence 01 if it is not already open. You will be exporting this short video project to an autoplay DVD with no menus. But first you'll add a chapter marker so users can click ahead with the DVD remote.

Note: Encore chapter markers are not clip markers or Timeline markers. Clip markers and Timeline markers help you position and trim clips. Adobe Premiere Pro uses Encore chapter markers solely for DVD menu creation and button links.

2 To place an Encore chapter marker, position the current-time indicator where you want the marker to be, and then click the Set Encore Chapter Marker button (located near the top left of the Timeline). Place the marker at the beginning of the third clip (about 00;00;23;25 on the Timeline).

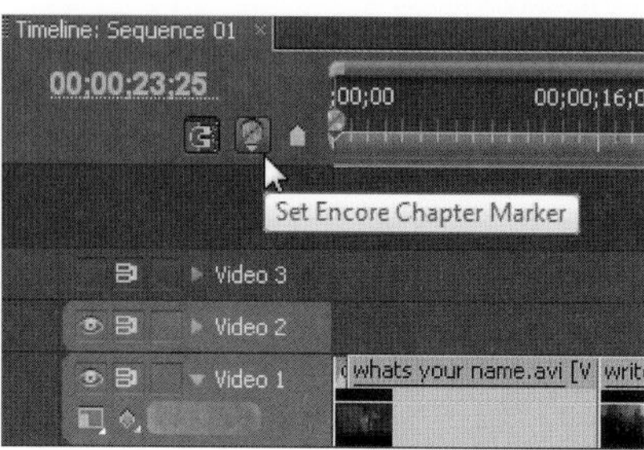

Note: Adobe Premiere Pro automatically places an Encore chapter marker on the first frame of every sequence. You cannot move or remove this marker. You can move, remove, or rename any other chapter markers you add.

3 Name this chapter marker **Dixie**.

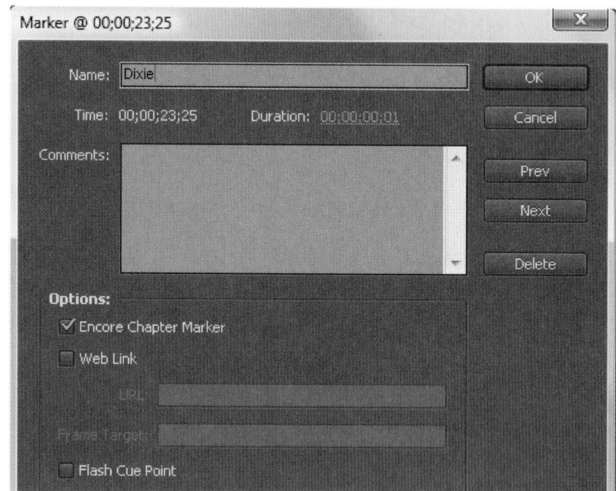

Creating an autoplay DVD

Next, you'll create an autoplay DVD that will begin playing your movie automatically when a user plays the disc in a DVD player:

1 Choose File > Adobe Dynamic Link > Send to Encore. Encore launches.

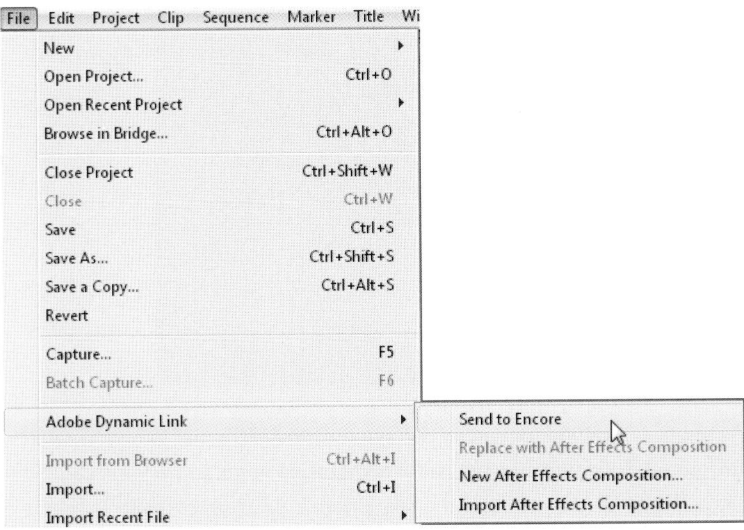

2 Name the disc Auto Play DVD and choose the Lesson 21 folder for the location.

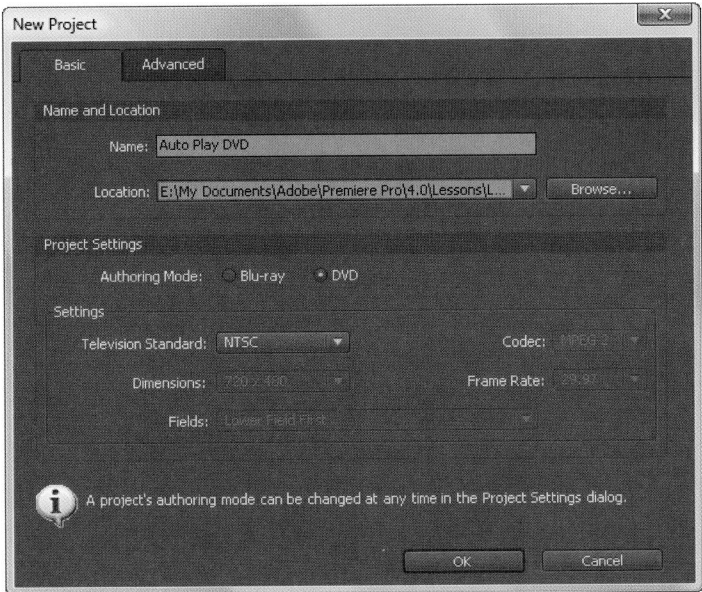

3 Select DVD as the authoring mode.

4 Click OK.

Encore opens with the Adobe Premiere Pro sequence you selected in the Encore Project panel. This also creates an Encore Timeline of the same name.

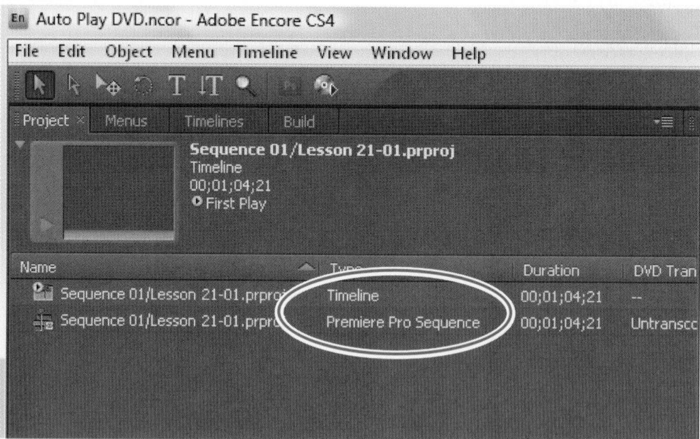

5 Double-click the Timeline object in the Encore Project panel, which opens a Timeline panel in Encore and a monitor window so you can preview the video. Play or scrub the video to see it is the sequence you exported from Adobe Premiere Pro.

This video sequence is loaded into Encore via Dynamic Link. This technology allows Encore to play the Adobe Premiere Pro sequence without first having to render it anywhere. To demonstrate that this link is dynamic, you'll now make a change to the Adobe Premiere Pro sequence and see that it is reflected immediately in Encore.

6 Toggle from Encore to Adobe Premiere Pro.

7 Choose Effects > Video Effects > Image Control and drag the Black & White filter to the first clip on the Adobe Premiere Pro Timeline.

8 Do not save the Adobe Premiere Pro project after you make this change. Toggle back to Encore and play the Timeline. You will see that the change you made appears in Encore without rendering or even saving the project.

To complete the creation of an autoplay DVD, you need to set a couple of parameters, and then you'll be ready to burn the DVD.

Note: If an Adobe Premiere Pro sequence is dynamically linked to an Encore project, it is not even necessary for Adobe Premiere Pro to be running for Encore to use the linked sequence.

9 Select the Sequence 01/Lesson 21-01 Timeline object in the Project panel and notice the End Action on the Properties panel is Not Set. This means the DVD will not know what to do when the Timeline finishes playing. Set the Timeline to stop after playing by setting End Action to Stop.

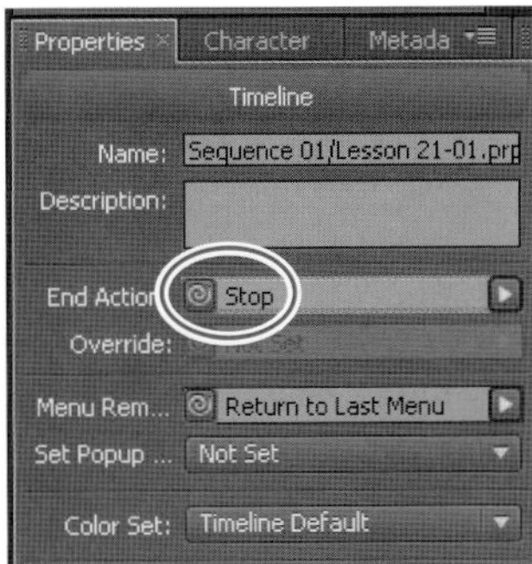

10 A DVD player must also know what to do if the Title button is pressed on the DVD remote. Set this by clicking a blank area of the Project panel. The properties of the disc now appear in the Properties panel. Set Title Button to Sequence 01/Lesson 21-01 by using the Pickwhip tool to select the Timeline object in the Project panel.

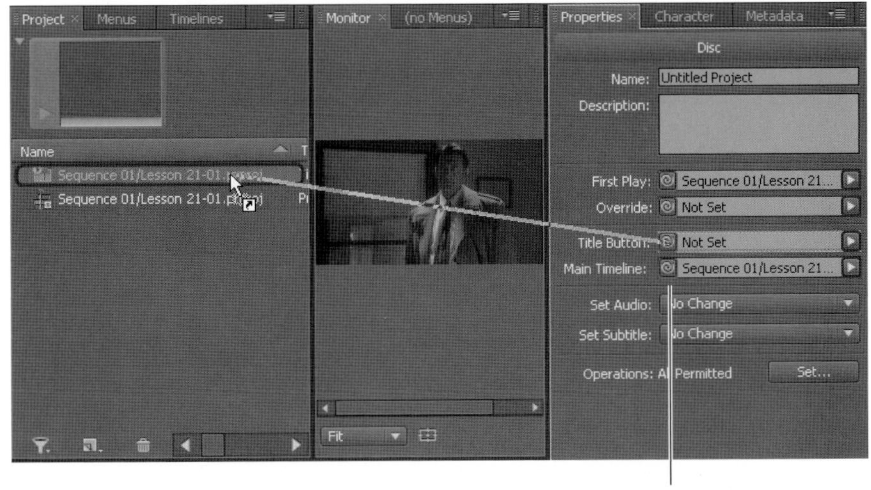

Note: To actually create a DVD, place a blank DVD in your DVD burner drive. If you do not have a DVD drive or do not want to burn a physical DVD, you can proceed, but won't be able to complete the final burn process.

11 Choose File > Build > Disc.

12 You can adjust several settings in the Build panel. Typically you will leave them at the defaults to burn your DVD. Check that you have the correct DVD recorder selected if you have more than one burner in your system, and give the project an appropriate name. Click Build to start burning your DVD.

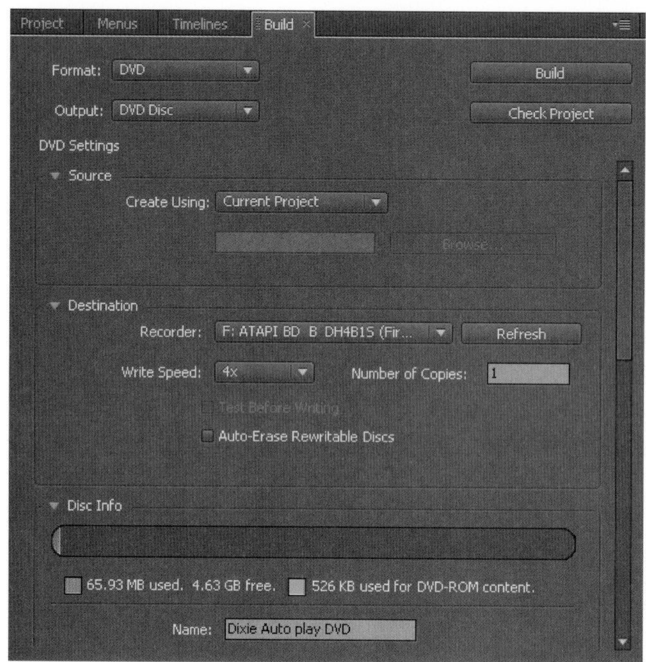

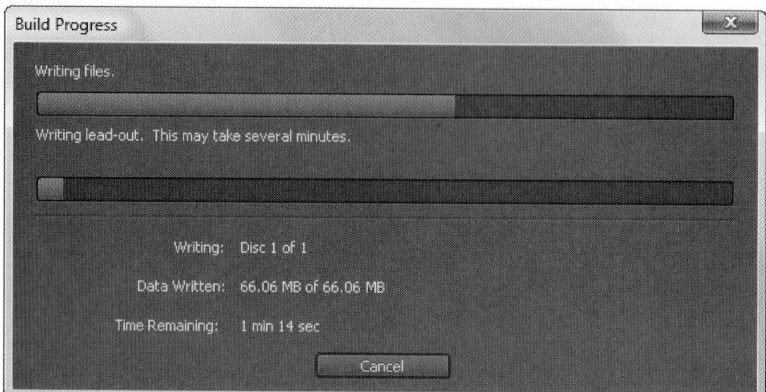

13 If there are errors in your project, Encore will prompt you with a dialog box letting you know where they are so you can correct them before burning the disc. If there are no errors in your project, Encore will burn your DVD and alert you when it is complete. Leave the Encore project open; you will use it in the next exercise.

Creating a menu DVD

Adobe Premiere Pro does not have tools to create DVD menus directly. However, you can transfer the Encore chapter markers you place on the Timeline to Encore and then use them to create buttons or chapters. You use Adobe Premiere Pro to pass the video assets along with the chapter markers to Encore, and you use Encore to build the menus and burn the DVD.

For this exercise, you do not need Adobe Premiere Pro running. Switch to the Encore project that should still be open from the previous section.

You will select a DVD menu from a list of menu templates included with Encore:

1 Select the Library panel to see a list of assets. You'll see several sets of menu and button styles. Choose the General set.

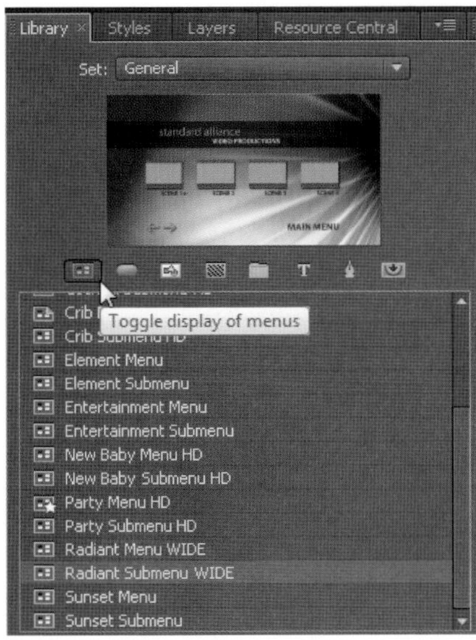

2 Scroll to locate the menu named Radiant Submenu WIDE. Double-click this menu item to add it to the Project panel and display it in the Menus panel.

3 Drag the Sequence 01/Lesson 21-01 Timeline from the Project panel to the Scene 1 button on the menu.

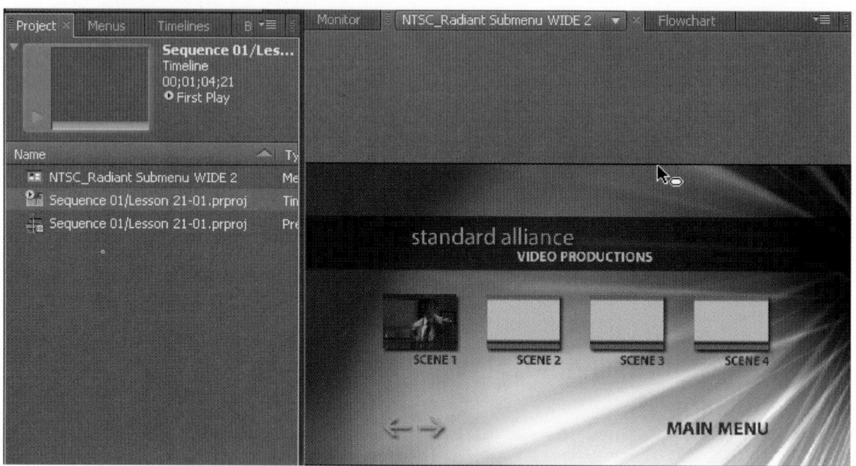

A DVD menu with only one scene to select is a little boring, so you will add another sequence from Adobe Premiere Pro without even having to open Adobe Premiere Pro. You will add this sequence via Dynamic Link from Encore. Remember that the first sequence was added to Encore via Dynamic Link from Adobe Premiere Pro.

4 Choose File > Adobe Dynamic Link > Import Premiere Pro Sequence. In the Import Premiere Pro Sequence dialog box, navigate to the Lesson 17 folder and click Lesson 17-4.prproj. This reveals the sequences contained in that project on the right. Click the completed sequence to select it and then click OK.

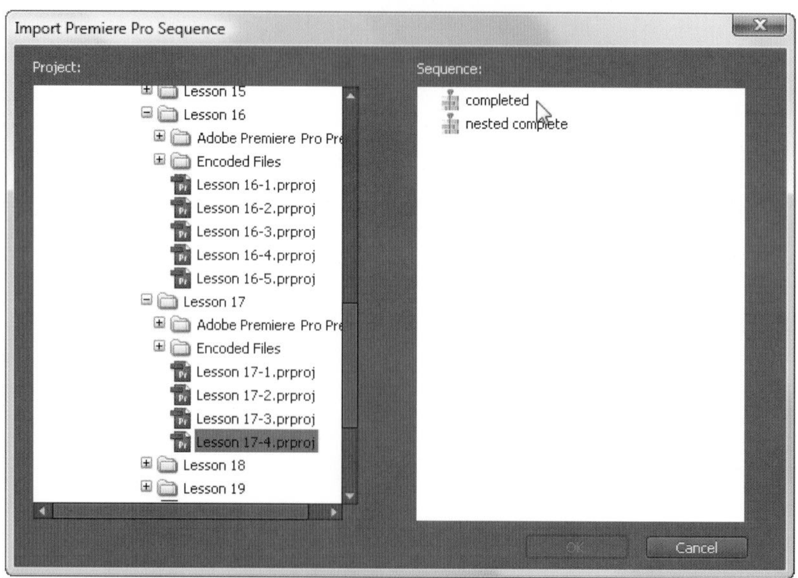

5 Drag the completed/Lesson 17-4 sequence from the Project panel to the Scene 2 button on the menu.

You can add as many sequences as you want like this. In this exercise, you will stop at two and clean up the menu a little before burning it.

6 Since you don't have multiple menus, delete the Main Menu text and the navigation arrows. You can delete them by selecting them and pressing the Delete button on your keyboard.

7 Since you have only two sequences, also delete Scene 3 and Scene 4.

8 Select each scene button, and drag them to be larger and evenly spaced on the menu. The menu should look like the one shown here.

9 Click the Timelines panel to select it. This panel filters the assets so you see only the Timeline assets. Select each Timeline and set End Action to Return to Last Menu.

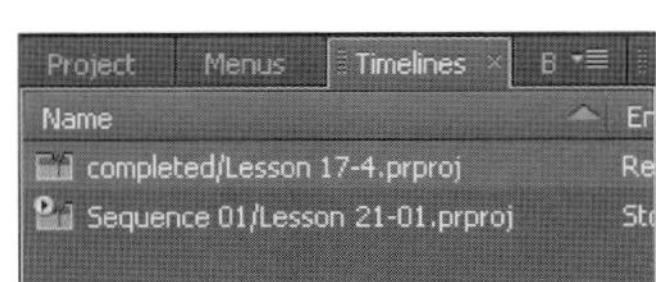

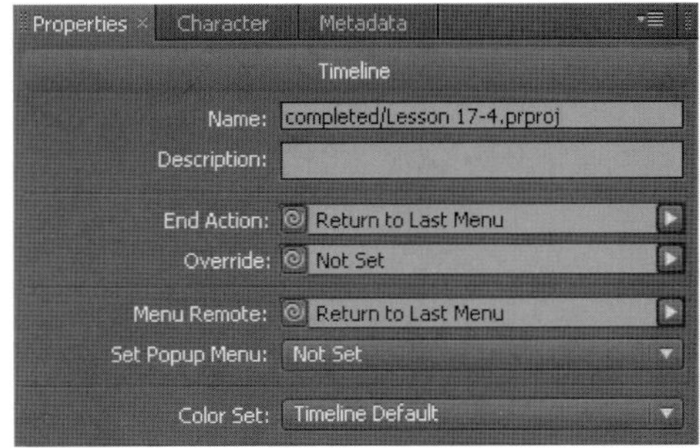

Encore makes the first object you import the First Play object, meaning it's the first object the DVD player plays when the DVD is inserted. The first thing imported into this project was the Sequence 01/Lesson 12-01 object. Notice that it has a First Play status added to its icon. That worked well for an autoplay DVD. But now you want the menu to be the first thing that plays. Fortunately, this is easy to change.

completed/Lesson 17-4.prproj
completed/Lesson 17-4.prproj
NTSC_Radiant Submenu WIDE 2
Sequence 01/Lesson 21-01.prproj
Sequence 01/Lesson 21-01.prproj

First Play indicator

10 Right-click the menu object and choose Set as First Play from the menu. Notice the First Play indicator is now on the menu icon.

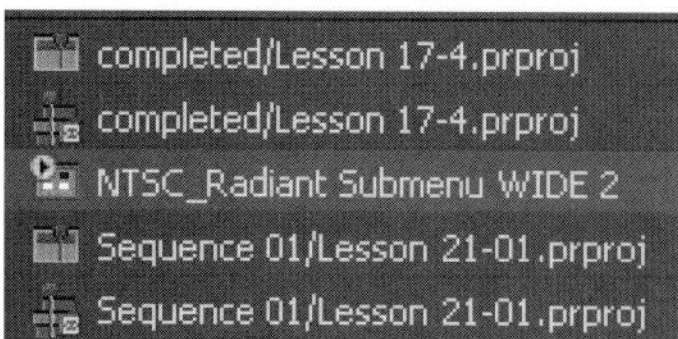

Previewing the DVD

You can preview the menu in Encore before burning it to DVD to make sure it looks and works as you expect:

1 Choose File > Preview. Use the pointer as your DVD remote to click the buttons. Click each button to ensure they all play as expected.

2 You can burn this DVD in the same way you burned the autoplay DVD earlier. Choose File > Build > Disc and proceed as you did in the autoplay exercise.

Creating a Blu-ray Disc

Blu-ray Disc is a format that supports HD video. HD video has a higher resolution than SD video, so it will not fit on a standard DVD. Burning a Blu-ray Disc requires a Blu-ray Disc–capable burner and Blu-ray Disc media, and to play the Blu-ray Disc, you need a Blu-ray Disc–capable player connected to a high-definition TV. Fortunately, Encore is ready to handle this new technology when you are. Burning a Blu-ray Disc is as easy as burning a standard-definition DVD.

Start where you left off with the Encore project still open and follow these steps:

1 Select the Build panel.
2 Change Format to Blu-ray.
3 Change Output to Blu-ray Disc.
4 Click Build.

Yes, it *is* that easy. As with standard DVD, you can also output to a folder or image file if you do not want to burn directly to a disc.

Blu-ray Disc pop-up menus

The Blu-ray Disc standard has additional functionality not found in standard-definition DVDs. One enhancement the Blu-ray Disc format has is that menus can pop up over video when a user presses the Menu button on the remote. When creating menus for Blu-ray Disc, you will notice a Pop-up panel. Use this panel to specify the pop-up details.

Exporting DVD projects to Flash

Creating Flash content from a DVD menu is an innovative feature in Encore. Encore not only converts the video to Flash Video, but it converts the whole menu system to a SWF file that is viewable in a web browser. This allows you to demo DVD projects over the Web with no knowledge of Flash, HTML, or scripting—pretty amazing! The Flash controls even allow you to skip to chapter points via Flash web-friendly video controls.

In this exercise, you will export the project you just created for DVD to Flash. If you want to load that project from the included example, open Lesson 21 example.ncor in the Lesson 21 folder.

1 Select the Build panel.
2 Change Format to Flash.

3 Specify a location under Destination and a project name under Settings. Remember the folder and filename you use here, because you will need to navigate to the file later with a browser.

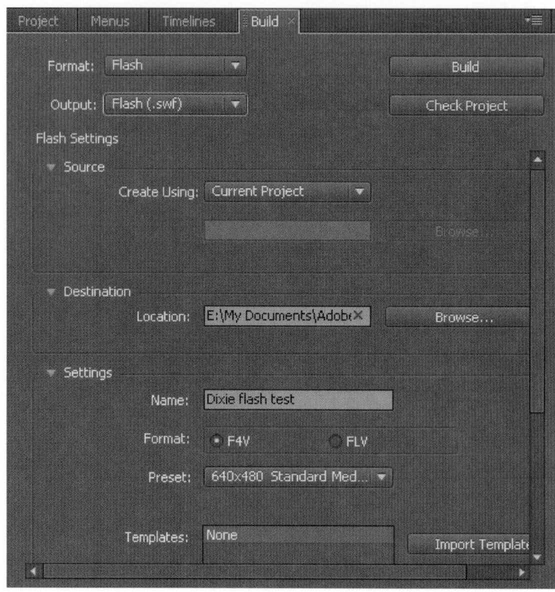

4 Leave all the other parameters at the defaults and then click Build. You will see progress bars that provide details of the export process and a "Complete" message when it's done.

Encore converts your DVD project into an interactive Flash file that you can view in a web browser.

5 Open a web browser. (The browser needs to have the Flash plug-in to view Flash content.)

6 Navigate to the folder where you saved the Flash file.

7 Within the folder you specified, there will be an HTML file called index.html. Open this file in your browser to view your Flash application.

You will notice that the menu is fully functional, including a background, button highlights, and even semitransparent buttons. Clicking a button will play the video and then return you to the menu, preserving the end actions you set up in Encore. All this is possible without you needing to know Flash and without writing a single line of code.

Note: If you upload this to a web server, be sure to upload the subfolder called Sources and all its content.

As we've said before, Encore is a complete DVD-authoring and DVD-burning tool (and more!). In this lesson, you've seen a very brief example of building a fairly simple menu from Adobe Premiere Pro sequences. It is beyond the scope of this book to explore all the menu-authoring capabilities of Encore, but this lesson should have given you a taste of the amazing possibilities you have with Encore.

Review questions

1 Why send a project to Encore via Dynamic Link rather than exporting an MPEG-2 file for Encore to import?

2 What is the purpose of Encore chapter markers in Adobe Premiere Pro?

3 What is the significance of the First Play object in Encore?

4 Is it possible to export the same Encore project to DVD and Blu-ray Disc?

5 When you upload an Encore Flash project to a web server, which files must you upload?

Review answers

1 Using Dynamic Link eliminates the need to render or encode before working on a sequence in Encore. Dynamic Link allows you to make changes to the sequence in Adobe Premiere Pro and have them show up in Encore.

2 Encore chapter markers in Adobe Premiere Pro will be passed to Encore when you export. These markers can be used in Encore to set chapter points and to name buttons.

3 The First Play object in Encore is the object executed when a user inserts a DVD into a player. Typically, the First Play object is the main menu, but it can be a video Timeline that plays automatically.

4 Yes. You cannot export to the two formats simultaneously, but you can burn the same project to DVD or Blu-ray Disc and then export it to Flash by changing the Build panel's parameters.

5 You must upload the contents of the folder you specified in the Build panel, plus the Sources subfolder and its contents.

INDEX

NUMBERS

A

D

G

H

I

J

K

Q

R

S

T

U

V

W

X

Z